Python
PROGRAMMING

Late Ch Satyanarayana
Former Professor, Department of CSE
and
Director of Academics and Planning
JNTU Kakinada

M Radhika Mani
Head, Department of CSE
Pragati Engineering College
Surampalem, Andhra Pradesh

B N Jagadesh
Head, Department of CSE
Srinivasa Institute of Engineering and Technology
Amalapuram, Andhra Pradesh

Universities Press

PYTHON PROGRAMMING

UNIVERSITIES PRESS (INDIA) PRIVATE LIMITED

Registered Office
3-6-747/1/A & 3-6-754/1, Himayatnagar, Hyderabad 500 029, Telangana, India
info@universitiespress.com; www.universitiespress.com

Distributed by
Orient Blackswan Private limited

Registered Office
3-6-752 Himayatnagar, Hyderabad 500 029, Telangana, India

Other Offices
Bengaluru, Chennai, Guwahati, Hyderabad, Kolkata
Mumbai, New Delhi, Noida, Patna

First published 2018
Reprinted 2019, 2021, 2022, 2024

ISBN: 978-93-86235-63-3

Cover and book design

502069

Typeset in Dehuti 9.5/11.5 *by*
Cameo Corporate Services, Coimbatore, Tamil Nadu, India

Printed at
SS Colour Impression Pvt Ltd, Chennai 600 106

Published by
Universities Press (India) Private Limited
3-6-747/1/A & 3-6-754/1, Himayatnagar, Hyderabad 500 029, Telangana, India

We dedicate this book to all our teachers
and our respective family members

Table of Contents

Preface

We live in a time when computer applications have revolutionized all enterprises and changed the substance of our society. Because of their boundless utility and expanding ubiquity, a study of computer applications and their impact on our daily life has become mandatory. Programming languages are required to develop efficient and effective computer applications. Python Programming gains significance in this context in that it is an elegant and powerful language aimed at non-professional programmers.

Python is an easy-to-use, powerful and interpreted high-level programming language for general-purpose programming. Developed under open-source license, it supports object oriented programming with classes and multiple inheritance. It also supports addition of new modules implemented in a compiled language such as C or C++. Python contains advanced programming features such as generators and list comprehensions. It can run on almost all platforms.

ABOUT THE BOOK

This book is designed to bring readers up to speed on Python language fundamentals and will be useful to undergraduate students of computer science and information technology as well as to those pursuing masters degree in computer applications. The objective of this book is to improve the efficiency of students in using Python to solve real-world problems.

The book begins with an introduction to computer systems and analyzes the defining features of the Python Programming language. With a thorough discourse on the basics of Python programming, it elaborates on the language's characteristic elements before exploring ways to apply it in common application domains and realistically scaled tasks. At the end of each chapter, there are numerous Sample Programs, MCQs, Fill in the Blanks and True/False questions for the students' benefit. In addition, there are case studies that demonstrate how decision making and looping statements, along with Python's built-in and user-defined functions, can be adopted for practical applications.

ORGANIZATION

The book contains 19 chapters and four appendices. **Chapter 1** provides an introduction to computer systems and covers the concept of generations of computers, while also providing an insight into the applications and classification of computers. It also includes computer hardware and software, giving detailed information on various levels of programming languages and problem solving approaches such as algorithms, pseudo code and flowcharts. **Chapter 2** discusses about the features and applications of Python programming language. It compares the essential elements of Python with those of C and Java programming languages and illustrates installation of the Python software, step by step. **Chapter 3** elaborates on the syntax and style used in Python programming language and describes the various operators and expressions supported by Python. **Chapter 4** explains the different types of decision making statements such as if, if.. else and nested if and analyzes the use of while loop, for loop, break statement, continue statement and pass statement in Python programs. **Chapter 5** deals with Sequences (strings, lists, tuples, byte arrays, buffers and range objects) in the Python programming language. It also spells out the properties of List Function.

Chapter **6** focuses on the concept of tuples and their immutable properties and shows how these form efficient sequences in Python. The chapter also discusses the various operations that can be performed on a tuple object. Chapter **7** expounds on the concept of Dictionaries and shows the different ways of creating a dictionary object. Chapter **8** deals with functions in Python programming language. It examines defining and calling functions, recursive functions and the four types of arguments, viz., required arguments, default arguments, keyword arguments and variable length arguments. Chapter **9** delves into the creation of a module and the various ways of importing elements from a module. Chapter **10** exemplifies the object oriented properties of encapsulation, abstraction, inheritance and polymorphism.

Chapter **11** elucidates the handling of packages in Python. It also covers installation of packages and importing packages. Chapter **12** explores how strings are handled in Python. This chapter also depicts the use of regular expressions to handle text patterns efficiently. Chapter **13** scrutinizes the various operations performed on files such as `read`, `write`, `open` and `close`. The chapter also covers serialization and de-serialization, hash files and dictionary access. Chapter **14** discusses about the various types of errors and exceptions with simple examples. Chapter **15** reveals how multithreading is handled in Python and deals at length with thread synchronization. Chapter **16** delineates the use of Tkinter based GUI and asserts its use for the design of GUI based applications using various widgets such as label, button, entry and list box. Chapter **17** is dedicated to the handling of events in Python. Chapter **18** lays out the standard libraries available in Python. Chapter **19**, the last chapter of the book, outlines the concept of testing in Python programming with emphasis on unit testing and loading and running tests.

The book has four useful appendices: Appendix A deals with networking concepts in Python; Appendix-B explains Simple Mail Transfer Protocol (SMTP) for sending the mails from one account to another; Appendix C deals with the installation of the plotly package for graphs while Appendix-D provides basic information on Common Gateway Interface (CGI).

With adequate focus and effort, we are sure that students will find this book rewarding since it has been written to shorten their start-up time to familiarize themselves with Python and provide a solid foundation in Python's manifold application domains.

ACKNOWLEDGEMENTS

At the outset, we convey our special thanks to Universities Press (India) Private Limited for giving us an opportunity to work with them. We take this moment to thank Ramesh and Kallol Das, editors, who added value to our book. We also thank the entire team that was involved in this assignment.

We are obliged to the management of our respective colleges for their support, which helped us in no small measure while we were working on the manuscript. We are also indebted to our college staff for their constant encouragement and support.

Finally, we thank our respective family members without whose love and understanding, this work may not have come to fruition.

Ch Satyanarayana
M Radhika Mani
B N Jagadesh

CHAPTER 1 Introduction

1.1 Introduction to Computer Systems

The computer is a collection of hardware and software components used to perform a specific operation on an existing hardware. There are several characteristics of a computer system such as its speed, accuracy, storage etc. which are used to evaluate its efficiency.

1.1.1 Generations of computers

The generations of computers are characterized by the hardware used in them. There are five generations of computers and in each generation, there was a major technological advancement that fundamentally changed the way computers operate.

- The first-generation computers were designed based on vacuum tubes. It had magnetic drum-based memory and punch card-based inputs. The size of the first-generation computer was large.
- The second-generation computers were designed using transistors. Thus, the size of the second-generation computer was less when compared with first-generation computer. It contained magnetic core-based memory.
- The third-generation computers were designed with Integrated Circuits (ICs). The integrated circuit is smaller in size when compared with the transistor, whereas its memory capacity is much higher. Thus the size of the third generation computer is smaller when compared with the second-generation computer. It contains enhanced magnetic core-based memory.
- During the fourth generation, the micro computer, personal computers were introduced. The size of fourth-generation computer is lesser than that of the third-generation computer.
- The fifth generation saw the advent of multi-core computers that have now become indispensible for performing artificial intelligence, machine vision, virtual reality etc.

1.1.2 Applications of computers

Today, computers are used in various fields and they have become an integrated part of our life. Computers are routinely used in the areas of

- Education
- Business
- Industry
- Automation
- Textile
- Transportation
- Navigation
- Surveillance
- Weather forecasting
- Medicine

1.1.3 Classification of computers

The computers are classified into various types as listed below.

- Micro computer
- Laptop computer
- Work station
- Super computer
- Main Frames
- Hand held computer
- Multi core computer

1.2 Computer Hardware

The computer is mainly used to perform various operations on data. The computer hardware represents the physical elements in the computer. The block diagram of a computer is shown in Fig. 1.1.

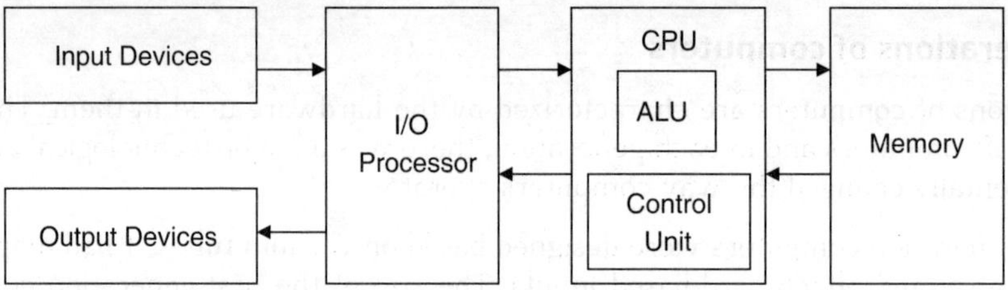

Figure **1.1** Computer Hardware

1.2.1 Input/ Output devices

The input devices are used to obtain data from the user. The data given by the user is transferred to the CPU. Examples of input devices are keyboard, scanner etc. The output devices are used to deliver data to the user. The data from the CPU are transferred to the output devices. Monitor, printer etc. are examples of output devices. The speed of the CPU is high and the speed of the Input/Output (I/O) devices is low. Thus, during the communication between CPU and the I/O devices, CPU becomes idle. To avoid the wastage of CPU time, the I/O processor is introduced between the CPU and I/O devices.

1.2.2 CPU

The Central Processing Unit (CPU) coordinates the complete computer. In the computer, CPU is responsible for performing any operation. For this, CPU contains two elements. They are the control unit and Arithmetic Logical and Shift Unit (ALU). The ALU is responsible for performing the operation on the given operands. The control unit generates control signals. With these control signals, CPU can have control over all the other components.

1.2.3 Memory

In addition to the execution of operation on the data, the computer is responsible for maintaining data. For this, the computer uses memory. The memory is responsible to maintain data and can be represented as M×N size. Thus, the memory contains M number of locations, with each location storing a word size of N bits. On any memory location, either read operation or write operation can be performed. There are various types of memory elements in the computer. The CPU can have a direct connection with main memory. There are two types of main memory. They are i) Random Access Memory (RAM) and ii) Read Only Memory (ROM). The RAM allows performing both read and writing operations whereas the ROM allows performing only read operation. Other than main memory, various other types of memory elements are allowed in the computer. They are cache memory, virtual memory and auxiliary memory.

1.3 Computer Software

Computer software is a set of programs that can be executed by a processor. With the software, the computer can able to perform a specific task. There are two types of computer software. They are

1. System software
2. Application software

1.3.1 System software

System software is a collection of programs used to perform the operation or task for the computer. In general, operating system is considered as system software. With the system software, the computer can be handled efficiently.

1.3.2 Application software

Application software is a collection of programs intended to perform a particular application. They are also called as applications and are end-user programs. Application software can be executed on top of the system software.

1.4 Programming Languages

Programming languages are used for the development of a solution to a problem. There are three types of programming languages. They are machine-level, assembly-level and high-level programming languages.

1.4.1 Machine-level programming language

During the early days of the computer development, programmers had developed the code only in computer readable format. The computer can understand everything in digital format only. So, the instructions were written in the form of 0 and 1. This machine-level code is in the format which can be directly understood by the computer. The programmer had to remember the length of the complicated machine-level instructions for the development of a program. It was observed that the complexity of the machine code was high but the time required to execute the machine code was less. The programs developed by using machine-level language were system-dependent.

1.4.2 Assembly-level programming language

In case of machine-level programming language, the complexity is high for the programmers to develop their programs. The assembly-level language was introduced to overcome this. The assembly-level language allows the programmer to write the instructions with short codes of the operation. These short codes are also called as “pneumonics”. The assembly-level language instruction consists of the operational code (also called as "opcode") and the operand. The operands represent the data on which the opcode should be performed. As the computer can understand only the machine code, it is necessary to convert the assembly-level language code to machine code. This conversion process is performed by the "Assembler". When compared to the execution of machine-level language program, the assembly-level language programs required additional time for the conversion process. Hence, programmers still feel that the assembly-level language code is complex.

1.4.3 High-level programming language

To overcome the complexity of the assembly-level language program, the high-level programming language was introduced. High-level programming language is programmer friendly since the building blocks of this language could be easily read and understood by humans. For example, the addition operation can be represented in various languages as shown below.

Machine level: 10101000100000100. . . (Binary format)

Assembly level: ADD

High level: +

The "+" is used regularly. So, writing the programs with regular symbols becomes easy for the programmer. But the computer can understand only the machine code. Thus, the high-level code should be converted into machine code. For this conversion, two elements are available. They are "compiler" and "interpreter". Both compiler and interpreter are used for converting high-level codes to machine codes. The compiler will read the entire high-level code and then start the conversion process. The interpreter will read a line of high-level code and then convert it to machine code, performing line-by-line conversion.

1.5 Algorithmic Problem Solving

Programming languages are used for developing programs that help in solving problems. For solving a problem, various steps are to be followed as given below.

- Initially, the problem for which the solution has to be given has to be analyzed. With this step, the problem should be reviewed thoroughly and the developer should understand the definition of the problem. Finally, the developer should learn the inputs and outputs required for the problem and the implementation plan.
- In the second step, the methodology for the implementation plan should be identified. Further, the implemented methodology should be decomposed into various small parts. Each small part is considered as a task.
- In the third step, an algorithm has to be developed for the methodology and its tasks. With the help of algorithm, the developer will understand the step-by-step instruction to be performed to get the desired end output for solving the problem.
- In the fourth step, a program is developed by following the algorithm. For this, the developer has to use any one of the programming languages.
- Finally, the developed program should be compiled and then executed to get the solution for the given problem.

1.5.1 Algorithms

Algorithm is a step-by-step approach for representing the problem solving process. The algorithm can be written in any language such as English etc. It is a blue-print of the methodology which will be developed by any one of the programming language. With an algorithm, the solution for a problem can be derived in a finite number of steps. The algorithm should ensure the termination of the methodology. It should be efficiently developed. With an efficient algorithm, the developed program will have less complexity. The complexity of the algorithm can be represented in terms of time and space. Time complexity represents the time required for the completion of program execution while space complexity represents the total amount of memory space required for the completion of program execution. Space complexity includes the memory space allocated for all elements in the program during execution.

1.5.2 Characteristics of algorithm

- The algorithm should be simple.
- The algorithm should be written in a sequential order of steps. The developer should not write the (n+1)th step before the nth step of the algorithm.
- The algorithm should consist of a finite number of steps.
- The algorithm should start and terminate properly.
- The algorithm should give the solution of the problem.
- The algorithm should use have less space and time complexities.
- The algorithm should have at least one input and output.

1.5.3 Advantages and disadvantages of algorithm

Algorithms have the following advantages:

- They are simple to develop
- They provide better understanding of the methodology.
- Debugging is easy with sequential steps.
- Development of program with the programming language is easy

However, an important disadvantage is that it is time-consuming for developing an algorithm and its corresponding program.

1.5.4 Algorithm notation

Algorithm notations are used to represent the algorithm in various formats. There are various notations used for an algorithm as listed below.

Step form

The step form allows the developer to write the algorithm with various statements. Each statement represents a task of the problem solution and a group of statements will give the final solution to the problem. The step form is written with the help of statements. It consists of sequenced steps for each statement.

Example: The step form of the algorithm the problem "Read and display the number."

```
1. Start
2. Read the number
3. Display the number
4. Stop
```

Pseudo code

The written format of the algorithm is called as pseudo code. This is a limited edition of the step form. In this notation, the statements are written with limited terminology of the general language. It focuses on high-level description of each statement of the algorithm. It does not reflect on the actual programming language code but it contains the short codes for the development of the program.

Example: The pseudo code of the algorithm the problem “Read and display the number.”

```
1. Start
2. INPUT N
3. PRINT N
4. Stop
```

Flowchart

The graphical representation of an algorithm is called as flowchart. The flowchart contains various symbols and simple statements for representing each element of the algorithm. Some of them are listed below.

S.No.	Symbol	Representation
1	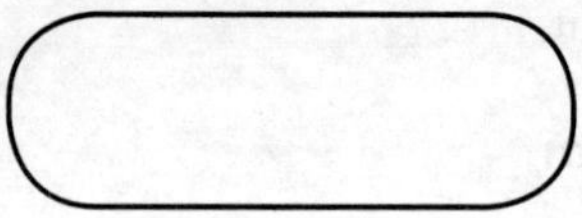	start/stop
2		Relationship between symbols
3	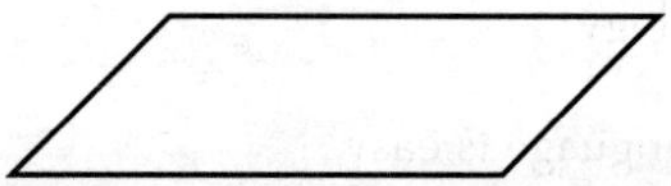	Input/Output operations
4		Process
5	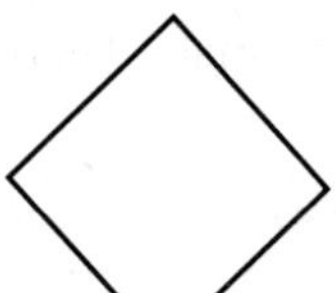	Decision making
6		Predefined process
7	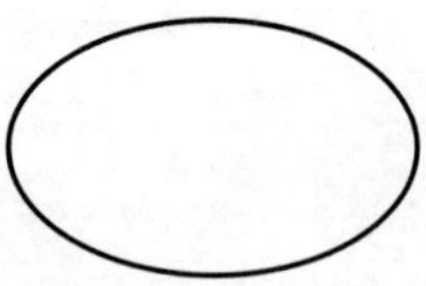	Connector between shapes
8		Internal storage

Example:

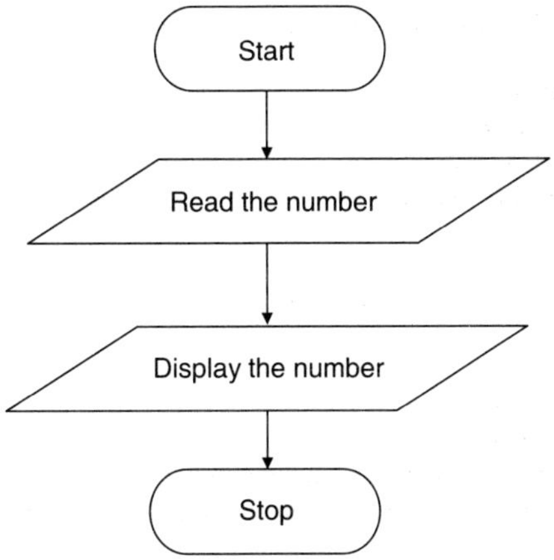

1.5.5 Building blocks of algorithms

The algorithm should derive an efficient solution to a problem. The various elements of an algorithm are listed below.

- The "statement" is used to express an action or event. In an algorithm, statements should be written in sequential order. The statement can have multiple sub-statements. The statement can either be simple statement or compound statement.
- The state of the algorithm represents its current status. The first state of the algorithm is its initial state. From the initial state, it enters into successive states and finally enters the ending state. With the final ending state, the algorithm will be terminated.
- The control flow or flow of control is used to evaluate the statements in an order to get the result. The control flow starts with the start statement and ends with the stop statement.
- A function is a collection of ordered sub-statements which can be grouped into a single entity. They are also called as subroutine. The function can be executed multiple times.

There are three building blocks of the algorithm. They are listed below.

Sequence structure

The sequence structure of the algorithm is used to represent an action or event. In the sequential structure, the current action or event leads to the next ordered action or event. Skipping of action or event is not permitted in this structure.

Example: "Read a number and display the absolute value of the number."

1. Start
2. Read the number
3. Compute the absolute value of the number
4. Display the absolute value of the number
5. Stop

Selection structure

The selection structure of the algorithm contains the decision making statements. The outcome of the decision is a Boolean value, i.e., True or False. Based on the outcome of the decision making statement, the decision is made whether to ignore the set of statements or not. Various examples of selection structure are if. . . then and if. . .then. . .else.

Example:
"Read a number and check whether the number is positive."

```
1. Start
2. Input N
3. if N is positive then
   identify the number as positive number
4. Stop
```

"Read a number and check whether the number is positive or negative."

```
1. Start
2. Input N
3. if N is positive then
   identify the number as positive number
   else identify the number as negative number
4. Stop
```

Iteration structure

The iteration process of the algorithm is made up of repetition or loop statements. The iteration structure is used to repeat the statements for a finite number of times; for example, **Repeat** and **While** Statements. The repetition is performed based on the evaluation of condition.

Example of iterative statement: "Read an N value and print the hello message N times."

```
1. Start
2. Input N
3. Repeat
     Print "hello"
     Decrement N value
     until N is non positive number
4. Stop
```

```
1. Start
2. Input N
3. While N is non positive number
4. begin
5. Print "hello"
6. Decrement N value
7. end
8. Stop
```

1.5.6 Steps for developing algorithms

Algorithmic problem solving uses the following steps.

- Prepare a detailed report of the problem to be solved.
- Conduct a detailed analysis of the problem report.
- Develop a well-defined algorithm for the analyzed problem.
- Review the algorithm and update it with additional features, if required.
- Test and evaluate the validity of the algorithm.
- Develop the program for the algorithm.

1.5.7 Simple strategies for developing algorithms

The iterative approach of the algorithm includes repeated execution of statements until the condition is satisfied. In an algorithm, repeat, while and for are used for iteration.

Example: "Read an N value and print the factorial of N" by using iterative approach.

```
1. Start
2. Input N
3. Initialize X with 1
4. Repeat
5. multiply X with N
6. Decrement N value by 1
7. until N is greater than 1
8. Print the value of X
9. Stop
```

The recursive approach of the algorithm includes calling function repeatedly until the condition is satisfied.

Example: "Read an N value and print the factorial of N" by using recursive approach.

Algorithm 1: FACT (Positive integer K)

```
1. Start
2. If N is 1
   then return 1
   else return FACT(N-1)
3. Stop
```

Algorithm 2:

```
1. Start
2. Input N
3. Store the result of FACT(N) in X
4. Print the value of X
5. Stop
```

1.5.8 Find minimum in a list

```
 1. Start
 2. Input N values and store them in list L
 3. X← L[0]
 4. I←1
 5. Repeat
 6. if X >L[I]
 7. then X←L[I]
 8. until I is less than or equal to N
 9. Print the value of X
10. Stop
```

1.5.9 Insert a card in a list of sorted cards

```
1. Start
2. Input N sorted cards and store them in list L
3. Input the new card C
4. Identify the position of the card where the current position value is>C and next position value<C
5. If position is not identified
6. then consider the end of the list as the position
7. Insert C into the identified position of L
8. Print the value of X
9. Stop
```

1.5.10 Guess an integer number in a range

```
1. Start
2. Input N
3. Generate a random number between 1 and 100 and store it in X
4. If X is equal to N
5. then print "matched"
6. else if X is less than N
7. then print "less value"
8. else print "greater value"
9. Stop
```

1.5.11 Towers of Hanoi algorithm

```
1.  Start
2.  Function H(disk, source, destination, aux)
3.      IF disk == 0, THEN
4.          move disk from source to destination
5.      ELSE
6.          H(disk - 1, source, aux, destination)
7.          move disk from source to destination
8.          H(disk - 1, aux, destination, source)
9.      END IF
10. END Function
11. Stop
```

1.6 Building Blocks of Program

The collection of instructions grouped into a single place called as program. A program consists of multiple instructions. Each instruction in a program is called as a statement. After developing a program for the required application, the programmer will save the program. Thus, the program will be stored into the memory. After compilation process, the corresponding machine level code will be stored in the memory. During the execution of the program, the memory will be read, statement by statement, and the processor will carry out the instructions of the corresponding statement. Various building blocks of a program are listed below.

- Statements
- Data types
- Variables
- Keywords
- Expressions
- Operands
- Operators
- Functions
- Conditions and loops

1.7 Background of Learning to Write Programs

- Learn the character set which refers to the set of alphabets, letters and some special characters that are valid in the programming language.

- Learn the tokens that are valid in the programming language. With this, the programmer will know the valid words.
- Then, learn the instruction format allowed in the programming language. With this, the programmer will be able to write valid sentences.
- Finally, the programmer should be able to group valid multiple instructions into a program in the programming language.

1.8 Sample Algorithms

Algorithm **1**: Read a string and check whether it is palindrome or not.

1. Start
2. Input String S
3. l←length of S
4. i←l-1
5. while i>=0
6. begin
7. Store the cuurent character of S into string T
8. Decrement i value
9. end
10. If S is equal to T
11. then print "palindrome"
12. else print "not palindrome"
13. stop

Algorithm **2**: Read N number of values and add N values

1. Start
2. Read N numbers
3. i←0
4. S←0
5. while i<N
6. begin
7. S←S+i
8. i←i+1
9. end
10. print S
11. stop

Algorithm **3**: Read N and print the Fibonacci series with N numbers

1. Start
2. Read N
3. Fib[0]←0
4. Fib[1]←1
5. i←2
6. while i<=N
7. begin
8. Fib[i]←Fib[i-1]+Fib[i-2]
9. i←i+1
10. End
11. Print Fib
12. Stop

Glossary

- The computer program consists of a set of instructions that provide solution to a given problem.
- An algorithm is a step-by-step approach for the development of a program.
- A flowchart is a graphical representation of the program.

Summary

- A computer program helps in solving complex problems.
- To develop a computer program, initially an algorithm should be developed and then a programming language should be used to develop a program for the algorithm.

Multiple Choice Questions

1. Which of the following are the characteristic of a computer?
   (a) Speed (b) Accuracy
   (c) Storage (d) All the above
2. How many generations of computer are available?
   (a) 3 (b) 4
   (c) 5 (d) 6
3. Which of the following are applications of computer?
   (a) Automation (b) Textile
   (c) Transportation (d) All the above
4. Which of the following is used for storing the data?
   (a) CPU (b) Memory
   (c) Input (d) Output
5. How many types of computer software are available?
   (a) 1 (b) 2
   (c) 3 (d) 4
6. Which of the following characteristics are valid for an algorithm?
   (a) Simple (b) Easy
   (c) Termination (d) All the above
7. Algorithm development consumes
   (a) less time
   (b) more time
   (c) Both (a) and (b)
   (d) None of the above
8. The algorithm notation with a sequence of statements is called as?
   (a) Step form (b) Pseudo code
   (c) Flowchart (d) All the above
9. The written format of algorithm with limited terminology is called as?
   (a) Step form (b) Pseudo code
   (c) Flowchart (d) All the above
10. The graphical representation of algorithm is called as?
    (a) Step form (b) Pseudo code
    (c) Flowchart (d) All the above

Fill in the Blanks

1. The first generation computers are designed with ____________.
2. There are ____________ number of computers are available in the classification.
3. To overcome the speed mismatch between CPU and I/O devices, ____________ is used.
4. Operating system is a ____________ software.
5. ____________ is a step-by-step approach for representing problem solution.
6. Algorithm representation in various formats is called as ____________.
7. In a flow chart, the symbol for relationship is ____________.
8. In an algorithm, ____________ is used to express the action or event.
9. The flow of control ends with ____________ statement.
10. The ____________ structure of algorithm, uses loop statements.

State True/False

1. Magnetic core based memory is used in second generation.
2. Main frame is not one of the types of computer?
3. The speed of cache memory speed is higher than other types of memory.
4. Applications are end user programs.
5. Algorithm contains infinite steps.
6. There are three types of algorithm notation.
7. In a flowchart, different symbols are used for initial and terminating states.
8. The current status of the algorithm is represented by a statement.
9. A function is also called as subroutine.
10. The selection structure of an algorithm contains decision making statements.

Find the Output

1.
   1. Start
   2. Input N
   3. A=3.14×N×N
   4. Print A
   5. Stop

2.
   1. Start
   2. Input N
   3. i←0
   4. S←0
   5. While N>0
   6. Begin
   7. r←remainder of n/10
   8. S←S+r
   9. n←n/10
   10. End
   11. Print S
   12. Stop

Find the Error

1.
   1. Start
   2. Input N
   3. Print N

2.
   1. Start
   2. Print
   3. Stop

Long Answer Questions

1. State and explain the building blocks of algorithm.
2. With an example, explain in detail about flowchart.
3. Illustrate computer hardware and discuss with a detailed note.
4. List and explain the various types of programming languages.
5. What are the various notations of algorithm?
6. Write the algorithm for Towers of Hanoi.

Short Answer Questions

1. List and explain various control flow statements in algorithm.
2. Differentiate algorithm, pseudo code and flowchart.
3. Briefly discuss about the generations of computer.
4. Differentiate application software and system software.
5. List the various states in an algorithm.
6. Explain algorithmic problem solving.
7. List the various applications of a computer.

Exercise Algorithms

1. Write an algorithm to check whether a given number is Armstrong number or not.
2. Write an algorithm to print the sum of all digits in a given number.
3. Write an algorithm to find the largest number among given N numbers.
4. Write an algorithm to check whether the given number is prime number or not.
5. Write an algorithm to print the Nth multiplication table.
6. Write an algorithm to find the roots of a quadratic equation.
7. Write an algorithm to swap two numbers.
8. Write an algorithm to find the GCD/LCM of a given number.

Answers

Multiple Choice Questions

1. (d)
2. (c)
3. (d)
4. (b)
5. (b)
6. (d)
7. (b)
8. (a)
9. (b)
10. (c)

Fill in the Blanks

1. vacuum tubes
2. 7
3. I/O processor
4. system
5. Algorithm
6. notation
7. ⟶
8. statement
9. end/stop
10. Iteration

State True/False

1. True
2. False
3. True
4. True
5. False
6. True
7. False
8. False
9. True
10. True

Find the Output

1. Prints the area of the circle
2. Prints the reverse of the given number

Find the Error

1. No terminate statement in the algorithm.
2. For print statement, the value is not provided.

CHAPTER

2 Fundamentals of Python Programming

The present chapter discusses about the features, applications of Python programming language. It compares C, Java and Python programming languages and illustrates installation of the Python software, step by step.

2.1 Introduction to Python

Python is a simple and powerful language. It helps the programmer find solution to a given problem without worrying about the technical details of the programming language viz., structure and syntax. It supports high-level programming language with both procedure and object-oriented properties and is suitable for scripting and development of various applications. The python programming language is introduced by Guido van Rossum. Various popular programming languages such as C, C++ and Java can be coupled with Python. It contains built-in libraries for data structures and GUI (graphical user interface). In Python, a control routine program is an additional feature. This program feature helps Python to connect to different programs. There is also a built-in garbage collector feature, which helps Python to handle memory management efficiently. In Python, inclusion of various libraries is not required. Further, usage of code blocks is made easy with the indentation (white space).

In Python, declaration of a variable does not require the specification of the data type. So, it is called a dynamic typed language. It is applicable for derived types also. The Python is a platform-independent programming language. It contains an interpreter which will read the source program line by line and convert it into machine code. Similar to Java programming language, the Python also supports platform-independent feature with the help of Byte code. The interpreter of Python will generate the Byte code as the output. This byte code file can be used by any platform and within each platform, the Byte code is executed. The Python uses the interpreter more than the compiler; so it takes more time. The advantage of using interpreter is that the syntax errors can be identified immediately while reading a program line. The Python programming language is popular for program prototyping and is used for developing programs within a short time. It can support program modifications with the support of graphical user interfaces (GUIs).

The Python supports both procedural oriented and object oriented programming language. In a single Python program, both these programming language features can be used. So, Python programming supports the top-down approach which allows the usage of functions. It also supports bottom-up approach which allows the usage of classes and objects.

2.2 Features of Python

- Unsophisticated

  It is an unsophisticated language. It allows the user to write the programs without following strict rules viz., declaring the variable data types, usage of curly braces etc. It allows the programmer to provide the solution program rather than focusing on the structure and syntax.

- Easy
  Learning of Python programming language is very easy, even for beginners. Python is a Free/ Libre and Open Source Software (FLOSS). This is a software given by FLOSS community for knowledge sharing.
- High-level
  The programmer need not worry about various low-level details required for the program.
- Portable
  The Python is a platform-independent programming language. With the Byte code, the Python Program can be executed by any platform and hence, Python programs are portable.
- Interpreted
  Python programs can be directly executed from the Byte code. The Byte code is an executable code but it is an interpreted code. It translates the original source code into platform-independent code.
- Object Oriented
  Python supports all the principles of object-oriented programming (OOP). Python programs can be designed around the objects which concentrate on data. Implementing various OOP principles in Python is simple as compared to C++ or Java.
- Extensibility
  These programs can be executed by the Python and are extensible to C, C++ and Java. In this case, the programs can be treated as disabled codes.
- Embeddable
  The scripting feature can be provided by embedding the Python program into C or C++ programs.
- Extensive Libraries
  The Python consists of a huge standard library for handling regular expressions, threading, GUI etc.

2.3 Applications of Python

The Python can be useful for various real-time applications as listed below.

2.3.1 Web and internet development

The Python provides various features for handling the Web and the Internet. It is used for development of various frameworks (Pyramid and Django etc.), Micro frameworks (Bottle and Flask etc.) and content management systems (CMS and Plone etc.). For this, Python extensive libraries should support HTML, FTP, XML, JSON, Socket and E-mail processing. For supporting asynchronous network programming, Twisted Python framework is used.

2.3.2 Scientific and numeric

Python is widely used in scientific and numeric computing. For handling mathematics, engineering and science, SciPy framework is used. To analyze and model the data, Pandas framework is used. For parallel computation and visualization, IPython framework is used.

2.3.3 Education

For students, Python is a powerful language to learn programming skills. By learning Python programming, the student will be able to develop various real-time applications. Issues that may arise while teaching the language are discussed in the Education Special Interest Group.

2.3.4 Desktop GUIs

For Python, Tk GUI library provides the binary distribution. There are also platform-specific libraries such as GTK+. Kivy and wxWidgets are widely used toolkits for various platforms.

2.3.5 Software development

Nowadays, Python is widely used as a standard programming language for developing software. Python can be used for various applications such as building, controlling, management and testing. For building and controlling, sCons framework is used; for testing, Buildbot framework is used and for management, Trac framework is used.

2.4 Installation of Python

2.4.1 Windows operating system

Step1: Download the Python software from the following URL
https://www.python.org/downloads/windows/

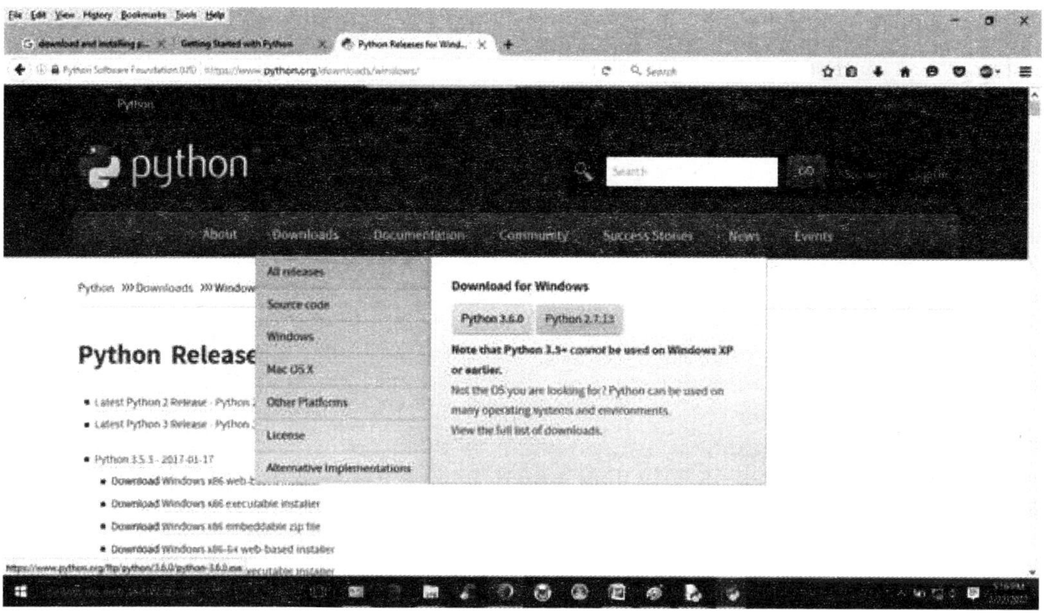

Step2: Install the downloaded Python software

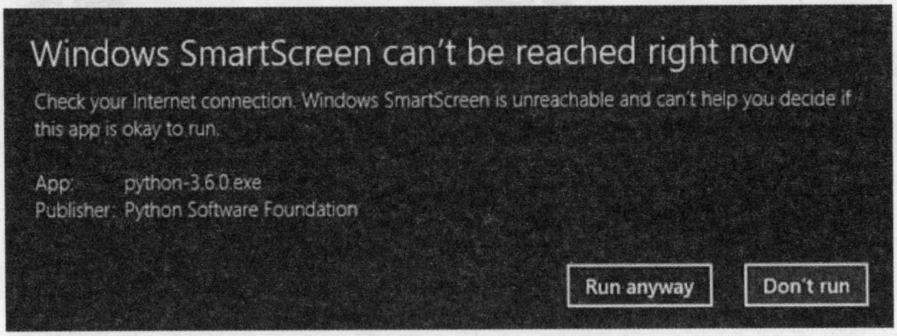

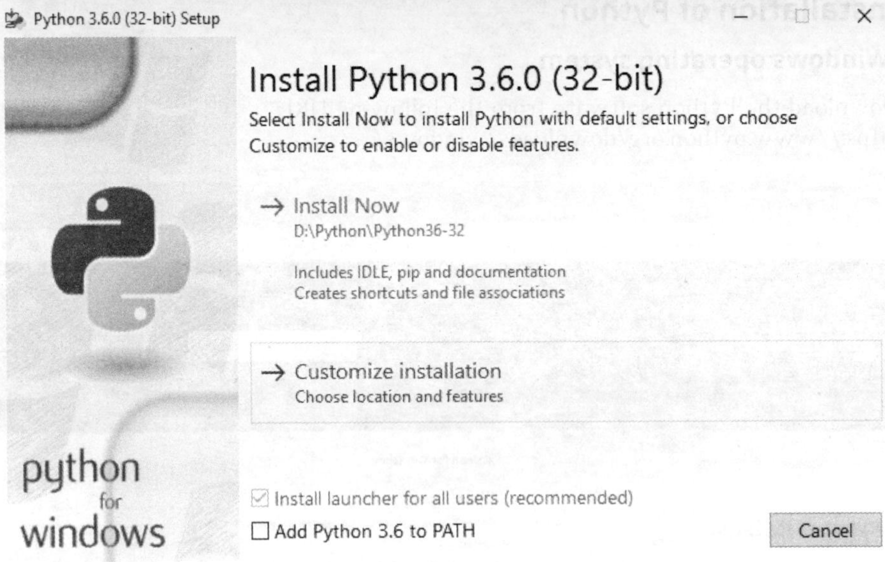

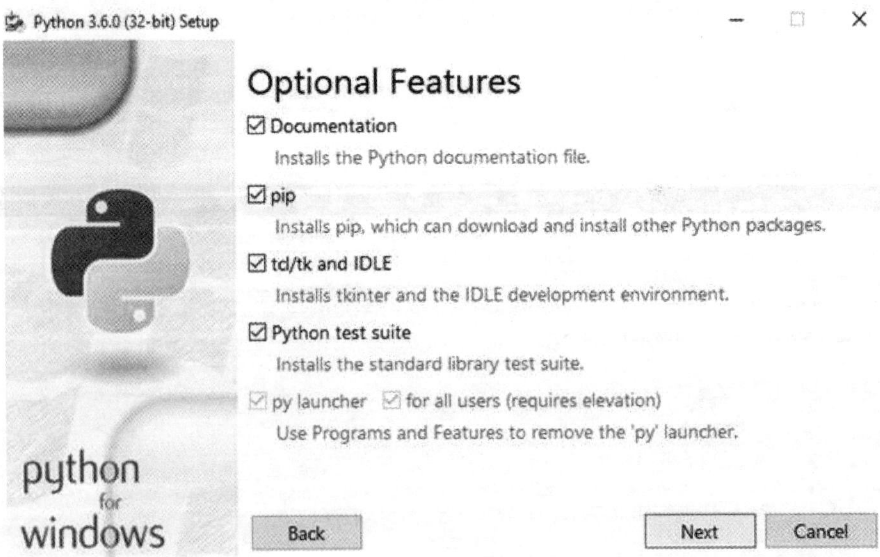

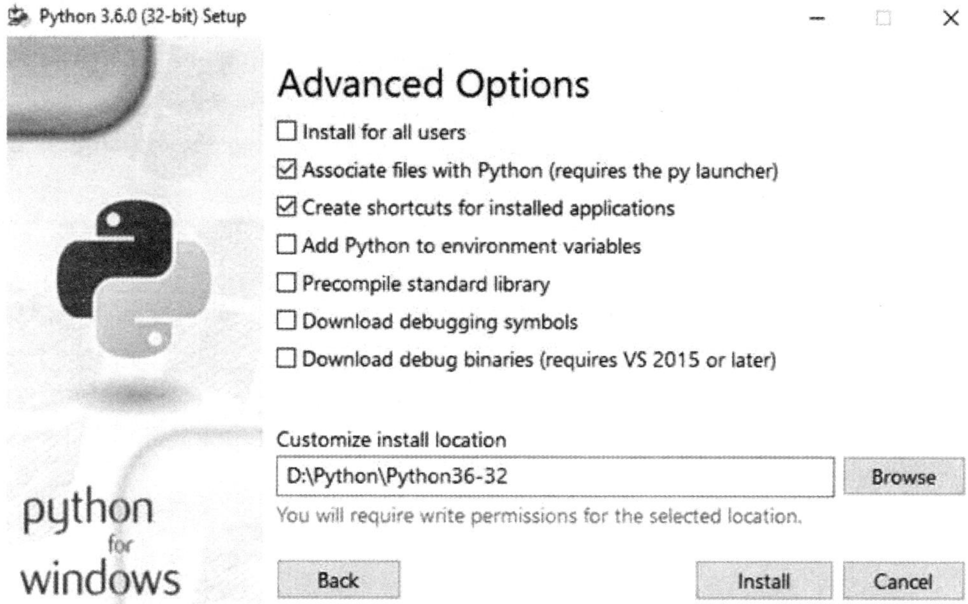

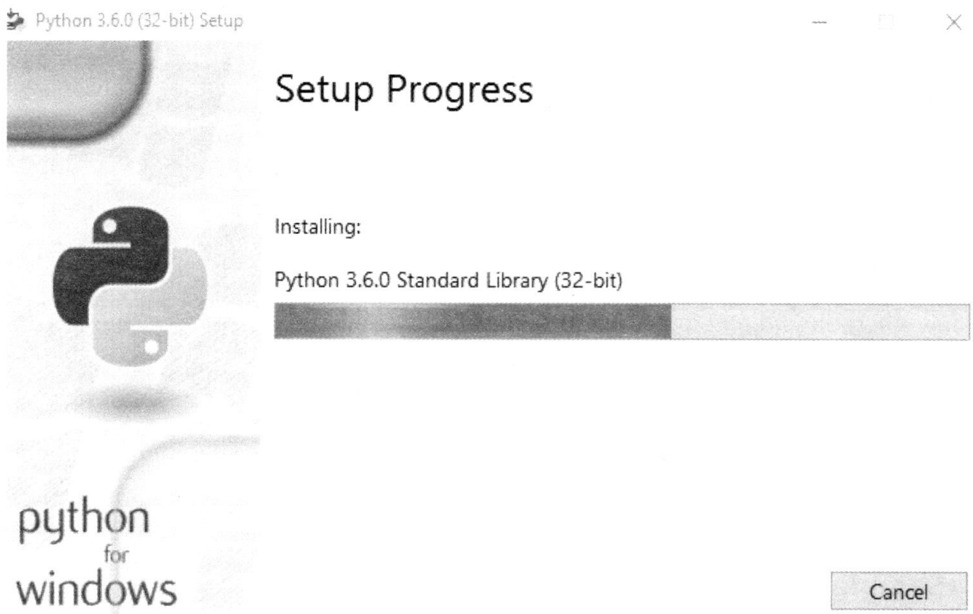

Step3: Add Python to the System Variable

- Click on *Start* → *My Computer* → *Properties* → *Advanced System Settings* → *Environment Variables* → *System Variables* → *Path* → *Edit.*
- In the Text box, at the end paste the path of the Python "D:\Python\Python36-32;"
- Click *OK.*

2.4.2 Linux operating system

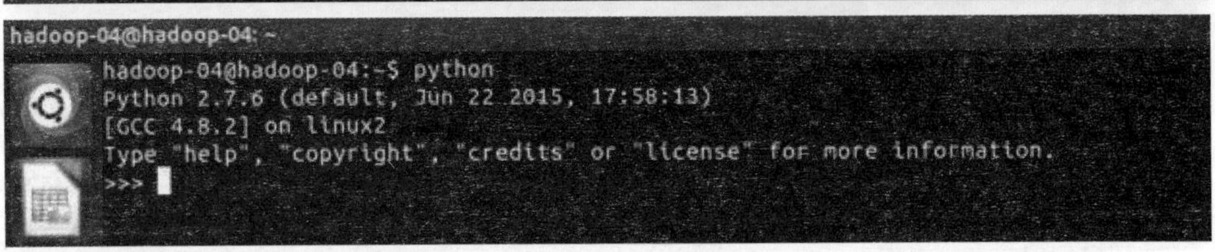

2.5 Sample Program

Program 1: Write a Python program to print "Hello World!" Program

Step 1: Open notepad and type the following line

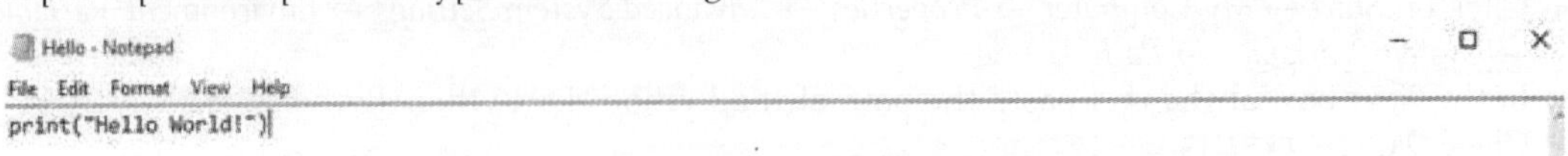

Step 2: Save the file as Hello.py
Step 3: Click Start → run → cmd → PythonProgramdirectory → python Hello.py

C:\Windows\system32\cmd.exe

```
Microsoft Windows [Version 10.0.10240]
(c) 2015 Microsoft Corporation. All rights reserved.

C:\Users\T SRIKANTH>d:

D:\>cd ythonPrograms

D:\ythonPrograms>python Hello.py
Hello World!

D:\ythonPrograms>
```

2.6 Python Virtual Machine

The Python Virtual Machine (PVM) is used to provide platform independence while developing application software. The PVM is a part of the Python interpreter that helps to understand the pre-compiled or byte code of the source python program. The compiled byte code is available in ".pyc" file. This file contains a magic tag and a modification time stamp tag. Each tag has a length of 4 bytes. The .pyc file is simple and can be transferred. Its loading capacity is high and it provides more security. These files are not compatible between various versions of Python.

2.7 Frozen Binaries

For any Python program, the frozen binary file can be created with various components such as the byte code of the source program, interpreter or PVM and the corresponding supported files. All these files are packaged into a single binary file which is executable. "py2exe", "PyInstaller" and "freeze" are used for creating frozen binaries.

2.8 Memory Management in Python

In Python, the memory is considered as private heap. All the Python objects are created by using private heap only. The Python memory manager is responsible for allocating and deallocating the memory for the objects. The raw memory allocator will interact directly with the operating system and can manage all Python data. The object-specific allocators are used to manage the specific object data only.

- PyMem_RawMalloc(), PyMem_RawCalloc(), PyMem_RawRealloc() and PyMem_RawFree() functions are used by the raw memory allocator.
- PyMem_GetAllocator(), PyMem_SetAllocator() and PyMem_SetupDebugHooks() functions are used by the object specific allocators.

2.9 Comparison Between C and Python

- Developing the code in C is complex; whereas it is easy in Python.
- In C, indentation is not mandatory; whereas in Python, indentation is mandatory.

- In C, each variable requires declaration; whereas in Python, declaration is not required for a variable.
- In-line assignments are supported in C; whereas in Python, they are not supported.
- In C, pointers can be used; whereas in Python, pointers are not used.
- In C, garbage collector is not used; whereas in Python, garbage collector is used.
- In C, there are no automatic memory management tools; whereas in Python, there are automatic memory management tools.
- In C, the semicolon is used for ending the statements; whereas in Python, the statement is ends with new line character.

2.10 Comparison Between Java and Python

- Developing the code in Java is complex; whereas it is easy in Python.
- In Java indentation is not mandatory; whereas in Python, indentation is mandatory.
- In Java, each variable requires declaration; whereas in Python, declaration is not required for a variable.
- In Java, a class can have multiple constructors; whereas in Python, only one constructor is allowed in a class.
- Handling strings in Java is weak; whereas handling strings in Python is strong.
- Java uses static typing; whereas Python uses dynamic typing.
- The execution speed of Java is higher than that in Python.

2.11 Python vs. Similar Tools

Various other similar tools for Python are listed below

- SAS
- R-programming
- MATLAB

SAS contains a wide variety of functions for performing statistical operations. But SAS is not open-source software. To overcome this, R-programming was introduced. It is open-source software that can be distributed to anyone. The Python provides various functions for performing statistical operations and other operations also. MATLAB software is also popular and widely used software but it is not open source software.

2.12 Python Keywords

Various keywords in Python are listed in Table 2.1.

Table 2.1 Keywords in Python

FALSE	finally	return	class	is
None	for	try	continue	lambda
TRUE	from	while	def	nonlocal
and	global	with	del	not
as	if	yield	elif	or
assert	import	else	pass	
break	in	except	raise	

2.13 Python Identifiers

The identifier represents the names used in the Python program. The length of the identifier can be varied from one to another. The rules for validating the identifier are listed below.

- The identifier can be a combination of various elements viz., uppercase letters, lowercase letters, digits and underscore.
- Any one of the keyword is not permitted to act as identifier.
- The first letter of the identifier should not be a digit.
- Special alphabets viz., !,@,# etc. . . are also not permitted to be a part of identifier.

2.14 Python Statements

Various Python statements are listed below.

- Simple statement
- Expression statement
- Assignment statement
- Assert statement
- Pass statement
- Del statement
- Return statement
- Yield statement
- Raise statement
- Break statement
- Continue statement
- Import statement
- Global statement
- Nonlocal statement

2.15 Python Indentation

In Python programming language, a group of code or statements are arranged in an individual block. Each block can be separated with the indentation as shown in Fig. 2.1.

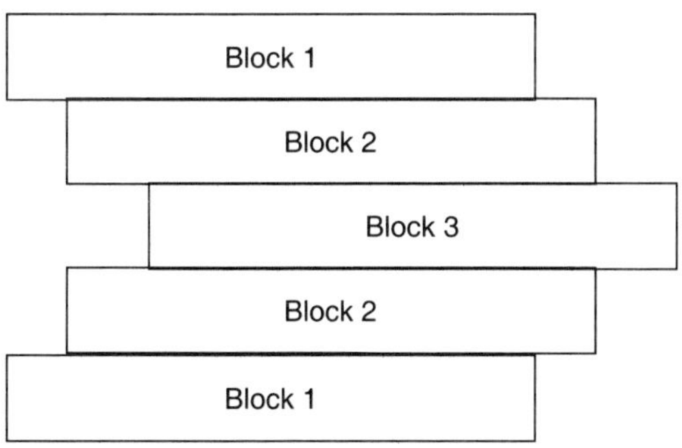

Figure 2.1 Structure blocks in Python with indentation.

2.16 Comments in Python

In Python, the comments can be specified in any one of the following two ways.

- "#" is used to represent the single line comment.
- Multiple line comment statements are started and ended with the """ delimiter.

2.17 Differences Between Python 2.x and 3.x

- In Python 2.x, the print statement is used; whereas in 3.x, the print() function is used.
- In Python 2.x, integer division returns only integer result; whereas in 3.x, it can return floating value. For example, for 3/2 operation, the result is 1 in 2.x while the result is 1.5 in 3.x.
- The input() function of 3.x is same as raw_input() function in 2.x.
- In 2.x, "file" command should be used to open the file; whereas in 3.x., "open()" function should be used.
- The "xrange()" function of 2.x is the same as "range()" function in 3.x.
- In 2.x, the implicit type string code is ASCII; whereas in 3.x, the implicit string code is UNICODE.
- In Python 3.x, additional "as" keyword should be used for handling exception; whereas in 2.x, it is not required.
- _future_module is required to upgrade from Python 2.x to 3.x.

2.18 Coding Styles in Python

In Python, there are four different types of coding styles. They are

- Functional
- Imperative
- Procedural
- Object oriented

Functional

In this style of coding, the given problem is decomposed into various functions. It is widely used for lambda calculus.

```
import functools
M = [10, 20, 30, 40, 50]
res = functools.reduce(lambda a, b: a + b, M)
print("result=",res)
```

> Programming Tip:
> In Python, print() is used for printing the input value on the monitor.

Output

```
D:\PythonPrograms>python s1.py
result=150
```

In the above sample code, "functools" module is used. This module is used for higher-order functions. The "lambda" is used to create the anonymous functions at runtime. The "reduce()" is used to reduce the iterable to a single value.

Imperative

In this style of coding, the order of the operations should be defined explicitly. It is widely used for handling various operations of data structures.

```
M = [10, 20, 30, 40, 50]
res = 0
for a in M:
    res=res+a
print("result=",res)
```

Output

```
D:\PythonPrograms>python s1.py
result= 150
```

Procedural

In this style of coding, focus is given on the code. The given problem is described in terms of list of instructions. The code is efficiently handled with multiple functions. It uses iteration, modularization etc. for avoiding code redundancy.

```
def su(N):
    res = 0
    for a in N:
        res=res+a
    return(res)
M = [10, 20, 30, 40, 50]
print("result=",su(M))
```

Output

```
D:\PythonPrograms>python s1.py
result= 150
```

Object oriented

In this style of coding, focus is given on the data. The data is considered as a real-time object. The code that works with the object data is grouped into a single entity and is called as a "class". The class contains members and methods. Some of the object oriented principles are

- Abstraction
  Abstraction allows the programmer to use the object without knowing the details of the object.
- Inheritance
  Inheritance allows one class to derive the properties of the other class. With this, the properties of the base class are derived into sub-class.
- Encapsulation
  Encapsulation binds all the properties, viz., members and methods into single entity called as "class."
- Polymorphism
  Polymorphism allows the same entity to be used in different forms. There are two types of polymorphism i) Compile-time polymorphism and ii) Run-time polymorphism.

```
class X:
    def su(self,x,y):
        return(x+y)
y=X();
print("result=",y.su(10,20))
```

Output

```
D:\PythonPrograms>python s1.py
result= 30
```

In the above sample code, the class "X" contains method "su()". For the class "X", an object "y" is created.

Glossary

- The Python Virtual Machine (PVM) is used to provide platform-independent feature for Python scripts.

Summary

- In the present chapter, the advantages of Python programming language over other programming languages, viz., C and Java are discussed.
- The Python language is platform-independent because of the use of Python Virtual Machine (PVM).
- Indentation should be followed in Python programming.

Multiple Choice Questions

1. Python is a case sensitive language?
   (a) Yes (b) No
   (c) Maybe (d) Never
2. Which variable does Python use for locating the module files?
   (a) PYTHONPATH
   (b) PYTHONSTARTUP
   (c) PYTHONCASEOK
   (d) PYTHONHOME
3. Python source code file initialization is represented by which variable?
   (a) PYTHONPATH
   (b) PYTHONSTARTUP
   (c) PYTHONCASEOK
   (d) PYTHONHOME
4. In an import statement, the first non case-sensitive match is identified by which variable?
   (a) PYTHONPATH
   (b) PYTHONSTARTUP
   (c) PYTHONCASEOK
   (d) PYTHONHOME
5. Which is an alternative module search path.?
   (a) PYTHONPATH
   (b) PYTHONSTARTUP
   (c) PYTHONCASEOK
   (d) PYTHONHOME
6. Who is the developer of the Python?
   (a) Guido van Rossum (b) James Gosling
   (c) Steve Jobs (d) Bill Gates
7. In command prompt, which command is used to start Python?
   (a) run python (b) execute python
   (c) go python (d) python
8. Which of the following is correct to execute the t.py file?
   (a) run python t.py (b) python t.py
   (c) execute python t.py (d) go python t.py
9. Which of the following languages can be coupled with Python?
   (a) C (b) C++
   (c) Java (d) All the above
10. Code block is made easy with?
    (a) Indentation
    (b) Comma operator
    (c) Both a and b
    (d) None of the above
11. Which of the following are features of Python?
    (a) High level (b) Easy
    (c) Portable (d) All of the above
12. Regular expressions are handled with?
    (a) Extensibility
    (b) Object oriented
    (c) Extensive libraries
    (d) None of the above
13. Which of the following supports Web and Internet development applications?
    (a) HTML (b) FTP
    (c) XML (d) All the above
14. Which of the following framework supports asynchronous network programming application?
    (a) Python
    (b) Twisted Python
    (c) Twisted
    (d) None of the above
15. Which of the following framework supports build control?
    (a) Twisted Python (b) Buildbot
    (c) sCons (d) Trac
16. Which of the following framework supports testing?
    (a) Twisted Python (b) Buildbot
    (c) sCons (d) Trac
17. Which of the following framework supports management?
    (a) Twisted Python (b) Buildbot
    (c) sCons (d) Trac
18. Which of the following library provides binary distribution?
    (a) Tk (b) SciPy
    (c) All the above (d) None

19. The compiled code of Python program saves in which file?
(a) .py (b) .pyc
(c) .pyz (d) .ycz

20. The compiled code contains
(a) magic tag
(b) time stamp tag
(c) Both (a) and (b)
(d) None of the above

21. Which of the following are used to create frozen binaries?
(a) py2exe (b) PyInstaller
(c) freeze (d) All the above

22. Frozen binary file is created with
(a) byte code
(b) byte code, PVM
(c) byte code, PVM, supported files
(d) All the above

23. In Python, memory is considered as
(a) heap
(b) static
(c) heap and static
(d) None of the above

24. The raw memory allocator uses which of the following functions?
(a) PyMem_RawMalloc()
(b) PyMem_RawCalloc()
(c) PyMem_RawRealloc()
(d) All the above

25. A variable in Python
(a) should be declared
(b) should be declared and defined
(c) should not be declared
(d) None of the above

26. The Python statement ends with?
(a) comma
(b) new line character
(c) semi-colon
(d) None of the above

27. How many constructors are allowed in a Python class?
(a) 1
(b) 2
(c) 3
(d) None of the above

28. Python uses:
(a) static typing
(b) dynamic typing
(c) heap typing
(d) None of the above

29. Other similar tools for Python:
(a) SAS (b) R-programming
(c) MATLAB (d) All the above

30. SAS is used for:
(a) Statistical operations
(b) Analytical operations
(c) Management operations
(d) None of the above

31. Which of the following are Python keywords?
(a) Finally (b) Return
(c) Class (d) All the above

32. The first letter of the Python identifier should not be:
(a) an upper-case letter
(b) a lower-case letter
(c) a digit
(d) None of the above

33. Each block of Python is separated by:
(a) indentation
(b) comma
(c) semi-colon
(d) None of the above

34. Single-line comment in Python contains:
(a) # (b) ?
(c) % (d) !

35. Multi-line comment in Python contains:
(a) # (b) ?
(c) """ (d) !

36. Which of the following functions are used to read data in Python **3**.x and **2**.x?
(a) input() and raw_input()
(b) raw_input() and raw_input()
(c) input() and input()
(d) None of the above

37. What are the various coding styles in Python?
(a) Functional (b) Procedural
(c) Object oriented (d) All the above

38. Which of the following functions are used to open the file in Python **3**.x and **2**.x??
(a) file() and open() (b) file and open()
(c) file and open (d) file() and open

Fill in the Blanks

1. ___________ makes Python to connect different programs.

2. Python uses ___________ for compiling the source program.

3. ____________ is the output of the compilation process.
4. Python is given by ____________ community.
5. Python is a ____________ language
6. In case of extensibility, Python codes are considered as ____________
7. In Python, Bottle and Flask are ____________
8. Pandas framework is used for ____________
9. For parallel computation and visualization, ____________ is used
10. Platform-independent feature is supported with ____________
11. PVM consists of ____________
12. Combination of byte code, PVM and others is called ____________
13. Frozen binary is a ____________
14. To create a frozen binaries ____________ are used
15. All Python objects are created by using ____________ only.
16. ____________ will interact directly with operating system.
17. ____________ functions are used by object specific allocators
18. Python uses ____________ typing.
19. Statistical operations are performed with ____________.
20. ____________ are not permitted to be a part of an identifier.
21. ____________ should not be a first letter of the identifier.
22. ____________ is not permitted to act as identifier.
23. Individual blocks are separated with ____________.
24. range() is used in Python ____________
25. xrange() is used in Python ____________
26. In Python ____________, "as" keyword is used for handling exceptions.
27. There are ____________ number of coding styles in Python.
28. Length of the identifier can be ____________.
29. The code of Python is ____________ when compared with Java coding.
30. The execution speed of Python is ____________ when compared with Java.

State True/False

1. The Python is a simple and powerful language.
2. The Python cannot be coupled with other programming languages.
3. Garbage collector is responsible for handling memory efficiently.
4. In Python, declaration of a variable does not require specification of the data type.
5. Python is a platform-dependent programming language.
6. Python contains compiler and interpreter.
7. PVM is responsible for platform-independent feature.
8. The syntax errors can be efficiently identified by the interpreter.
9. Python supports prototyping efficiently.
10. Python follows either top-down or bottom-up approach.
11. Python is free and open-source software.
12. Python programs are not portable.
13. Python supports disabled codes
14. Pyramid is one of the development frameworks of Python.
15. SciPy framework is not used for mathematics, engineering and science.
16. Ipython framework can be used in both online and offline modes.
17. Kivy is one of the desktop GUI frameworks in Python.
18. "Python" is used for executing the Python program.
19. Python source code files are saved with ".pyc"
20. Compiled Python files are saved with ".pyc'

Long Answer Questions

1. Write about Python programming language.
2. List and explain the various features of Python programming language.

3. What are the applications of Python programming language?
4. Is Python is a platform-independent programming language? Justify your answer.

Short Answer Questions

1. What is the advantage of using white spaces in Python?
2. What are the various data types used in Python?
3. Does Python support procedure-oriented or object-oriented programming language?
4. What is Bytecode? What is its advantage?
5. What is the default GUI library available in Python?

Answers

Multiple Choice Questions

1. (a)
2. (a)
3. (b)
4. (c)
5. (d)
6. (a)
7. (d)
8. (b)
9. (d)
10. (a)
11. (d)
12. (c)
13. (d)
14. (c)
16. (b)
17. (d)
18. (a)
19. (b)
20. (c)
21. (d)
22. (c)
23. (a)
24. (d)
25. (c)
26. (b)
27. (a)
28. (b)
29. (d)
30. (a)
31. (d)
32. (c)
33. (a)
34. (a)
35. (c)
36. (a)
37. (d)
38. (b)

Fill in the Blanks

1. Control routine program
2. Interpreter
3. Byte code
4. FLOSS
5. platform-independent
6. disabled codes
7. micro frameworks
8. data visualization
9. IPython framework
10. Python Virtual Machine (PVM)
11. Interpreter
12. Frozen binary
13. Binary file
14. py2exe, PyInstaller and freeze
15. private heap
16. Raw memory allocator
17. PyMem_GetAllocator(), PyMem_SetAllocator() and PyMem_SetupDebugHooks()
18. dynamic
19. SAS, R-programming and MATLAB
20. Special alphabets
21. Digit
22. Keyword
23. indentation
24. 3.x
25. 2.x
26. 3.x
27. 4
28. varied
29. easy
30. slow

State True/False

1. True
2. False
3. True
4. True
5. False
6. False
7. True
8. True
9. True
10. False
11. True
12. False
13. True
14. True
15. False
16. True
17. True
18. True
19. False
20. True

CHAPTER 3 Syntax and Styles

In this chapter, we discuss the syntax and styles used in Python programming language. Based on the initialized value, the data type will be automatically assigned to the variable. The values are represented by literals. Like other programming languages, Python also supports various operators and expressions.

3.1 Data Types

In Python programming language, the data can be maintained by variables. The type of variable represents the value stored within the variable. Type inferencing is allowed in Python. So, general keywords like int, float etc. are not required for the variable.

```
D:\Python>python
Python 3.6.0 (v3.6.0:41df79263a11, Dec 23 2016, 07:18:10) [MSC v.1900 32 bit (Intel)] on win32
Type "help", "copyright", "credits" or "license" for more information.
>>> 10
10
>>> 35.76
35.76
>>> 'abcd'
'abcd'
>>> 1,00,000
(1, 0, 0)
```

In Python, type keyword is used to get the data type assigned to the input data.

```
>>> type(100)
<class 'int'>
>>> type(15.27)
<class 'float'>
>>> type('abcd')
<class 'str'>
```

The bool data type contains two possible values viz., "True" and "False".

```
>>> bool
<class 'bool'>
```

The "False" value can be considered in any one of the following cases.

- If the value is "None"
- If the value is "0" or "0.0"
- If the input value is an empty list, tuple or string.

```
>>> bool('a')
True
>>> bool('')
False
```

3.2 Literal

A literal is a value that can be parsed and turned into an object. In Python, literals can be any one of the following.

- Int
- Float
- Unicode
- Tuple
- Complex
- String
- List
- dict literal

3.3 Numeric Literal

- The integer literal converts the input integer value to **int** object.

```
>>> type(12)
<class 'int'>
```

- The float literal converts the input float value to **float** object.

```
>>> type(12.5)
<class 'float'>
```

- The complex literal converts the input complex value to **complex** object.

```
>>> type(2+5j)
<class 'complex'>
```

3.4 Boolean Literal

The Boolean literal will convert either True or False value to **bool** object.

```
>>> type(True)
<class 'bool'>
>>> type(False)
<class 'bool'>
```

3.5 String Literal

The string value defined in single quote or double quotes can be considered as string literal. The string literal can convert the input string value to a string object.

```
>>> type('hello')
<class 'str'>
>>> type("hello")
<class 'str'>
```

3.6 Variable

In Python, variables can be initialized without declaration. Based on the value of the input data, the type of the variable will be automatically considered. A variable name should start with a letter followed by sequence of letters, numbers or underscore (_) special character.

Integer data, floating point data and string data will be considered as primitive data type. Character data will be considered as string data with length 1.

```
>>> a=65
>>> b=78.24
>>>c='hai'
>>>a
65
>>>b
78.24
>>>c
'hai'
```

In Python, the string data will be considered as an array. The array index will start from 0.

```
>>> a='chapter-2'
>>> a
'chapter-2'
>>> a[1]
'h'
>>> a[0]
'c'
>>> a[5]
'e'
```

For string data, '+' represents the concatenation operation and '*' represents the repetition operation.

```
>>> a=('ha'+'i')
>>> a
'hai'
>>> a=('ha'*2)
>>> a
'haha'
```

Other than the primitive variables, Python also supports the following variables.

Tuples

A tuple is a list with a fixed number of elements. It uses parentheses for specification of data.

```
>>> x=(4,5,6)
>>> x[0]
4
>>> x[1]
5
>>> x[-1]
6
>>> x[2]
6
```

The index '-1' represents the last element in the tuple. In case of tuple variable, change of values is not permitted.

```
>>> x[2]=10
Traceback (most recent call last):
File "<stdin>", line 1, in <module>
TypeError: 'tuple' object does not support item assignment
```

Lists

Lists are different from tuples. A list does not have a fixed number of elements. It uses square brackets for specification of data. The change of values of a list variable is allowed.

```
>>> x=[4,5,6]
>>> x[0]
4
>>> x[1]
5
>>> x[-1]
6
>>> x[2]
6
>>> x[0]=10
>>> x
[10, 5, 6]
```

Dictionaries

It is a variable used to maintain multiple typed elements. It uses curly braces for specification of data. It maintains the data by using {key:value,. . .} format. Multiple entries are separated by the comma operator. The change of values is allowed.

```
>>> x={1:'a',2:2,3:5.8}
>>> x
{1: 'a', 2: 2, 3: 5.8}
>>> x[1]
'a'
>>> x[2]
2
>>> x[3]
5.8
>>> x[1]='b'
>>> x
{1: 'b', 2: 2, 3: 5.8}
```

3.7 Operators and Expressions

The Python programming language supports the following operators.

- Arithmetic operators
- Comparison (Relational) operators
- Assignment operators
- Logical operators

- Bitwise operators
- Membership operators
- Identity operators

3.7.1 Arithmetic operators

Arithmetic operators are used to perform arithmetic operations between any two operands. The various arithmetic operators supported by Python are given below:

- The '+' operator is used to perform the addition operation between the two input data values.
- The '-' operator is used to perform the subtraction operation between the two input data values.
- The '*' operator is used to perform the multiplication operation between the two input data values.
- The '/' operator is used to perform the division operation between the two input data values.
- The '%' operator is used to return the remainder of the division operation performed between the two input data values.
- The '**' operator is used for calculating the exponential.
- The '//' operator is used to perform the floor division operation between the two input data values. It returns the quotient of the division operation. The decimal points in the quotient result will be removed. If any one of the input is negative, then the quotient result is rounded towards negative infinity.

  For example, if the two numbers considered are 20 and 10, then the result of

  a + b = 30

  a - b = 10

  a * b = 200

  a / b = 2

  a % b = 0 (remainder is 0)

  a ** 2 = 400 (202)

  -a//b = -2 (a is negative, so the quotient will be rounded towards negative infinity)

3.7.2 Comparison (relational) operators

These operators are used to estimate the relation between two given input values. The various relational operators are given below:

- The '==' operator is used to compare whether the two given input values are equal or not. It returns True when both are equal; otherwise it returns False.
- The '!=' operator is used to compare whether the two given input values are equal or not. It returns True when both are not equal; otherwise it returns False.
- The '>' operator is used to compare the two given input values, whether the left side value is greater than right side value or not. It returns True if the left side value is greater than the other value otherwise it returns False.
- The '<' operator is used to compare the two given input values, whether the left side value is less than right side value or not. It returns True if the left side value is less than the other value otherwise it returns False.
- The '>=' operator is used to compare the two given input values, whether the left side value is greater than or equal to right side value or not. It returns True if the left side value is greater than or equal to the other value otherwise it returns False.
- The '<=' operator is used to compare the two given input values, whether the left side value is less than or equal to right side value or not. It returns True if the left side value is less than or equal to the other value otherwise it returns False.

For example, if the two numbers considered are 20 and 10 then the result of

(a == b) → False
(a != b) → True
(a > b) → True
(a < b) → False
(a >= b) → True
(a <= b) → False

3.7.3 Assignment operators

The assignment operator is used to assign the input value to the variable. The assignment operator can be grouped with arithmetic operators and are called as compound assignment operators. The various assignment operators are as follows:

- The '=' operator is used to assign the input value (right-side value) to the variable (left-side variable).
- The '+=' is used to add the right-side value and the left-side value and assigns the result to the left-side variable.
- The '-=' is used to subtract the right-side value from the left-side value and assigns the result to the left-side variable.
- The '*=' is used to multiply the right-side value and the left-side value and assigns the result to the left-side variable.
- The '/=' is used to divide the left-side value by the right-side value and assigns the result to the left-side variable.
- The '**=' is used to compute the exponential of the left-side value raised to the right-side value and assigns the result to the left-side variable.
- The '//=' is used to compute the result of floor division of the left-side value by the right-side value and assigns the result to the left-side variable.

The results of the following operators are

(a = 20) → value of a is 20
(a = 20), (a += 10) → value of a is 30
(a = 20), (a -= 10) → value of a is 10
(a = 20), (a *= 10) → value of a is 200
(a = 20), (a /= 10) → value of a is 2
(a = 20), (a **= 2) → value of a is 400
(a = 20), (a //= 10) → value of a is -2

3.7.4 Logical operators

The logical relation between two input values is computed by logical operators. The various logical operators are

- The 'and' is called as Logical AND operator. It returns True only when both the inputs are True.
- The 'or' is called as Logical OR operator. It returns True when at least one of input is True.
- The 'not' is called as Logical NOT operator. It returns the negativity of the input value.

For example, if two input numbers a and b are 1 and 0, then the results of the following operations are

(a and b) → False
(a or b) → True
(not (a)) → False

3.7.5 Bitwise operators

The bitwise operators work bit by bit, on the input data value. For each value, the 8-bit ASCII code will be considered and on these bits, the following operations are performed.

- The '&' is called as binary AND operation. It will select the resultant bit to True only when the corresponding two input bit values are True; otherwise it is False.
- The '|' is called as binary OR operation. It will select the resultant bit to True when at least one of the corresponding two input bit values are True; otherwise it is False.
- The '^' is called as binary XOR operation. It will select the resultant bit to True only when the corresponding two input bit values are different; otherwise it is False.
- The '~' is called as binary ones complement operation. It will set the resultant bit to the complemented input bit value.
- The '<<' is called as binary Left Shift Operation. It will left shift the left-side value. The right-side value will specify the required number of shift operations.
- The '>>' is called as binary Right Shift Operation. It will right shift the left-side value. The right-side value will specify the required number of shift operations.

For example, if the two numbers considered are a = 101 and b = 011. The results of the following operations are

(a & b) → 001
(a | b) → 111
(a ^ b) → 110
(~ a) → 010

3.7.6 Membership operators

The membership operators in Python are used for strings, lists or tuples. They focus on testing the membership in the sequence. The various operators are

- The 'in' operator is used to search the input element in the sequence. If the input element is found, then it returns True; otherwise it returns False.
- The 'not in' operator is used to search the input element in the sequence. If the input element is not found then returns it True; otherwise it returns False.

```
x=(1,2,3)
y=2
a=(y in x)
print("in operator result=",a)
b=(y not in x)
print("not in operator result=",b)
```

Output

```
D:\PythonPrograms\aa>python a2.py
in operator result= True
not in operator result= False
```

3.7.7 Identity operators

Identity operators are used to evaluate whether the given two objects point to the same memory location or not. The various operators are

- The 'is' operator is used to return True if both objects points to the same memory location; otherwise it returns False.
- The 'is not' operator is used to return True if both objects are not pointing to the same memory location; otherwise it returns False.

```
x=(1,2,3)
y=2
a=(y is x)
print("is operator result=",a)
b=(y is not x)
print("not is operator result=",b)
```

Output

```
D:\PythonPrograms\aa>python a2.py
is operator result= False
not is operator result= True
```

3.8 Expressions and Order of Evaluations

Atom is a basic element of Python expression. An atom can be an identifier or literal. An Atom also consists of various forms enclosed in brackets, parentheses or braces. Name is an atom representing an identifier. Both the Byte and String literals are allowed in Python. Multiple expressions are separated by comma operator in a parenthesized form. The order of precedence of operators is evaluated based on the following Table 3.1.

Table **3.1** Operator Precedence in Python.

S. No.	Operator and Description
1	**
2	~ + -
3	* / % //
4	+ -
5	>> <<
6	&
7	^ |
8	<= < > >=
9	<> == !=
10	= %= /= //= -= += *= **=
11	Identity operators
12	Membership operators
13	Logical operators

3.9 Numbers

In Python programming, when numerical values are assigned to a variable, the numeric objects are automatically created. The 'del' keyword is used to delete reference to the numeric objects. The syntax of 'del' keyword is

```
del numericalobject-1[,......,numericalobject-n]
```

- If the 'del' keyword is applied on the numeric object where it is not initialized, then a runtime error will be generated.

```
b=20
print("Value of B=",b)
del(a)
print("Value of A=",a)
```

Output

```
D:\PythonPrograms>python del.py
Value of B= 20
Traceback (most recent call last):
File "del.py", line 3, in <module>
del(a)
NameError: name 'a' is not defined
```

In Python programming language, there are three types of numerical objects. They are

i. integers
ii. floating point numbers
iii. complex numbers

3.9.1 Integers

Integers represent fixed point numerical data. So, Python maintains integer numbers with no decimal point. In early versions, there were integers and long integers. However, in Version3, only int with unlimited size is allowed. With this, both the positive and negative numbers can be represented. A subset of integers is allowed to represent the Boolean values. An integer value can be represented in binary, decimal, hexa-decimal or octal form.

```
>>> a=10          #decimal integer value
>>> a
10
>>> a=0b100       #binary integer value
>>> a
4
>>> a=0x16        #hexa-decimal integer value
>>> a
22
>>> a=0o24        #octal integer value
>>> a
20
```

3.9.2 Floating point numbers

Floating point numbers are used to represent floating point numerical data. So, it maintains real numbers with decimal point separating the integer and fractional parts. Scientific notation may also be used to represent the data. The exponential power is represented with 'E' or 'e' in the decimal system.

3.9.3 Complex numbers

Complex numbers are used to represent the numerical data in terms of $x + iy$, where x represents the real part and y represents the imaginary part. Both x and y values are floating point numbers.

3.10 Functions Applicable to All Types of Numbers

In Python programming, one type of numerical data can be converted to another type of data by using number type conversion functions. Common number type conversion functions are listed below.

- int() function will convert and return the input data to a integer number. It requires one argument.
- long() function will convert and return the input data to a long integer number. It requires one argument.
- float() function will convert and return the input data to a real number. It requires one argument.
- complex() will convert and return the input data to a complex number. It can take one or two arguments. If one argument is provided, then it will be placed in real value with zero imaginary value. If two are provided, then they will be considered for both real and imaginary values.

Various mathematical functions are defined in math module and are listed below.

- The ceil(arg1) function will return the ceiling value of the argument (arg1)
- The fabs(arg1) function will return the absolute value of the input float arg1.
- The abs(arg1) function will return the absolute value of the input integer arg1.
- The floor(arg1) function will return the floor value of the arg1.
- The copysign(arg1,arg2) function will copy the sign of *y* into *x*.
- The isinf(arg1) function will return the TRUE if arg1 is infinity; otherwise it returns FLASE.
- The isnan(arg1) function will return the TRUE if arg1 is a NaN; otherwise it returns FLASE.
- The exp(arg1) function returns the exponential value of arg1.
- The log2(arg1) function returns the log2 value of arg1.
- The pow(arg1,arg2) function returns the arg1arg2 value.
- The acos(arg1) function returns the arc cosine value of arg1.
- The sin(arg1) function returns the sine value of arg1.
- The atan(arg1) function returns the arc tangent value of arg1.
- The radians(arg1) function returns the radian value of arg1(degrees)
- pi is a mathematical constant used to represent the π value
- e is a mathematical constant used to represent the constant value of 'e'

3.11 Sample Programs

Program 1: Write a Python program to display the data.

```
a=20
b=10.5
print(a)
print(b)
```

Output

```
D:\PythonPrograms>python "arithmetic operator.py"
20
10.5
```

Program 2: Write a Python program to read and display the data.

```
a=input("Enter the value of a:")
b=input("Enter the value of b:")
print("Value of A:"+a)
print("Value of B:"+b)
print(type(a))
print(type(b))
```

Output

```
D:\PythonPrograms>python a1.py
Enter the value of a:20
Enter the value of b:10
Value of A:20
Value of B:10
<class 'str'>
<class 'str'>
```

Program 3: Write a Python program to read and display the integer and float values. input() in Python 3.x and raw_input() in Python 2.x always return strings. So, conversion from string to int/float type is required.

```
a=int(input("Enter the value of a:"))
b=float(input("Enter the value of b:"))
print(type(a))
print(type(b))
```

Output

```
D:\PythonPrograms>python a1.py
Enter the value of a: 20
Enter the value of b: 35.78
<class 'int'>
<class 'float'>
```

***Program 4*:** Write a Python program to perform various arithmetic operations.

```
a=int(input("Enter the value of a:"))
b=int(input("Enter the value of b:"))
print("Value of A=",a)
print("Value of B=",b)
c=a+b
print ("Addition Result=",c)
c=a-b
print("Subtraction Result=",c)
c=a*b
print("Multiplication Result=",c)
c=a/b
print("Division Result=",c)
c=a%b
print("Remainder Result=",c)
c=a**2
print("Exponential Result=",c)
c=(-a)//b
print("Floor Division Result=",c)
```

Output

```
Enter the value of a: 20
Enter the value of b: 10
Value of A = 20
Value of B = 10
Addition Result = 30
Subtraction Result = 10
Multiplication Result = 200
Division Result = 2.0
Remainder Result = 0
Exponential Result = 400
Floor Division Result = -2
```

***Program 5*:** Write a Python program to perform various relational operations.

```
a=int(input("Enter the value of a:"))
b=int(input("Enter the value of b:"))
print("Value of A=",a)
print("Value of B=",b)
print ("Result of a==b",a==b)
print ("Result of a!=b",a!=b)
print ("Result of a>b",a>b)
print ("Result of a<b",a<b)
print ("Result of a>=b",a>=b)
print ("Result of a<=b",a<=b)
```

Output

```
D:\PythonPrograms>python "relational operator.txt"
Enter the value of a:20
Enter the value of b:10
Value of A= 20
Value of B= 10
Result of a==b False
Result of a!=b True
Result of a>b True
Result of a<b False
Result of a>=b True
Result of a<=b False
```

***Program 6*:** Write a Python program to perform various assignment operations.

```
a=int(input("Enter the value of a:"))
print("Value of A=",a)
print ("Result of a",a)
a+=10
print ("Result of a+=10",a)
a-=10
print ("Result of a-=10",a)
a*=10
print ("Result of a*=10",a)
a/=10
print ("Result of a/=10",a)
a**10
print ("Result of a**=10",a)
a//=-10
print ("Result of a//=10",a)
```

Output

```
D:\PythonPrograms>python assignment.py
Enter the value of a:20
Value of A= 20
Result of a 20
Result of a+=10 30
Result of a-=10 20
Result of a*=10 200
Result of a/=10 20.0
Result of a**=10 20.0
Result of a//=10 -2.0
```

Program 7: Write a Python program to perform various logical operations.

```
a=int(input("Enter the value of a:"))
b=int(input("Enter the value of b:"))
print("Value of A=",a)
print("Value of B=",b)
print("Result of Logical AND=",(a and b))
print("Result of Logical OR=",(a or b))
print("Result of Logical NOT of Logical AND=",(not (a and b)))
```

Output

```
D:\PythonPrograms>python "logical operator.py"
Enter the value of a:1
Enter the value of b:0
Value of A= 1
Value of B= 0
Result of Logical AND= 0
Result of Logical OR= 1
Result of Logical NOT of Logical AND= True
```

Program 8: Write a Python program to perform various bitwise operations.

```
a=int(input("Enter the value of a:"))
b=int(input("Enter the value of b:"))
print("Value of A=",a)
print("Value of B=",b)
print("Result of Bitwise AND=",(a&b))
print("Result of Bitwise OR=",(a|b))
print("Result of Bitwise EXOR=",(a∧b))
print("Result of Bitwise NOT=",~(a&b))
print("Result of Bitwise LeftShift=",(a<<b))
print("Result of Bitwise RightShift=",(a>>b))
```

Output

```
D:\PythonPrograms>python bitwise.py
Enter the value of a:20
Enter the value of b:2
Value of A= 20
Value of B= 2
Result of Bitwise AND= 0
Result of Bitwise OR= 22
Result of Bitwise EXOR= 22
Result of Bitwise NOT= -1
Result of Bitwise LeftShift= 80
Result of Bitwise RightShift= 5
```

Program 9: Write a Python program to perform various membership operations.

```
a=[1,2,3,4,5]
b=3
print("Value of a=",a)
print("Value of b=",b)
print("Result of b in a=",(b in a))
print("Result of b not in a=",(b not in a))
```

Output

```
D:\PythonPrograms>python member op.py
Value of a= [1, 2, 3, 4, 5]
Value of b= 3
Result of b in a= True
Result of b not in a= False
```

Program 10: Write a Python program to perform various identity operations.

```
a=100
b=200
print("Value of a=",a)
print("Value of b=",b)
print("Result of a is a=",(a is a))
print("Result of b is a=",(b is a))
print("Result of b is not a=",(b is not a))
```

Output

```
D:\PythonPrograms>python identity.py
Value of a= 100
Value of b= 200
Result of a is a= True
Result of b is a= False
Result of b is not a= True
```

Program 11: Write a Python program to use the number type conversion functions.

```
a='10' #char data
b=int(a)
print("int() result=",b)
a=50 #int data
b=float(a)
print("float() result=",b)
a=67.47 #float data
b=complex(a)
print("complex(arg1) result=",b)
a=67.47 #float data
a1=38      #int data
b=complex(a,a1)
print("complex(arg1,arg2) result=",b)
```

Output

```
D:\PythonPrograms>python ntc.py
int() result= 10
float() result= 50.0
complex(arg1) result= (67.47+0j)
complex(arg1,arg2) result= (67.47+38j)
```

Program 12: Write a Python program to delete the reference to a numeric object.

```
a=10
b=20
print("Value of A=",a)
print("Value of B=",b)
del(a)
print("Value of A=",a)
print("Value of B=",b)
```

Output

```
D:\PythonPrograms>python del.py
Value of A= 10
Value of B= 20
Traceback (most recent call last):
File "del.py", line 6, in <module>
print("Value of A=",a)
NameError: name 'a' is not defined
```

Program 13: Write a Python program to use the mathematical functions.

```
import math
print("Value of abs(10)=",abs(10))
print("Value of fabs(-47.56)=",math.fabs(-47.56))
print("Value of ceil(34.85)=",math.ceil(34.85))
print("Value of floor(34.85)=",math.floor(34.85))
print("Value of exp(2)=",math.exp(2))
print("value of fabs(-24.37)=",math.fabs(-24.37))
print("Value of log(20)=",math.log(20))
print("Value of log10(20)=",math.log10(20))
print("Max Value of 20,4,39=",max(20, 4, 39))
print("Min Value of 20,4,39=",min(20, 4, 39))
print("Value of pow(20,2)=",math.pow(20,2))
print("Value of round(5.456,1)=",round(5.456,1))
print("Value of sqrt(16)=",math.sqrt(16))
```

Output

```
D:\PythonPrograms>python "math functions.py"
Value of abs(10)= 10
Value of fabs(-47.56)= 47.56
Value of ceil(34.85)= 35
Value of floor(34.85)= 34
Value of exp(2)= 7.38905609893065
value of fabs(-24.37)= 24.37
Value of log(20)= 2.995732273553991
Value of log10(20)= 1.3010299956639813
Max Value of 20,4,39= 39
Min Value of 20,4,39= 4
Value of pow(20,2)= 400.0
Value of round(5.456,1)= 5.5
Value of sqrt(16)= 4.0
```

Program 14: Write a Python program to use the mathematical trigonometric functions.

```
import math
print("Value of acos(0.5)=",math.acos(0.5))
print("Value of asin(0.5)=",math.asin(0.5))
print("Value of atan(0.5)=",math.atan(0.5))
print("Value of atan2(0.5,0.1)=",math.atan2(0.5,0.1))
print("Value of cos(0.5)=",math.cos(0.5))
print("Value of sin(0.5)=",math.sin(0.5))
print("Value of tan(0.5)=",math.tan(0.5))
print("Value of degrees(10)=",math.degrees(10))
print("Value of radians(10)=",math.radians(10))
```

Output

```
D:\PythonPrograms>python randfunc.py
Value of acos(0.5)= 1.0471975511965979
Value of asin(0.5)= 0.5235987755982989
Value of atan(0.5)= 0.4636476090008061
Value of atan2(0.5,0.1)= 1.373400766945016
Value of cos(0.5)= 0.8775825618903728
Value of sin(0.5)= 0.479425538604203
Value of tan(0.5)= 0.5463024898437905
Value of degrees(10)= 572.9577951308232
Value of radians(10)= 0.17453292519943295
```

***Program 15*:** Write a Python program to use the mathematical constants, π and *e*.

```
import math
print("Value of pi=",math.pi)
print("Value of e=",math.e)
```

Output

```
D:\PythonPrograms>python randfunc.py
Value of pi= 3.141592653589793
Value of e= 2.718281828459045
```

***Program 16*:** Write a Python program to compute the factorial of a given number.

```
import math
a=int(input("Enter the number:"))
b=math.factorial(a)
print(b)
```

Output

```
D:\PythonPrograms>python s1.py
Enter the number:4
24
```

***Program 17*:** Write a Python program to compute the sum of array elements.

```
import math
a=[10.5,23.54]
b=math.fsum(a)
print(b)
```

Output

```
D:\PythonPrograms>python s1.py
34.04
```

***Program 18*:** Write a Python program to truncate the given floating point data.

```
import math
a=10.54
b=math.trunc(a)
print(b
```

Output

```
D:\PythonPrograms>python s1.py
 10
```

***Program 19*:** Write a Python program convert the rectangular coordinates to polar coordinates.

```
import cmath
a=10
b=cmath.polar(a)
print("r value=",b[0])
print("phi value=",b[1])
```

Output

```
D:\PythonPrograms>python s1.py
r value= 10.0
phi value= 0.0
```

***Program 20*:** Write a Python program to convert polar coordinates to rectangular coordinates.

```
import cmath
a=60
b=40
b1=cmath.rect(a,b)
print("b value=",b1)
```

Output

```
D:\PythonPrograms>python s1.py
b value= (-40.01628369913571+4
4.70678962876093j)
```

Glossary

- Literal is a value which can be parsed and further turned into an object.
- A variable can be initialized with a value without declaration in Python
- Operator indicates the operation to be performed on the operands.

Summary

- In Python, int, string and float are considered as primitive data types. Other than these, tuples, lists and dictionaries are also considered as primitive data type.
- Literals are converted to primitive data objects.
- There are various operators to perform operations in the statement.
- The Python programming supports integer, floating and complex numbers.

Multiple Choice Questions

1. Which division will drop the remainder?
(a) Dropping division
(b) Truncating division
(c) Partial division
(d) Alpha division

2. set={} is a
(a) tuple (b) dictionary
(c) set (d) list

3. Python dictionaries are also called as
(a) Associative Arrays (b) Hash Tables
(c) Both A and B (d) None

4. Which of the following is immutable?
(a) tuple (b) list
(c) dictionary (d) All the above

5. In order to store value in terms of key and values, we use
(a) tuple (b) list
(c) dictionary (d) All the above

6. The output for print({'a':'b','a':'c'}) is
(a) Error (b) {'a':'b','a':'c'}
(c) {'a':'c'} (d) {'a':'b'}

7. list=['a','b','b','d','e']

Print list[10:]. What is the output?
(a) Index Error (b) []
(c) ['a'] (d) ['e']

8. The data type of fabs() argument is
(a) int (b) float
(c) complex (d) long int

9. Comments in Python use the following symbol:
(a) ! (b) & (c) # (d) %

10. acos() function argument is
(a) Radian (b) Degree
(c) Both a and b (d) None

11. Any module function can be used by using the following keyword
(a) main (b) super
(c) sub (d) import

12. What will be the default value of the imaginary part in a complex number?
(a) 0 (b) 1 (c) 2 (d) 3

13. In a complex number, both real and imaginary values are
(a) int,int (b) int,float
(c) float,float (d) float,int

14. In Python3, what is the size of 'int' type?
(a) 16 bytes (b) 24 bytes
(c) 34 bytess (d) Unlimited

15. Which function is used to convert the string to int type?
(a) int() (b) float()
(c) complex() (d) none

16. How many mathematical constants are available in Python?
(a) 0 (b) 1 (c) 2 (d) 3

17. What are the mathematical constants available in Python?
(a) pi and x (b) x and e
(c) e and chi (d) pi and e

18. Data is maintained by
(a) variables
(b) values
(c) variables and values
(d) None of the above

19. Boolean variable can have the following value(s)?
(a) True (b) False
(c) True and False (d) None of the above

20. The false value contains
(a) 0
(b) None
(c) Empty list, tuple or string
(d) All the above

21. Which of the following are valid literals in Python?
(a) Int
(b) Int, String
(c) Int, String, Float
(d) Int, String, Float and Char

22. The string literal can be represented with?
(a) single quote
(b) double quote
(c) Both (a) and (b)
(d) None of the above

23. Which of the following will be considered as primitive data type?
(a) Integer data
(b) Floating point data
(c) String data
(d) All the above

24. The string data is represented with?
(a) integer
(b) array
(c) structure
(d) None of the above

25. String repetition is performed with?
(a) + (b) *
(c) % (d) None of the above

26. String concatenation is performed with?
(a) + (b) *
(c) % (d) None of the above

27. In a tuple, "-**1**" index represents
(a) first element
(b) second element
(c) last element
(d) None of the above

28. The values of the Tuple cannot be
(a) deleted
(b) modified
(c) Both (a) and (b)
(d) None of the above

29. The Tuple uses
(a) []
(b) ()
(c) Either (a) or (b)
(d) None of the above

30. The list uses
(a) []
(b) ()
(c) Either (a) or (b)
(d) None of the above

31. Dictionary maintains
(a) Key
(b) Value
(c) Both Key and Value
(d) None of the above

32. The exponential calculation is performed with?
(a) * (b) **
(c) *** (d) None of the above

33. The floor division operation is performed with?
(a) // (b) ///
(c) //// (d) All the above

34. Which of the following are relational operators?
(a) == (b) !-
(c) > (d) All the above

35. The compound assignment operators are?
(a) = (b) +
(c) += (d) None of the above

36. Which of the following are logical operators?
(a) and (b) or
(c) not (d) All the above

37. Membership operator can be used for
(a) strings
(b) strings or lists
(c) strings, lists or tuples
(d) None of the above

38. Membership operators are
(a) in
(b) not in
(c) Both (a) and (b)
(d) None of the above

39. Identity operators are
(a) is
(b) is not
(c) Both (a) and (b)
(d) None of the above

40. If uninitialized object is deleted, then
(a) memory is free
(b) syntax error
(c) runtime error
(d)None of the above

41. Examples of various numerical objects are
(a) integer numbers
(b) floating point numbers
(c) complex numbers
(d) All the above

42. Examples of various number type conversion functions are
(a) int() (b) long()
(c) float() (d) All the above

Fill in the Blanks

1. In Python ____________ is used to get the data type assigned to the variable.

2. ____________ can be passed and turned into an object.

3. ____________ literal converts the integer into int object.
4. Types of numerical literals are ____________
5. In Python, a variable can be initialized without ____________.
6. Character data will be considered as ____________ data.
7. The length of the character data is ____________.
8. The initial index of an array is ____________.
9. List with a fixed number of elements is called as ____________.
10. List without a fixed number of elements is called as ____________.
11. The initial index of tuple is ____________.
12. The initial index of lists is ____________.
13. Multi-typed elements can be represented with ____________.
14. ____________ operator will separate multiple entries of dictionary.
15. Compound assignment operator consists of ____________.
16. "***" is used for ____________.
17. The result of comparison operator is ____________.
18. The result of assignment operator is ____________.
19. The result of Logical operator is ____________.
20. The binary left shift operator is ____________.
21. The binary right shift operator is ____________.
22. The one's complement operator is ____________.
23. The membership operators are ____________
24. The identity operators are ____________.
25. ____________ is a basic element of Python expression.
26. Multiple expressions are separated with ____________.
27. ____________ form is used for multiple expressions.
28. ____________ atom represents identifier.
29. ____________ keyword is used for deleting the numeric objects.
30. In Python 3, Only 'int' with ____________ size is allowed.

State True/False

1. In Python, type referencing is not allowed.
2. Unicode is a literal in Python.
3. Tuple is not a literal in Python
4. Complex is a literal in Python
5. For a variable declaration, data type has to be specified.
6. "type" keyword is used to display the value of the variable.
7. Value 'None' can be considered as True.
8. Empty string can be considered as False.
9. An object consists of a literal.
10. Complex is not a valid literal in Python.
11. String literal can be represented without any quote.
12. String literal can be represented with single or double quotes.
13. '_' is permitted in the variable name.
14. In Python, type of the variable is considered automatically.
15. Character data and string data are handled differently in Python.
16. The string data is used to handle character data.
17. Tuples, dictionaries and lists are primitive data types.
18. Tuples allow change of data.
19. Lists allow change of data.
20. Dictionaries do not allow change of data.
21. Tuples maintain data as a {key, value} pair.
22. Dictionaries maintain data as a {key, value} pair.
23. List maintains data as a {key, value} pair.
24. Tuples uses []
25. Tuples uses ()
26. Lists uses []
27. Lists uses ()
28. Membership operator does not focus on the membership in the sequence.

29. The identity operator checks whether the given set of objects are related to the same memory location or not.

30. Atom also consists of various forms enclosed in brackets, parentheses or braces.

Find the Output

1.
```
a=100
print("a value=",a)
```

2.
```
a=100
print("a value=",a+100)
```

3.
```
x=(1,2,3)
y=(2, 1)
a=(y in x)
print(a)
```

4.
```
x=[1, 2, 3]
y=x[-2]
a=(y in x)
print(a)
```

5.
```
x=[1, 2, 3]
y=x[-2]
a=(y in x)
print(a)
```

6.
```
x=[1, 2, 3]
y=x[-2]**2
print(y)
```

7.
```
x=[1, 2, 3]
print("Original:",x)
del(x[-1])
print("After Deletion:",x)
```

8.
```
a=0b110
b=0x16
print("valuesof a, b, a+b:",a,b,a+b)
```

9.
```
import math
a=math.nan
b=math.isnan(a)
print(b)
```

10.
```
import math
a=math.inf
b=~(math.isinf(a))
print(b)
```

Find the Error

1.
```
a=100
print("a value=",a++)
```

2.
```
a=100
print("a value=",a)
```

3.
```
a=100
printf("a value=",a)
```

4.
```
a=100
print("a value="a)
```

5.
```
a=input("enter number:")
b=a+1
```

6.
```
a=input("enter number:")
b=a[-10]
print(b)
```

7.
```
a=int(input("enter number:"))
b=a[-1]
print(b)
```

8.
```
a=complex(5+2j)
b=a∧1
print(b)
```

9.
```
a=3
b and= 0
print(b)
```

10.
```
x=(1+2j)
y=1
a=(y in x)
print(a)
```

Long Answer Questions

1. Discuss in detail about various operators in Python.

2. How can one type of number be converted to another type?

3. Explain about various functions applicable to all types of numbers.

Short Answer Questions

1. List the operator precedence in Python.
2. Write about math module.
3. What is the importance of import statement?

Exercise Programs

1. Write a Python program to print the sum of two complex numbers.
2. Write a Python program to use the identity operator.
3. Write a Python program to print the mantissa and exponent of the given number.
4. Write a Python program for performing angular conversion.
5. Write a Python program to print the hyperbolic function result of the given 'x' value.
6. Write a Python program to perform arithmetic operations on lists.
7. Write a Python program to perform arithmetic operations on tuples.
8. Write a Python program to perform arithmetic operations on dictionary.
9. Write a Python program to perform logical operations on lists.
10. Write a Python program to perform logical operations on tuples.
11. Write a Python program to perform logical operations on dictionary.
12. Write a Python program to perform relational operations on lists.
13. Write a Python program to perform relational operations on tuples.
14. Write a Python program to perform relational operations on dictionary.
15. Write a Python program to read the temperature in Celsius/Fahrenheit and convert it to another form.
16. Write a Python program to handle all primitive data types.
17. Write a Python program to print the data type assigned to a variable.
18. Write a program to read the string value and convert it to float value.
19. Write a program to read the radius of the circle and display the area of the circle.
20. Write a program to compute the exponential value of the given number.
21. Write a program to compute the slope of a given line.
22. Write a program to handle the various decimal arithmetic operations.

Answers

Multiple Choice Questions

1. b	10. a	19. c	28. b	37. c
2. b	11. d	20. d	29. b	38. c
3. c	12. a	21. c	30. a	39. c
4. a	13. c	22. c	31. c	40. c
5. c	14. d	23. d	32. b	41. d
6. c	15. a	24. b	33. b	42. d
7. b	16. c	25. b	34. d	
8. b	17. d	26. a	35. c	
9. c	18. a	27. c	36. d	

Fill in the Blanks

1. type
2. Literal
3. Integer literal
4. Int, Float and Complex
5. declaration
6. string data.
7. 1
8. 0
9. Tuples
10. Lists
11. 0
12. 0
13. dictionaries
14. Comma
15. Arithmetic operator and Assignment operator
16. Exponential calculation
17. Boolean value
18. Initialized variable
19. Boolean value
20. <<
21. >>
22. ~
23. 'in' and 'not in'
24. 'is' and 'is not'
25. Atom
26. Comma operator
27. Parenthesized
28. Name
29. Del
30. unlimited.

State True/False

1. False
2. True
3. False
4. True
5. False
6. False
7. False
8. True
9. True
10. False
11. False
12. True
13. True
14. True.
15. False
16. True
17. True
18. False
19. True
20. False
21. False
22. True
23. False
24. False
25. True
26. True
27. False
28. False
29. True
30. True

Find the Output

1. a value= 100
2. a value= 200
3. False
4. True
5. False
6. 4
7. Original: [1, 2, 3]
   After Deletion: [1, 2]
8. valuesof a, b, a+b: 6 22 28
9. True
10. -2

Find the Error

1. SyntaxError: invalid syntax (++ operator is not available in Python)
2. IndentationError: unexpected indent
3. NameError: name 'printf' is not defined
4. SyntaxError: invalid syntax ("," is not used for separation)
5. TypeError: must be str, not int
6. IndexError: string index out of range
7. TypeError: 'int' object is not subscriptable
8. TypeError: unsupported operand type(s) for ^: 'complex' and 'int'
9. SyntaxError: invalid syntax (compound assignment is applicable for only arithmetic operators)
10. TypeError: argument of type 'complex' is not iterable

CHAPTER

4 Control Flow

This chapter discusses about the decision making statements and looping statements. Decision making statements evaluate the condition and execute the associated block of statements for a single time. Looping statements evaluate the condition and execute the associated block of statements repeatedly until the condition has failed.

4.1 If Statement

In Python programming, decision making statements are used to identify the set of codes to be executed according to the given conditions. The condition will be evaluated and the result can be either TRUE or FALSE. Any non-null or non-zero value will be considered as TRUE and any zero or null value will be considered as FALSE. There are three types of decision making statements. They are

i. if statement
ii. if..else statement
iii. nested if statement

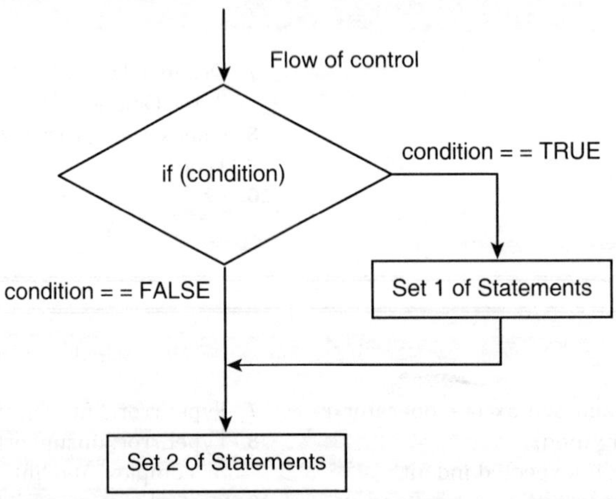

Figure 4.1 Flowchart for if statement.

The flowchart for if statement is illustrated in Fig. 4.1. For the if statement, only one condition is allowed. When the flow of control reaches the if statement, the condition given in the if statement is evaluated. If the evaluated result of the condition is FALSE, then the flow of control will not enter into the if statement block but continue the execution of Set 2 of statements. If the evaluated result of the condition is TRUE, then the flow of control enters into the if statement block and executes the Set 1 of statements. After completing the execution of the if statement block, the flow of control will continue the execution of Set 2 of statements.

If statement is used to evaluate the given condition and the block of statements is executed only if the condition is TRUE. If the condition is FALSE, then the block of statements will not be executed. For if statements, only one block of statements are allowed. The syntax is

if(condition):

#set of statements to be executed when the condition is TRUE

An example is

```
a=int(input("Enter the number:"))
if(a>0):
    print("The given number is positive")
```

Output

```
D:\PythonPrograms>python a1.py
Enter the number:4
The given number is positive
D:\PythonPrograms>python a1.py
Enter the number:-1
```

In the above example program, initially, the value of 'a' is read followed by print "The given number is positive" statement. The **if** statement is used to check the given condition. If the condition (a>0) is true, then the statement will be printed. If the condition is FALSE, then nothing will be printed.

Example **1**: Write a Python program to check whether a given character is a vowel or not.

```
a=input("Enter the character:")
if((a=='a') or (a=='e') or (a=='i') or (a=='o') or (a=='u')):
    print("The given character is vowel")
```

Output

```
D:\PythonPrograms>python b1.py
Enter the character: e
The given character is vowel
```

Example **2**: Write a Python program to check whether or not the given number is less than 5. If the number is less than 5, then print the square of the number?

```
a=int(input("Enter the given number:"))
if(a<5):
    print("square of the number:",a*a)
```

Output

```
D:\PythonPrograms>python b1.py
Enter the given number:3
square of the number: 9
```

Example **3**: Write a Python program to check whether or not the given number is divisible by 10.

```
a=int(input("Enter the given number:"))
if((a%10)==0):
    print("The given number is divisible by 10")
```

Output

```
D:\PythonPrograms>python b1.py
Enter the given number:100
The given number is divisible by 10
```

Example **4**: Write a Python program to count the number of 100-rupee notes required for a given amount and print whether or not more than one 100-rupee note is required.

```
a=int(input("Enter the Amount:"))
x=a/100;
if(x>1):
    print("More than one 100-rupee note required")
```

Output

```
D:\PythonPrograms>python b1.py
Enter the Amount:200
More than one 100-rupee note
required
```

The problem of if statement is that no block of statements will be executed when the condition is FALSE. To overcome this problem, the if..else statement is used.

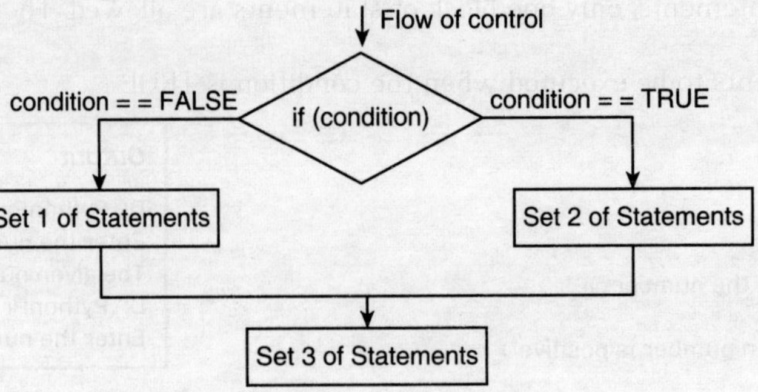

Figure 4.2 Flowchart for **if-else** statement

The flowchart for **if-else** statement is illustrated in Fig. 4.2. For the **if-else** statement, only one condition is allowed. When the flow of control reaches the **if-else** statement, then the condition given in the **if-else** statement is evaluated. If the evaluated result of the condition is FALSE, then the flow of control will enter into the FALSE block and execute the Set 1 of statements and then continue the execution of Set-3 of statements. If the evaluated result of the condition is TRUE, then the flow of control enters into the TRUE block and executes Set 2 of statements and then continues the execution of Set 3 of statements. So, irrespective of the condition for the **if-else** statement, only one block, i.e., either TRUE or FALSE block will be executed and then Set 3 of statements will be executed finally.

In **if..else** statement, two blocks of statements (TRUE block and FALSE block) can be used. The condition is specified within the **if** statement. Initially, the condition will be evaluated and if the condition is TRUE, then the TRUE block will be evaluated. If the condition is FALSE, then the FALSE block will be evaluated. The syntax is

```
if(condition):
    # TRUE block of statements
else:
    # FALSE block of statements
```

An example is

```
a=int(input("Enter the number:"))
if(a>0):
    print("The given number is positive")
else:
    print("The given number is negative")
```

Output

```
D:\PythonPrograms>python a1.py
Enter the number:6
The given number is positive
D:\PythonPrograms>python a1.py
Enter the number:-2
The given number is negative
```

In the above example, only the condition for **if** statement is given. So, the drawback of **if..else** statement is that it can only evaluate one condition.

Example 5: Write a Python program to check if the given character is a vowel or consonant.

```
a=input("Enter the character:")
if((a=='a') or (a=='e') or (a=='i') or (a=='o') or (a=='u')):
    print("The given character is vowel")
else:
    print("The given character is consonant")
```

Output

```
D:\PythonPrograms>python b1.py
Enter the character: b
The given character is consonant
```

Example 6: Write a Python to check if the given number is greater than 5. If the number is greater than 5, then print the cube of the number. If the number is less than or equal to 5, then print the square of the number.

```
a=int(input("Enter the given number:"))
if(a>5):
    print("Cube of the number:", a*a*a)
else:
    print("Square of the number:",a*a)
```

Output

```
D:\PythonPrograms>python b1.py
Enter the given number:6
Cube of the number: 216
```

Example 7: Write a Python program to check the profit or loss.

```
a=int(input("Enter the cost price:"))
b=int(input("Enter the selling price:"))
if(b>a):
    print("Profit")
else:
    print("Loss")
```

Output

```
D:\PythonPrograms>python b1.py
Enter the cost price: 100
Enter the selling price: 75
Loss
```

Example 8: Write a Python program to check whether the given character is an uppercase letter or a lower case letter.

```
a=input("Enter the character:")
if(a.islower()):
    print("the given character is lower case letter")
else:
    print("the given character is upper case letter")
```

Output

```
D:\PythonPrograms>python b1.py
Enter the character: V
The given character is upper case letter
```

To overcome this problem **if..elif..else** statement is used. In **if..elif..else** statement, multiple conditions can be specified for **if** and multiple **elif** statements. The else will be executed only when all the conditions are evaluated to be FALSE. The syntax for **if..elif..else** statement is

```
if(condition1):
    # TRUE block1 of statements
elif(condition2):
    # TRUE block2 of statements
else:
    # FALSE block of statements
```

An example is

```
a=int(input("Enter the number:"))
if((a>90)and(a<=100)):
    print("The given number is between 90 and 100")
elif((a>80)and(a<=90)):
    print("The given number is between 80 and 90")
elif((a>70)and(a<=80)):
    print("The given number is between 70 and 80")
elif((a>60)and(a<=70)):
    print("The given number is between 60 and 70")
elif((a>50)and(a<=60)):
    print("The given number is between 50 and 60")
else:
    print("The given number is below 50")
```

Output

```
D:\PythonPrograms>python a1.py
Enter the number: 69
The given number is between 60 and 70
```

In the above example, if any one of the condition is evaluated as TRUE, then the corresponding TRUE block of statements will be executed but no other conditions will be evaluated. The **nested if** statement overcomes this problem by allowing **if, if..else** and **if..elif..else** statements with **if/elif/else** statements. The syntax is

```
if(condition1):
    # TRUE block1 of statements
    if(condition2):
        # TRUE block2 of statements
        .....
else:
    # FALSE block1 of statements
    if(condition3):
        # TRUE block3 of statements
        .....
```

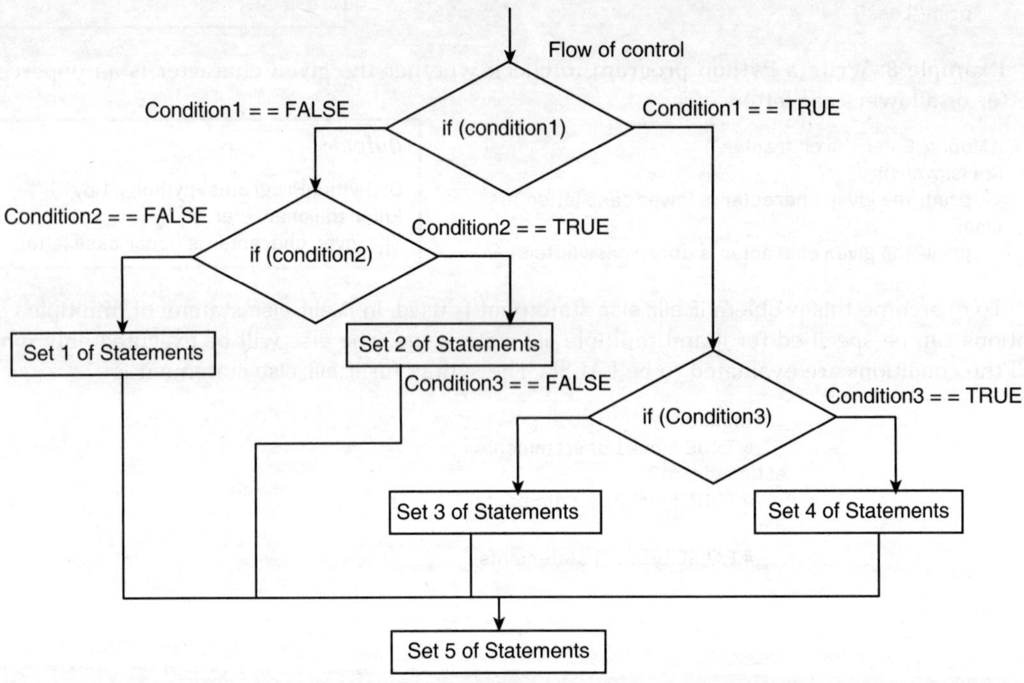

Figure 4.3 Flowchart for **nested if** statement.

The flowchart of **nested if** statement is illustrated in Fig. 4.3. For the **nested if** statement, multiple conditions are allowed. When the flow of control reaches the **nested if** statement, then the condition1 given in the **if** statement will be evaluated. If the evaluated result of the condition is FALSE, then the flow of control will enter the FALSE block and Condition 2 will be evaluated. If the Condition 2 is evaluated as FALSE then the Set 1 of statements will be executed. If the Condition 2 is evaluated as TRUE, then the Set 2 of statements will be executed. After executing either Set 1 or Set 2 of statements, the flow of control is continued to execute the Set 5 of statements.

If Condition 1 is evaluated as TRUE, then another corresponding Condition 3 will be evaluated. If the Condition 3 is evaluated as FALSE, then Set 3 of statements will be executed. If the Condition 3 is evaluated as TRUE, then the Set 4 of statements will be executed. After executing Set 3 or Set 4 of statements, the flow of control is continued to execute the Set 5 of statements.

An example is

```
a=int(input("Enter the number: "))
if(a>0):
    print("first true block")
    if(a>10):
        print("second true block")
    else:
        print("first false block")
else:
    print("second false block")
    if(a>-10):
        print("third true block")
    else:
        print("third false block")
```

Output

```
D:\PythonPrograms>python a1.py
Enter the number: 15
first true block
second true block
D:\PythonPrograms>python a1.py
Enter the number: 4
first true block
first false block
D:\PythonPrograms>python a1.py
Enter the number: -3
second false block
third true block
D:\PythonPrograms>python a1.py
Enter the number: -34
second false block
third false block
```

Example **9**: Write a Python program to check whether or not a given number is less than 50. If the number is less than 50, then check if the number is greater than 25 or not. If the number is less than 25, then check whether the number is even or odd.

```
a=int(input("Enter the number:"))
if(a<50):
    print("The number is less than 50.")
    if(a>25):
        print('The number is greater than 25.')
    else:
        print('The number is less than 25.')
    if(a%2==0):
        print("The number is even number.")
    else:
        print("The number is odd number.")
else:
    print("The number is greater than or equal to 50.")
```

Output

```
D:\PythonPrograms>python b1.py
Enter the number:47
The number is less than 50.
The number is greater than 25.
The number is odd number.
```

Example **10**: Write a Python program to check whether a given character is a digit or not. If the given character is a digit, check whether or not it is less than 5.

```
a=input("Enter the character:")
if(a.isdigit()):
    print("The given character is a digit")
    b=int(a)
    if(b<5):
        print("The number is less than 5")
    else:
        print("The number is greater than or equal to 5")
else:
    print("The character is not a digit")
```

Output

```
D:\PythonPrograms>python b1.py
Enter the character:3
The given character is a digit
The number is less than 5
```

Example **11**: Write a Python program to check whether the given two numbers are same or not. If they are not same, then check if the first number is greater than second number.

```
a=int(input("Enter the first number:"))
b=int(input("Enter the second number:"))
if(a==b):
    print("The two numbers are same")
else:
    if(a>b):
        print("The first number is greater than second number")
    else:
        print("The first number is less than the second number")
```

Output

```
D:\PythonPrograms>python b1.py
Enter the first number:6
Enter the second number:4
The first number is greater than
second number
```

4.2 While Statement

In addition to decision making statements, Python programming also supports looping statements. There are two loops in Python. They are i) while and ii) for.

The while loop checks the condition initially and repeats the execution of the block of statements until the evaluated condition becomes False. The syntax for the while loop is

```
while(condition):
    #block of statements
```

The condition is evaluated initially and if the condition is TRUE, then it will execute the block of statements. After this, the condition is evaluated again and the process is repeated until the condition becomes False.

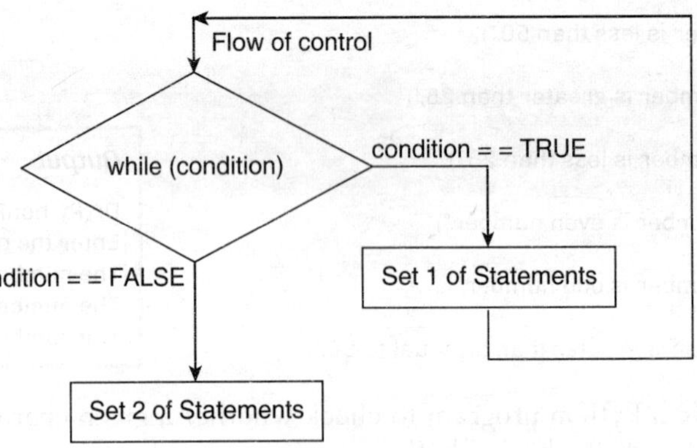

Figure 4.4 Flowchart for while loop

The flowchart of while loop is illustrated in Fig. 4.4. For the while loop, one condition will be evaluated multiple times. Each time, when the condition becomes TRUE, the flow of control enters into the while block and executes the Set 1 of statements whereas when the condition becomes FALSE, the repeated evaluation of the condition and execution of the while block is terminated. Thus, when the condition becomes FALSE, the flow of control executes the Set 2 of statements.

An example is

```
a=int(input("Enter the number: "))
i=0
print("Numbers from 0 to ",a)
while(i<a):
    print(i)
    i=i+1
```

Output

```
Enter the number: 5
Numbers from 0 to 5
0
1
2
3
4
```

Example **12**: Write a Python program to count the number of digits in any number.

```
a=int(input("Enter the value of n:"))
x=0
while(a>0):
    a=int(a/10)
    x=x+1
print("No of Digits:",x)
```

Output

```
D:\PythonPrograms>python a1.py
Enter the value of n:87963
No of Digits: 5
```

Example **13**: Write a Python program to print the sum and product of the digits of a number.

```
a=int(input("Enter the value of n:"))
x=0
s=0
pr=1
while(a>0):
    t=a
    a=int(a/10)
    di=t%10
    s=s+di
    pr=pr*di
print("Sum of Digits:",s)
print("Product of Digits:",pr)
```

Output

```
D:\PythonPrograms>python a1.py
Enter the value of n: 54
Sum of Digits: 9
Product of Digits: 20
```

Example **14**: Write a Python program to read a number and print the reverse of the number

```
a=int(input("Enter the value of n:"))
x=0
s=0
pr=1
while(a>0):
    t=a
    a=int(a/10)
    di=t%10
    s=(s*10)+di
print("Reverse of the number:",s)
```

Output

```
D:\PythonPrograms>python a1.py
Enter the value of n:98765
Reverse of the number: 56789
```

Example **15**: Write a Python program to print the Fibonacci series up to the given number.

```
a=int(input("Enter the value of n:"))
x1=0
x2=1
print("The Series:",x1,end=",")
print(x2,end=",")
i=0
while(i<=a):
    s=x1+x2
    x1=x2
    x2=s
    i=i+1
    print(s,end=",")
```

Output

```
D:\PythonPrograms>python a1.py
Enter the value of n:20
The Series: 0,1,1,2,3,5,8,13,21,34,55,89,144,233,377,610,9
87,1597,2584,4181,6765,10946,17711,
```

4.3 For Statement

The for loop is used to repeat the execution of a block of code for a fixed number of times. In Python, the for loop is repeated for all the members of a sequence in order, executing the block each time, whereas in while loop the condition is evaluated for each iteration. The syntax of for loop is

```
for variable in range(val1,val2,inr):
    #block of statements
```

In the above syntax val1 and val2 represents minimum and maximum number of the specified range. The 'inr' specifies the increment value.

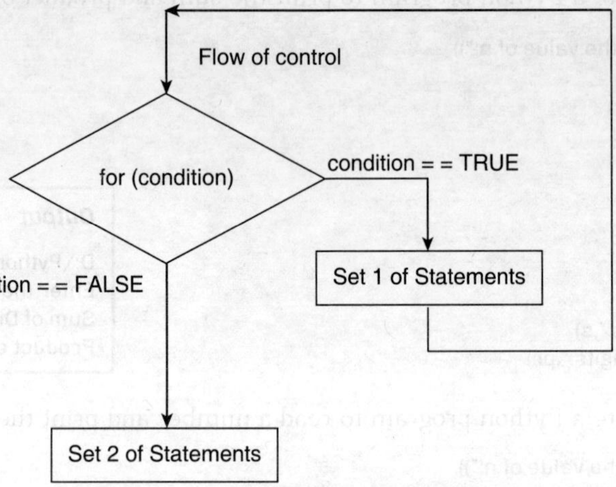

Figure 4.5 Flowchart for for loop

The flowchart of for loop is illustrated in Fig. 4.5. In the for loop, one condition will be evaluated multiple times. Each time, when the condition becomes TRUE, then flow of control enters into the for loop block and executes the Set 1 of statements, whereas when the condition becomes FALSE, the repeated evaluation of condition and execution of for loop block is terminated. Thus, when the condition becomes FALSE, the flow of control executes the Set 2 of statements.

An example is

```
a=int(input("Enter the number: "))
for i in range(a):
    print(i)
```

Output

```
D:\PythonPrograms>python a1.py
Enter the number: 5
0
1
2
3
4
```

In the above example, only one value is given in the range. This will be considered as maximum value of the range.

An example is

```
a=int(input("Enter the number: "))
for i in range(1,a):
    print(i)
```

Output

```
D:\PythonPrograms>python a1.py
Enter the number: 4
1
2
3
```

In the above example, the minimum and maximum value of the range is specified. The 'inr' value is not specified; it is automatically assigned as 1.

An example is

```
a=int(input("Enter the number: "))
for i in range(1,a,2):
    print(i)
```

Output

```
D:\PythonPrograms>python a1.py
Enter the number: 10
1
3
5
7
9
```

4.4 Break Statement

In Python programming, loops are used to execute a block of statements repeatedly. The body of the loop will be executed when the condition of the loop is evaluated as TRUE. During the execution of the loop, if an emergency exit from the loop is required then break statement is used. The break statement is used to quit the running loop statements. The syntax of the break statement is

```
loop (condition):
    #block of statements
    break
else:
    #block of statements
```

An example is

```
a=int(input("Enter the number: "))
i=0
while(i<a):
    print("Entered into while loop with value of i=",i)
    if(i==2):
        break
    i=i+1
else:
    print("break is not executed")
```

Output

```
D:\PythonPrograms>python a1.py
Enter the number: 5
Entered into while loop with value of i= 0
Entered into while loop with value of i= 1
Entered into while loop with value of i= 2
D:\PythonPrograms>python a1.py
Enter the number: 2
Entered into while loop with value of i= 0
Entered into while loop with value of i= 1
break is not executed
```

In case no break statement of the running loop is executed, then the else part of the loop will be executed.

4.5 Continue Statement

The continue statement is used to skip the current iteration of the loop. If the condition of the loop is evaluated as TRUE, then the body of the loop is executed. During the execution, the continue statement stops the current execution of the body and continues the next iteration. The syntax is

```
loop(condition):
    #block of statements
    continue
```

An example is

```
a=int(input("Enter the number: "))
i=0
while(i<a):
    if(i==2):
        i=i+1
        continue
    else:
        print("Entered into while loop with value of i=",i)
        i=i+1
```

Output

```
D:\PythonPrograms>python a1.py
Enter the number: 5
Entered into while loop with value of i= 0
Entered into while loop with value of i= 1
Entered into while loop with value of i= 3
Entered into while loop with value of i= 4
```

4.6 Pass Statement

The **pass** statement can be called as a do-nothing statement. It does not perform any action. This statement is mainly used to keep the CPU busy for some time. The 'pass' keyword is used for specifying the pass statement.

An example is

```
a=int(input("Enter the number: "))
i=0
while(i<a):
    if(i<=2):
        i=i+1
        pass
    else:
        print("Entered into while loop with value of i=",i)
        i=i+1
```

Output

```
D:\PythonPrograms>python a1.py
Enter the number: 5
Entered into while loop with value of i= 3
Entered into while loop with value of i= 4
```

In this program, the **pass** statement is used in **while** loop. During the iteration, the **pass** statement will not execute anything and looks similar to the **continue** statement. However, there is a difference between **continue** and **pass** statements. The **continue** statement will skip the execution of current iteration and save the execution time, whereas the **pass** statement will waste the execution time.

4.7 Entry Controlled Loop

Entry controlled loops evaluate the condition at the time of entry into the loop. The flowchart for entry controlled loop is shown in Fig. 4.6. **While** loop and **for** loop are examples for entry controlled loop.

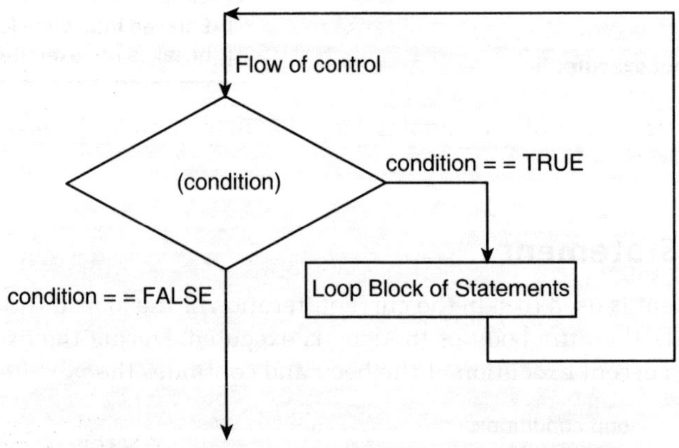

Figure 4.6 Flowchart for entry controlled loop

4.8 Exit Controlled Loop

Exit controlled loops evaluate the condition at the time of exiting from the loop. The flow chart for exit controlled loop is shown in Fig. 4.7. Do-while loop is considered as an exit controlled loop.

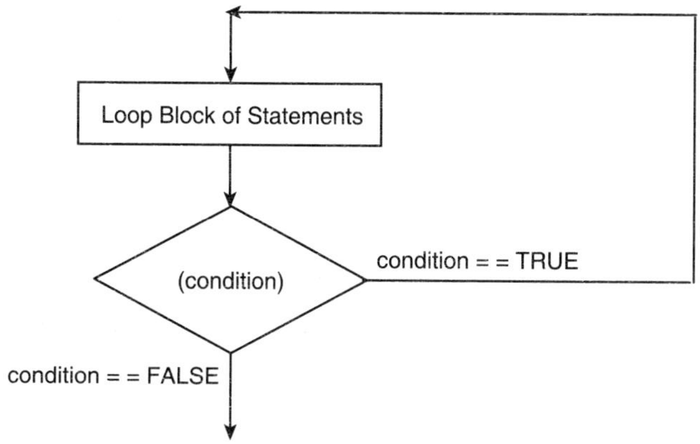

Figure 4.7 Flowchart for exit controlled loop

In Python, do-while loop should be simulated with an entry controlled loop as shown in the example below.

```
a=0
while(1):
    print("hai")
    a=a+1
    if(a>3):
        break
```

Output

```
D:\PythonPrograms>python b1.py
hai
hai
hai
hai
```

4.9 Counter Controlled Loop

Counter controlled loops are loops which can iterate based on the counter value. If the counter value is reached, then the loop will be terminated; otherwise, the loop will be repeated. The flowchart is shown in Fig. 4.8.

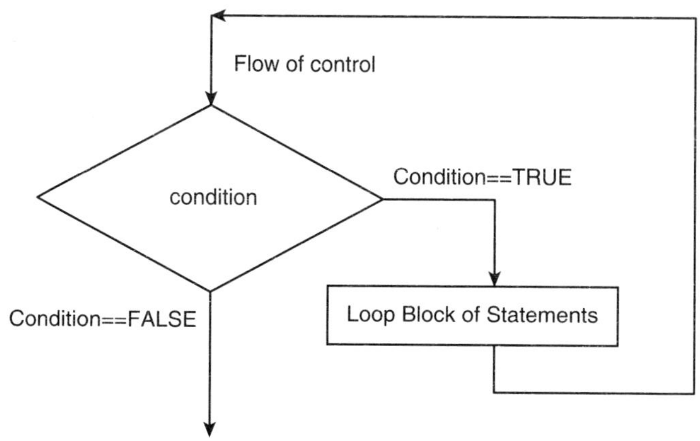

Figure 4.8 Flowchart for counter controlled loop

For the counter controlled loop, the condition indicates whether the maximum value of the counter is reached or not. If the maximum value of the counter is reached, then the loop is terminated; otherwise, the flow of control enters into the loop and executes the block of statements within the loop.

```
for a in ['a','e','i','o','u']:
    print(a," is a vowel")
```

Output

```
D:\PythonPrograms>python b1.py
a is a vowel
e is a vowel
i is a vowel
o is a vowel
u is a vowel
```

4.10 Condition Controlled Loop

Condition controlled loops are loops which can iterate based on the specified condition. If the condition is evaluated as FALSE, then the loop is terminated; otherwise, the loop is repeated. The flowchart is shown in Fig. 4.9. For the condition controlled loop, the condition is evaluated as TRUE or FALSE.

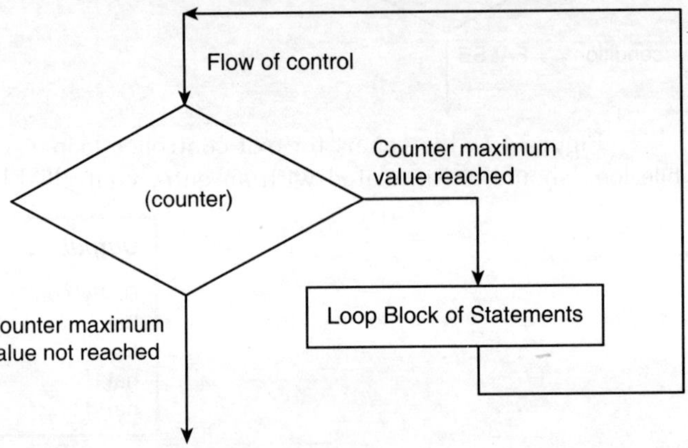

Figure 4.9 Flowchart for counter controlled loop

4.11 Nested Loops

Python allows the usage of nested loops. A nested loop allows the usage of one loop inside another loop. Thus, in a **for** loop, another **for** or **while** loop is allowed. Similarly, within a **while** loop, another **for** or **while** loop is allowed. The flowchart for nested loops is shown in Fig. 4.10.

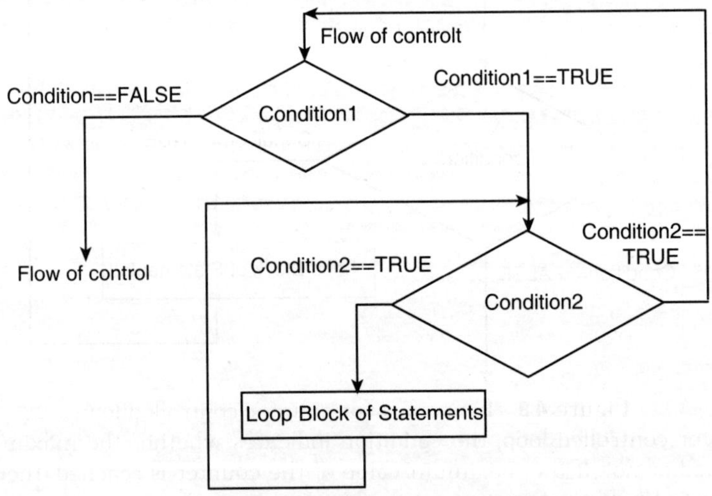

Figure 4.10 Flowchart for nested loops

Various examples are given below.

1.
```
for a in range(3):
    for b in range(3):
        print(a,",",b)
```

Output

```
D:\PythonPrograms>python b1.py
0 , 0
0 , 1
0 , 2
1 , 0
1 , 1
1 , 2
2 , 0
2 , 1
2 , 2
```

2.
```
i=0
while(i < 3):
    j = 0
    while(j <3):
        print(i,",",j)
        j=j+1
    i = i + 1
```

Output

```
D:\PythonPrograms>python b1.py
0 , 0
0 , 1
0 , 2
1 , 0
1 , 1
1 , 2
2 , 0
2 , 1
2 , 2
```

3.
```
i=1
while(i < 5):
    j=1
    while(j<=i):
        print("* ",end="")
        j=j+1
    print("\r")
    i = i + 1
```

Output

```
D:\PythonPrograms>python b1.py
*
* *
* * *
* * * *
```

4.
```
x=5
m = 2*x - 2
for a in range(0, x):
    for b in range(0, m):
        print(end=" ")
    for b in range(0, a+1):
        print("* ", end="")
    m = m - 2
    print("\r")
```

Output

```
D:\PythonPrograms>python b1.py
        *
      * *
    * * *
  * * * *
* * * * *
```

4.12 Sample Programs

Program 1: Write a Python program to check whether the given number is even or odd.

> Programming Tip:
> The decision making statements used to evaluate the decision.

```
a=int(input("Enter the number: "))
if((a%2)== 0):
    print(a, "is an even number")
else:
    print(a, "is an odd number")
```

Output

```
D:\PythonPrograms>python a1.py
Enter the number: 6
6 is an even number
D:\PythonPrograms>python a1.py
Enter the number: 3
3 is an odd number
```

Program 2: Write a Python program to find the biggest number among given two numbers.

```
a=int(input("Enter the first number: "))
b=int(input("Enter the second number: "))
if(a>b):
    print("Maximum Number is:",a)
else:
    print("Maximum Number is:",b)
```

Output

```
D:\PythonPrograms>python a1.py
Enter the first number: 4
Enter the second number: 9
Maximum Number is: 9
```

Program 3: Write a Python program to find the greatest number among given four numbers

```
a=float(input("Enter the first number: "))
b=float(input("Enter the second number: "))
c=float(input("Enter the third number: "))
d=float(input("Enter the fourth number: "))
if((a>b)and(a>c)and(a>d)):
    print("Greatest Number is:",a)
elif((b>a)and(b>c)and(b>d)):
    print("Greatest Number is:",b)
elif((c>a)and(c>b)and(c>d)):
    print("Greatest Number is:",c)
else:
    print("Greatest Number is:",d)
```

Output

```
D:\PythonPrograms>python a1.py
Enter the first number: 20.54
Enter the second number: 12.78
Enter the third number: 56.38
Enter the fourth number: 08.94
Greatest Number is: 56.38
```

Program 4: Write a Python program to check whether a given year is a leap year or not.

```
a=int(input("Enter the year:"))
if((a%4)==0):
    print(a,"is a leap year")
else:
    print(a,"is not a leap year")
```

Output

```
D:\PythonPrograms>python a1.py
Enter the year: 2012
201   is a leap year
```

Program 5: Write a Python program to print all natural numbers from 1 to n.

> Programming Tip:
> Loops are used for repeated execution of code based on the evaluation of condition.

```
a=int(input("Enter the value of n:"))
print("The natural numbers:")
for i in range(1,(a+1)):
    print(i,end=', ')
```

Output

```
D:\PythonPrograms>python a1.py
Enter the value of n:10
The natural numbers:
1, 2, 3, 4, 5, 6, 7, 8, 9, 10,
```

Program 6: Write a Python program to print all the natural numbers from 1 to n in the reverse order.

```
a=int(input("Enter the value of n:"))
print("The natural Numbers:")
for i in range(a,0,-1):
print(i,end=', ')
```

Output

```
D:\PythonPrograms>python a1.py
Enter the value of n:10
The natural Numbers:
10, 9, 8, 7, 6, 5, 4, 3, 2, 1,
```

Program 7: Write a Python program to print all even numbers in the range from 1 to n.

```
a=int(input("Enter the value of n:"))
print("The Even Numbers:")
for i in range(2,a,2):
    print(i, end=" ")
    print("\n")
```

Output

```
D:\PythonPrograms>python a1.py
Enter the value of n:20
The Even Numbers:
2 4   6   8 10 12 14 16 18
```

Program 8: Write a Python program to print the multiplication table of a given number.

```
a=int(input("Enter the value of n:"))
for i in range(1,11):
    print(a,"*",i,"=",a*i)
```

Output

```
D:\PythonPrograms>python a1.py
Enter the value of n:10
10 * 1 = 10
10 * 2 = 20
10 * 3 = 30
10 * 4 = 40
10 * 5 = 50
10 * 6 = 60
10 * 7 = 70
10 * 8 = 80
10 * 9 = 90
10 * 10 = 100
```

Program 9: Write a Python program to print the sum of all odd numbers and the sum of all even numbers in a given range.

```
a=int(input("Enter the value of n:"))
esum=0;
osum=0;
for i in range(1,(a+1)):
    if((i%2)==0):
        esum=esum+i
    else:
        osum=osum+i
print("Sum of Even Numbers:",esum)
print("Sum of Odd Numbers:",osum)
```

Output

```
D:\PythonPrograms>python a1.py
Enter the value of n:50
Sum of Even Numbers: 650
Sum of Odd Numbers: 625
```

Program 10: Write a Python program to print the number pattern.

```
a=int(input("Enter n:"))
for i in range(1, a+1):
    for j in range(i,0,-1):
        print(j,end=' ')
    print(" ")
```

Output

```
D:\PythonPrograms>python a1.py
Enter n:10
1
2 1
3 2  1
4 3  2  1
5 4  3  2 1
6 5  4  3 2 1
7 6  5  4 3 2 1
8 7  6  5 4 3 2 1
9 8  7  6 5 4 3 2 1
10 9  8  7 6 5 4 3 2 1
```

4.13 Case Studies

4.13.1 Simple temperature converter

```
while(1):
    print("1. Conversion of temperature form Fahrenheit to Celsius:")
    print("2. Conversion of temperature form Celsius to Fahrenheit:")
    print("3. Exit")
    a=int(input("Enter your choice:"))
if(a==1):
    b=float(input("Enter temperature in Fahrenheit:"))
    res=(b-32)/1.8
    print("The Equivalent temperature in Celsius=",res)
elif(a==2):
    b=float(input("Enter temperature in Celsius:"))
    res=(b*1.8)+32
    print("The Equivalent temperature in Fahrenheit=",res)
else:
    break
```

```
Output
D:\PythonPrograms>python b1.py
    1. Conversion of temperature form Fahrenheit to Celsius:
    2. Conversion of temperature form Celsius to Fahrenheit:
    3. Exit
Enter your choice:1
Enter temperature in Fahrenheit:40
The Equivalent temperature in Celsius= 4.444444444444445
    1. Conversion of temperature form Fahrenheit to Celsius:
    2. Conversion of temperature form Celsius to Fahrenheit:
    3. Exit
Enter your choice:2
Enter temperature in Celsius:4.4445
The Equivalent temperature in Fahrenheit= 40.0001
    1. Conversion of temperature form Fahrenheit to Celsius:
    2. Conversion of temperature form Celsius to Fahrenheit:
    3. Exit
Enter your choice:3
```

4.13.2 Simple number system converter

```
while(1):
    print(" 1. binary \n 2. octal \n 3. hexadecimal \n 4. exit")
    i=int(input("Enter your choice:"))
    if(i==4):
        break
    else:
        a=int(input("Enter the decimal number:"))
        if(i==1):
            print("binary equivalent= ",bin(a))
        elif(i==2):
            print("octal equivalent= ",oct(a))
        else:
            print("hexa decimal equivalent= ",hex(a))
```

```
Output
D:\PythonPrograms>python b2.py
    1. binary
    2. octal
    3. hexadecimal
    4. exit
Enter your choice:1
Enter the decimal number:10
binary equivalent= 0b1010
    1. binary
    2. octal
    3. hexadecimal
    4. exit
Enter your choice:2
Enter the decimal number:10
octal equivalent= 0o12
    1. binary
    2. octal
    3. hexadecimal
    4. exit
Enter your choice:3
Enter the decimal number:10
hexa decimal equivalent= 0xa
    1. binary
    2. octal
    3. hexadecimal
    4. exit
Enter your choice:4
```

4.13.3 Generation of vowel alphabet pattern

```
a=input("Enter the vowel character:")
if(a[0]=="a"):
    m=""
    for i in range(0,7):
```

```
        for j in range(0,7):
        if (((j == 0 or j == 6) and i != 0 and i != 1) or
((i == 1) and (j == 1 or j == 5)) or
((i==0) and j > 1 and j < 5) or ((i==3) and j >0 and j < 7)):
     m=m+"#"
    else:
     m=m+" "
     m=m+"\n"
    print(m)
elif(a[0]=="e"):
    m=""
    for i in range(0,7):
     for j in range(0,7):
    if ( ((i==0 or i==3 or i==6) and j >0 and j <7) or
((j==0) and i>=0 and i<=7)
):
     m=m+"#"
    else:
     m=m+" "
     m=m+"\n"
    print(m)
elif(a[0]=="i"):
    m=""
    for i in range(0,7):
     for j in range(0,7):
    if ( ((i==0 or i==6) and j >=0 and j <=7) or
((j==3) and i>=0 and i<=7)
):
     m=m+"#"
    else:
     m=m+" "
     m=m+"\n"
    print(m)
elif(a[0]=="o"):
    m=""
    for i in range(0,7):
     for j in range(0,7):
    if (((j == 1 or j == 5) and i != 0 and i != 6) or ((i == 0 or i == 6) and j > 1 and j < 5)):
     m=m+"#"
    else:
     m=m+" "
     m=m+"\n"
    print(m)
elif(a[0]=="u"):
    m=""
    for i in range(0,7):
     for j in range(0,7):
    if ( ((i==6) and j >0 and j <7) or
((j==0 or j==6) and i>=0 and i<=7)
):
     m=m+"#"
    else:
     m=m+" "
     m=m+"\n"
    print(m)
else:
print("The given character is not a vowel alphabet")
```

```
Output
D:\PythonPrograms>python b2.py
Enter the vowel character:i
#######
   #
   #
   #
   #
   #
#######
```

Glossary

- Decision making statements are used to perform an operation based on evaluation of a given condition.
- Loop statements are used for repeated execution of a code based on evaluation of the condition.
- Break statement is used to terminate the execution of a loop.

Summary

- A single-block decision can be made with **if** statement.
- The **if..else** statement is used to handle two blocks with single condition.
- Multiple conditions can be handled with the **nested if** statement.
- Python allows two looping statements. The **for** and **while** loops are used in Python.
- The **break** statement will stop the loop and the **continue** statement will skip the current iteration of the loop.
- The **pass** statement is a do-nothing statement and is used to keep the CPU busy for some time.

Multiple Choice Questions

1. **Pass** statement
   (a) performs nothing
   (b) skips the current iteration
   (c) continues the current iteration
   (d) breaks the loop
2. Which statement will recognize the execution of **break** statement?
   (a) continue (b) switch
   (c) break (d) else
3. What are various loops available in Python?
   (a) for
   (b) for, while
   (c) for, while, do-while
   (d) while, do-while
4. Which decision statement is used for one condition?
   (a) if (b) if..else
   (c) if..elif..else (d) nested if
5. **Nested if** represents
   (a) if within if
   (b) else within else
   (c) if..else with in if
   (d) if..elif..else within if..elif..else
6. The minimum number of iterations for loops in Python is
   (a) 0 (b) 1 (c) 2 (d) 3
7. A loop within a loop is called as
   (a) Loop loop
   (b) Nested loop
   (c) Omega loop
   (d) None of the above
8. which symbol is used for decision making and looping?
   (a) * (b) #
   (c) : (d) %
9. In case a given condition is FALSE, which decision making statement is used for providing another condition?
   (a) if (b) if..else
   (c) if..elif..else (d) nested if

10. In case of **for** loop, specification of increment value is
    (a) optional
    (b) compulsory
    (c) Both a and b
    (d) None of the above

11. Decision statements work based on
    (a) statement
    (b) operator
    (c) condition
    (d) None of the above

12. The condition statement yields a
    (a) Boolean value
    (b) String value
    (c) Both (a) and (b)
    (d) None of the above

13. Non-zero values are considered as
    (a) False (b) True
    (c) False and True (d) False or True

14. Non-null values are considered as
    (a) False (b) True
    (c) False and True (d) False or True

15. Which of the following statements are decision making statements?
    (a) **if**
    (b) **if..else**
    (c) **nested if**
    (d) All the above

16. How many blocks are allowed for **if** statement?
    (a) 0 (b) 1 (c) 2 (d) 3

17. If condition is True, then the number of blocks executed by **if** statement is
    (a) 0 (b) 1 (c) 2 (d) 3

18. If condition is False, then the number of blocks executed by **if** statement is
    (a) 0 (b) 1 (c) 2 (d) 3

19. If condition is True, then the number of blocks executed by **if..else** statement is
    (a) 0 (b) 1 (c) 2 (d) 3

20. If condition is False, then the number of blocks executed by **if..else** statement is
    (a) 0 (b) 1 (c) 2 (d) 3

21. How many blocks are allowed for **if..else** statement?
    (a) 0 (b) 1 (c) 2 (d) 3

22. The number of condition statements in **if** statement is
    (a) 0 (b) 1 (c) 2 (d) 3

23. The number of condition statements in **if..else** statement is
    (a) 0 (b) 1 (c) 2 (d) 3

24. Multiple conditions can be specified with
    (a) **if**
    (b) **if..else**
    (c) **if..elif..else**
    (d) All the above

25. In **if..elif..else** statement, when will the **else** block be executed?
    (a) When all conditions have failed
    (b) When all conditions are satisfied
    (c) Both (a) and (b)
    (d) None of the above

26. How many blocks can be executed for **if..elif..else** statement?
    (a) 1 (b) 2 (c) 3 (d) 4

27. **Nested if** statement consists of
    (a) **if**
    (b) **if..else**
    (c) **if..elif..else**
    (d) All the above

28. How many blocks can be executed for **nested if** statement?
    (a) None (b) One
    (c) Two (d) Many

29. Examples of looping statements in Python are
    (a) **while**
    (b) **for**
    (c) Both (a) and (b)
    (d) None of the above

30. How many condition statements are allowed in **while** loop?
    (a) 1 (b) 2 (c) 3 (d) 4

31. How many condition statements are allowed in **for** loop?
    (a) 0 (b) 1 (c) 2 (d) 3

32. In case of looping, when is infinite execution allowed?
    (a) Condition is sometimes True
    (b) Condition is sometimes False
    (c) Condition is always True
    (d) Condition is always False

33. In which loop is **range()** function used?
    (a) **for**
    (b) **while**
    (c) Both (a) and (b)
    (d) None of the above

34. What are **x,y** in **range(x,y)**?
    (a) 0 and 1
    (b) 10, 20
    (c) Maximum and minimum of range
    (d) Minimum and maximum of range

35. Emergency exit is supported by
    (a) **Break**
    (b) **For**
    (c) **While**
    (d) None of the above

36. When will the **else** part of a loop be executed?
    (a) When **break** executed
    (b) When **break** is not executed
    (c) When condition is failed
    (d) None of the above

37. CPU can be made busy with
    (a) **for** (b) **while**
    (c) **pass** (d) **continue**

38. CPU time is saved with
    (a) **for** (b) **while**
    (c) **pass** (d) **continue**

Fill in the Blanks

1. The decision making statements are used for __________.
2. The looping statements are used for __________.
3. The control flow is decided with the __________.
4. In case of decision statements, the block of statements are __________ number of times executed.
5. In case of looping statements, the block of statements is __________ number of times executed.
6. If the condition results a positive integer greater than **0**, then it is considered as __________.
7. If the condition result is string!=null , then it is considered as __________.
8. If the condition result is string==null , then it is considered as __________.
9. If the condition result is zero, then it is considered as __________.
10. The result of a condition statement is always __________.
11. In **if** statement, when __________,then the block will be executed.
12. In **if** statement, when condition is False it executes __________.
13. To overcome the problem of **if** statement, __________ is used.
14. To overcome the problem of **if..else** statement, __________ is used
15. To overcome the problem of **if..elif..else** statement, __________ is used.
16. If condition is not given for **if** statement, then __________ is executed.
17. If condition is not given for **if..else** statement, then __________ is executed.
18. An empty condition is considered as __________.
19. Multiple blocks can be executed with __________ statement.
20. If condition is not given in for a statement, then __________ is executed.
21. If condition is not given in **while** statement, then __________ is executed.
22. The looping is stopped with __________
23. The execution of **break** statement is identified by __________.
24. **Pass** statement is used to perform __________.
25. The do-nothing statement is __________.
26. The keyword for the **pass** statement is __________.
27. The current iteration is skipped with __________.
28. In case of **nested if**, the **else** block is executed when __________.
29. __________ is used to specify two conditions.
30. __________ is used to specify two blocks.

State True/False

1. The control flow is performed with variables.
2. Loops are considered as control flow statement.

3. Decision making statement is considered as control flow statement.
4. Switch...case is allowed in Python.
5. **Break** statement is applicable to loops.
6. **Continue** statement is applicable to decision making statements.
7. **Pass** statement can be used for loops.
8. **Pass** statement can be used for a variable.
9. **Continue** will execute the current iteration of the loop.
10. The iteration of the loop can be skipped.
11. The condition statement can yield any integer value.
12. The condition statement cannot yield any string value.
13. **Else** can be used in decision making statements.
14. **Else** block cannot be used with loops.
15. **Else** block can be used with decision statements.
16. An empty condition results True value.
17. A null string results False value.
18. A condition can have complex values.
19. Control flow statements use ":"
20. Multiple conditional blocks can be specified with **if** statement.
21. Multiple conditional blocks can be specified with **if..else** statement.
22. Multiple conditional blocks can be specified with nested **if** statement.
23. **Case** keyword is allowed in control flow statements.
24. **Default** keyword is allowed in control flow statements.
25. **Case** and **default** are used with **for** loop.
26. Multi decision statements are allowed in Python.
27. In Python, CPU time can be wasted.
28. In Python, CPU speed can be improved.
29. Loops are decision making statements.
30. **If** statement is used for looping.

Find the Output

1.
```
a=100
if(a):
    print("True Block")
```

2.
```
a=""
if(a):
    print("True Block")
else:
    print("False Block")
```

3.
```
if():
    print("True Block")
else:
    print("False Block")
```

4.
```
if(0+1j):
    print("True Block")
else:
    print("False Block")
```

5.
```
if(1+1j):
    print("True Block")
else:
    print("False Block")
```

6.
```
for i in range(1,5):
    if(i==3):
        break
    else:
        print(i)
```

7.
```
for i in range(1,5):
    if(i==6):
        break
    else:
        print(i)
else:
    print("Break")
```

8.
```
for i in range(1,5):
    if(i==3):
        continue
    else:
        print(i)
```

9.
```
for i in range(1,5):
    if(i==3):
        pass
    else:
        print(i)
```

10.
```
if("abc"):
    print("ok")
elif(""):
    print("not ok")
else:
    print("else")
```

Find the Error

1.
```
while()
    print("hai")
```

2.
```
for i in range():
    print(i)
```

3.
```
for i in range(1.5,2.8):
    print(i)
```

4.
```
a=10
while(a<15):
    passed
```

5.
```
a=10
while(a<15):
    a++
```

6.
```
a=10
if(a):
    print("1")
else:
    print("2")
elif(a==1):
    print("3")
```

7.
```
a=[1 2 3]
while(a):
    print(a)
```

8.
```
a=(1 2 3)
while(a):
    print(a)
```

9.
```
a=""
b=a*3.8
if(b):
    print("hai")
```

10.
```
a="x"
b=a+3
for i in b:
    print("hai")
```

Long Answer Questions

1. With a real-time example, explain the need of using branching statements.
2. Give justification for not supporting **switch** statement.
3. Write a detailed note on looping statements.
4. Differentiate entry controlled and exit controlled loops with suitable example programs.
5. How does Python support the development of **do-while** loop?
6. List the differences between decision making and looping conditions.

Short Answer Questions

1. List the differences between branching and looping statements.
2. Describe briefly about **pass** statement.
3. Write the difference between **pass**, **break** and **continue** statements.
4. Define the counter controlled loop.
5. Describe the condition controlled loop.

Exercise Programs

1. Write a program to compute distance between two points taking input from the user (Pythagorean Theorem)
2. Write a program add.py that takes two numbers as command line arguments and prints its sum.
3. Using a for loop, write a program that prints out the decimal equivalents of 1/2, 1/3, 1/4, . . . , 1/10.
4. Write a program using a for loop that loops over a sequence. What is the sequence?
5. Write a program using a while loop that asks the user for a number, and prints a countdown from that number to zero.

6. Write a program to find the sum of all the primes below two thousand.
7. Each new term in the Fibonacci sequence is generated by adding the previous two terms. By starting with 1 and 2, the first 10 terms will be: 1, 2, 3, 5, 8, 13, 21, 34, 55, 89, ... Write a program to generate the Fibonacci sequence.
8. By considering the terms in the Fibonacci sequence whose values do not exceed four million, write a program to find the sum of the even-valued terms.
9. Write a Python program to read a number and check whether the given number is Armstrong or not.
10. Write a Python program to read a string and check whether the given string is a palindrome or not.
11. Write a Python program to compute the factorial of the given number.
12. Write a Python program to find the roots of a quadratic equation.
13. Write a Python program to check whether the given number is positive, negative or zero.
14. Write a Python program to find whether the given character is a digit, alphabet or special character
15. Write a Python program to read the week day number and print the week day name.
16. Write a Python program to check whether the given number is divisible by 2, 5 and 9.
17. Write a Python program to read the marks in five subjects and compute the percentage and grade. Grade A: >90%; Grade B: >80%; Grade C: >70%; Grade D: >60% and Grade E: <60%
18. Write a Python program to perform matrix multiplication.
19. Write a Python program to perform matrix addition and subtraction operations.
20. Write a Python program to compute the product of digits in a given number.
21. A perfect number is a positive integer that is equal to the sum of its proper divisors. Write a Python program to find whether or not a given number is a perfect number.
22. Write a Python program to print the Pascal triangle up to n rows.
23. Write a Python program to print the frequency of negative and positive numbers in a given array.
24. Write a Python program to print the sorted order of an input array.
25. Write a Python program to design a simple calculator.
26. Write a Python program to read the date of birth and calculate the age of a person.
27. Write a Python program to read the range and display the numbers that are divisible by 3 and 5 within the range?
28. Write a Python program to check whether a triangle is valid or not.
29. Write a Python program to read the date of birth and display the week day?
30. Write a Python program to check whether a given triangle is equilateral or not?

Answers

Multiple Choice Questions

1. (a)	9. (c)	17. (b)	25. (a)	33. (a)
2. (d)	10. (a)	18. (a)	26. (a)	34. (d)
3. (d)	11. (c)	19. (b)	27. (d)	35. (a)
4. (a)	12. (a)	20. (b)	28. (d)	36. (b)
5. (d)	13. (b)	21. (c)	29. (c)	37. (c)
6. (a)	14. (b)	22. (b)	30. (a)	38. (d)
7. (b)	15. (d)	23. (b)	31. (b)	
8. (c)	16. (b)	24. (c)	32. (c)	

Fill in the Blanks

1. control flow
2. control flow
3. condition statement
4. either 0 or 1.
5. 0 to infinite
6. True
7. True
8. False
9. False
10. Boolean
11. condition is True
12. nothing.
13. if..else
14. if..elif..else
15. nested if
16. nothing
17. else block
18. False
19. Nested if
20. nothing
21. nothing
22. break
23. else statement of loop.
24. nothing
25. Pass statement
26. pass
27. Continue statement
28. all the conditions are failed.
29. if..elif..else
30. if..else

State True/False

1. False
2. True
3. True
4. False
5. True
6. False
7. True
8. False
9. False
10. True
11. True
12. False
13. True
14. False
15. True
16. False
17. True
18. False
19. True
20. False
21. False
22. True
23. False
24. False
25. False
26. True
27. True
28. True
29. False
30. False

Find the Output

1. True Block
2. False Block
3. False Block
4. False Block
5. True Block
6. 1
   2
7. 1
   2
   3
   4
   Break
8. 1
   2
   4
9. 1
   2
   4
10. ok

Find the Error

1. SyntaxError: invalid syntax ":" is not used
2. TypeError: range expected 1 arguments, got 0
3. TypeError: 'float' object cannot be interpreted as an integer
4. NameError: name 'passed' is not defined
5. SyntaxError: invalid syntax (++ is not allowed)
6. SyntaxError: invalid syntax (elif should be used before else)
7. SyntaxError: invalid syntax (, is not used in defining a)
8. SyntaxError: invalid syntax (, is not used in defining a)
9. TypeError: can't multiply sequence by non-int of type 'float'
10. TypeError: must be str, not int

CHAPTER

5 Sequences – Lists

In this chapter, we shall discuss about sequences in the Python programming language. The array is not a primitive data type in Python. There are six sequences in Python. The list is an ordered set of data elements. It is a mutable, i.e., changes are allowed on list elements.

5.1 Arrays

In Python, an array is used to represent a group of similar data values. It is similar to a list except that the list contains multiple dissimilar data values. In Python, array is not a built-in data type. So, an **array** module should be imported to use the array in the program. To declare an array use the **array( )** function. This function takes two arguments. The first argument specifies the type code and the second argument specifies the elements of the array. Individual elements can be accessed with [ ] operator.

```
from array import *
a1 = array('i',[1,2,3])
print("Array: ",a1)
print("First element of array: ",a1[0])
```

Output

```
D:\PythonPrograms>python bb.py
Array: array('i', [1, 2, 3])
First element of array: 1
```

5.2 Sequences

Python programming supports sequences to store multiple values to improve the efficiency of organization. There are six sequence types. They are

- Strings
- Lists
- Tuples
- Byte arrays
- Buffers
- Range objects

String

String is a collection of character data. It is also called as character array.

```
s=input("Enter the String:")
print("The entered string is:",s)
print(type(s))
```

Output

```
D:\PythonPrograms>python a1.py
Enter the String:hello
The entered string is: hello
<class 'str'>
```

List

List is similar to string. It is used to represent the ordered list of values.

```
x=[10,20,30]
print("The numbers in the list:")
for i in range(0,3):
    print(x[i])
```

Output

```
D:\PythonPrograms>python a1.py
The numbers in the list:
10
20
30
```

Tuple

Tuple is similar to list except that it is immutable. No changes are allowed on Tuple.

```
x=(10,20,30)
print("The numbers in the Tuple:")
for i in range(0,3):
    print(x[i])
```

Output

```
D:\PythonPrograms>python a1.py
The numbers in the Tuple:
10
20
30
```

Byte

Byte is a small range of integers between 0 and 256. It is an immutable sequence; thus, no changes are allowed. Bytearray is a mutable sequence to represent byte.

```
>>> a=b"100"
>>> print(a)
b'100'
```

In the above example code, a byte object 'a' is initialized with value 100 and is displayed. In the example code given next, a byte array object is initialized with the byte object.

```
>>> a=bytes([10, 20, 30])
>>> a
b'\n\x14\x1e'
>>> b=bytearray(a)
>>> b
bytearray(b'\n\x14\x1e')
```

Buffer

Buffer is a sequence used to maintain the object of the argument value. In Python 3, it is renamed as 'memory view'. It mainly used to provide a buffer for maintaining the input value even by applying the slice operation. The slice operation is used to extract elements from a given input object.

```
import numpy
a = numpy.ndarray(1000000)
print(a.data)
```

Output
```
D:\PythonPrograms>python a1.py
<memory at 0x058FFC60>
```

Range object

range( ) function is used to create a Range object. Generally, it is used in loops to maintain the range value. It is an immutable sequence.

```
print("The numbers from 0 to 10 with increment 3:")
for i in range(0,10,3):
    print(i)
```

Output
```
D:\PythonPrograms>python a1.py
The numbers from 0 to 10 with
increment 3:
0
3
6
9
```

Dictionaries and sets

Dictionaries and sets are not sequences. They are containers to maintain the sequential data. Dictionaries are used to maintain the values by using keys.

```
d={1:'ab',2:'cd',3:'ef'}
print("The elements in the dictionary:")
for i in range(1,4):
    print(d[i])
```

Output
```
D:\PythonPrograms>python a1.py
The elements in the dictionary:
ab
cd
ef
```

A set is an unordered set of list. It does not allow duplicated values. The set is a mutable sequence, while frozen set is an immutable set. Set is implemented by using hash table.

```
s={"ghi","abc","def"}
print("The elements in the set:")
print(s)
a="ghi" in s
if(a==True):
    print("ghi is available in the set")
else:
    print("ghi is not available in the set")
```

Output
```
D:\PythonPrograms>python a1.py
The elements in the set:
{'ghi', 'abc', 'def'}
ghi is avaiable in the set
```

5.3 Using Lists

Python supports data structures with the help of sequences. Sequences mainly focus on efficient representation and maintenance of large data. Large data can be maintained in ordered and unordered form. If the data is maintained, say, according to serial number, then it is maintained in an ordered way. The list is similar to array in C, C++ or Java.

In Python, the list is represented with [] (square brackets). The list is created by providing values separated by ",". A list can maintain homogeneous type of elements.

```
>>> x=[1,2,3]
>>> x
[1, 2, 3]
>>> x=[10.5,23.67,34.87,45.95]
>>> x
[10.5, 23.67, 34.87, 45.95]
>>> x=["q","s","e","d"]
>>> x
['q', 's', 'e', 'd']
```

A list allows duplicated ordered set of values.

```
>>> li=[20,30,20,30]
>>> li
[20, 30, 20, 30]
```

A list contains an ordered set of elements. So, the elements of a list can be accessed by using the index. As with array, the index for list also starts with 0.

```
>>> l=[54,47,35,99]
>>> l[0]
54
>>> l[1]
47
>>> l[2]
35
>>> l[3]
99
>>> l[4]
Traceback (most recent call last):
File "<stdin>", line 1, in <module>
IndexError: list index out of range
```

In a list, if the index value is greater than range of the list then an error will be generated. The index value can also be negative value. If the index value is negative, then it will be subtracted from the maximum index value of the list.

```
>>> l=[54,47,35,99]
>>> l[-1]
99
```

An empty list can be created in two different ways. An empty list is represented with [].

```
>>> a=list()
>>> a
[]
>>> b=[]
>>> b
[]
```

In list, the elements can be updated.

```
>>> l=[87,65,45,34]
>>> l[0]
87
>>> l[0]=10
>>> l
[10, 65, 45, 34]
```

5.4 List Assignment and Equivalence

The list assignment process is used to assign all elements of one list to another list. In this, memory will be allocated for the two list objects. So, if one list object element is updated then it will not reflect on another list.

i. By using list( ) function, one list can be copied into another list.

```
>>> a=[5,2,3]
>>> c=list(a)
>>> c
[5, 2, 3]
>>> c[0]=10
>>> c
[10, 2, 3]
>>> a
[5, 2, 3]
```

In the above example, memory is allocated for both a and c list objects.
To assign individual elements from one list to another, we can use "=" operator.

```
>>> l1=["a","b","c"]
>>> l2=["b","d","e"]
>>> l1
['a', 'b', 'c']
>>> l2
['b', 'd', 'e']
>>> l2[1]="x"
>>> l1
['a', 'b', 'c']
>>> l2
['b', 'x', 'e']
>>> l1[0]=l2[0]
>>> l1
['b', 'b', 'c']
>>> l2
['b', 'x', 'e']
```

In the above example, two lists l1 and l2 are created with different elements. We updated a few elements of the lists. Then, element from l2 list was assigned to l1 list element.

Within a single statement, multiple variables can also be assigned with the list.

```
>>> l1,l3=["ab","cd"]
>>> l1
'ab'
>>> l3
'cd'
```

The elements from list1 and list2 can also be compared to check whether they are equal. For this, Equivalent "==" operator is used. If both the lists are same, then it will return TRUE; otherwise it will return FALSE.

```
>>> a=[1,2,3]
>>> b=list(a)
>>> a
[1, 2, 3]
>>> b
[1, 2, 3]
>>> a==b
True
>>> a[0]=10
>>> a==b
False
```

An individual element of the list can also be compared with the another element by using the same operator.

```
>>> l1=["a","b","a","c"]
>>> l1[0]==l1[1]
False
>>> l1[0]==l1[2]
True
```

Other than this operator, all the operators available in Python can be applied on elements of the list.

5.5 List Bounds

In list assignment, memory is allocated to both the list objects. So, updates made on one list object will not be reflected in another list. To overcome this problem, the list bound is used. In this process, only one copy of the list object is maintained in memory and is shared by all other multiple list objects. Thus, if one list object updates the content of the list, it will reflect in all other list objects.

```
>>> lis1=[10,20,30]
>>> lis2=lis1
>>> lis1
[10, 20, 30]
>>> lis2
[10, 20, 30]
>>> lis1[0]=100
>>> lis1
[100, 20, 30]
>>> lis2
[100, 20, 30]
```

5.6 List Slicing

List slicing is used to copy selected elements from one list to another list. By using [:], all elements of one list can be assigned to another list.

```
>>> c=[10,2,3]
>>> d=c[:]
>>> d
[10, 2, 3]
>>> d[1]=20
>>> d
[10, 20, 3]
>>> c
[10, 2, 3]
```

We can specify the start position and end position for slicing operator.

```
>>> lis1=[100,200,300,400,500,600,700,800,900]
>>> lis2=lis1
>>> lis2
[100, 200, 300, 400, 500, 600, 700, 800, 900]
>>> lis1
[100, 200, 300, 400, 500, 600, 700, 800, 900]
>>> lis3=lis1[1:3]
>>> lis3
[200, 300]
```

We can also specify an increment value for the slice operator. This is called as extending slices. In the below example code, the range is started from index 3 and the index is incremented by 2 each time until it reaches index 8.

```
>>> lis1=[100,200,300,400,500,600,700,800,900]
>>> lis1
[100, 200, 300, 400, 500, 600, 700, 800, 900]
>>> lis4=lis1[3:8:2]
>>> lis4
[400, 600, 800]
```

5.7 List Cloning

In Python, the cloning operation will copy the list from one object to another and the changes made to one list cannot be reflected to another list.

```
x=[1,2,3]
y=x
k=x[:]
z=x.copy()
print(«list x:»,x)
print(«list y:»,y)
print("list k:",k)
print("list z:",z)
print("Results with assignment copy:")
y[0]=10
print(«list x:»,x)
print("list y:",y)
print("Results with clone:")
k[0]=1000
print("list x:",x)
print("list k:",k)
print("Results with copy():")
z[0]=100
print(«list x:»,x)
print(«list z:»,z)
```

Output

```
D:\PythonPrograms>python s1.py
list x: [1, 2, 3]
list y: [1, 2, 3]
list k: [1, 2, 3]
list z: [1, 2, 3]
Results with assignment copy:
list x: [10, 2, 3]
list y: [10, 2, 3]
Results with clone:
list x: [10, 2, 3]
list k: [1000, 2, 3]
Results with copy():
list x: [10, 2, 3]
list z: [100, 2, 3]
```

5.8 Nested Lists

In Python, a list can consist of another list(s) as elements. In this, the item can be accessed with the index of the sub-list and the index of the item in the sub-list.

```
x=[[1,2,3],['a','b','c']]
for a in x:
    for b in a:
        print(b)
```

Output

```
D:\PythonPrograms>python s1.py
1
2
3
a
b
c
```

5.9 List Comprehensions

In Python, list comprehension allows the programmer to define the list elements according to mathematical equations. For example, list comprehension for the equation $A = \forall_{i=0}^{4} y^{i}$ A is

```
>>> A = [y**2 for y in range(5)]
>>> print(A)
[0, 1, 4, 9, 16]
```

5.10 Lists and Functions

We can perform various operations on a list, as given below.

- The del( ) function is used to delete the list element. The del( ) is also used to delete a list object. Once the list object is deleted, the memory allocated for the list is deallocated.

```
>>> lis4=[400,600,800]
>>> lis4
[400, 600, 800]
>>> del lis4[0]
>>> lis4
[600, 800]
>>> del lis4
>>> lis4
Traceback (most recent call last):
File "<stdin>", line 1, in <module>
NameError: name 'lis4' is not defined
```

- The len( ) function is used to return the length of the list object. It specifies the number of elements in the list.

```
>>> g=[9.56,6.45,8.94,2.78]
>>> len(g)
4
```

- Two list objects can be concatenated or merged with the help of '+' operator.

```
>>> g=[4.8,7.2,6.5,9.2]
>>> f=[1,2,3]
>>> e=f+g
>>> e
[1, 2, 3, 4.8, 7.2, 6.5, 9.2]
```

```
>>> g=[4.8,7.2,6.5,9.2]
>>> f=[1,2,3]
>>> h=g[2:5]+f[1:2]
>>> h
[6.5, 9.2, 2]
```

- The list elements can be repeated by using the '*' operator. For this, the factor of repetition should be provided.

```
>>> a=[444,77,22]
>>> b=a*3
>>> a
[444, 77, 22]
>>> b
[444, 77, 22, 444, 77, 22, 444, 77, 22]
```

- The max( ) function will return the maximum element within the given list.

```
>>> k1=[6,3,9,23,1,4]
>>> max(k1)
23
>>> k2=[2.6, 30]
>>> max(k2)
30
>>> k3=["a","b","c"]
>>> max(k3)
'c'
```

- The min( ) function will return the minimum element within the given list.

```
>>> k1=[6,3,9,23,1,4]
>>> k2=[2.6, 30]
>>> k3=["a","b","c"]
>>> max(k3)
'c'
>>> min(k1)
1
>>> min(k2)
2.6
>>> min(k3)
'a'
```

- The in keyword is used to test whether an item forms part of the list. It returns True when the item is available in the input list.
- List Membership is also tested with the not in keyword. It returns True when the item is not available within the input list.
- The sum( ) function returns the sum of all items in the input list.
- The all( ) function checks whether the list contain all True values or not.
- The any( ) function checks whether the list contains at least one True element.
- The list( ) function will convert any iterable element to a list.
- The sorted( ) function returns the sorted list.

5.11 Prime Generation with a List

A prime number is a number which can be divided by only by itself and 1. To develop a program for finding the prime numbers within a series, list can be used.

```
a=int(input("Enter the starting number of the series:"))
b=int(input("Enter the ending number of the series:"))
l=list(range(a,b))
m=len(l)
f=[]
for j in range(m):
    x=l[j]
    flag=0;
    for i in range(2,x):
        if((x%i)==0):
            flag=1
            break
    if(flag==0):
        v=[x]
        f=f+v
print("The prime numbers:",f)
```

Output

```
D:\PythonPrograms>python a1.py
Enter the starting number of the series: 2
Enter the ending number of the series: 20
The prime numbers: [2, 3, 5, 7, 11, 13, 17, 19]
```

In the code given above, initially the starting and ending values of the series are stored in two variables, a and b, respectively. Then list 'l' is used to maintain all the consecutive numbers between a and b. For this, **range( )** is used. Then every number of the list 'l' is verified to check if it is a prime number. If the number is a prime number, then it is stored in a new list 'f'. Whenever a new prime number is identified then it is concatenated to the previous 'f' list. Finally, the list 'f' is displayed.

To add the current number to the list, the following code is used.

```
a=[]
b=10
c=[b]
d=a+c
print(a)
print(b)
print(c)
```

```
Output
D:\PythonPrograms>python a1.py
[]
10
[10]</01>
```

5.12 Adding List Elements

In a list, new elements can be added by using built-in functions. These built-in functions are discussed below.

- The **append( )** method is used to add a new list as a sub-list of the current list object.

```
>>> l1=["a","b","c"]
>>> l2=["d","e"]
>>> l1.append(l2)
>>> l1
['a', 'b', 'c', ['d', 'e']]
>>> l1[0]
'a'
>>> l1[1]
'b'
>>> l1[2]
'c'
>>> l1[3]
['d', 'e']
>>> l1[3][0]
'd'
>>> l1[3][1]
'e'
```

- The **extend( )** method is similar to **append( )** except that the new list elements are not appended as a sub-list.

```
>>> l1=["a","b","c"]
>>> l2=["d","e"]
>>> l1.extend(l2)
>>> l1
['a', 'b', 'c', 'd', 'e']
>>> l1[0]
'a'
>>> l1[1]
'b'
>>> l1[4]
'e'
```

- The **count( )** method is used to count the frequency of occurrence of an element in the current list object.

```
>>> s=[4,8,1,9,2,4,1,7,1]
>>> s
[4, 8, 1, 9, 2, 4, 1, 7, 1]
>>> s.count(1)
3
>>> s.count(7)
1
```

- The **index( )** method will return the index of the input element within a list. If there are duplicated elements in a list, then the least index value will be returned.

```
>>> x=["abc","def","abc","ghi","abc"]
>>> x.index("abc")
0
>>> x.index("ghi")
3
```

- The **inset( )** method is used to add the new list object to the current list object at the specified index position.

```
>>> x=["abc","def","abc","ghi","abc"]
>>> x
['abc', 'def', 'abc', 'ghi', 'abc']
>>> y=[«hello»]
>>> y
['hello']
>>> x.insert(3,y)
>>> x
['abc', 'def', 'abc', ['hello'], 'ghi', 'abc']
```

- The **pop( )** method deletes the element at the given index in the list
- The **remove( )** method deletes the given element in the list.
- The **reverse( )** method is used to reverse the order of elements in the list.
- The **sort( )** method returns the sorted list in ascending order.

5.13 Mutability

In Python, mutability feature allows the data objects to be updated. Mutable objects can be modified with new elements whereas immutable elements do not accept any modifications of their data. For example, string objects are immutable objects and string modifications lead to error.

```
>>> s1="def"
>>> s1
'def'
>>> s1[0]
'd'
>>> s1[0]="a"
Traceback (most recent call last):
File "<stdin>", line 1, in <module>
TypeError: 'str' object does not support item assignment
```

Various immutable data types are int, float, complex, string, tuple, frozenset and bytes. Various mutable data types are list, bytearray, set, dictionary, class and class instances.

List items are mutable objects. Hence, they can be modified.

```
>>> x=[5,1,9,2]
>>> x.sort()
>>> x
[1, 2, 5, 9]
>>> x.reverse()
>>> x
[9, 5, 2, 1]
>>> x.remove(9)
>>> x
[5, 2, 1]
>>> x.pop()
1
```

- The sort( ) method is used to sort the elements of a current list object
- The reverse( ) method is used to return the reverse list of a current list object.
- The remove( ) method will remove the specified element in a current list object.
- The pop( ) method will pop the top of the element in a stack

5.14 List Unpacking

List elements can be unpacked and stored in corresponding variables. To avoid assigning values in the input list, the *_ can be used.

```
x=(1,2,3)
y,z,*_=x
print(x)
print(y)
print(z)
```

Output

```
D:\PythonPrograms\aa>python
a2.py
(1, 2, 3)
1
2
```

5.15 Stack

A stack is a data structure used to maintain the data in Last-In-First-Out Order (LIFO). In the stack, two operations can be performed. They are push( ) and pop( ). The push( ) operation is used to insert a data element into the stack. The pop( ) operation is used to remove a data element from the stack. To perform the push( ) and pop( ) operations, the position is represented as TOP (Top of the Stack). Various operations of a stack are shown in Fig. 5.1.

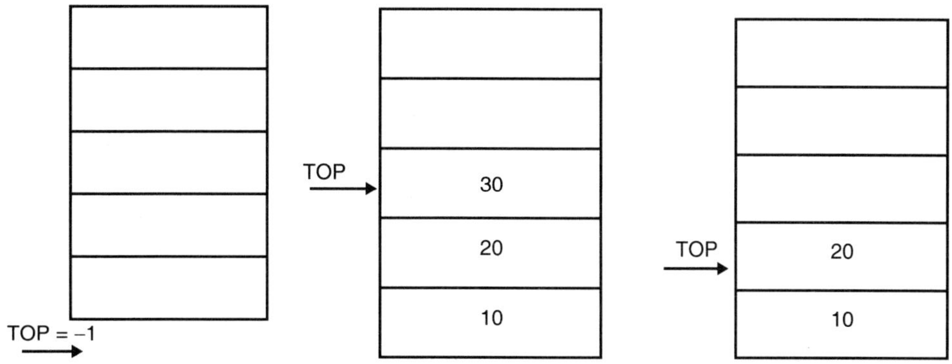

Figure. 5.1 (a) Initial stack (b) push(10,20,30) (c) pop( )

In Fig. 5.1 (a), the original stack with no values is shown. When nothing is available inside the stack, then the value of TOP is -1. If the element is pushed into the stack, then the TOP will be incremented and in the corresponding location, the value will be pushed as shown in Fig. 5.1(b). When the element is popped from the stack, then automatically the TOP will be decremented as shown in Fig. 5.1(c).

```
s=[]
top=-1
while(1):
    print("Menu for Stack operations:")
    print("1. Push")
    print("2. Pop")
    print("3. Display")
    print("4. Exit:")
    ch=int(input("Enter the choice:"))
    if(ch==1):
        top=top+1
        x=int(input("Enter the number:"))
        s.insert(top,x)
    elif(ch==2):
        y=s.pop()
        print("The popped element: ",y)
        top=top-1
    elif(ch==3):
        print("Stack:",s)
    elif(ch==4):
        exit()
    else:
        print("Invalid Choice:")
```

Output

```
D:\PythonPrograms>python st.py
Menu for Stack operations:
    1. Push
    2. Pop
    3. Display
    4. Exit:
Enter the choice:1
Enter the number:10
Menu for Stack operations:
    1. Push
    2. Pop
    3. Display
    4. Exit:
Enter the choice:3
Stack: [10]
Menu for Stack operations:
    1. Push
    2. Pop
    3. Display
    4. Exit:
Enter the choice:1
Enter the number:20
Menu for Stack operations:
    1. Push
    2. Pop
    3. Display
    4. Exit:
Enter the choice:3
Stack: [10, 20]
Menu for Stack operations:
    1. Push
    2. Pop
    3. Display
    4. Exit:
Enter the choice:2
The popped element: 20
Menu for Stack operations:
    1. Push
    2. Pop
    3. Display
    4. Exit:
Enter the choice:3
Stack: [10]
Menu for Stack operations:
    1. Push
    2. Pop
    3. Display
    4. Exit:
Enter the choice:4
```

5.16 Queue

A Queue is a data structure used to handle the data in the First-In-First-Out (FIFO) order. The data element can be inserted at one end of the queue and deleted from another end. The insertion position is represented with **rear** pointer and deletion is represented with **front** pointer.

```
q=[]
a=1
while a==1:
    print("Menu for Queue operations:")
    print("1. Insert")
    print("2. Delete")
    print("3. Display")
    print("4. Exit:")
    ch=int(input("Enter the choice:"))
    if(ch==1):
        x=int(input("Enter the number:"))
        q.insert(0,x)
    elif(ch==2):
        y=q.pop()
    elif(ch==3):
        print(«Queue:»,q)
    elif(ch==4):
        exit()
    else:
        print("Invalid Choice:")
```

```
Output
D:\PythonPrograms>pythonQueue
s1.py
Menu for Queue operations:
  1. Insert
  2. Delete
  3. Display
  4. Exit:
Enter the choice:1
Enter the number:10
Menu for Queue operations:
  1. Insert
  2. Delete
  3. Display
  4. Exit:
Enter the choice:1
Enter the number:20
Menu for Queue operations:
  1. Insert
  2. Delete
  3. Display
  4. Exit:
Enter the choice:3
Queue: [20, 10]
Menu for Queue operations:
  1. Insert
  2. Delete
  3. Display
  4. Exit:
Enter the choice:2
Menu for Queue operations:
  1. Insert
  2. Delete
  3. Display
  4. Exit:
Enter the choice:3
Queue: [20]
Menu for Queue operations:
  1. Insert
  2. Delete
  3. Display
  4. Exit:
Enter the choice:4
```

5.17 Functional Programming

In Python, functional programming is supported with three functions as listed below.

- map( )
- filter( )
- reduce( )

map( ) function

The map( ) function will take the input list and applies the specified function on the list elements. It returns a list of elements.

```
a = [1,2,3,4]
b = [10,20,30,40]
c=list(map(lambda x,y:x+y, a,b))
print("a= ",a)
print("b= ",b)
print("map() result= ",c)
```

```
Output
D:\PythonPrograms>python a.py
a= [1, 2, 3, 4]
b= [10, 20, 30, 40]
map() result= [11, 22, 33, 44]
```

filter( ) function

The filter( ) function takes two arguments. The first argument is the function to be applied on the input list. The second argument is the list of elements on which the function should be performed. After generating the result, the filter( ) will filter only the elements which are True values.

```
a = [15,20,24,35]
c=list(filter(lambda x:x%2==0, a))
print("a= ",a)
print("filter() result= ",c)
```

```
Output
D:\PythonPrograms>python a.py
a= [15, 20, 24, 35]
filter() result= [20, 24]
```

reduce( ) function

The **reduce( )** function repeatedly applies itself on the input list of elements and finally generates a single value as the final result.

```
from functools import reduce
a = [15,20,24,35]
c=reduce(lambda x,y:x+y, a)
print("a= ",a)
print("filter() result= ",c)
```

Output
```
D:\PythonPrograms>python a.py
a= [15, 20, 24, 35]
filter() result= 94
```

5.18 Sample Programs

***Program 1*:** Write a Python program to show the difference between a string and byte object.

```
a="hello"
y=b"hello"
print(a)
print(y)
```

Output
```
D:\PythonPrograms>python a1.py
hello
b'hello'
```

In this program, string maintains the ASCII characters whereas byte maintains the UNICODE characters.

***Program 2*:** Write a Python program to find whether the given number is a prime number or not.

```
x=int(input("Enter the input number:"))
flag=0;
if((x==1)or(x==2)):
    print("number is prime")
else:
    flag=0;
    for i in range(2,x):
        if((x%i)==0):
            flag=1
            break
if(flag==0):
    print("number is a prime number")
else:
    print("number is not a prime number")
```

Output
```
D:\PythonPrograms>python a1.py
Enter the input number:9
number is not a prime number
D:\PythonPrograms>python a1.py
Enter the input number:7
number is a prime number
```

***Program 3*:** Write a Python to find the frequency of occurrence of each element in a list.

```
a=int(input("Enter the length of the list:"))
l=[]
for i in range(a):
    m=input("Enter element in the list:")
    x=[m]
    l.extend(x)
print("The Input List:",l)
for i in range(a):
    f=0
    q=l[i]
    f=l.count(q)
    print("Frequency occurrence of ",q,": ",f)
```

Output
```
D:\PythonPrograms>python a1.py
Enter the length of the list:5
Enter element in the list:4
Enter element in the list:3
Enter element in the list:1
Enter element in the list:4
Enter element in the list:1
The Input List: ['4', '3', '1', '4', '1']
Frequency occurrence of 4 : 2
Frequency occurrence of 3 : 1
Frequency occurrence of 1 : 2
Frequency occurrence of 4 : 2
Frequency occurrence of 1 : 2
```

Program 4: Write a Python program to check whether or not a given string is a palindrome.

```
a=input("Enter the string:")
b=len(a)
c=int(b/2)
flag=1;
for i in range(c):
    j=(b-1)-i
    if(a[i]!=a[j]):
        flag=0
        break
if(flag==1):
    print("Input String is palindrome")
else:
    print("Input String is not a palindrome")
```

Output

```
D:\PythonPrograms>python a1.py
Enter the string:abba
Input String is palindrome
D:\PythonPrograms>python a1.py
Enter the string:abcde
Input String is not a palindrome
```

Program 5: Write a Python program to read and display the matrix with the help of a list.

> Programming Tip: The list sequencer contains ordered elements.

```
r=int(input("Enter the row size of the matrix: "))
c=int(input("Enter the col size of the matrix: "))
m=[]
for i in range(r):
    n=[]
    print("Enter the elements in the row:")
    for j in range(c):
        l=int(input())
        k=[l]
        n.extend(k)
    m.append(n)
print("The matrix list: ",m)
```

Output

```
D:\PythonPrograms>python a1.py
Enter the row size of the matrix: 2
Enter the col size of the matrix: 2
Enter the elements in the row:
1
2
Enter the elements in the row:
3
4
The matrix list: [[1, 2], [3, 4]]
```

Program 6: Write a Python program to print the sub-list of a given list according to the specified range.

```
r=int(input("Enter the size of the list: "))
m=[]
for i in range(r):
    print("Enter the elements in the list:")
    l=input()
    k=[l]
    m.extend(k)
print("The input list: ",m)
print("the index starts from 1:")
q1=int(input("Enter the start index of the range: "))
q2=int(input("Enter the ending index of the range: "))
if((q1>0)and(q2<=r)):
    sub=m[q1-1:q2-1]
print("The sub list at specified index is: ",sub)
```

Output

```
D:\PythonPrograms>python a1.py
Enter the size of the list: 5
Enter the elements in the list:
d
Enter the elements in the list:
y
Enter the elements in the list:
e
Enter the elements in the list:
h
Enter the elements in the list:
j
The input list: ['d', 'y', 'e', 'h', 'j']
the index starts from 1:
Enter the start index of the range: 2
Enter the ending index of the range:
4
The sub list at specified index is:
['y', 'e']
```

Program 7: Write a Python program to add two matrices and display the result.

```
r=int(input("Enter the row size of the matrix: "))
c=int(input("Enter the col size of the matrix: "))
print("Enter the elements in the Matrix1:")
m1=[]
for i in range(r):
    n=[]
    print("Enter the elements in the row:")
    for j in range(c):
        l=int(input())
        k=[l]
        n.extend(k)
    m1.append(n)
print("Enter the elements in the Matrix2:")
m2=[]
for i in range(r):
    n1=[]
    print("Enter the elements in the row:")
    for j in range(c):
        l=int(input())
        k=[l]
        n1.extend(k)
    m2.append(n1)
print("The matrix1: ",m1)
print("The matrix2: ",m2)
f=[]
for i in range(r):
    ss=[]
    for j in range(c):
        s=m1[i][j]+m2[i][j]
        e=[s]
        ss.extend(e)
    f.append(ss)
print("The result of addition: ",f)
```

Output

```
D:\PythonPrograms>python a1.py
Enter the row size of the matrix: 2
Enter the col size of the matrix: 2
Enter the elements in the Matrix1:
Enter the elements in the row:
1
2
Enter the elements in the row:
3
4
Enter the elements in the Matrix2:
Enter the elements in the row:
5
6
Enter the elements in the row:
7
8
The matrix1: [[1, 2], [3, 4]]
The matrix2: [[5, 6], [7, 8]]
The result of addition: [[6, 8], [10, 12]]
```

Program 8: Write a Python program to display the sum of all elements in the list.

```
l=[54,32,98,7]
print("the original list= ",l)
print("sum= ",sum(l))
```

Output

```
D:\PythonPrograms>python b2.py
the original list= [54, 32, 98, 7]
sum= 191
```

Program 9: Write a Python program to display the list in a sorted order.

```
l=[54,32,98,7]
print("the original list= ",l)
print("sorted order= ",sorted(l))
```

Output

```
D:\PythonPrograms>python b2.py
the original list= [54, 32, 98, 7]
sorted order= [7, 32, 54, 98]
```

Program 10: Write a Python program to check whether or not the input list is empty.

```
l=[54,32,98,7]
print("the original list= ",l)
a=any(l)
if(a):
    print("Input list is not empty")
else:
    print("Input list is empty")
```

Output

```
D:\PythonPrograms>python b2.py
the original list= [54, 32, 98, 7]
Input list is not empty
```

Program 11: Write a Python program to display each element of the list with membership operator.

```
l=[54,32,98,7]
print("the original list= ",l)
print("Elements in the list are:")
for i in l:
    print(i)
```

Output

```
D:\PythonPrograms>python b2.py
the original list= [54, 32, 98, 7]
Elements in the list are:
54
32
98
7
```

Glossary

- An array represents a group of similar data values.
- Sequences are used to store multiple dissimilar values.
- Buffer sequence is used to maintain the object of an argument value.
- List contains an ordered set of elements. List object is a mutable object.

Summary

- There are six sequences in Python programming language, viz., string, lists, tuples, bytearray, buffer and range.
- The present chapter discussed in detail about the properties of list.
- Empty lists can be created in two different ways.
- Various operations can be performed on the list object.

Multiple Choice Questions

1. What is the initial value of the index of a list?
   (a) 1 (b) 0
   (c) -1 (d) 2
2. Mutability data type
   (a) allows change of elements
   (b) does not allow change of elements
   (c) may allow change of elements
   (d) None of the above.
3. List is
   (a) an unordered set of data items
   (b) a string data type
   (c) an ordered set of data items
   (d) a primitive data type
4. Which method gives the index of an element?
   (a) position() (b) range()
   (c) place() (d) index()
5. list1=list2 will create how many copies?
   (a) 1 (b) 2
   (c) 3 (d) 4
6. Slicing operator is
   (a) ? (b) /
   (c) : (d) #
7. Set is
   (a) an ordered list of elements
   (b) an unordered list of elements
   (c) Both a and b
   (d) None of the above.

8. l=[] is
   (a) an empty list
   (b) a list with one element
   (c) a list with null character
   (d) None of the above.

9. + operator is used for
   (a) Remove (b) Modification
   (c) Creation (d) Concatenation

10. Which keyword is used to delete the element and the list?
   (a) del, remove (b) del, del
   (c) remove, del (d) remove, remove

11. An array consists of
   (a) similar data values
   (b) dissimilar data values
   (c) equal values
   (d) None of the above

12. A list consists of
   (a) similar data values
   (b) dissimilar data values
   (c) equal values
   (d) None of the above.

13. Array is a
   (a) primitive data type
   (b) secondary data type
   (c) Both (a) and (b)
   (d) None of the above.

14. array() is used for
   (a) defining an array
   (b) declaring and defining array
   (c) declaring an array
   (d) None of the above.

15. array() function takes how many arguments?
   (a) 0 (b) 1
   (c) 2 (d) 3

16. In Python, how many sequence types are available?
   (a) 5 (b) 6
   (c) 7 (d) 8

17. String is also called as
   (a) character array
   (b) integer array
   (c) empty array
   (d) None of the above.

18. List is
   (a) an ordered set of values
   (b) a disordered set of values
   (c) Both (a) and (b)
   (d) None of the above.

19. List and tuple are
   (a) both mutable
   (b) both immutable
   (c) immutable and mutable respectively
   (d) mutable and immutable respectively

20. Byte is
   (a) mutable
   (b) immutable
   (c) Both (a) and (b)
   (d) None of the above.

21. Byte array is
   (a) mutable
   (b) immutable
   (c) Both (a) and (b)
   (d) None of the above.

22. Buffer is renamed as
   (a) memory
   (b) view
   (c) memory view
   (d) None of the above.

23. Byte array object can be initialized with
   (a) integer object
   (b) byte object
   (c) array object
   (d) None of the above.

24. After applying slicing, the argument can be stored in
   (a) view
   (b) array
   (c) buffer
   (d) None of the above.

25. The range object is created with
   (a) range()
   (b) rangeobj(0)
   (c) Both (a) and (b)
   (d) None of the above

26. Range object is a
   (a) mutable sequence
   (b) immutable sequence
   (c) Both (a) and (b)
   (d) None of the above.

27. Loops use the following function:
   (a) range() (b) list()
   (c) box() (d) All the above.

28. Which of the following are not sequences?
   (a) Dictionaries
   (b) Sets
   (c) Both (a) and (b)
   (d) None of the above.

29. Dictionary is a
   (a) list
   (b) sequencer
   (c) container
   (d) None of the above.

30. Set is a
   (a) list
   (b) sequencer
   (c) container
   (d) None of the above.

31. Set is implemented by using
   (a) hash table
   (b) key table
   (c) Both (a) and (b).
   (d) None of the above.

32. The set does not allow
   (a) empty values
   (b) duplicate values
   (c) Null values
   (d) None of the above.

33. Dictionaries maintain
   (a) key
   (b) value
   (c) key and value
   (d) None of the above

34. A frozen set is
   (a) mutable
   (b) immutable
   (c) empty
   (d) None of the above.

35. In Python, data structures is supported by
   (a) sequences
   (b) arrays
   (c) class
   (d) None of the above.

36. Huge data can be maintained as
   (a) ordered
   (b) unordered
   (c) Both (a) and (b).
   (d) None of the above.

37. The ordered data requires
   (a) cells
   (b) sequential number
   (c) random number
   (d) None of the above.

38. The list allows
   (a) empty values
   (b) duplicated values
   (c) Both (a) and (b).
   (d) None of the above.

39. List elements can be accessed with
   (a) index
   (b) value
   (c) Both (a) and (b).
   (d) None of the above.

40. The initial value of index is
   (a) -1
   (b) 0
   (c) 1
   (d) 2

Fill in the Blanks

1. If the index value is ___________ than the size, then an error is generated.
2. An empty list can be created in ___________ different ways.
3. b=[] will create an ___________ list.
4. b=list() will create an ___________ list.
5. In list, elements can be ___________.
6. With list assignment, updating one list ___________ on another list.
7. One list can be copied into another list by using ___________.
8. List equivalence is obtained with ___________.
9. The result of list equivalence is ___________.
10. With ___________, only one copy of list is maintained.
11. With ___________, updating one list can reflect other copies of list.
12. Selected tem of list can be copied with ___________.
13. ":" is used for ___________ operation.
14. For slicing, ___________ positions should be specified.
15. For slicing operator, ___________ can be specified along with positions.
16. List cloning will create ___________.
17. Nested list means ___________.
18. ___________ is used to define the list elements based on mathematical equation.
19. ___________ is used to delete the list element.
20. ___________ is used to delete the list object.

21. __________ is used for repetition.
22. To add a list as a sub-list of another list, use __________.
23. To add a list to another list, use __________.
24. To add a list to another list at a specified position, use __________.
25. List unpacking is performed with __________.
26. Stack follows __________ order.
27. Queue follows __________ order.
28. In a stack, __________ number of pointers is used.
29. In a queue, __________ number of pointers is used.
30. Various operations on stack are __________.

State True/False

1. Python supports both arrays and lists.
2. There is no difference between array and list.
3. List can use ().
4. List index starts with 1.
5. Array is not a primary data type.
6. Array requires importing array module.
7. Character array is a sequence.
8. String is not a sequence.
9. Range object specifies the range of the index.
10. Sequences can be either mutable or immutable.
11. Data structures can be supported with sequences.
12. Negative index starts with ending.
13. Positive index starts with ending.
14. List is used to represent the ordered values.
15. Tuple uses []
16. Tuple uses ()
17. Byte represents a small range of integers.
18. Byte range is from 0 to 256.
19. Byte object value is represented with 'b'
20. byte() is used to represent the byte array.
21. Buffer and Memory view are not same.
22. List slicing and list cloning are same.
23. List slicing uses ":"
24. List can have empty values.
25. List should not have null values.
26. List elements can be accessed without index.
27. Empty lists are not allowed in Python.
28. Compound assignment operators can be applied on list.
29. List bounds will create a copy of the list.
30. List assignment will create a copy of the list.

Find the Output

1.
```
a=[]
print(a)
```
2.
```
a=list()
print(a)
```
3.
```
a=list("z")
print(a)
```
4.
```
b=bytes(5)
print(b)
```
5.
```
b=bytes([5])
print(b)
```
6.
```
b=bytes([5,6])
print(b)
```
7.
```
b=bytes([5,6])
print(b)
c=bytearray(b)
print(c[0])
```
8.
```
b=bytes(5)
c=bytearray(b)
print(c[0])
```
9.
```
a=[10, 20, 30, 40]
c=a[1:2]
print(c)
```
10.
```
a=[10, 20, 30, 40]
c=a
print(c)
```
11.
```
l=[1,2,3]
print(list(reversed(l)))
```

12. l=[1,2,3]
    print(reversed(l))

13. l=[1,2,3]
    print(sorted(l))

14. l=[1,2,3]
    print((l[-1]))

15. l=[1,2,3]
    print((10 in l))

16. l=[1,2,3]
    print(l.index(2))

17. l=[1,2,3]
    l.pop()
    print(l)

Find the Error

1. a=[1,1]
   print(a[2])

2. a=[1,2]
   b+=a
   print(b)

3. a=list(1,"z")
   print(a)

4. a=list(10)
   print(a)

5. a='abcd"
   print(a)

6. a='abcd'
   print(a)
   print("len=",a.len())

7. b=byte(100)
   print(b)

8. b=bytes(5,6)
   print(b)

9. b=bytes([])
   print(b)
   c=bytearray(b)
   print(c[0])

10. b=buffer()
    print(b)

Long Answer Questions

1. What is a sequence? How does Python support sequence? Explain all types of sequences.
2. In Python, what is the importance of list? How is list used?
3. With an example, write a detailed note on various the operations of list.
4. List the various methods available in list class object. Write an example program.

Short Answer Questions

1. Give the difference between set and list.
2. List the various mutable data types and immutable data types?
3. Write a program to print the reverse of the input list?

Exercise Programs

1. Write a Python program to represent the stack with list. Perform all operations of stack.
2. Write a Python program to represent a circular queue with list. Perform all operations of circular queue.
3. Write a Python program to display the result of matrix multiplication.
4. Write a Python program to perform the various operations on array.
5. Write a Python program to show the difference between FIFO and LIFO.
6. Write a Python program to convert the infix expression to postfix expression.
7. Write a Python program to convert the infix expression to prefix notation.
8. Write a Python program to convert prefix expression to postfix expression.
9. Write a Python program to evaluate arithmetic expressions using stacks?
10. Write a Python program to solve the towers of Hanoi problem.
11. Write a Python program to develop the various operations of priority queue.

Answers

Multiple Choice Questions

1. (b)
2. (a)
3. (c)
4. (d)
5. (a)
6. (c)
7. (b)
8. (a)
9. (d)
10. (b)
11. (a)
12. (b)
13. (d)
14. (c)
15. (c)
16. (b)
17. (a)
18. (a)
19. (d)
20. (b)
21. (a)
22. (c)
23. (b)
24. (c)
25. (a)
26. (b)
27. (a)
28. (c)
29. (c)
30. (c)
31. (a)
32. (b)
33. (c)
34. (b)
35. (a)
36. (c)
37. (b)
38. (c)
39. (a)
40. (b)

Fill in the Blanks

1. greater
2. 2
3. empty
4. empty
5. updated
6. will not reflect
7. list()
8. ==
9. Boolean
10. list bound
11. list bound
12. list slicing
13. list slicing
14. start and end
15. increment value
16. a copy of the original list.
17. list within another list.
18. List comprehension
19. del()
20. del()
21. *
22. append().
23. extend()
24. insert()
25. *_
26. LIFO
27. FIFO
28. 1
29. 2
30. push() and pop()

State True/False

1. True
2. False
3. False
4. False
5. True
6. True
7. True
8. False
9. False
10. True
11. True
12. True
13. False
14. True
15. False
16. True
17. True
18. True
19. True
20. True
21. False
22. False
23. True
24. True
25. False
26. False
27. False
28. False
29. True
30. True

Find the Output

1. [] (empty list)
2. [] (empty list)
3. ['z']
4. b'\x00\x00\x00\x00\x00'
5. b'\x05'
6. b'\x05\x06'
7. b'\x05\x06'
   5
8. 0
9. [20]
10. [10, 20, 30, 40]
11. [3, 2, 1]
12. <list_reverseiterator object at 0x0331AA90>
13. [1, 2, 3]
14. -3
15. False
16. 1
17. [1, 2]

Find the Error

1. IndexError: list index out of range
2. NameError: name 'b' is not defined
3. TypeError: list() takes at most 1 argument (2 given)
4. TypeError: 'int' object is not iterable
5. SyntaxError: EOL while scanning string literal
6. AttributeError: 'str' object has no attribute 'len'
7. NameError: name 'byte' is not defined
8. TypeError: bytes() argument 2 must be str, not int
9. IndexError: bytearray index out of range
10. NameError: name 'buffer' is not defined

CHAPTER

6 Tuples

In addition to lists, Tuples are also efficient sequences in Python. While lists are mutable objects and tuples are immutable objects. So, updating and deleting operations are not allowed in tuples. The present chapter discusses in detail about tuples.

6.1 Need of Tuple

Tuple is similar to list except that it is immutable. That is, once the data is defined in tuple, then changes are not permitted on the data. The advantages of immutability are listed below:

- During the copy operation of immutable objects, the efficiency is increases when compared with the mutable object.
- During comparison operation of immutable objects, the efficiency is increases when compared with the mutable object.
- For any immutable object value, only one copy can be stored.
- During concurrent code, development of synchronized access to immutable objects is not required.
- Supports const correctness feature.
- Lists are used to maintain data that is dynamic whereas tuples are used to maintain data of fixed size.
- For tuples, new elements cannot be added.
- For tuples, the existing elements cannot be removed.
- Tuples are used for maintaining the data by restricting add and remove features. Tuples allow only accessing of elements.
- In general, constant values can be maintained with tuple.
- Tuples can be executed faster than lists.
- Tuples can also be allowed to act as keys of dictionary, whereas this is not allowed for lists.
- The portability of lists is more than that of tuples.

Tuples is declared similar to the list except that it uses ().

```
>>> a=(4,"t",6.5)
>>> a
(4, 't', 6.5)
>>> type(a)
<class 'tuple'>
```

Any object can be converted to tuple by using **tuple( )** function.

```
a=[10,20]
print(a)
print(type(a))
b=tuple(a)
print(b)
print(type(b))
```

Output

```
[10, 20]
<class 'list'>
(10, 20)
<class 'tuple'>
```

In Tuples object, the index starts with 0. The index -1 represents the index from the highest index onwards.

```
>>> a[0]
4
>>> a[1]
't'
>>> a[2]
6.5
>>> a[-1]
6.5
>>> a[3]
Traceback (most recent call last):
File "<stdin>", line 1, in <module>
IndexError: tuple index out of range
```

In the above example code, the length of the tuple is 3. So, the index range is 0 to 2. For the index value=3, it returned an error. Tuples are immutable. So, changing any value of the Tuple object element will generate an error.

```
>>> a[0]=10
Traceback (most recent call last):
File "<stdin>", line 1, in <module>
TypeError: 'tuple' object does not support item assignment
>>> a[1]='e'
Traceback (most recent call last):
File "<stdin>", line 1, in <module>
TypeError: 'tuple' object does not support item assignment
```

We can declare a tuples within another tuples; this is called as Nested Tuples.

```
>>> a=(2,"b",3.2,10,(4,2))
>>> a
(2, 'b', 3.2, 10, (4, 2))
>>> a[0]
2
>>> a[1]
'b'
>>> a[2]
3.2
>>> a[3]
10
>>> a[4]
(4, 2)
>>> a[4][0]
4
>>> a[4][1]
2
```

6.2 Sequence Unpacking

Sequence unpacking allows assigning multiple values at a time. The unpacking will take the elements of Tuples object and assign them to individual variables. Nested sequencing unpacking allows assigning nested sub-tuples to individual variables. For this, it uses( ).

```
>>> a
(2, 'b', 3.2, 10, (4, 2))
>>> i1,i2,i3,i4,i5=a
>>> i1
2
>>> i2
'b'
>>> i3
3.2
>>> i4
10
>>> i5
(4, 2)
>>> (i6,i7)=i5
>>> i6
4
>>> i7
2
```

Sequence unpacking is also applicable to loops. In this, the range elements can be unpacked into multiple variables. For this type of unpacking, we should use tuples.

```
for x,y in [(10,20)]:
    `print(x,y)
```

Output

```
D:\PythonPrograms>python a1.py
10 20
```

If tuples are not used, then the values cannot be unpacked into multiple variables. In this case, it will generate an error.

```
for x,y in (10,20):
    print(x,y)
```

Output

```
D:\PythonPrograms>python a1.py
Traceback (most recent call last):
File "a1.py", line 1, in <module>
    for x,y in (10,20):
TypeError: 'int' object is not iterable
```

The benefits of the packing and unpacking concepts in Python programming are listed below.

- Validates the function arguments
- Defines the initial values of positional arguments
- Allows to create and use different adaptors
- Maintains log for function calls
- Helps in the development of resilient wrappers.

During unpacking, the left side contains variables and right side contains values. The number of variables should match with the number of values provided at the left and right positions respectively. Otherwise, it is an error.

```
>>> (a1,a2,a3)=(200,"bns")
Traceback (most recent call last):
File "<stdin>", line 1, in <module>
ValueError: not enough values to unpack (expected 3, got 2)
```

6.3 Methods

An empty tuple can be created by not providing any values. A single valued tuple can be created by using ",". If the single value is provided without "," then it is considered as string.

```
>>> t1=()
>>> type(t1)
<class 'tuple'>
>>> t1
()
>>> t1=(«a»)
>>> t1
'a'
>>> type(t1)
<class 'str'>
>>> t1
'a'
>>> t1=(«a»,)
>>> type(t1)
<class 'tuple'>
>>> t1
('a',)
```

Multiple values can also be separated with ",". The index of the tuple starts with 0.

```
>>> t1=(«a»,»b»)
>>> type(t1)
<class 'tuple'>
>>> t1
('a', 'b')
>>> t1[0]
'a'
>>> t1[1]
'b'
```

The 'del' keyword is used to delete the entire tuples. Once the tuples object is deleted, the memory allocated for it also gets de-allocated. Removing individual elements from the tuple is not allowed.

```
>>> t1=("ad","adadfd","er",23,5656)
>>> t1
('ad', 'adadfd', 'er', 23, 5656)
>>> del(t1[0])
Traceback (most recent call last):
File "<stdin>", line 1, in <module>
TypeError: 'tuple' object doesn't support item deletion
>>> del t1
>>> t1
Traceback (most recent call last):
File "<stdin>", line 1, in <module>
NameError: name 't1' is not defined
```

Various basic operations of a tuple are listed below.

- The **len( )** function is used to return the length of the Tuple.

```
a=(30,"a",40.67)
print("Type of a: ",type(a))
print("Elements of a: ",a)
print("The length of a: ",len(a))
```

Output

```
D:\PythonPrograms>python a1.py
Type of a: <class 'tuple'>
Elements of a: (30, 'a', 40.67)
The length of a: 3
```

- The **count( )** function is used to count the frequency occurrence of each element in the input tuple.

```
a=(30,"a",40.67,30,50,30)
print("Elements of a: ",a)
for i in a:
    print("The count of ",i," is= ",a.count(i))
```

Output

```
D:\PythonPrograms>python a1.py
Elements of a: (30, 'a', 40.67, 30, 50, 30)
The count of 30 is= 3
The count of a is= 1
The count of 40.67 is= 1
The count of 30 is= 3
The count of 50 is= 1
The count of 30 is= 3
```

- The '+' operator is used to concatenate multiple tuples.

```
a=(30,"a",40.67)
print("Type of a: ",type(a))
print("Elements of a: ",a)
print("The length of a: ",len(a))
b=(15,25.3+4j)
print("Type of b: ",type(b))
print("Elements of b: ",b)
print("The length of b: ",len(b))
c=a+b
print("Type of c: ",type(c))
print("Elements of c: ",c)
print("The length of c: ",len(c))
```

Output

```
D:\PythonPrograms>python a1.py
Type of a: <class 'tuple'>
Elements of a: (30, 'a', 40.67)
The length of a: 3
Type of b: <class 'tuple'>
Elements of b: (15, (25.3+4j))
The length of b: 2
Type of c: <class 'tuple'>
Elements of c: (30, 'a', 40.67, 15, (25.3+4j))
The length of c: 5
```

- The zip() function takes two list inputs and combines them into a Tuple object.

```
a=[30,40,50]
b=['a','b','c']
c=set(zip(a,b))
print("Elements of a: ",a)
print("Elements of b: ",b)
print("Result of zip(): ",c)
```

Output

```
D:\PythonPrograms>python a1.py
Elements of a: [30, 40, 50]
Elements of b: ['a', 'b', 'c']
Result of zip(): {(30, 'a'), (50, 'c'), (40, 'b')}
```

- The '*' operator is used to repeat the elements of the tuples.

```
a=(30,"a",40.67)
print("Type of a: ",type(a))
print("Elements of a: ",a)
print("The length of a: ",len(a))
b=(15,25.3+4j)
print("Type of b: ",type(b))
print("Elements of b: ",b)
print("The length of b: ",len(b))
c=(a*2)+(b*3)
print("Type of c: ",type(c))
print("Elements of c: ",c)
print("The length of c: ",len(c))
```

Output

```
D:\PythonPrograms>python a1.py
Type of a: <class 'tuple'>
Elements of a: (30, 'a', 40.67)
The length of a: 3
Type of b: <class 'tuple'>
Elements of b: (15, (25.3+4j))
The length of b: 2
Type of c: <class 'tuple'>
Elements of c: (30, 'a', 40.67, 30, 'a',
40.67, 15, (25.3+4j), 15, (25.3+4j),
15, (25.3+4j))
The length of c: 12
```

- The membership operator and iteration operator can be applied on the tuple.

```
a=(30,"a",40.67)
#iteration operator
for z in a:
    print(z)
#membership operator
if 40.67 in a:
    print("40.67 is in Tuples")
if 100 in a:
    print("100 is in Tuples")
else:
    print("100 is not in Tuples")
```

Output

```
D:\PythonPrograms>python a1.py
30
a
40.67
40.6   is in Tuples
100   is not in Tuples
```

- Slicing operation is allowed for tuples. The slicing operator will select the sub-elements of the tuples. For this, we should provide the starting index, ending index and index increment values. The default value of the start index is 0; ending index is the length of the tuples. The default value of the index increment value is 1.

```
>>> a=(45,65,95)
>>> b=a[]
File "<stdin>", line 1
    b=a[]
^
SyntaxError: invalid syntax
>>> b=a[:]
>>> b
(45, 65, 95)
```

If the slicing operator is not used, then it will treat **a** as an array and generate an error. To overcome this problem, slicing operator ":" is used. In the above example, no values are provided for the slicing operator. So, it will copy all the values from Tuple **a** to **b**. The index value always starts with 0.

```
>>> a=(45,65,95)
>>> a
(45, 65, 95)
>>> c=a[1:]
>>> c
(65, 95)
```

In this example, the start index for slicing operator is 1. So, the elements from Index 1 will be copied into Tuple c.

```
>>> a=(45,"mhj","nfhg",76.34,89.45,"kjkjh",6+7j)
>>> a
(45, 'mhj', 'nfhg', 76.34, 89.45, 'kjkjh', (6+7j))
>>> b=a[:5]
>>> b
(45, 'mhj', 'nfhg', 76.34, 89.45)
```

In this example, the ending index for slicing operator is 5. So, the elements from Index 0 to Index 5 will be copied into Tuple c.

```
>>> c=a[2:5]
>>> c
('nfhg', 76.34, 89.45)
```

In this example, the index from 2 to 5 will be used to select the elements in Tuple a.

```
>>> c=a[2:6:2]
>>> c
('nfhg', 89.45)
```

In this example, the index from 2 to 6 will be used to select the elements in Tuple a. The index will be incremented by 1.

- The == operator is used to compare the given two tuples.

```
>>> a=(3,4,5)
>>> b=(4,5,6)
>>> a==b
False
>>> a==a
True
>>> b==b
True
>>> b==a
False
```

- The max() function will return the maximum value of the Tuple and min() will return the minimum value of the Tuple.

```
>>> a=(3,4,5)
>>> max(a)
5
>>> min(a)
3
```

- The elements of Tuples cannot be changed. But an element of mutable object can be changed.

```
>>> a=(10,20,30,(40, 50))
>>> a
(10, 20, 30, (40, 50))
>>> a[0]=100
Traceback (most recent call last):
File "<stdin>", line 1, in <module>
TypeError: 'tuple' object does not support item assignment
>>> a[3][0]=400
Traceback (most recent call last):
File "<stdin>", line 1, in <module>
TypeError: 'tuple' object does not support item assignment
>>> b=("aa","bb","cc",[10, 20])
>>> b
('aa', 'bb', 'cc', [10, 20])
>>> b[3][0]=100
>>> b
('aa', 'bb', 'cc', [100, 20])
```

6.4 Sample Programs

Program 1: Write a Python program to pack and unpack a Tuple.

> **Programming Tip:** The elements of a tuple cannot be modified.

```
#Tuple Packing
x=(10,20,30,40)
print("Type of x: ",type(x))
print("Values of x: ",x)
#Tuple Unpacking
(v1,v2,v3,v4)=x
print("value1: ",v1)
print("value2: ",v2)
print("value3: ",v3)
print("value4: ",v4)
```

Output

```
D:\PythonPrograms>python a1.py
Type of x: <class 'tuple'>
Values of x: (10, 20, 30, 40)
value1: 10
value2: 20
value3: 30
value4: 40
```

Program 2: Write a Python program to swap two numbers by using Tuple.

```
(a,b)=(10,20)
print("The numbers before swapping:",a,b)
(a,b)=(b,a)
print("The numbers after swapping:",a,b)
```

Output

```
D:\PythonPrograms>python a1.py
The numbers before swapping: 10 20
The numbers after swapping: 20 10
```

***Program 3*:** Write a Python program to concatenate two tuples.

```
a=(30,"a",40.67)
b=("cd",89,23.21,41)
print("Tuple1 Values: ",a)
print("Tuple2 Values: ",b)
c=a+b
print("Concatenated Tuple Values: ",c)
```

Output

```
D:\PythonPrograms>python a1.py
Tuple1 Values: (30, 'a', 40.67)
Tuple2 Values: ('cd', 89, 23.21, 41)
Concatenated Tuple Values: (30, 'a', 40.67, 'cd', 89,
23.21   41)
```

***Program 4*:** Write a Python program to read and print the values of tuples from console I/O.

```
l=int(input("Enter the length of tuples:"))
t=()
for i in range(l):
    x=input("Enter the element: ")
    y=(x,)
    t=t+y
print(«The tuples elements: «,t)
```

Output

```
D:\PythonPrograms>python a1.py
Enter the length of tuples:3
Enter the element: 300
Enter the element: 400
Enter the element: a
The tuples elements: ('300', '400', 'a')
```

***Program 5*:** Write a Python program to convert a tuple into a string.

```
l=int(input("Enter the length of tuples:"))
t=()
for i in range(l):
    x=input("Enter the element: ")
    y=(x,)
    t=t+y
print(«The tuples elements: «,t)
str = ''.join(t)
print("The string is: ",str)
```

Output

```
D:\PythonPrograms>python a1.py
Enter the length of tuples:5
Enter the element: a
Enter the element: b
Enter the element: c
Enter the element: d
Enter the element: e
The tuples elements: ('a', 'b', 'c', 'd', 'e')
The string is: abcde
```

***Program 6*:** Write a Python program to search for an element in Tuples.

```
l=int(input("Enter the length of tuples:"))
t=()
for i in range(l):
    x=input("Enter the element: ")
    y=(x,)
    t=t+y
print(«The tuples elements: «,t)
s=int(input("Enter the element to be searched: "))
flag=1;
for s in t:
    flag=0
    break
if(flag==1):
    print("The element is not available in Tuples:")
else:
    print("The element is available in Tuples:")
```

Output

```
D:\PythonPrograms>python a1.py
Enter the length of tuples:5
Enter the element: 10
Enter the element: 40
Enter the element: 20
Enter the element: 60
Enter the element: 30
The tuples elements: ('10', '40', '20',
'60', '30')
Enter the element to be searched: 30
The element is available in Tuples:
```

Program 7: Write a Python program to print the sum of all elements of a tuple.

```
a=(10,20,30,40)
print("Elements of a:",a)
b=sum(a)
print("Sum of all elements: ",b)
```

Output

```
D:\PythonPrograms>python a1.py
Elements of a: (10, 20, 30, 40)
Sum of all elements: 100
```

Program 8: Write a Python program to print the sorted order of a tuple.

```
a=(400,900,50,96.78)
print("Elements of a:",a)
b=sorted(a)
print("Sorted Tuple: ",b)
```

Output

```
D:\PythonPrograms>python a1.py
Elements of a: (400, 900, 50, 96.78)
Sorted Tuple: [50, 96.78, 400, 900]
```

Glossary

- Tuple is an immutable object and no modifications are allowed on the tuple object.
- Sequence unpacking assigns multiples of tuple to individual variables.
- The slicing operator allows selection of sub-elements of the sequence.

Summary

- The present chapter discusses in detail about the creation of tuples and their immutable properties.
- Deleting entire tuples is allowed.
- Sequence unpacking is also allowed on tuple.
- Various operations can be performed on a tuple object.

Multiple Choice Questions

1. Tuples are
   (a) mutable
   (b) immutable
   (c) Both a and b.
   (d) None of the above.
2. Sort() can be applicable for a tuple that consists of elements
   (a) int, float
   (b) int, float, complex
   (c) int, float, complex, string
   (d) None of the above.
3. Which function is used to convert tuple to string?
   (a) cmp() (b) convert()
   (c) to() (d) join()
4. Which of the following is used for tuples?
   (a) []
   (b) {}
   (c) ()
   (d) None of the above.
5. a=(10,20,30). Which of the following is used to access the element "30"?
   (a) a[1] (b) a[-1]
   (c) a[0] (d) None
6. any() returns FALSE when
   (a) the tuple is empty
   (b) the tuple is full
   (c) both a and b
   (d) None of the above.
7. An empty tuple 'b' is defined by
   (a) b
   (b) b=NULL
   (c) b=()
   (d) None of the above.

8. A tuple 'b' with element '100' is defined by
(a) b=(100) (b) b=[100]
(c) b=(100,NULL) (d) b=(100,)

9. Wich statement is used to select the element abc from tuple x=("c", "d", "a", "b", "c", "e")?
(a) x[] (b) x[:]
(c) x[2:5] (d) x[2:4]

10. x=(10, 20, [30])
(a) Valid statement
(b) Invalid statement
(c) Both a and b.
(d) None of the above.

11. Tuple uses?
(a) ()
(b) []
(c) {}
(d) None of the above.

12. Tuple is
(a) mutable (b) immutable
(c) empty (d) All the above

13. For copying immutable object, the efficiency
(a) increases
(b) decreases
(c) is stable
(d) None of the above.

14. For comparing immutable objects, the efficiency
(a) increases
(b) decreases
(c) is stable
(d) None of the above.

15. How many copies of immutable objects are maintained?
(a) 3 (b) 2
(c) 1 (d) 0

16. For concurrent mode of operation, immutable objects
(a) are not required
(b) are required
(c) may be required
(d) may not be required

17. Tuples support
(a) const
(b) correctness
(c) feature
(d) const correctness feature

18. The size of tuples is
(a) fixed
(b) variable
(c) empty
(d) All the above.

19. Tuples maintain
(a) null values
(b) empty values
(c) constant values
(d) None of the above.

20. The portability of tuples is
(a) less (b) high
(c) moderate (d) average

21. Tuples index starts with
(a) -1 (b) 0
(c) 1 (d) 2

22. Declaring tuples within another tuple is called as?
(a) inner tuples (b) outer tuples
(c) merged tuples (d) nested tuples

23. Tuples can have
(a) heterogeneous data
(b) homogeneous data
(c) empty data
(d) None of the above

24. Multiple values in Tuples are separated with?
(a) : (b) ;
(c) , (d) ^

25. Multiple values of tuples can be assigned to individual variables. This is called as?
(a) sequence packing
(b) sequence unpacking
(c) sequence generating
(d) sequence degenerating

26. Sequence unpacking of tuples uses
(a) = (b) ==
(c) += (d) -=

27. Sequence unpacking is also applicable to
(a) variable
(b) literal
(c) decision making statements
(d) loops

28. In case of sequence unpacking in loops, how many variables are required?
(a) 1 (b) 2
(c) 3 (d) Many

29. Sequence unpacking can be applied
(a) to validate the arguments
(b) to define the positional arguments of initial values
(c) Both (a) and (b).
(d) None of the above.

30. Function calls log is maintained with?
   (a) sequence packing
   (b) sequence unpacking
   (c) Both (a) and (b).
   (d) None of the above.

31. An empty tuple can be created with?
   (a) []
   (b) {}
   (c) ()
   (d) None of the above.

Fill in the Blanks

1. The Tuple is ____________________.
2. Changes to Tuples are ____________________.
3. With Tuples, the efficiency is increased for ____________________ operations.
4. ____________________ number of copies can be maintained for Tuples object.
5. Tuples maintain data of ____________________ size.
6. Restricted operations on Tuples are ____________________.
7. Tuples use ____________________ for creation.
8. In the Tuple object, index value -1 represents ____________________.
9. Nested sub-tuples are unpacked with ____________________.
10. For unpacking multiple values, ____________________ has to be used.
11. For unpacking [(10,20,30)], ____________________ are required.
12. Tuples are used for developing ____________________.
13. For defining positional arguments, ____________________ are used.
14. During unpacking, ____________________ are placed at left side.
15. During unpacking, ____________________ are placed at right side.
16. A tuple single value without "," is considered as ____________________.
17. A tuple without any value is considered as ____________________.
18. In tuple, multiple values are separated with ____________________.
19. The del keyword will delete the ____________________.
20. Removing an individual element of tuple is ____________________.
21. The size of the tuple is estimated with ____________________.
22. The "+" operator is used for ____________________.
23. The repetition is performed with ____________________.

State True/False

1. The tuples and lists are same.
2. The tuples and lists are not same
3. Tuples and lists are sequences.
4. Tuples and dictionaries are same.
5. Lists maintain dynamic data.
6. Tuples maintain static data.
7. Addition of elements is allowed in tuples.
8. Deletion of elements is not allowed in tuples
9. Tuples uses []
10. Tuples uses ()
11. Empty tuples are not allowed.
12. String can be represented as single-valued tuple.
13. Tuples are less portable than lists
14. Comma operator is not allowed in tuple.
15. In tuples, ":" is used for separating multiple elements.
16. Multiple tuples can be combined.
17. For combining multiple tuples, **append()** is used.
18. **Size()** is used for estimating the length of the tuple.
19. Constant values can be maintained with tuples.
20. Removing individual elements of tuple is allowed.

21. Removing multiple elements of tuple is allowed.
22. Removing entire tuple is allowed.
23. Removing a tuple will not de-allocate memory
24. Tuple index starts with -1.
25. Unpacking is not allowed with tuples.
26. Multiple values in tuple can be unpacked into a single variable.

Find the Output

1.
```
a=()
print(a)
```
2.
```
a=(10,)
print(a)
```
3.
```
a=(10,)
b=len(a)
print(b)
```
4.
```
a=(10)
print(type(a))
```
5.
```
a=(10,20)
print(type(a))
```
6.
```
a=(10,20,30)
del()
print("Tuple is deleted")
```
7.
```
a=(10,20)
x,y=a
print(x,y)
```
8.
```
l=(10,20,30)
print(l[0])
```
9.
```
l=(10,20,30)
print(l[1:2])
```
10.
```
l=(10,20,30)
print(l.index(20))
```
11.
```
l=(60,100,30)
print(sorted(l))
```
12.
```
l=(60,100,30)
print(tuple(reversed(l)))
```
13.
```
l=(60,100,30)
print(reversed(l))
```
14.
```
l=(60,100,30)
print(30 in l)
```

Find the Error

1.
```
a=(,)
print(a)
```
2.
```
a=(10,)
print(a[1])
```
3.
```
a=(10,20,30)
del(a[0])
print(type(a))
```
4.
```
a=(10,20,30)
a[0]=40
print(type(a))
```
5.
```
a=(10,20)
x,y=a
del(x)
print(x,y)
```
6.
```
a=(10,20,30)
x,y=a
print(x,y)
```
7.
```
a=(10x)
print(a)
```

Long Answer Questions

1. Write in detail about Tuples in python programming. How are they immutable objects?
2. What is sequence packing and unpacking? With an example, explain the process of sequence packing and unpacking.
3. List and explain the various operations and functions applicable to a tuple object.

Short Answer Questions

1. How is the tuple deleted?
2. What are the various operators allowed on a tuple?
3. Discuss about len() function.

Exercise Programs

1. Write a Python program to categorize all the elements of a given tuple according to their data type. Store the results of each category into a new sub-tuple. Display the sorted order of each sub-tuple.
2. Write a Python program to create a tuples without using (). (Hint: use ",").
3. Write a Python program to read the values in tuples from console I/O and compute the first order statistical operations.
4. Write a Python program to search for a given element in tuples by using "in" operator.
5. Write a Python program to use index operator on tuples.
6. Write a Python program to display the sliced tuple result.
7. Write a Python program for reassigning the tuple.
8. Write a Python program for enumerating tuple.
9. Write a Python program for displaying the sorted order of tuple.
10. Write a Python program for performing membership test on tuple.
11. Write a Python program for iterating a tuple.
12. Write a Python program to unpack a tuple into various variables.
13. Write a Python program to convert tuple into a string.
14. Write a Python program to find duplicated items in the input tuple.

Answers

Multiple Choice Questions

1. (b)	9. (c)	17. (d)	25. (b)
2. (a)	10. (a)	18. (a)	26. (a)
3. (d)	11. (a)	19. (c)	27. (d)
4. (c)	12. (b)	20. (a)	28. (d)
5. (b)	13. (a)	21. (b)	29. (c)
6. (a)	14. (a)	22. (d)	30. (b)
7. (c)	15. (c)	23. (a)	31. (c)
8. (d)	16. (b)	24. (c)	

Fill in the Blanks

1. immutable
2. not allowed
3. copy and comparison
4. One
5. fixed.
6. Adding and Removing elements.
7. ()
8. the last element
9. nested sequencing
10. Tuple
11. multiple variables
12. resilient wrappers
13. tuples.
14. variables
15. values
16. string
17. empty tuple
18. comma
19. entire tuple
20. not allowed
21. len( )
22. concatenating two tuples
23. T*

State True/False

1. False
2. True
3. True
4. False
5. True
6. True
7. False
8. True
9. False
10. True
11. False
12. True
13. True
14. False
15. True.
16. True
17. False
18. False
19. True
20. False
21. False
22. True
23. False
24. False
25. False
26. False

Find the Output

1. ()
2. (10,)
3. 1
4. <class 'int'>
5. <class 'tuple'>
6. Tuple is deleted
7. 10 20
8. 10
9. (20,)
10. 1
11. [30, 60, 100]
12. (30, 100, 60)
13. <reversed object at 0x032EAAB0>
14. True

Find the Error

1. SyntaxError: invalid syntax
2. IndexError: tuple index out of range (a[1])
3. TypeError: 'tuple' object doesn't support item deletion
4. TypeError: 'tuple' object does not support item assignment
5. NameError: name 'x' is not defined
6. ValueError: too many values to unpack (expected 2)
7. SyntaxError: invalid syntax

CHAPTER 7 Dictionaries

Python programming supports both sequence and mapping objects. The present chapter discusses about the mapping object called as "dictionary". Dictionary is a mutable object used to maintain heterogeneous elements. It is a mutable object. Various operations are allowed on the dictionary object.

7.1 Making a Dictionary

Python supports various built-in data types for data structures. They are sequence or mapping objects. There are two types of sequencers. They are i) List ii) Tuple. The sequencer will access elements of the input set of elements by using an index value. The values are maintained in a sequential order. The mapping object is mainly used to access the elements without index value. Dictionary is an unordered set of elements.

Python programming supports dictionary data type. The dictionary is a mapping object. Hence, in dictionary heterogeneous values can be maintained. Each of the values is mapped to the corresponding key. The dictionary contains a set of key, value pairs. Within a dictionary, the value is accessed only with the help of corresponding key.

List is a mutable object, whereas the dictionary is an implementation of hash table and key-value pair. The list is an ordered object whereas the dictionary is an unordered object. The list elements can be any type. The elements can be accessed with the help of index value. The dictionary can also have multi-typed values. The elements can be accessed with the help of a key.

Dictionary is a mutable object. So, all the elements of the dictionary can be changed, updated, or removed. The dictionary takes O(1) look-up speed. Hence, they are found to be efficient for memory over operations and for improving look-up speed efficiency.

There are three different ways to create a dictionary. They are given below.

i. By using literal dictionary literals "{" and "}"

There are two literals for dictionary. They are { and }. By using these, we can create a new dictionary.

```
>>> d1={}
>>> type(d1)
<class 'dict'>
>>> d1
{}
```

In the above example code, a new dictionary name d1 is created without any key, value pairs. So, it is called as empty dictionary. We can also provide the key, value pairs.

```
>>> d1={10:20}
>>> d1
{10: 20}
>>> d1[10]
20
```

In the above example code, a new dictionary d1 is created with a single key, value pair. The key and value are separated by using ":" operator. The left side of ":" is considered as key value and the right side of ":" is considered as value. After creating the dictionary, the value is accessed by specifying the corresponding key. For this, [] should be used.

If only value is specified without assigning a key, then it will be considered as set data type.

```
>>> d2={10}
>>> d2
{10}
>>> type(d2)
<class 'set'>
```

The dictionary is a mutable object; so we can add multiple key, value pairs to the existing dictionary.

```
>>> a={}
>>> a
{}
>>> a["one"]=1
>>> a[2]=10
>>> a[3.5]=30
>>> a
{'one': 1, 2: 10, 3.5: 30}
>>> a['one']
1
>>> a[2]
10
>>> a[3.5]
30
```

Within a dictionary, multiple key-value pairs can be specified by using ",".

```
>>> b={1:100,2:200,3:300}
>>> b
{1: 100, 2: 200, 3: 300}
>>> b[1]
100
>>> b[2]
200
>>> b[3]
300
>>> b[4]
Traceback (most recent call last):
  File "<stdin>", line 1, in <module>
KeyError: 4
```

In the above example code, the dictionary contains keys {1,2,3}. Accessing the dictionary with wrong key "4" will generate an error.

ii. By using list of tuples

A dictionary can also be constructed from the multiple lists of tuples as shown below. It uses the dict keyword.

```
>>> d=dict([("x",50)])
>>> type(d)
<class 'dict'>
>>> d
{'x': 50}
>>> d["x"]
50
```

This type of dictionary creation is useful for dynamic list of elements.

iii. By using parallel lists

This is similar to the previous method of dictionary creation except that, here multiple lists of tuples can be used to create the dictionary.

```
>>> a=("x",50)
>>> b=("y",60)
>>> c=[a,b]
>>> a
('x', 50)
>>> b
('y', 60)
>>> c
[('x', 50), ('y', 60)]
>>> d=dict(c)
>>> d
{'x': 50, 'y': 60}
```

7.2 Basic Operations

- Dictionary values can be updated by proving new value for the existing key in the existing dictionary.

```
>>> x={1:"a",2:"b"}
>>> x
{1: 'a', 2: 'b'}
>>> type(x)
<class 'dict'>
>>> x[1]="c"
>>> x
{1: 'c', 2: 'b'}
```

- In a dictionary, duplicate keys are not allowed. In case of duplicate keys, only the last value will be maintained by the dictionary.

```
>>> q={1:100,1:200}
>>> q
{1: 200}
```

- In dictionary, key can be anyone of the basic built-in data type. In addition to this, a tuple object can also be considered as key. But a list object is not allowed for key.

```
>>> q1={('key'):100}
>>> q1
{'key': 100}
>>> q1={['key']:100}
Traceback (most recent call last):
    File "<stdin>", line 1, in <module>
TypeError: unhashable type: 'list'
```

- The "==" operator is used to compare the given two dictionaries. If both are same then it will return TRUE; otherwise it will return FALSE.

```
>>> d={1.0:"abc",2.0:"def"}
>>> d1={1:"abc",2:"def"}
>>> d2={"a":100,"b":500.30}
>>> d1
{1: 'abc', 2: 'def'}
>>> d2
{'a': 100, 'b': 500.3}
>>> d
{1.0: 'abc', 2.0: 'def'}
>>> d1==d
True
>>> d1==d2
False
>>> d2==d
False
```

- The **str()** function will convert the input dictionary to a string.

```
>>> d={1:"hai"}
>>> d
{1: 'hai'}
>>> str(d)
"{1: 'hai'}"
```

- The **len()** function will return the length of the dictionary.

```
>>> d1
{1: 'abc', 2: 'def'}
>>> len(d1)
2
```

- The **del()** function is used to delete an element from the dictionary. Within a dictionary, to delete a value, the corresponding key should be provided.

```
>>> d1
{1: 'abc', 2: 'def'}
>>> del(d1[1])
>>> d1
{2: 'def'}
```

- The del() is also used to delete the complete dictionary object.

```
>>> d1
{2: 'def'}
>>> del(d1)
>>> d1
Traceback (most recent call last):
  File "<stdin>", line 1, in <module>
NameError: name 'd1' is not defined
```

7.3 Dictionary Operations

The dictionary contains keys and values. The details of a dictionary can be ascertained by various built-in methods of a dictionary class. They are listed below.

- The list of keys available within a dictionary are listed by using **keys()** method.

```
>>> d1={1:"a",2:"b",3:"c",4:"d"}
>>> d1
{1: 'a', 2: 'b', 3: 'c', 4: 'd'}
>>> d1.keys()
dict_keys([1, 2, 3, 4])
```

- The list of values available within a dictionary are listed by using **values()** method.

```
>>> d1={1:"a",2:"b",3:"c",4:"d"}
>>> d1
{1: 'a', 2: 'b', 3: 'c', 4: 'd'}
>>> d1.values()
dict_values(['a', 'b', 'c', 'd'])
```

- The elements in the dictionary can be cleared by using **clear()** method. This will create the input dictionary as an empty dictionary.

```
>>> d1={1:"a",2:"b",3:"c",4:"d"}
>>> d1
{1: 'a', 2: 'b', 3: 'c', 4: 'd'}
>>> d1.clear()
>>> d1
{}
```

- Dictionaries can be copied in using two ways, viz., shallow copy or deep copy. In deep copy, the copied object will share the same memory locations as the original object. So, changes made in one object will reflect on the other object. In shallow copy, memory will be allocated for the copied object. So, changes made in one object will not be reflected on the other object. The **copy()** method will perform shallow copy of one dictionary object to another object.

```
>>> d1={1:100.50, 2:"abc", 3:"5+9j"}
>>> d1
{1: 100.5, 2: 'abc', 3: '5+9j'}
>>> type(d1)
<class 'dict'>
>>> d2=d1.copy()
>>> d2
{1: 100.5, 2: 'abc', 3: '5+9j'}
>>> type(d2)
<class 'dict'>
>>> d1[1]=986
>>> d1
{1: 986, 2: 'abc', 3: '5+9j'}
>>> d2
{1: 100.5, 2: 'abc', 3: '5+9j'}
```

- The fromkeys() method is used to created a new dictionary. For the new dictionary, the sequential keys can be provided as another dictionary by the user. The user can also specify the values. If no values are provided, then none values will be initialized automatically. This method is called with "dict" class.

```
>>> k={1,'a',2,'b'}
>>> d=dict.fromkeys(k)
>>> d
{1: None, 2: None, 'a': None, 'b': None}
>>> d1=dict.fromkeys(k,100)
>>> d1
{1: 100, 2: 100, 'a': 100, 'b': 100}
```

In the above code, the keys are defined a dictionary "k". A new dictionary "d" is created by using dict.fromkeys() method. With this method, a new dictionary "d" is created with keys in "k" dictionary. As values are not provided, the default value is assigned to all these key pairs.

In the second case, "100" is specified as the value and the key dictionary "k" is specified for keys. So, a new dictionary "d1" is created and the value is initialized to 100 for the keys.

The list of values can be provided as an argument.

```
>>> v=[1]
>>> d2=dict.fromkeys(k,v)
>>> d2
{1: [1], 2: [1], 'a': [1], 'b': [1]}
>>> v=[1,2]
>>> d2=dict.fromkeys(k,v)
>>> d2
{1: [1, 2], 2: [1, 2], 'a': [1, 2], 'b': [1, 2]}
```

In the above code, the list of values is copied to all keys in the dictionary. To overcome this, dictionary comprehension is used.

```
>>>k={1,2,3}
>>> v=['ab','cd','ef']
>>> d3=dict(zip(k,v))
>>> d3
{1: 'ab', 2: 'cd', 3: 'ef'}
```

- The get() is used find the input key and return the corresponding value.

```
>>> d3
{1: 'ab', 2: 'cd', 3: 'ef'}
>>> d3.get()
Traceback (most recent call last):
    File "<stdin>", line 1, in <module>
TypeError: get expected at least 1 arguments, got 0
>>> d3.get(1)
'ab'
>>> d3.get(5)
>>>
>>> d3.get(5,"None")
'None'
```

In the above code, the get() without any arguments will generate an error. We should give at least one argument to the get() method. In the input dictionary, there is no key-value pair for the key="5". So, for get(5) call, nothing is displayed. In this case, we can provide the default value.

- The setdefault() method is used to set initialize the key value to a default value..

```
>>> d1={}
>>> d1.setdefault(1,"none")
'none'
>>> d1
{1: 'none'}
```

- The key-value pairs in the input dictionary are listed by using items() method.

```
>>> d3
{1: 'ab', 2: 'cd', 3: 'ef'}
>>> d3.items()
dict_items([(1, 'ab'), (2, 'cd'), (3, 'ef')])
```

- The update()method is used to update the current dictionary object by adding a new dictionary object.

```
>>> d1={1:"a",2:"b",3:"c"}
>>> d2={100:"abc",200:"def"}
>>> d1
{1: 'a', 2: 'b', 3: 'c'}
>>> d2
{100: 'abc', 200: 'def'}
>>> d1.update(d2)
>>> d1
{1: 'a', 2: 'b', 3: 'c', 100: 'abc', 200: 'def'}
>>> d2
{100: 'abc', 200: 'def'}
```

- The pop() method returns the element from the current dictionary object. This method takes two arguments.
  - i. The first argument specifies the key to be searched.
  - ii. The second argument specifies the default value to be returned when the key is not found.

When the argument key is found in the dictionary, then its value will be popped from the dictionary.

```
>>> d1={1:10,2:"a",3:55.43,4:"c",5:"d"}
>>> d1
{1: 10, 2: 'a', 3: 55.43, 4: 'c', 5:'d'}
>>> d1.pop(2)
'a'
>>> d1
{1: 10, 3: 55.43, 4: 'c', 5: 'd'}
```

The pop() method searches the dictionary for key "2" and the value for key "2" is popped from the dictionary. If the key is not found then if the default value is not provided, keygen error will be displayed. If the default value is provided, then it will be returned.

```
>>> d1.pop(10)
Traceback (most recent call last):
   File "<stdin>", line 1, in <module>
KeyError: 10
>>> d1.pop(10,"no key found")
'no key found'
```

- The popitem() method removes the topmost item from the current dictionary object. The popitem() method takes no arguments.

```
stack = {'a': 10, 'b': 'str', 'c': 46.3}
print('stack = ',stack)
popresult = stack.popitem()
print('stack = ',stack)
print('popitem() result = ',popresult)
```

Output

```
D:\PythonPrograms\aa>python
a2.py
stack = {'a': 10, 'b': 'str', 'c': 46.3}
stack = {'a': 10, 'b': 'str'}
popitem() result = ('c', 46.3)
```

- Dictionary comprehension is a technique to create new dictionary with an expression. The expression consists of a pair of key and value. Within the curly braces, the expression followed by the for loop will be used to iterate the expression.

```
stack = {y: y*2 for y in range(10)}
print('stack = ',stack)
popresult = stack.popitem()
print('stack = ',stack)
print('popitem() result = ',popresult)
```

Output

```
D:\PythonPrograms\aa>python
a2.py
stack = {0: 0, 1: 2, 2: 4, 3: 6, 4: 8, 5:
10, 6: 12,
7: 14, 8: 16, 9: 18}
stack = {0: 0, 1: 2, 2: 4, 3: 6, 4: 8, 5:
10, 6: 12,
7: 14, 8: 16}
popitem() result = (9, 18)
```

7.4 Sets

A set is an unordered list of elements. It is a mutable object. So, changes in the set elements are allowed.

```
>>> s=set("hai")
>>> s
{'h', 'a', 'i'}
>>> type(s)
<class 'set'>
```

- An empty set can be created by using **set()**.

```
>>> s1=set()
>>> type(s1)
<class 'set'>
```

- Multiple elements can be provided in a set by using (). Within () each value can be separated by using ",".

```
>>> se2=set((1,2,3,))
>>> se2
{1, 2, 3}
>>> type(se2)
<class 'set'>
```

- New elements can be added to a set by using **add()** method.

```
>>> se1.add(50)
>>> se1
{1, 2, 3, 50}
>>> se1.add((100,200))
>>> se1
{1, 2, 3, (100, 200), 50}
```

- In a set, duplicate values are not allowed.

```
>>> s1=set((10,20,10))
>>> s1
{10, 20}
```

- In a set, elements cannot be accessed by using index.
- Adding an iterable element to a set yields error. To overcome this problem, **update()** method is used.

```
>>> s1
{10, 20}
>>> s1.add([40,50])
Traceback (most recent call last):
  File "<stdin>", line 1, in <module>
TypeError: unhashable type: 'list'
>>> s1.update([40,50])
>>> s1
{40, 10, 20, 50}
```

- **discard()** and **remove()** methods are used for deleting elements from the set. If the specified element is not found then **remove()** will result an error.

```
>>> s1
{40, 10, 20, 50}
>>> s1.remove(10)
>>> s1
{40, 20, 50}
>>> s1.discard(20)
>>> s1
{40, 50}
>>> s1.remove(100)
Traceback (most recent call last):
    File "<stdin>", line 1, in <module>
KeyError: 100
>>> s1.discard(100)
>>> s1
{40, 50}
```

- The **clear()** method is used to clear all elements in a set and makes the current set an empty set.

```
>>> se1
{1, 2, 3, 50}
>>> se1.clear()
>>> se1
set()
```

- The **pop()** method will pop the element from the current set.

```
>>> s1
{'a', 40, 10, 20, 'b', 30}
>>> s1.pop()
'a'
```

- The "|" operator is used to perform the set union operation.

```
>>> s1
{40, 10, 20, 'b', 30}
>>> s2
{10, 300, 400, 20, 500}
>>> s3=s1|s2
>>> s3
{40, 10, 300, 400, 20, 500, 'b', 30}
```

- The 'intersection()' method is used to find the set difference result.

```
>>> s4=s1.intersection(s2)
>>> s4
{10, 20}
```

- The "-" is used for perform the set difference operation.

```
>>> s5=s1-s2
>>> s5
{40, 'b', 30}
```

- The len() function returns the length of the set.
- The all() function will return TRUE when all the elements of the set are TRUE; otherwise it returns FALSE.
- The any() function returns TRUE if any of the set element is TRUE; otherwise it returns FALSE.

```
>>> s1
{40, 10, 20, 'b', 30}
>>> len(s1)
5
>>> all(s1)
True
>>> any(s1)
True
```

- The max() and min() functions returns the maximum and minimum values in the input set.

```
>>> s1=set([10, 20, 30, 40])
>>> s1
{40, 10, 20, 30}
>>> max(s1)
40
>>> min(s1)
10
```

7.5 Iterators and Generators

In Python programming, an iterator is used to represent the object. With iterator, the sequence of elements is accessed with the next() method. The iter() will take iterable object and returns an iterator. If there are no next elements, then it will raise StopIteration exception.

```
st1="hello"
i=iter(st1)
print(next(i))
print(next(i))
print(next(i))
print(next(i))
print(next(i))
print(next(i))
```

Output

```
D:\PythonPrograms>python s1.py
h
e
l
l
o
Traceback (most recent call last):
  File "s1.py", line 8, in <module>
    print(next(i))
StopIteration
```

A Generator is an iterator which controls the iteration of a loop. The generator will return a sequence of values. During iteration of a loop, the statements up to "yield" statement and the generator object with the sequence of values will be returned.

```
def fun():
    a,b,c=1,2,3
    yield a,b,c
    a = a+1
    b = b+2
    c= c+3
    yield a,b,c
    a = a*2
    b = b*2
    c= c*2
    yield a,b,c
gen1 = fun()
print(next(gen1))
print(next(gen1))
print(next(gen1))
print(next(gen1))
```

Output

```
D:\PythonPrograms>python s1.py
(1, 2, 3)
(2, 4, 6)
(4, 8, 12)
Traceback (most recent call last):
    File "s1.py", line 21, in <module>
    print(next(gen1))
StopIteration
```

7.6 Sample Programs

Program 1: Write a Python program to read the elements of dictionary from console I/O and display the dictionary.

Programming Tip:

Dictionary is a mapping object.

```
d={}
n=int(input("Enter the length:"))
for i in range(n):
    k=input("enter the key: ")
    v=input("enter the value: ")
    x={k:v}
    d.update(x)
print("The dictionary: ",d)
```

Output

```
D:\PythonPrograms>python a1.py
Enter the length:3
enter the key: 1
enter the value: a
enter the key: 2
enter the value: b
enter the key: 3
enter the value: c
The dictionary: {'1': 'a', '2': 'b', '3': 'c'}
```

Program 2: Write a Python program to read and display a frozen set.

Frozen set is a set which does not allow changes in the set elements. Thus, frozen set is an immutable object.

```
a=frozenset('a')
print("Elements of frozen set are:",a)
a1=frozenset(['a','b'])
print("Elements of frozen set are:",a1)
a.add('c')
```

Output

```
D:\PythonPrograms>python a1.py
Elements of frozen set are: frozenset({'a'})
Elements of frozen set are: frozenset({'b', 'a'})
Traceback (most recent call last):
    File "a1.py", line 7, in <module>
        a.add('c')
AttributeError: 'frozenset' object
    has no attribute 'add'
```

Program 3: Write a Python program to check whether or not the user-provided keys are available in the dictionary with 'in' operator.

The 'in' operator is used to search for a given element available in the dictionary.

```
d={}
n=int(input("Enter the length:"))
for i in range(n):
    k=input("Enter the key: ")
    v=input("Enter the value: ")
    x={k:v}
    d.update(x)
for k, v in d.items():
    print('\nKey and Value: ', k, v)
s=input("Enter the key to be searched:")
if(s in d.keys()):
    print("The key is available")
else:
    print("The key is not available")
```

Output

```
D:\PythonPrograms>python a1.py
Enter the length:3
Enter the key: 1
Enter the value: a
Enter the key: 2
Enter the value: b
Enter the key: 3
Enter the value: c
Key and Value: 1 a
Key and Value: 2 b
Key and Value: 3 c
Enter the key to be searched:2
The key is available
```

Program 4: Write a Python program to print the sorted dictionary.

```
d = {10: 100, 30: 90, 50: 250, 70: 490, 90: 810}
print("original= ",d)
a=sorted(d)
print("sorted= ",a)
```

Output

```
D:\PythonPrograms>python b2.py
original= {10: 100, 30: 90, 50: 250,
70: 490, 90: 810}
sorted= [10, 30, 50, 70, 90]
```

Program 5: Write a Python program to print the length of the dictionary.

```
d = {10: 100, 30: 90, 50: 250, 70: 490, 90: 810}
print("original= ",d)
a=len(d)
print("length= ",a)
```

Output

```
D:\PythonPrograms>python b2.py
original= {10: 100, 30: 90, 50: 250,
70: 490, 90: 810}
length= 5
```

Program 6: Write a Python program to compare two dictionaries.

```
d = {10: 100, 30: 90, 50: 250, 70: 490, 90: 810}
d1 = {10: 100, 30: 90, 50: 250, 70: 490, 90: 810}
print("original dict1= ",d)
print("original dict2= ",d1)
a=set(d.items()) ^ set(d1.items())
if(len(a)==0):
    print("The two dictionaries are same")
else:
    print("The two dictionaries are not same")
```

Output

```
D:\PythonPrograms>python b2.py
original dict1= {10: 100, 30: 90, 50:
250, 70: 490, 90:
810}
original dict2= {10: 100, 30: 90, 50:
250, 70: 490, 90:
810}
The two dictionaries are same
```

Program 7: Write a Python program to check whether the dictionary is empty or not.

```
d = {1: 1, 3: 9, 5: 25, 7: 49, 9: 81}
a=any(d)
if(a==1):
    print("The dictionary is not empty")
else:
    print("The dictionary is empty")
```

Output

```
D:\PythonPrograms>python b2.py
The dictionary is not empty
```

Program 8: Write a Python program to iterate through the dictionary.

```
d = {1: 1, 3: 9, 5: 25, 7: 49, 9: 81}
print("iteration result")
for i in d:
    print(i)
```

Output

```
D:\PythonPrograms>python b2.py
iteration result
1
3
5
7
9
```

Program 9: Write a Python program to print the even squares.

```
squares = {x: x*x for x in range(6)}
print(squares)
```

Output

```
D:\PythonPrograms>python b2.py
{0: 0, 1: 1, 2: 4, 3: 9, 4: 16, 5: 25}
```

Program 10: Write a Python program to display the keys and items in the input dictionary.

```
d = {1: 1, 3: 9, 5: 25, 7: 49, 9: 81}
print("keys= ",d.keys())
print("values= ",d.values())
print("items= ",d.items())
```

Output

```
D:\PythonPrograms>python b2.py
keys= dict_keys([1, 3, 5, 7, 9])
values= dict_values([1, 9, 25, 49, 81])
items= dict_items([(1, 1), (3, 9), (5, 25),
(7, 49), (9,
81)])
```

Program 11: Write a Python program to remove all the items in the dictionary.

```
d = {1: 1, 3: 9, 5: 25, 7: 49, 9: 81}
print("original= ",d)
print("removed result= ",d.clear())
```

Output

```
D:\PythonPrograms>python b2.py
original= {1: 1, 3: 9, 5: 25, 7: 49, 9: 81}
removed result= None
```

Glossary

- Dictionary is a mutable object used to maintain heterogeneous elements.
- Dictionary is a mapping object which maps the key and value pairs.
- Dictionary comprehension is a technique to create new dictionary with an expression.

Summary

- There are three different ways to create a dictionary object.
- Elements in a dictionary object can be updated and deleted.
- For each value in the dictionary, a key should be maintained.
- The values of the dictionary object can be accessed with the associated key value.
- Set is a subset of the dictionary.

Multiple Choice Questions

1. The set is
   (a) an ordered list
   (b) an unordered list
   (c) Both a and b
   (d) None of the above
2. The frozen set is
   (a) an immutable set
   (b) a mutable set
   (c) an ordered set
   (d) an unordered set
3. The dictionary contains a
   (a) key
   (b) value
   (c) key and value
   (d) none of the above
4. Which of the following will remove the elements of a dictionary?
   (a) discard()
   (b) remove()
   (c) Both a and b
   (d) None of the above
5. Which of the following is not a sequence object?
   (a) List
   (b) Tuple
   (c) Dictionary
   (d) None of the above
6. In how many ways can the dictionary be created?
   (a) 1 (b) 2
   (c) 3 (d) 4
7. Which will generate all the keys in the input dictionary?
   (a) dict.items() (b) dict.keys()
   (c) dict.values() (d) dict.pairs()
8. Which of the following will create the dictionary by using tuples?
   (a) dict(tuples)
   (b) tuples(dict)
   (c) Either a or b
   (d) None of the above
9. Dictionary contains
   (a) duplicate values
   (b) no duplicate values
   (c) Both a and b
   (d) None of the above
10. clear() function
    (a) prints the dictionary
    (b) deleted the dictionary
    (c) removes the dictionary
    (d) clears the dictionary
11. The sequence object will access the elements by
    (a) using index
    (b) without index
    (c) Both a and b
    (d) None of the above
12. The sequencer will maintain data in
    (a) random order
    (b) sequential order
    (c) Both a and b
    (d) None of the above
13. The mapping object will maintain data in
    (a) random order
    (b) sequential order
    (c) All the above
    (d) None of the above
14. The mapping object will access the elements by using
    (a) index
    (b) without index
    (c) All the above
    (d) None of the above

15. Lists is a
(a) sequence object
(b) mapping object
(c) Both a and b
(d) None of the above

16. Tuples is a
(a) sequence object
(b) mapping object
(c) Both a and b
(d) None of the above

17. Dictionary is a
(a) sequence object
(b) mapping object
(c) Both a and b
(d) None of the above

18. List is
(a) a null set
(b) an empty set
(c) a sorted set of elements
(d) a unordered set of elements

19. Tuple is
(a) a null set
(b) an empty set
(c) a sorted set of elements
(d) an unordered set of elements

20. Dictionary is
(a) a null set
(b) an empty set
(c) a sorted set of elements
(d) an unordered set of elements

21. In dictionary, each value is mapped with?
(a) index (b) size
(c) key (d) null

22. Dictionary contains
(a) key
(b) value
(c) All the above
(d) None of the above

23. Within a dictionary, value is accessed based on
(a) index (b) size
(c) key (d) null

24. In how many ways, can a dictionary be created?
(a) 0 (b) 1
(c) 2 (d) 3

25. Dictionary literals?
(a) {
(b) {}
(c) Both a and b
(d) None of the above

26. With dictionary literals, what type of dictionary is created?
(a) empty dictionary
(b) single-valued dictionary
(c) multi-valued dictionary
(d) All the above

27. The key and value are separated with
(a) , (b) ;
(c) : (d) #

28. If single value without key is specified within a dictionary, then it is considered as
(a) a frozen set
(b) a set
(c) an empty dictionary
(d) a single-valued dictionary

29. Dictionary is
(a) a mutable object
(b) an immutable object
(c) Both a and b
(d) None of the above

30. Updating the dictionary elements is?
(a) allowed
(b) not allowed
(c) May or may not be allowed
(d) None of the above

31. Deleting a tuple is?
(a) allowed
(b) not allowed
(c) May or may not be allowed
(d) None of the above

32. The 'dict' keyword is used
(a) to delete a tuple
(b) to add a tuple
(c) to create a tuple
(d) None of the above

33. keys() method will give
(a) values in the dictionary
(b) keys in the dictionary
(c) empty dictionary
(d) None of the above

34. values() method will give
(a) values in the dictionary
(b) keys in the dictionary
(c) empty dictionary
(d) None of the above

35. clear() method will create
(a) a single-valued dictionary
(b) a multi-valued dictionary
(c) an empty dictionary
(d) None of the above

Fill in the Blanks

1. Dictionaries can be copied using ____________________________.
2. Same memory location will be maintained in ____________________________ copy.
3. Different memory locations will be maintained in ____________________________ Copy.
4. The **fromkeys()** method is used to ____________________________ dictionary.
5. In case of **fromkeys()** method, ____________________________ are the default values.
6. The argument for **get()** method is ____________________________.
7. The **get()** method returns ____________________________.
8. Listing the pairs in dictionary is performed with ____________________________.
9. Dictionary with expression can be created with ____________________________.
10. Set is ____________________________ list of elements.
11. Changes in set are ____________________________.
12. **set()** will create ____________________________.
13. In set, ____________________________ values are not allowed.
14. The union operation is performed with ____________________________.
15. The set difference is performed with ____________________________.
16. Iterator is used to represent ____________________________.
17. ____________________________ is used to access the sequence elements in iterator.
18. ____________________________ exception is generated with **next()**.
19. A ____________________________ is an iterator which controls the iteration of a loop.
20. ____________________________ statement is required with generator.

State True/False

1. List is a mapping object.
2. Dictionary is a mapping object.
3. Dictionary supports homogeneous data.
4. Dictionary and Array are same
5. Dictionary uses key,value pair.
6. Empty dictionaries cannot be created.
7. Dictionary, list and tuples are same
8. Dictionary is a mutable object
9. Dictionary takes O(1) loop speed.
10. Dictionaries are used for memory over operations.
11. Dictionaries are not used for improving lookup speed efficiency.
12. There are three types of dictionary literals.
13. { and {} are dictionary literals.
14. Dictionary literals will create empty dictionary.
15. Dictionary[key] will return the associated value.
16. The key and value are separated in the dictionary pair.
17. For accessing dictionary value, [] is used
18. Set is a sub-type of dictionary.
19. Set is a mutable object.
20. Frozen set is not a set.
21. Dictionary can be created from multiple lists.
22. **dict** keyword will take only values.
23. Dictionary allows duplicated keys.
24. Dictionary allows duplicate values.
25. Tuple can be considered as a key in dictionary
26. **list** can be considered as a key in dictionary.
27. Dictionary can be converted to string.

Find the Output

1.
```
a={}
print(a)
```
2.
```
a=dict({})
print(a)
```
3.
```
a=dict({(4,'a')})
print(a)
```
4.
```
a={'x':10,'y':20}
for i in a.values():
    print(i)
```
5.
```
a={'x':10,'y':20}
for i in a.keys():
print(i)
```
6.
```
a={'x':10,'y':20}
b=dict.fromkeys(a)
print(b)
```
7.
```
a={1:100,2:200,3:300,4:400}
s=a.pop(4,"h")
print(s)
```
8.
```
s=set([10,20])
print(s)
```
9.
```
s=set((10,20,40,50))
print(s)
```
10.
```
s=set((10,20,10,50))
print(s)
```
11.
```
x={10:100,20:200,30:300}
print(x[20])
```
12.
```
x={10:1,20:2,30:3}
y={1:100,2:200,3:300}
print(y[x[30]])
```
13.
```
x={(1,2):100, 3:200}
print(x)
```
14.
```
x={(1,2):100, 3:200}
print(x[(1,2)])
```
15.
```
x={1:100, 3:200}
y=x.copy()
print(y)
```
16.
```
x={1:100, 3:200}
y=x.copy()
y.clear()
print(y)
```
17.
```
x={1:100, 3:200}
y={2:500}
x.update(y)
print(x)
```

Find the Error

1.
```
a={{}}
print(a)
```
2.
```
a=dict({[4,'a']})
print(a)
```
3.
```
a={'x':10,'y':20}
b=dict.fromkeys(a)
print(b[0])
```
4.
```
a={'x':10,'y':20}
del(a)
print(a)
```
5.
```
a={}
a.setdefault(10,20,30,40)
print(a)
```
6.
```
a={1:100,2:200,3:300,4:400}
s=a.pop()
print(s)
```
7.
```
a={1:100,2:200,3:300,4:400}
s=a.pop(100)
print(s)
```
8.
```
s=set([10,20],[40,50])
print(s)
```
9.
```
s=set({10,20})
print(s[0])
```
10.
```
s=set()
s.add(10)
s.remove(50)
```

Long Answer Questions

1. In how many ways can dictionary be created in Python? Discuss in detail.
2. List and explain the various operations on dictionary?
3. Differentiate the set and frozen set with examples.

Short Answer Questions

1. What is the importance of dictionary?
2. List the various operations on a dictionary.
3. List the various operations on a set.

Exercise Programs

1. Write a Python program to read the user option for performing the dictionary operations. The program should support all operations of dictionary.
2. Write a Python program to read the user option for performing set operations. The program should support all operations of set.
3. Write a Python program to count the numbers of characters in a string and store them in a dictionary data structure.
4. Write a program to use split and join methods in the string and trace a birthday with a dictionary data structure?
5. Write a Python program to create linked list using dictionary.
6. Write a Python program to create stack using dictionary.
7. Write a Python program to create queue using dictionary.
8. Write a Python program to read the student name and subject-wise marks and maintain the input data by using dictionary.
9. Write a program to read the student name and subject-wise marks and maintains the input data by using set.
10. Write a Python program to read two set values and print the union and intersection results between them.
11. Write a Python program to perform membership test on a set.
12. Write a Python program to perform membership test on a dictionary.
13. Write a Python program to print the symmetric difference between two sets.
14. Write a Python program to create a set with frozen set.
15. Write a Python program to search for an element in the input set.

Answers

Multiple Choice Questions

1. (b)	8. (a)	15. (a)	22. (c)	29. (a)
2. (a)	9. (b)	16. (a)	23. (c)	30. (a)
3. (c)	10. (d)	17. (b)	24. (d)	31. (a)
4. (c)	11. (a)	18. (c)	25. (c)	32. (c)
5. (c)	12. (b)	19. (c)	26. (a)	33. (b)
6. (c)	13. (a)	20. (d)	27. (c)	34. (a)
7. (b)	14. (b)	21. (c)	28. (b)	35. (c)

Fill in the Blanks

1. shallow copy or deep copy	8. item()	15. -
2. deep	9. dictionary comprehension	16. object
3. shallow	10. unordered	17. next()
4. create a new	11. allowed	18. StopIteration
5. none	12. empty set	19. Generator
6. key	13. duplicate values	20. yield
7. value	14. |	

State True/False

1. False
2. True
3. False
4. False
5. True
6. False
7. False
8. True
9. True
10. True
11. False
12. False
13. True
14. True
15. True
16. False
17. True
18. True
19. True
20. False
21. True
22. False
23. False
24. True
25. True
26. False
27. True

Find the Output

1. {}
2. {}
3. {4: 'a'}
4. 10
   20
5. x
   y
6. {'x': None, 'y': None}
7. 400
8. {10, 20}
9. {40, 10, 20, 50}
10. {10, 20, 50}
11. 200
12. 300
13. {(1, 2): 100, 3: 200}
14. 100
15. {1: 100, 3: 200}
16. {}
17. {1: 100, 3: 200, 2: 500}

Find the Error

1. TypeError: unhashable type: 'dict'
2. TypeError: unhashable type: 'list'
3. KeyError:0 print(b[0]))
4. NameError: name 'a' is not defined
5. TypeError: setdefault expected at most 2 arguments, got 4
6. TypeError: pop expected at least 1 arguments, got 0
7. KeyError: 100
8. TypeError: set expected at most 1 arguments, got 2
9. TypeError: 'set' object does not support indexing
10. KeyError: 50 (s.remove(50))

CHAPTER

8 Functions

In this chapter, we shall discuss the user-defined functions in Python. In Python, there are built-in and user-defined functions. The built-in functions are defined within the Python program. The user-defined functions, on the other hand, are defined by the user.

8.1 Introduction

In Python programming, functions are used for code reduction. A function represents some part of code which can be executed only when it is required. Functions are mainly used for performing a particular task. Various advantages of functions are

- Duplicated codes in a program can be reduced.
- Complex codes can be divided into smaller parts.
- Improves the efficiency of the code.
- Code can be reused.
- Provides additional flexibility.
- Improves modularity.
- The information contained in one function can be hidden from other functions.

In Python programming, functions are similar to basic data type objects. There are two types of functions viz., i) built-in functions and ii) user-defined functions.

Built-in functions are defined within the Python programming language. In any Python program, the programmer can call these functions without providing the definition.

```
x=input("Enter the data:")
print("The Entered Data is: ",x)
```

Output

```
D:\PythonPrograms>python a1.py
Enter the data: 10
The Entered Data is: 10
```

In the above example code, two built-in functions are used. They are print() and input(). In the program, the user has not provided the definition of these two functions. The definitions are available in Python. With these predefined definitions, the input() function reads the data from the console I/O and print() function displays the data on the console I/O. In the program, whenever the function is called, a control is shifted automatically to the user-defined function definition and it will be executed and if required the results will be returned as shown in Fig. 8.1.

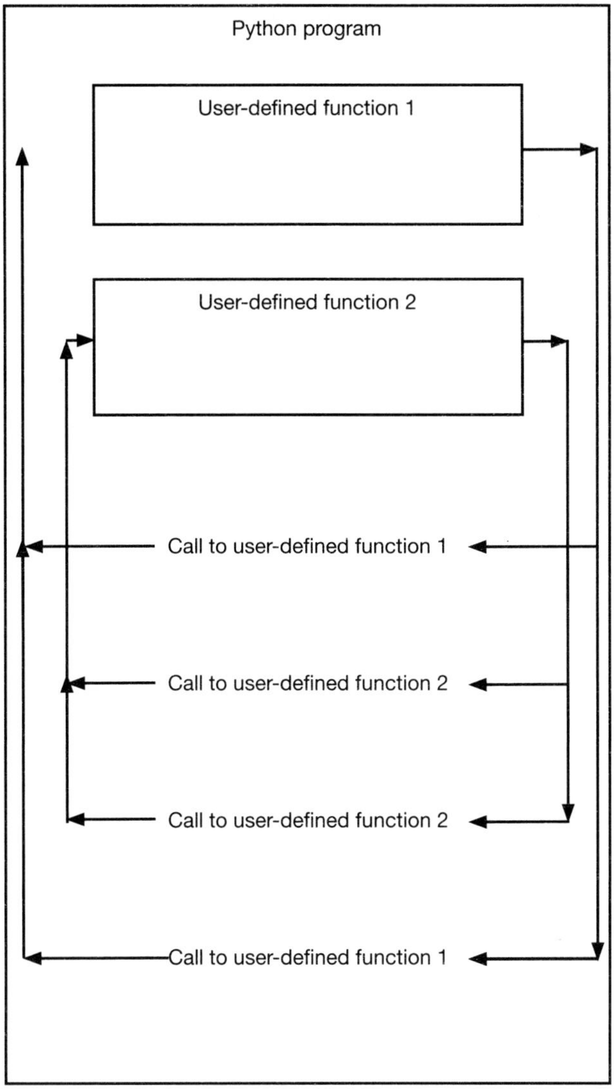

Figure. **8.1** The user-defined functions in Python programming.

8.2 Defining Functions

In python, user-defined functions can be defined by using "def". Function definition is allowed within a class, module or another user-defined function. The syntax of the user-defined function is

```
def user_defined_function_name(list_of_arguments):
    body of the user-defined function
```

An example of user-defined function is given below.

```
..........
..........
..........
print("hello")
print("this is first prg")
..........
..........
print("hello")
print("this is first prg")
..........
..........
..........
print("hello")
print("this is first prg")
..........
..........
print("hello")
print("this is first prg")
..........
..........
```

In the above example code, two statements are repeated. So, with the duplicated set of statements, the length of the code becomes 8 lines. To reduce this, the user-defined functions can be used. The reduced code with 4 lines is shown below.

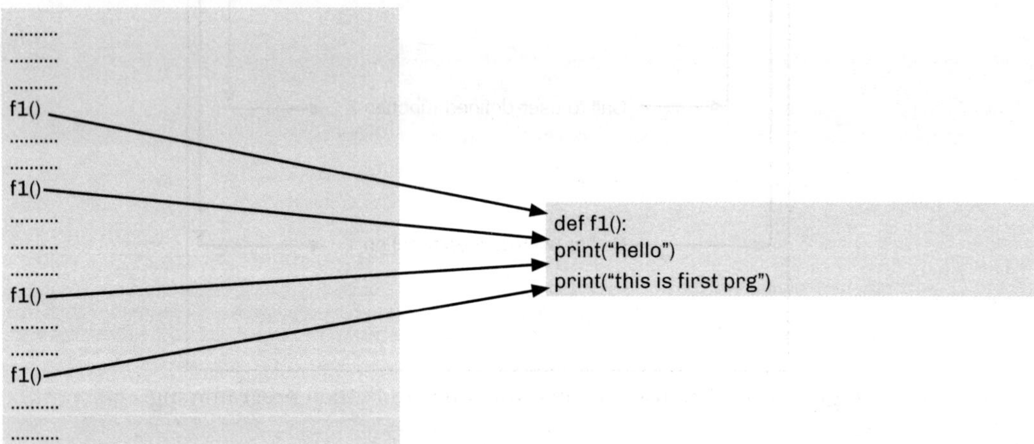

8.3 Calling Functions

In a Python program, user-defined functions will reduce the duplication of data. In the above example code, the 8 lines of duplicated code is reduced to 4 lines of code with the help of user-defined function. The user-defined function should be defined with 'def' keyword. In the program, whenever, the user-defined function execution is required, then the function should be called. The syntax for calling the user-defined function is given below.

```
user_defined_function_name(list_of_arguments)
```

An example code for calling a user-defined function is given below.

```
def f1():
    print("hello")
    print("this is first prg")
f1()
f1()
f1()
```

Output

```
D:\PythonPrograms>python a1.py
hello
this is first prg
hello
this is first prg
hello
```

In the above code, **f1()** is a user-defined function. The **f1()** definition is given in the program (print "hello" and "this is first prg"). In the program, "f1()" statement is used to call the user-defined function. This statement will call the user-definition function **f1()**, execute its body of statements and return to the statement where the call is made. The function call can be made in a repetitive manner by using loops.

```
def f1():
    print("hello")
    print("this is first prg")
for i in range(5):
    f1()
```

Output

```
D:\PythonPrograms>python a1.py
hello
this is first prg
hello
this is first prg
hello
this is first prg
hello
this is first prg
hello
this is first prg
```

In the above example code, the function **f1()** is called for 5 times.

In the next example code, there are two user-defined functions, **f1()** and **f2()**. The program will read the integer value from the user if the value is even; then **f1()** function will be called otherwise **f2()** function will be called.

```
def f1():
    print("Function is called for even number")
def f2():
    print("Function is called for odd number")
n=int(input("Enter the value of n: "))
if((n%2)==0):
    f1()
else:
    f2()
```

Output

```
D:\PythonPrograms>python a1.py
Enter the value of n: 5
Function is called for odd number
D:\PythonPrograms>python a1.py
Enter the value of n: 8
Function is called for even number
```

8.4 Passing Arguments

When the user-defined function is called, the values are transferred from **calling** function to **called** function. These values are called as arguments. In Python programming, there are four types of arguments.

i. Required arguments
ii. Keyword arguments
iii. Default arguments
iv. Variable length arguments

The arguments list can be none. Thus, user-defined functions can also have no arguments. The required arguments are values passed from **calling** function to **called** function. In this type, the number of arguments should be matched in function call and function definition. Otherwise, it yields an error.

```
def f1(x):
    print("The value of x: ",x)
x=input("Enter the value of argument: ")
f1(x)
```

Output

```
D:\PythonPrograms>python a1.py
Enter the value of argument: abcd
The value of x: abcd
```

In the above example code, the user-defined function **f1()** contains one argument. So, during function call, variable 'x' is transferred as an argument to **f1()**. It matches with the number of arguments in the definition of **f1()**. If there is a mismatch in the number of arguments in the function call and the function definition, then it will raise an error.

```
def f1(x,y):
    print("The value of x,y: ",x,y)
x=input("Enter the value of argument: ")
f1(x)
```

Output

```
D:\PythonPrograms>python a1.py
Enter the value of argument: 5
Traceback (most recent call last):
File "a1.py", line 5, in <module>
f1(x)
TypeError: f1() missing 1 required
positional argument: 'y'
```

8.5 Keyword Arguments

The arguments can also be classified as keyword arguments. Keyword arguments can be recognized based on the keywords. These arguments do not follow their positions. That is, the position of the arguments can be varied. Keyword arguments are used when there are some functions with many parameters and only some of them need to be specified.

```
def add(x,y):
    s=x+y
    print("x value: ",x)
    print("y value: ",y)
    print("sum: ",s)
n1=int(input("Enter the number:"))
n2=int(input("Enter the number:"))
add(x=n1,y=n2)
add(y=n2,x=n1)
```

Output

```
D:\PythonPrograms>python a1.py
Enter the number: 5
Enter the number: 6
x value: 5
y value: 6
sum: 11
x value: 5
y value: 6
sum: 11
```

In the above example code, the user-defined function **add()** has two arguments "x" and "y". In the program, two numbers n1 and n2 are used to maintain the values. The two values are passed to **add()** function. The positions of the arguments are changed in these two function calls.

If the arguments are not passed with keyword, then the values will be considered as positional arguments.

```
def add(x,y):
    s=x+y
    print("x value: ",x)
    print("y value: ",y)
    print("sum: ",s)
n1=int(input("Enter the number:"))
n2=int(input("Enter the number:"))
add(x=n1,y=n2)
add(y=n2,x=n1)
add(100,200)
```

Output

```
D:\PythonPrograms>python a1.py
Enter the number:4
Enter the number:7
x value: 4
y value: 7
sum: 11
x value: 4
y value: 7
sum: 11
x value: 100
y value: 200
sum: 300
```

8.6 Default Arguments

Default arguments are used to initialize the arguments with default values. If the argument is not passed during the function call then the default values will be initialized for default arguments. The below code explains the usage of default arguments.

In the below example code, the **add()** function contains two default arguments "x" and "y". These two values are initialized with default values "0" and "0". In the program, two numbers are maintained by the variables "n1" and "n2". The **add()** function is called four times.

- During the first call **add()**, no arguments are passed. So, during the execution of the function, x and y argument values are initialized with 0.
- During the second call **add(x=n1)**, only x value is passed with n1. So the value of y is initialized with 0.
- During the third call **add(y=n2)**, only y value is with n2. So, the value of x is initialized with 0.
- During the fourth call **add(n1,n2)**, both the values x and y are passed with n1 and n2. So, no default arguments are initialized.

```
def add(x=0,y=0):
    s=x+y
    print("x value: ",x)
    print("y value: ",y)
    print("sum: ",s)
n1=int(input("Enter the number:"))
n2=int(input("Enter the number:"))
add()
add(x=n1)
add(y=n2)
add(n1,n2)
```

Output

```
D:\PythonPrograms>python a1.py
Enter the number:200
Enter the number:300
x value: 0
y value: 0
sum: 0
x value: 200
y value: 0
sum: 200
x value: 0
y value: 300
sum: 300
x value: 200
y value: 300
sum: 500
```

8.7 Required Arguments

For any function, the arguments can be either required or default. The default arguments are discussed in detail in Section 8.6. Other than default arguments, the other arguments are considered as required arguments. For the default arguments, if the value of the argument is not passed during the function call, then the default value is considered. In the case of required arguments, the value of the argument should be passed during the function call. So, the required arguments are mandatory for the function call. In Python function definition, first, the required arguments should be listed and then the default arguments should be listed.

```
def sum(a,b=10):
    return(a+b)
print("sum(10,20)=",sum(10,20))
print("sum(,20)=",sum(20))
print("sum(10,)=",sum(10))
```

Output

```
D:\PythonPrograms>python s1.py
sum(10,20)= 30
sum(,20)= 30
sum(10,)= 20
```

In the above sample code, the function sum() contains the required argument "a" and default argument "b".

```
def pr(a,b):
    if(a>b):
        print("profit=",(a-b))
    elif(a<b):
        print("loss=",(b-a))
    else:
        print("no profit or no loss")
x=float(input("Enter the selling price:"))
y=float(input("Enter the cost price:"))
pr(x,y)
```

Output

```
D:\PythonPrograms>python b2.py
Enter the selling price:50
Enter the cost price:60
loss= 10.0
```

```
def pr(a=0,b=0):
    if(a>b):
        print("profit=",(a-b))
    elif(a<b):
        print("loss=",(b-a))
    else:
        print("no profit or no loss")
pr()
```

Output

```
D:\PythonPrograms>python b2.py
no profit or no loss
```

8.8 Variable-length Arguments

Python programming supports an additional feature called as variable length argument. Thus, in python programming user-defined functions, the variable length need not be fixed. During the function call, more number of the arguments can be passed. For this purpose, an operator "*" should be used. Multiple arguments (more arguments) are maintained by using tuples.

```
def disp(x,*t):
    print(len(t))
    print(x,t)
n1=int(input("Enter the number:"))
n2=int(input("Enter the number:"))
disp(n1)
disp(n1,n2)
```

Output

```
D:\PythonPrograms>python a1.py
Enter the number:10
Enter the number:20
0
10 ()
1
10 (20,)
```

In the above example code, the disp() function is defined with variable length arguments. The disp() function contains one argument x and variable length tuple *t. In the program, n1 and n2 maintain the values of the input. The disp() function is called in two different ways.

- In the first call disp(n1), only one argument n1 is passed and is stored in argument x.
- In the second call disp(n1,n2), two arguments n1 and n2 are passed. The n1 argument is stored in x and argument n2 is passed and stored in variable length tuple t.

```
def disp(x,*t):
    print("values of argument: ",x)
    print("The length of the tuples: ",len(t))
    print("The elements of tuples: ")
    for i in t:
        print(i)
n1=int(input("Enter the number:"))
n2=int(input("Enter the number:"))
n3=int(input("Enter the number:"))
n4=int(input("Enter the number:"))
disp(n1,n2,n3,n4)
```

Output

```
D:\PythonPrograms>python a1.py
Enter the number:200
Enter the number:300
Enter the number:400
Enter the number:500
values of argument: 200
The length of the tuples: 3
The elements of tuples:
300
400
500
```

8.9 Return Statement

The return statement is used to return the values from user-defined function to the calling statement. return keyword is used to return the values.

```
def add(x,y):
    s=x+y
    return s
n1=int(input("Enter the number:"))
n2=int(input("Enter the number:"))
print("The two input values: ",n1,n2)
n3=add(n1,n2)
print("The sum of two numbers: ",n3)
```

Output

```
D:\PythonPrograms>python a1.py
Enter the number:100
Enter the number:200
The two input values: 100 200
The sum of two numbers: 300
```

In the above example code, only one value is returned from add() function to the calling statement and the value is stored in variable n3.

In Python programming, multiple values can also be returned with **return** statement.

```
def add(x,y):
    s=x+y
    x=x+1
    y=y+1
    return (s,x,y)
n1=int(input("Enter the number:"))
n2=int(input("Enter the number:"))
print("The two input values: ",n1,n2)
(n3,ix,iy)=add(n1,n2)
print("The sum of two numbers: ",n3)
print("The incremented x value: ",ix)
print("The incremented y value: ",iy)
```

Output

```
D:\PythonPrograms>python a1.py
Enter the number:40
Enter the number:30
The two input values: 40 30
The sum of two numbers: 70
The incremented x value: 41
The incremented y value: 31
```

```
def sq(x):
    return(x*x)
x=int(input("Enter the input number:"))
print("Original Number=",x)
print("Square of the Number=",sq(x))
```

Output

```
D:\PythonPrograms>python b2.py
Enter the input number:4
Original Number= 4
Square of the Number= 16
```

8.10 Nesting of Passing Arguments

In Python **nonlocal** keyword is used to bind the nested arguments. The following example code illustrates the usage of **nonlocal**.

```
def f(x):
    def g(n):
        nonlocal x
        if n < 10:
                x = x + 1
                print(" ",x)
                g(n + 1)
    g(0)
f(5)
```

Output

```
D:\PythonPrograms\aa>python a2.py
6
7
8
9
10
11
12
13
14
15
```

8.11 Anonymous Functions

In Python, a user-defined function without name is also allowed. This type of function is called as anonymous function. Anonymous functions are not defined with **def** keyword. Instead, **lambda** keyword is used. These functions consist of only one expression. The lambda functions can be used in the program like other user-defined functions. In anonymous function definition, multiple arguments are allowed but only one value can be returned. The syntax of the lambda function is given below.

```
return_var_name = lambda [list_of_multiple_arguments]:expression
```

In an anonymous function, the **lambda** keyword specifies that it is not a normal user-defined function. In this function, multiple arguments can be specified by using "," and are separated with the expression by using ":"

```
m=lambda x,y:x*y
n1=int(input("Enter the number:"))
n2=int(input("Enter the number:"))
print("The two input values: ",n1,n2)
print("The result: ",m(n1,n2))
```

Output

```
D:\PythonPrograms>python a1.py
Enter the number:10
Enter the number:20
The two input values: 10 20
The result: 200
```

8.12 Recursive Function

A function which calls itself is called as a recursive function.

```
def pr(a):
    if(a>0):
        print(a)
        pr(a-1)
    else:
        return()

pr(5)
```

Output

```
D:\PythonPrograms>python s1.py
5
4
3
2
1
```

- Greatest common divisor

```
def gcd(a,b):
    if(b!=0):
        return(gcd(b,a%b))
    else:
        return(a)
x=int(input("Enter the first number:"))
y=int(input("Enter the second number:"))
z=gcd(x,y)
print("The greatest common divisor value= ",z)
```

Output

```
D:\PythonPrograms>python b2.py
Enter the first number:18
Enter the second number:27
The greatest common divisor
value= 9
```

- Finding exponents

```
def po(a,b):
    if(b!=0):
        return(a*po(a,b-1))
    else:
        return(1)
x=int(input("Enter the number:"))
y=int(input("Enter the exponent value:"))
z=po(x,y)
print("The exponent value= ",z)
```

Output

```
D:\PythonPrograms>python b2.py
Enter the number:2
Enter the exponent value:3
The exponent value= 8
```

- The Fibonacci series

```
def fib(a):
    if(a<=1):
        return(a)
    else:
        return fib(a-1)+fib(a-2)


n=int(input("Enter the number:"))
for i in range (0,n):
    x=fib(i)
    print(x,"")
```

Output

```
D:\PythonPrograms>python b2.py
Enter the number:5
0
1
1
2
3
```

- Recursion vs. Iteration

Iteration occurs in loops. During the execution of the loops, the iteration indicates each cycle of the execution. Iteration includes the initialization, condition and increment/decrement of a loop control variable. The iteration of a loop can be terminated with **break** or **continue** statements. The **break** statement terminates all the possible iterations whereas the **continue** statement terminates only the current iteration. The recursion occurs in functions. During the execution of a function, recursion indicates the repeated execution of the entire function code. In general, the terminating condition should be written to exit the repeated execution of a recursive function.

8.13 Scope of Local and Global Variable

The variables can be of two types.

i. Local variable
ii. Global variable

Local variable is a variable defined within a user-defined function. The local variable value is available only within the given user-defined function.

```
def f1():
    x=10
    print("local variable x value in f1(): ",x)
f1()
print("local variable x value outside f1(): ",x)
```

Output

```
D:\PythonPrograms>python a1.py
Traceback (most recent call last):
File "a1.py", line 6, in <module>
print("local variable x value outside f1(): ",x)
NameError: name 'x' is not defined
```

In the above example code, the variable "x" is a local variable to **f1()** function. Accessing variable "x" outside **f1()** raises an error. To overcome this problem, the variable "x" can be declared as a global variable. The global variable is not defined in any function. It can be accessed throughout the program. In case of local variable, the changes made to it is available only within the corresponding function. In case of global variable, the changes made in any user-defined function will be reflected and available to all other user-defined functions. The below example codes highlight the use of global variable.

Example 1

```
x=10
def f1():
    print("global variable x value in f1(): ",x)
f1()
print("global variable x value outside f1(): ",x)
```

Output

```
D:\PythonPrograms>python a1.py
global variable x value in f1(): 10
global variable x value outside f1(): 10
```

Example 2

```
x=10
def f1():
    x=20
    print("variable x value in f1(): ",x)
f1()
print("variable x value outside f1(): ",x)
```

Output

```
D:\PythonPrograms>python a1.py
variable x value in f1(): 20
variable x value outside f1(): 10
```

Example 3

```
def f1():
    global x
    x=20
    print("variable x value in f1(): ",x)
f1()
print("variable x value outside f1(): ",x)
```

Output

```
D:\PythonPrograms>python a1.py
variable x value in f1(): 20
variable x value outside f1(): 20
```

- Using the Global Statement

In Python, **global** statement is used to declare the variable as global variables. Once the variable is declared as global, the corresponding variable can be available in any other function.

```
def f1():
    global x
    x=10
    print("x value inside f1() function: ", x)
f1()
print("x value outside f1() function: ", x)
```

Output

```
D:\PythonPrograms>python b2.py
x value inside f1() function: 10
x value outside f1() function: 10
```

- Resolution of Names

In Python, scope resolution for the names of variables follows the "LEGB" rule. Thus, for a variable name, the initial search is made in Local name space. If the variable is not found, then the search is made in Enclosed name space. The enclosed name space contains variables in the enclosing or wrapped function. If the variable is not found in the enclosed name space, then the search is made in Global name space. If the variable is not found in global name space, then finally search is made in Built-in name space.

Table 8.1 collates the attributes of global variable and local variable

Table 8.1 Comparison between global variables and local variables

S. No.	Local Variable	Global Variable
1	The declaration of a variable happens within the function	The declaration of a variable happens within the program
2	The scope of the variable is limited to the declared function only.	The scope of the variable is limited to the entire program.
3	The value of the variable can be accessed only within the declared function.	The value of the variable can be accessed by the entire program

8.14 Documentation Strings

Documentation strings in Python are also called as "docstrings." It provides an efficient way of providing documentation in a Python program. In Python, all functions can have docstrings. It is similar to comment but the docstring is considered as a string constant and it describes the functionality of the function. Docstrings consist of the following features.

- It begins and ends with """
- The first letter should be an upper case letter.
- The docstring should end with "."
- If the doctsring contains multiple lines then the second line should be left blank.
- The _doc_ is used to access the docstring value.

Example 4

```
def fun1():
    """This is docstring line1."""
    pass
print(fun1.__doc__)
```

Output

```
D:\PythonPrograms\aa>python a2.py
This is docstring line1.
```

Example 5

```
def fun1():
    """This is docstring line1.
    This is second line. """
    pass
print(fun1.__doc__)
```

Output

```
D:\PythonPrograms\aa>python a2.py
This is docstring line1.
This is second line.
```

8.15 Sample Programs

Program 1: Write a Python program to print the statement "Sample Program" for n times.

> Programming Tip:
> With the functions, the code can be efficiently organized

```
def f1():
    print("Sample Program")
n=int(input("Enter the value of n: "))
for i in range(n):
    f1()
```

Output

```
D:\PythonPrograms>python a1.py
Enter the value of n: 5
Sample Program
Sample Program
Sample Program
Sample Program
Sample Program
```

Program 2: Write a Python program to define a function within a function.

```
x = 1
def f1():
    x = 2
    def inner():
        print(x)
    inner()
f1()
```

Output

```
D:\PythonPrograms>python a1.py
2
```

Program 3: Write a Python program to print the multiplication table of a given number by using user-defined function.

```
def multable(x):
    for i in range(1,11):
        print(i,"*",x,"=",(i*x))
x=int(input("Enter the value of n: "))
multable(x)
```

Output

```
D:\PythonPrograms>python a1.py
Enter the value of n: 12
1 * 12 = 12
2 * 12 = 24
3 * 12 = 36
4 * 12 = 48
5 * 12 = 60
6 * 12 = 72
7 * 12 = 84
8 * 12 = 96
9 * 12 = 108
10 * 12 = 120
```

Program 4: Write a Python program to develop call by value.

```
def inr(x):
    x=x+1
    print("x value in inr(): ",x)
n=int(input("Enter the number:"))
print("original value of n: ",n)
inr(n)
print("After function call, value of n: ",n)
```

Output

```
D:\PythonPrograms>python a1.py
Enter the number:5
original value of n: 5
x value in inr(): 6
After function call, value of n: 5
```

Program 5: Write a Python program to develop call by reference.

```
def inr(x):
    x[0]=x[0]+1
    print("x value in inr(): ",x[0])
n=[]
n1=int(input("Enter the number:"))
n.append(n1)
print("Original value of n: ",n[0])
inr(n)
print("After function call, value of n: ",n[0])
```

Output

```
D:\PythonPrograms>python a1.py
Enter the number:100
Original value of n: 100
x value in inr(): 101
After function call, value of n: 101
```

Program 6: Write a Python program to swap two numbers by using user-defined functions.

```
def swap(x,y):
    temp=x
    x=y
    y=temp
return (x,y)
n1=input("Enter the number:")
n2=input("Enter the number:")
print("The two input values: ",n1,n2)
(n1,n2)=swap(n1,n2)
print("The swapped x value: ",n1)
print("The swapped y value: ",n2)
```

Output

```
D:\PythonPrograms>python a1.py
Enter the number: a
Enter the number :b
The two input values: a b
The swapped x value: b
The swapped y value: a
```

Program 7: Write a Python program to find the sum of the series 1!/1+2!/2+3!/3+4!/4+5!/5.

```
def f(x):
    s=1
    for i in range(1,x+1):
        s=(s*i)
    return(s)
a=int(input("Enter the number:"))
res=0
for j in range(1,a+1):
    res=res+(f(j)/j)
print("The final result= ",res)
```

Output

```
D:\PythonPrograms>python b2.py
Enter the number:6
The final result= 154.0
```

Program 8: Write a Python program to print all natural numbers between 1 to n using functions.

```
def f(x1,y1):
    for i in range(x1,y1+1):
        print(i)
x=int(input("Enter the lower limit:"))
y=int(input("Enter the upper limit:"))
f(x,y)
```

Output

```
D:\PythonPrograms>python b2.py
Enter the lower limit:4
Enter the upper limit:15
4
5
6
7
8
9
10
11
12
13
14
15
```

Program 9: Write a Python program to print all even or odd numbers in given range using functions.

```
def f(x1,y1):
    e=[]
    l=[]
    for i in range(x1,y1+1):
        if((i%2)==0):
            e.append(i)
        else:
            l.append(i)
    print("Even numbers: ",e)
    print("Odd numbers: ",l)
x=int(input("Enter the lower limit:"))
y=int(input("Enter the upper limit:"))
f(x,y)
```

Output

```
D:\PythonPrograms>python b2.py
Enter the lower limit:2
Enter the upper limit:10
Even numbers: [2, 4, 6, 8, 10]
Odd numbers: [3, 5, 7, 9]
```

Program 10: Write a Python program to find sum of elements of array using functions.

```
def su(a):
    l=len(a)
    s=0
    for i in range(0,l):
        s=s+a[i]
    return(s)
l=[10,20,30]
r=su(l)
print("result=",r)
```

Output

```
D:\PythonPrograms>python b2.py
result= 60
```

Program 11: Write a Python program to find maximum and minimum elements in array using functions.

```
def su(a):
    l=len(a)
    mi=a[0]
    mx=a[0]
    for i in range(1,l):
        if(a[i]>mx):
            mx=a[i]
        if(a[i]<mi):
            mi=a[i]
    print(«Max element=»,mx)
    print(«Min element=»,mi)
l=[10,20,30, 50, 5, 90, 32]
print(«Input=»,l)
su(l)
```

Output

```
D:\PythonPrograms>python b2.py
Input= [10, 20, 30, 50, 5, 90, 32]
Max element= 90
Min element= 5
```

Program 12: Write a Python program to find sum of all natural numbers between 1 to n using recursion.

```
def su(a,b):
    if(a==b):
        return(b)
    else:
        return a+su(a+1,b)
x=int(input("Enter the n value:"))
s=su(1,x)
print("The sum=",s)
```

Output

```
D:\PythonPrograms>python b2.py
Enter the n value:5
The sum= 15
```

Program 13: Write a Python program to find sum of all even numbers in given range using recursion.

```
def su(a,b):
    if(a>b):
        return(0)
    else:
        return a+su(a+2,b)
x=int(input("Enter the n value:"))
s=su(2,x)
print("The sum=",s)
```

Output

```
D:\PythonPrograms>python b2.py
Enter the n value:10
The sum= 30
```

Program 14: Write a Python program to find reverse of any number using function.

```
def r(x):
    res=0
    while(x>0):
        y=x%10
        res=(res*10)+y
        x=x//10
    return(res)
a=int(input("Enter the number:"))
print("Original Number: ",a)
print("Reverse Number :",r(a))
```

Output

```
D:\PythonPrograms>python b2.py
Enter the number: 789
Original Number: 789
Reverse Number : 987
```

Program 15: Write a Python program to check whether a number is palindrome or not using function.

```
def r(x):
    res=0
    while(x>0):
        y=x%10
        res=(res*10)+y
        x=x//10
    return(res)
a=int(input("Enter the number:"))
print("Original Number: ",a)
b=r(a)
if(a==b):
    print("The given number is a palindrome")
else:
    print("The given number is not a palindrome")
```

Output

```
D:\PythonPrograms>python b2.py
Enter the number:989
Original Number: 989
The given number is a palindrome
```

Program 16: Write a Python program to find sum of digits of a given number using recursion.

```
def s(x):
    if(x==0):
        return(0)
    else:
        return((x%10)+(s(x//10)))
a=int(input("Enter the number:"))
print("original number= ",a)
print("Sum of digits= ",s(a))
```

Output

```
D:\PythonPrograms>python b2.py
Enter the number:456
original number= 456
Sum of digits= 15
```

Program 17: Write a Python program to generate the nth Fibonacci term using recursion.

```
def s(x):
    if(x==0):
        return(0)
    elif(x==1):
        return(1)
    else:
        return(s(x-1)+s(x-2))
a=int(input("Enter the number:"))
print(a, "th fibonacci term is= ",s(a))
```

Output

```
D:\PythonPrograms>python b2.py
Enter the number:10
10 th fibonacci term is= 55
```

8.16 Case Studies

8.16.1 Recursive Binary Search

```
def bs(a, i, n, s):
    if n >= i:
        m =int((i+n)//2)
        if a[m]==s:
            return m
        elif a[m]>s:
            return bs(a, i, m-1, s)
        else:
            return bs(a, m+1, n, s)
        else:
            return(-1)
a=[];
n=int(input("Enter number of elements:"))
for i in range(0,n):
    b=int(input("Enter the element:"))
    a.append(b)
s=int(input("Enter the element to be searched:"))
re = bs(a,0,n-1,s)
if re>-1:
    print("The element is found at",re,"position")
else:
    print("The element is not found")
```

Output

```
D:\PythonPrograms>python b2.py
Enter number of elements:5
Enter the element:10
Enter the element:20
Enter the element:30
Enter the element:40
Enter the element:50
Enter the element to be searched:50
The element is found at 4 position
```

8.16.2 Substitution Cipher

```
def s(a):
l=['a','b','c','d','e','f','g','h','i','j','k','l','m',
'n','o','p','q','r','s','t','u','v','w','x','y','z']
    n=len(a)
    res=""
        for i in range(0,n):
            flag=0
            for j in range(0,26):
                if(l[j]==a[i]):
                    flag=1
                    break
                if(flag==1):
                    f=(j+2)%26
                    res=res+l[f]
                return(res)
x=input("Enter the string:")
print("Plain text=",x)
print("Cipher text=",s(x))
```

Output

```
D:\PythonPrograms>python b2.py
Enter the string:hello
Plain text= hello
Cipher text= jgnnq
```

Glossary

- Recursive function is a user-defined function which calls itself.
- Keyword arguments are recognized based on the keywords.
- Default arguments will have default values for argument initialization.
- Required arguments are the mandatory arguments to be provided during the function call.

Summary

- User-defined functions are used to reduce the code complexity and thus enable higher modularity.
- The functions can have various arguments and return values.
- In Python, there are four types of arguments, viz., required arguments, default arguments, keyword arguments and variable length arguments. T
- The required arguments should be matched during the function call. If there are not matched then, the default arguments will provide the default values.
- In Python, the order of the arguments can be varied and are identified by using the keywords in keyword arguments.
- The variable length arguments and return values are maintained by using tuple.

Multiple Choice Questions

1. Which keyword is used to define the user-defined function?
   (a) assign
   (b) return
   (c) def
   (d) None of the above.
2. Minimum number of arguments for a function is
   (a) 0 (b) 1
   (c) 2 (d) 3
3. How many types of arguments are available in Python?
   (a) 1 (b) 2
   (c) 3 (d) 4
4. Required arguments require
   (a) arguments of minimum of 1
   (b) matching of number of arguments

(c) Both a and b.
(d) None of the above.

5. Keyword arguments are
(a) positional arguments
(b) non-positional arguments
(c) May be a or b.
(d) None of the above.

6. Default arguments will be used to initialize the arguments
(a) with default values
(b) with default values when argument is not passed
(c) with default values when argument is passed
(d) None of the above.

7. Which of the following is used for variable-length arguments?
(a) * (b) ^
(c) ! (d) @

8. In case of variable-length arguments, the arguments are maintained by
(a) list (b) set
(c) tuples (d) dictionary

9. How many values can be returned with `return` statement
(a) 1 (b) 2
(c) 3 (d) multiple

10. Anonymous functions are created by using which keyword
(a) `def` (b) `lambda`
(c) `len` (d) `any`

11. The functions are used for
(a) code reduction
(b) deleting memory
(c) allocating memory
(d) None of the above.

12. Which of the following is correct?
(a) The duplicated code in the program can be reduced.
(b) The complex codes can be divided into various parts.
(c) Code can be reused.
(d) All the above.

13. Modularity can be improved with
(a) Decision statements
(b) Looping
(c) Functions
(d) None of the above.

14. Data from one function to another function can be
(a) passed
(b) hidden
(c) transparent
(d) None of the above.

15. The definition of built-in function is
(a) available within Python
(b) provided by the user
(c) Both a and b.
(d) None of the above.

16. The definition of user-defined function is
(a) available within Python
(b) provided by the user
(c) Both a and b.
(d) None of the above.

17. `input()` function is
(a) user-defined
(b) built-in
(c) a system call
(d) None of the above.

18. `xyz()` function is
(a) user-defined
(b) built-in
(c) a system call
(d) None of the above.

19. The definition of user-defined function should be
(a) within the function
(b) outside the function
(c) within the program
(d) outside the program

20. During function call
(a) control remains within the program
(b) control comes out of the program
(c) control goes to the nested class
(d) control goes to the called function

21. The function can be defined within
(a) class
(b) module
(c) another function
(d) All the above.

22. The function can be called with
(a) type of the function
(b) name of the function
(c) name of the function with associated arguments
(d) None of the above.

23. The function call can be made repetitive with
(a) loops
(b) `if` statement
(c) `if..else` statement `if..elif..else` statement
(d) None of the above.

24. Data passed during the function call are called as
(a) return values (b) arguments
(c) null values (d) empty values

25. Matching the number of arguments during function call is performed with
(a) required arguments
(b) keyword arguments
(c) default arguments
(d) variable-length arguments

26. The position of the arguments is not followed with
(a) required arguments
(b) keyword arguments
(c) default arguments
(d) variable-length arguments

27. The initialized arguments are used with
(a) required arguments
(b) keyword arguments
(c) default arguments
(d) variable-length arguments

28. The order of arguments specification is
(a) only default arguments
(b) only required arguments
(c) default arguments and required arguments
(d) required arguments and default arguments

29. In Python programming, the variable length
(a) should be fixed at compile time
(b) should not be fixed
(c) Should be fixed at run time
(d) None of the above.

30. Multiple arguments of variable length are
(a) static (b) dynamic
(c) mutable (d) immutable

31. The `return` keyword is used for
(a) receiving the arguments
(b) returning the arguments
(c) Both a and b.
(d) None of the above.

32. In Python, a function can return
(a) single value
(b) two values
(c) three values
(d) multiple values

33. Which of the following is used to bind nested arguments?
(a) local (b) non-local
(c) static (d) dynamic

34. Anonymous functions consist of
(a) one expression
(b) multiple expression
(c) one block of code
(d) multiple blocks of code

35. Anonymous functions consist of how many arguments?
(a) 1 (b) 2
(c) 3 (d) multiple

36. Anonymous functions consist of how many return values?
(a) 1 (b) 2
(c) 3 (d) multiple

37. Which of the following is used for separating the definition of anonymous function?
(a) , (b) :
(c); (d) *

38. A function that calls itself is called as
(a) nested function
(b) local function
(c) recursive function
(d) global function

39. In Python, documentation strings are called as
(a) docstrings
(b) documentstrings
(c) docstr
(d) documentstr

40. The first letter of the documentation string should be
(a) lower case
(b) upper case
(c) either lowercase or upper case
(d) None of the above

Fill in the Blanks

1. ___________ are used to reduce the duplicated code.
2. There are ___________ types of functions.
3. The types of functions are ___________.
4. The functions will take ___________.
5. The functions will send ___________.
6. With functions, code can be ___________.
7. With functions, modularity can be ___________.
8. A function call can be ___________.
9. Repetition of a function call is performed with ___________.

10. Multi arguments are maintained with ____________.
11. Control is shifted from one function to another function during ____________.
12. Control is shifted from called function to calling function with ____________.
13. The **def** keyword is used for ____________.
14. One example for built-in function is ____________.
15. The **def** keyword uses the ____________ operator.
16. The minimum number of arguments is ____________.
17. In Python, ____________ types of arguments are available.
18. The arguments can be either____________ or ____________.
19. ____________ arguments are initialized with predefined value.
20. ____________ arguments are not initialized with predefined value.
21. In Python, ____________ length of arguments is allowed.
22. The ____________ is used to specify the variable-length arguments.
23. With keyword arguments, ____________ can be varied.
24. With the varied position, the arguments can be identified with ____________.
25. The ____________ functions use expression.
26. The ____________ keyword is used for anonymous functions.
27. The nonlocal keyword is used for ____________.
28. The docstrings should end with ____________.
29. In case of multi-line docstring, the____________ should be left blank.
30. The ____________ is used to access the docstring value.

State True/False

1. The functions enhanc the code complexity.
2. With functions, the control will be shifted between the functions.
3. The functions can have both arguments and return values.
4. All the functions are only built-in functions.
5. All the functions are only user-defined functions.
6. The functions in Python can be either built-in or user-defined functions.
7. Python user-defined functions require a minimum of one argument.
8. Python user-defined functions require a minimum of one return value.
9. Multiple return values are considered as a list.
10. There are 7 types of arguments in Python.
11. All the arguments in Python function are default arguments.
12. The arguments in Python function are either default or required.
13. The keyword arguments can change their positions.
14. In Python, the length of the variables list can be varied.
15. The nesting of arguments is allowed in Python.
16. The non-local variable binds the arguments in nested functions.
17. The binded variables of nested arguments are mutable.
18. The **lambda** functions take multiple expressions.
19. The anonymous functions can return only one value at a time.
20. The ; is used in the anonymous function syntax.
21. The scope of variables can be either local or global.
22. Recursive functions are allowed in Python.
23. The global variable should be defined within the function.
24. The local variable should be defined within the function.
25. Documentation strings are used for providing efficient documentation.
26. The docstring and comment are same.
27. The documentation string is considered as string constant.
28. The documentation string begins and ends with “””

Find the Output

1. ```
def read():
    print("hi")
read()
```
2. ```
def pr():
    print("hi")
    return(10)
pr()
```
3. ```
def pr(a=10):
    print(a)
pr()
```
4. ```
def pr(a,b):
    print(a,b)
x=10
y=20
pr(b=y,a=x)
```
5. ```
def pr(a,*b):
    print(a,b)
x=10
y=20
pr(a=y)
```
6. ```
def pr(a,*b):
    print(a,b)
x=10
y=20
pr(x,y)
```
7. ```
def pr(a,*b):
    print(a,b)
    l=len(b)
    print(l)
x=10
y=20
z=30
pr(x,y,z)
```
8. ```
def pr(a,*b):
    print(a,b)
    l=len(b)
    return(l)
x=10
y=20
z=30
q=pr(x,y,z)
print(q)
```
9. ```
def pr():
    return()
q=pr()
print(q)
```
10. ```
def f(x):
    def g(n):
        x=10
        if n < 10:
        x = x + 1
        print(" ",x)
        g(n + 1)
    g(0)
f(5)
```
11. ```
def a():
    global j
    j=10
a()
print("value of j=",j)
```
12. ```
def a():
    return(10)
b=a()
print("value of b=",b)
```
13. ```
def a(x,y):
    if(x>=y):
        return(x)
    else:
        return(y)
b=a(10,20)
print("value of b=",b)
```
14. ```
m=lambda x,y:x+y
print("The result: ",m(5,6))
```
15. ```
def f1(a):
    if(a==1):
        return(1)
    else:
        return(a+f1(a-1))
print(f1(5))
```
16. ```
def f1(a):
    s=0
    if(a==1):
        return(1)
    else:
        return(s+f1(a-1))
print(f1(5))
```
17. ```
def f1(a):
    print(a)
def f1(a,b):
    print(a,b)
f1(5,4)
```
```

18.
```
def f1(a):
    i=0
    while(i<len(a)):
     print(a[len(a)-i-1],end="")
       i=i+1
       f1("hello")
```

19.
```
def f1(x):
    return(x*x*x)
print(f1(-3))
```

20.
```
def x():
        """hello."""
        pass
print(x.__doc__)
```

21.
```
def x():
        """hello."""
        pass
print(len(x.__doc__))
```

22.
```
def x():
        """hello."""
        pass
print(x.__doc__[3:-1])
```

23.
```
def f(x):
    return(x*2)
print(f(3.4))
```

24.
```
def f(x):
    return(x*2)
print(f("3.4"))
```

25.
```
def f(x):
    return(x+x)
print(f("3.4"))
```

26.
```
def f(x):
    return(x+"ab")
print(f("3.4"))
```

Find the Error

1.
```
def print():
    print("hi")
read()
```

2.
```
def print():
    print("hi")
print(10)
```

3.
```
def pr(a):
    print(a)
pr()
```

4.
```
def pr(a,b):
    print(a)
x=10
y=20
pr(p=x,q=y)
```

5.
```
def pr(a,*b):
    print(a,b)
x=10
y=20
pr(b=y)
```

6.
```
def pr(a,*b):
    print(a,b)
    b[0]=b[0]+1
    x=10
    y=20
pr(x,y)
```

7.
```
def pr():
    return(10,20)
q=pr()
q[0]=q[0]+1
print(q)
```

8.
```
def f(x):
    def g(n):
        if n < 10:
            x = x + 1
            print(" ",x)
            g(n + 1)
    g(0)
f(5)
```

9.
```
r=lambda a,b:
print("The result:
  ",r(10,20))
```

10.
```
r=lambda a,b:a+b
print("The result: ",r(10))
```

Long Answer Questions

1. In Python, how many types of arguments are supported? Explain each type with a suitable example?

2. What are the differences between call by value and call by reference?

3. Differentiate the various name spaces available in Python.
4. What are the advantages of recursion procedure in Python?
5. Explain about the anonymous functions.
6. Discuss in detail about nesting of passing arguments in a Python function.

Short Answer Questions

1. Define lambda function.
2. What is the scope of local and global variable?
3. List the various types of arguments available in Python functions.
4. Discuss about the documentation strings.
5. Differentiate recursion and iteration.

Exercise Programs

1. Write a function **ball_collide** that takes two balls as parameters and computes if they are colliding. Your function should return a Boolean representing whether or not the balls are colliding.
2. Find mean, median and mode for the given set of numbers in a list.
3. Write a function **nearly_equal** to test whether two strings are nearly equal. Two strings a and b are nearly equal when a can be generated by a single mutation on b.
4. Write a function **dups** to find all duplicates in the list.
5. Write a function **unique** to find all the unique elements of a list.
6. Write a function **cumulative_product** to compute cumulative product of a list of numbers.
7. Write a function **reverse** to reverse a list without using the reverse function.
8. Write function to compute the LCM of two numbers.
9. Write a Python program to check whether or not the given number is an Armstrong number.
10. Write a Python program to compute the mean, mode and median of the given group of numbers by using functions.
11. Write a Python program to check whether the given number is a perfect number or not by using functions.
12. Write a Python program to compute the area of circle, square, rectangle and triangle by using functions.
13. Write a Python program to display the calendar by using functions.
14. Write a Python program to display Floyd's triangle by using functions.
15. Write a Python program to display Pascal triangle program by using functions.
16. Write a Python program to perform the linear search by using functions.
17. Write a Python program to add, multiply and subtract complex numbers by using functions.
18. Write a Python program to add, subtract and multiply matrices by using functions.
19. Write a Python program to transpose the matrix by using functions.
20. Write a Python program to display the diamond pattern by using functions.

Answers

Multiple Choice Questions

1. (c)
2. (a)
3. (d)
4. (b)
5. (b)
6. (b)
7. (a)
8. (c)
9. (d)
10. (b)
11. (a)
12. (d)
13. (c)
14. (b)
15. (a)
16. (b)
17. (b)
18. (a)
19. (c)
20. (d)
21. (d)
22. (c)
23. (a)
24. (b)
25. (a)
26. (b)
27. (c)
28. (d)
29. (b)
30. (d)
31. (b)
32. (d)
33. (b)
34. (a)
35. (d)
36. (a)
37. (b)
38. (c)
39. (a)
40. (b)

Fill in the Blanks

1. Functions
2. two
3. built-in and user-defined
4. arguments.
5. return values.
6. reused
7. improved
8. repeated.
9. loops.
10. tuple
11. function call
12. `return` statement
13. defining the user-defined functions.
14. `print()`
15. :
16. zero
17. four
18. default, required.
19. Default
20. Required
21. variable
22. *
23. position
24. keyword
25. anonymous
26. `lambda`
27. nesting passing arguments.
28. “.”
29. second line
30. _doc_

State True/False

1. False
2. True
3. True
4. False
5. False
6. True
7. False
8. False
9. False
10. False
11. False.
12. True
13. True
14. True
15. True
16. True
17. True
18. False
19. True
20. False
21. True
22. True
23. False
24. True
25. True
26. False
27. True
28. True

Find the Output

1. hi
2. hi
3. 10
4. 10 20
5. 20 ()
6. 10 (20,)
7. 10 (20, 30)
   2
8. 10 (20, 30)
   2
9. ()
10. 11
    11
    11
    11
    11
    11
    11
    11
    11
    11
11. value of j= 10
12. value of b= 10
13. value of b= 20
14. The result: 11
15. 15
16. 1
17. 5 4
18. olleh
19. -27
20. hello.
21. 6
22. lo.
23. 6.8
24. 3.43.4
25. 3.43.4
26. 3.4ab

Find the Error

1. NameError: name 'read' is not defined
2. TypeError: print() takes 0 positional arguments but 1 was given
3. TypeError: pr() missing 1 required positional argument: 'a'
4. TypeError: pr() got an unexpected keyword argument 'p'
5. TypeError: pr() got an unexpected keyword argument 'b'
6. TypeError: 'tuple' object does not support item assignment
7. TypeError: 'tuple' object does not support item assignment
8. UnboundLocalError: local variable 'x' referenced before assignment
9. SyntaxError: invalid syntax
10. TypeError: <lambda>() missing 1 required positional argument: 'b'

CHAPTER 9

Modules

The Python allows definitions and executable codes to the outside of the current program. For this, Python uses module and package concepts. In this chapter, we shall discuss in detail about the creation of a module and the various ways of importing elements from a module.

9.1 Introduction

In Python programming, the definitions and executable codes are available only within the current file. They are not available for longer duration. To overcome this, Python supports two types of files. They are

- Module
- Package

A module is a single python file that contains various definitions and executable statements. The package contains a group of module files. The module is a single python file and so it should be saved with ".py" extension. The executable statements and the function/class definitions available in the module can be executed in other programs also. For this execution, the module should be imported in other programs. With modules, all related programs can be grouped into one place, thus making it simpler to use. Runnable code can also be included in a module. An example code for a module is given below.

```
v1=100
def s(x,y):
    return(x+y)
```

The above is saved as "sum.py". It represents that a module "sum" contains one variable "v1" and one function "s()".

9.2 Importing Modules

In Python programming, the module is used to arrange the codes logically into one place. After grouping the code into the corresponding module, module definitions and executable statements should be used in outside environment. For this, the module should be imported into the outside environment. The module can be imported in two different ways:

i. Importing all the elements of a module
ii. Importing the specific elements of a module

9.2.1 Importing all elements of a module

In this category, the import statement imports all executable statements and definitions into the requested environment. Then, a specific element is used with the corresponding module name. An example code is shown below.

sum.py

```
v1=100
def s(x,y):
    return(x+y)
```

terminal mode

```
>>> import sum
>>> sum.s(100,200)
300
```

main.py

```
import sum
print(sum.s(100,200))
print(sum.v1)
```

Output

```
D:\PythonPrograms>python main.py
300
100
```

The elements of a module can be imported by using "from. . .import *" statement also.

sum.py

```
v1=100
def s(x,y):
    return(x+y)
def m(x,y):
    return(x*y)
```

bb.py

```
from sum import *
print(s(100,200))
print(v1)
print(m(10,20))
```

Output

```
D:\PythonPrograms>python bb.py
300
100
200
```

9.2.2 Importing the specific elements of a module

In this category, the import statement imports only the specific executable statements and definitions into the requested environment. Once the requested elements are imported, a specific element is used without the corresponding module name. An example code is shown below.

sum.py

```
v=100
def s(x,y):
    return(x+y)
def m(x,y):
    return(x*y)
```

terminal mode

```
>>> from sum import(s,m)
>>> s(20,30)
50
>>> m(4,5)
20
>>> v
Traceback (most recent call last):
    File "<stdin>", line 1, in <module>
NameError: name 'v' is not defined
```

main.py

```
from sum import(s,v,m)
print(s(100,200))
print(v)
print(m(10,20))
```

Output

```
D:\PythonPrograms>python main.
py
300
100
200
```

9.3 Creating Modules

In Python programming, a module can be created with multiple definitions and executable statements. In other programs, we can import the required elements of the module or we can import the complete module.

sum.py

```
def add(x,y):
    return(x+y)
def mul(a,b):
    return(a*b)
def sub(x,y):
    return(x-y)
def div(x,y):
    return(x/y)
```

In the above example code, the "sum.py" represents a module with definitions for four functions, viz., add(), mul(), sub() and div(). In other programs, all these definitions or a few of these definitions can be imported. In the below example code, main.py, all these definitions are imported.

```
import sum
n1=int(input("Enter the first number: "))
n2=int(input("Enter the second number: "))
print("The result of add(): ",sum.add(n1,n2))
print("The result of sub(): ",sum.sub(n1,n2))
print("The result of mul(): ",sum.mul(n1,n2))
print("The result of div(): ",sum.div(n1,n2))
```

Output

```
D:\PythonPrograms>python bb.py
Enter the first number: 30
Enter the second number: 10
The result of add(): 40
The result of sub(): 20
The result of mul(): 300
The result of div(): 3.0
```

Instead of importing all the definitions, in the following sample codes, only a few of the definitions are imported. In these cases, from module import(lis_of_element) statement is used as import statement.

Example 1

```
from sum import add
n1=int(input("Enter the first number: "))
n2=int(input("Enter the second number: "))
print("The result of add(): ",add(n1,n2))
```

Output

```
D:\PythonPrograms>python xmain.py
Enter the first number: 40
Enter the second number: 50
The result of add(): 90
```

Example 2

```
from sum import sub
n1=int(input("Enter the first number: "))
n2=int(input("Enter the second number: "))
print("The result of sub(): ",sub(n1,n2))
```

Output

```
D:\PythonPrograms>python xmain.py
Enter the first number: 50
Enter the second number: 10
The result of sub(): 40
```

9.4 Use of __name__

In Python programming, there is no main module. The program that is currently executed is considered as the content of the main module. When any other module is imported into the top level main module, then the Python interpreter will maintain the current module that is used. For this, __name__ variable is used. When the Python program is executed, the value of __name__ variable is __main__. The elements of the imported module can be called when other modules are imported into the program. After the import statement, the value of __name__ variable is the name of the corresponding module. The example code below depicts the usage of __name__ variable.

sum.py

```
print(__name__)
def sub(x,y):
    return(x-y)
def div(x,y):
    return(x/y)
```

xmain.py

```
print(__name__)
from sum import sub
print(__name__)
n1=int(input("Enter the first number: "))
n2=int(input("Enter the second number: "))
print("The result of sub(): ",sub(n1,n2))
```

Output

```
D:\PythonPrograms>python xmain.py
__main__
sum
__main__
Enter the first number: 10
Enter the second number: 20
The result of sub(): -10
```

During the execution of the program of **xmain.py**, initially the value of **__name__** variable is assigned with **__main__**. Then the definition of **sub()** function from the module "sum" is imported into the main module. So, the value of **__name__** is sum. After importing the definition of the **sub()** function, the control is in the main module itself. So, the value of **__name__** variable is assigned with **__main__**.

9.5 Name Spacing

Namespace is used to represent the set of names used in a module. It is used to map the names to the corresponding objects and contains a collection of variable names, function names, class names, etc. In a module, the same name cannot be used for more than one element such as variable, class, function.

```
x=100
x="ab"
print(x)
```

Output

```
D:\PythonPrograms>python a1.py
ab
```

In the above example code, two values "100" and "ab" are not maintained with the same name "x". Only the latest value "ab" is maintained by name "x". So, in a module, the same name cannot be used for multiple elements.

In Python, any file can be considered as a module and each module has its own local and global namespaces. In the above example code, variable x is considered in global namespace. Similar to global namespace, each module can also maintain a local namespace. In any module, the same name can be used in both local and global namespaces.

```
x=100
def f1():
    x="ab"
    print("local name space:", x)
f1()
print("global name space:", x)
```

Output

```
D:\PythonPrograms>python a1.py
local name space: ab
global name space: 100
```

In the above example code, the name "x" is used in both local namespace and global namespace. If changes are made to one name space, these are not reflected in the other namespace.

In Python, there is another namespace called as "built-in namespace". All names used for the built in operations/variables/functions/classes of Python are represented with built-in namespace. In a Python program, built in names can also be used for our own global or local namespaces.

```
x=100
def len():
    x="ab"
    print("local name space:", x)
len ()
print("global name space:", x)
```

Output

```
D:\PythonPrograms>python a1.py
local name space: ab
global name space: 100
```

In Python programming, **len()** function is already available in built-in namespace. The built-in namespace name **len** is used in the above example code for global namespace.

9.5.1 Scope

A scope represents a program region from where a namespace can be accessed without a prefix. In Python, there are four types of scopes. They are listed below.

- Local scope is found inside a function or class method.
- Enclosed scope is found with its enclosing function
- Global scope refers to the current execution module
- Built-in scope represents the reserved names of Python

9.6 Reloading Module

In Python, when a loaded module is updated, the updated module can be reloaded by using **reload()** function.

```
import importlib
import sum
importlib.reload(sum)
```

9.7 Sample Programs

Program 1: Write a Python program to create a module by using command line arguments.

The command line arguments can be accessed with **sys** module. So, in the program, initially, the **sys** module should be imported. Once the module is imported, the **argv[]** array is used to represent the command line arguments.

```
import sys
from sum import(s,v,m)
print("The first command line argument: ",sys.argv[0])
print("The second command line argument: ",sys.argv[1])
print("The third command line argument: ",sys.argv[2])
a=int(sys.argv[1])
b=int(sys.argv[2])
print("The result of s() in module: ",s(a,b))
print("The value of variable v in module: ",v)
print("The result of m() in module",m(a,b))
```

Output

```
D:\PythonPrograms>python main.py 4 5
The first command line argument: main.py
The second command line argument: 4
The third command line argument: 5
The result of s() in module: 9
The value of variable v in module: 100
The result of m() in module 20
```

Program 2: Write a Python program to print the level of the program to be executed in Python.

sum.py

```
print("The top level execution:",__name__)
def add(x,y):
    return(x+y)
def mul(a,b):
    return(a*b)
def sub(x,y):
    return(x-y)
def div(x,y):
    return(x/y)
```

Programming Tip:

A module can have multiple definitions of functions.

xmain.py

```
if(__name__=="__main__"):
    print("The top level execution:",__name__)
    from sum import div
    print("The top level execution:",__name__)
    n1=int(input("Enter the first number: "))
    n2=int(input("Enter the second number: "))
    print("The result of div(): ",div(n1,n2))
```

Programming Tip:

The import statement is used to import the function from any module.

Output

```
D:\PythonPrograms>python xmain.py
The top level execution: __main__
The top level execution: sum
The top level execution: __main__
Enter the first number: 200
Enter the second number: 4
The result of div(): 50.0
```

Program 3: Write a Python program to print the factorial of a number by using module.

fact.py

```
def f1(x):
    s=1
    for i in range(1,x+1):
        s=s*i
    return(s)
```

b2.py

```
import fact
a=int(input("Enter the number:"))
print("Original number=",a)
print("Factorial result=",fact.f1(a))
```

Output

```
D:\PythonPrograms>python fact.py
D:\PythonPrograms>python b2.py
Enter the number:3
Original number= 3
Factorial result= 6
```

Program 4: Write a Python program to display the reverse of a number by using module.

fact.py

```
def r(x):
    res=0
    while(x>0):
        y=x%10
        res=(res*10)+y
        x=x//10
    return(res)
```

b2.py

```
import fact
a=int(input("Enter the number:"))
print("Original Number: ",a)
print("Reverse Number :",fact.r(a))
```

Output

```
D:\PythonPrograms>python fact.py
D:\PythonPrograms>python b2.py
Enter the number:654
Original Number: 654
Reverse Number : 456
```

Program 5: Write a Python program to display the natural, even and odd numbers by using module.

fact.py

```
def n(x):
    print("natural numbers:")
    for i in range(1,x+1):
        print(i,end=' ')
    print("")
def o(x):
    print("Odd numbers:")
    for i in range(1,x+1, 2):
        print(i,end=' ')
    print("")
def e(x):
    print("Even numbers:")
    for i in range(2,x+1, 2):
        print(i,end=' ')
    print("")
```

b2.py

```
import fact
a=int(input("Enter the number:"))
fact.n(a)
fact.o(a)
fact.e(a)
```

Output

```
D:\PythonPrograms>python fact.py
D:\PythonPrograms>python b2.py
Enter the number:5
natural numbers:
1 2  3  4 5
Odd numbers:
1 3  5
Even numbers:
2 4
```

Glossary

- Module is a single program with multiple definitions. Module allows the access of the code outside the program.
- Importing a module indicates the granted access to the content of the module.
- __name__ is a variable used to represent the name of the current module.

Summary

- In Python, code reusuability is greatly achieved with module and package.
- A module is a single file used for grouping multiple definitions and executable code.
- A module can be imported into another Python file and the elements of the module, accessed.

Multiple Choice Questions

1. Module is
   (a) a collection of executable statements
   (b) a collection of definitions
   (c) Both a and b.
   (d) None of the above.
2. Module elements can be accessed in external environment by using
   (a) import statement
   (b) access statement
   (c) module statement
   (d) None of the above.
3. In how many ways can the module be imported?
   (a) 4 (b) 3
   (c) 2 (d) 1
4. import module_name is used to access the elements by using
   (a) element
   (b) module_name
   (c) element.module_name
   (d) module_name.element
5. for module_name import(elements_list) is used to access the elements by using
   (a) element
   (b) module_name
   (c) element.module_name
   (d) module_name.element
6. Package is a
   (a) collection of executable statements
   (b) collection of definitions
   (c) Both a and b.
   (d) collection of modules
7. PYNOPATH contains a
   (a) list of directories of Python
   (b) list of files of Python
   (c) list of definitions of Python
   (d) list of executable statements of Python
8. Which variable is used to represent the currently executed module?
   (a) __main__ (b) __void__
   (c) __name__ (d) __none__
9. The value of __name__ for top level program execution
   (a) __void__
   (b) __null__
   (c) __main__
   (d) None of the above.
10. The namespace represents a
    (a) list of all names used in a module/class/object
    (b) list of functions defined
    (c) list of classes defined
    (d) None of the above.
11. In Python, how is a defined function available to all other files?
    (a) By using Module
    (b) By using Package
    (c) By using Module and Package
    (d) None of the above.
12. A Python module contains how many files?
    (a) 1 (b) 2
    (c) 3 (d) 4
13. The module file is saved with which extension?
    (a) .p (b) .y
    (c) .pym (d) .py
14. A module consists of
    (a) single definition
    (b) multiple definitions
    (c) executable statements
    (d) multiple definitions and executable statements
15. The set of names used in a module is represented with
    (a) namelist
    (b) namespacing
    (c) Both a and b.
    (d) None of the above.
16. The namespace contains
    (a) variable names
    (b) function names
    (c) class names
    (d) All the above.
17. Each module can maintain
    (a) local namespace
    (b) global namespace

(c) Both a and b.
(d) None of the above.

18. Names of Python built-in operations/variables/functions are available in
(a) built-in namespace
(b) default namespace
(c) initial namespace
(d) None of the above.

19. How many scopes are available in Python?
(a) 1 (b) 2
(c) 3 (d) 4

20. Which scope is found inside a function or class method?
(a) Local (b) Enclosed
(c) Global (d) Built-in

21. Which scope is found with its enclosing function?
(a) Local (b) Enclosed
(c) Global (d) Built-in

22. Which scope refers to the current execution module?
(a) Local (b) Enclosed
(c) Global (d) Built-in

23. Which scope represents the reserved names of Python?
(a) Local (b) Enclosed
(c) Global (d) Built-in

24. The reloading of the module is performed with?
(a) **update()** (b) **modify()**
(c) **reload()** (d) **assign()**

Fill in the Blanks

1. There are ____________ types are available for maintain the definitions for long duration.
2. ____________ and ____________ allow the executable code to external environment.
3. A module is a ____________ file.
4. A module file contains ____________ number of definitions.
5. A module consists of ____________, ____________.
6. A Module file is saved with ____________ extension.
7. To use the module definitions, module should be ____________.
8. For importing a module, there are ____________ number of ways in Python.
9. Import statement will import ____________ elements of the module.
10. After importing all elements, a specific element of the module can be accessed with ____________.
11. from..import statement will ____________.
12. A specific element of a module can be imported with ____________.
13. from..import * will import ____________.
14. from x import(y) statement will import ____________.
15. The definitions of a module should use ____________ keyword.
16. In Python, there is no ____________ module.
17. The currently imported module is represented with ____________ variable.
18. ____________ is used to map the names to the corresponding object.
19. The python built in operations names are represented with ____________.
20. In Python, there are ____________ types of scopes.

State True/False

1. Availability of executable code for longer duration is allowed in Python.
2. A python module can have only definitions.
3. A Python module can have only runnable code.
4. A Python module can have both executable statements and definitions.
5. A Python module can have only single definition.
6. A Python module can have multiple definitions.
7. There are three ways to maintain the definitions for longer durations.
8. Module is used for handling multiple definitions.

9. Package is used for handling multiple definitions.
10. A Module definition can be written in more than one file.
11. A Module file can be saved with ".py" extension.
12. Importing a module is required in any other program for using the module definitions.
13. A module can be imported in two different ways.
14. All the module definitions cannot be imported into another file.
15. Specific elements of the module can be imported into another file.
16. After importing a module, elements can be directly accessed.
17. Module name is required to access the elements of the module.
18. from.. import can import all the elements with &.
19. from..import is used to import specific elements of the module.
20. **import** statement can import all the elements of the module.

Find the Output

1. sum.py
```
def add(x,y):
   return(x+y)
def mul(a,b):
   return(a*b)
def sub(x,y):
   return(x-y)
def div(x,y):
   return(x/y)
```
s1.py
```
import sum
s=sum.add('a','20')
print(s)
```
2. sum.py
```
def add(x,y):
   return(x+y)
def add(x,y):
   return(x-y)
```
s1.py
```
import sum
print(sum.add(10,20))
s=sum.add(10,20)
print(s)
```
3. sum.py
```
def add(x,y):
   return(x+y)
```
s1.py
```
import sum
print(sum.add(10,20))
print(__name__)
```
4. sum.py
```
print(__name__)
def add(x,y):
   return(x+y)
```
s1.py
```
import sum
print(sum.add(10,20))
```

Find the Error

1. sum.py
```
def add(x,y):
   return(x+y)
def mul(a,b):
   return(a*b)
def sub(x,y):
   return(x-y)
def div(x,y):
   return(x/y)
```
s1.py
```
import sum *
s=sum(10,20)
print(s)
```
2. s1.py
```
import sum
s=sum(10,20)
print(s)
```
3. s1.py
```
import sum
s=sum.add(a,20)
print(s)
```
4. s1.py
```
import sum
s=sum.add('a',20)
print(s)
```
5. s1.py
```
from sum import mul
s=sum.add('a','20')
print(s)
```

6. s1.py
```
from sum import mul
s=sum.mul('a','20')
print(s)
```

7. s1.py
```
from sum import(mul)
s=mul('a','20')
print(s)
```

Long Answer Questions

1. What is a module? Explain the process of creating a module.
2. Explain the various ways of importing a module into another module.
3. Discuss in detail about reloading a module in Python.
4. Compare the function and module in Python.

Short Answer Questions

1. List the various scopes in Python.
2. What is the advantage of namespace?
3. Give the advantage of __name__ variable usage in Python.

Exercise Programs

1. Write a Python program to develop a simple calculator by using modules.
2. Write a Python program to display all types of scopes of a variable.
3. Write a Python program to display the GCD of the given number by using module.
4. Write a Python program to display the LCM of the given number by using module.
5. Write a Python program to display the exponent value of the given number by using module.
6. Write a Python program to compute the mean, mode and median of the given group of numbers by using module.
7. Write a Python program to check whether or not the given number is an Armstrong number by using module?
8. Write a Python program to check whether or not the given number is a perfect number by using module?
9. Write a Python program to compute the area of circle, square, rectangle and triangle by using module.
10. Write a Python program to display the calendar by using module.
11. Write a Python program to display Floyd's triangle by using module.
12. Write a Python program to display the Pascal triangle by using module.
13. Write a Python program to perform a linear search by using module.
14. Write a Python program to add, multiple and subtract the complex numbers by using module.
15. Write a Python program to add, subtract and multiply matrices by using module.
16. Write a Python program to transpose a matrix by using module.

Answers

Multiple Choice Questions

1. (c)	6. (d)	11. (c)	16. (d)	21. (b)
2. (a)	7. (a)	12. (a)	17. (c)	22. (c)
3. (c)	8. (c)	13. (d)	18. (a)	23. (d)
4. (d)	9. (c)	14. (d)	19. (d)	24. (c)
5. (a)	10. (a)	15. (b)	20. (a)	

Fill in the Blanks

1. two
2. Module, Package
3. single
4. multiple
5. Definitions, executable code.
6. ".py"
7. imported.
8. 2
9. all the elements
10. module name
11. import a single element or all elements from the module.
12. from..import
13. all elements of a module
14. element y from module x.
15. def
16. main
17. __name__
18. Namespace
19. built-in namespace
20. four

State True/False

1. True
2. False
3. False
4. True.
5. False
6. True.
7. False.
8. True
9. True.
10. False
11. True
12. True
13. True
14. False
15. True
16. False
17. True
18. False
19. True
20. True

Find the Output

1. a20
2. -10
-10
3. 30
__main__
4. sum
30

Find the Error

1. SyntaxError: invalid syntax 9**i**mport sum *)
2. TypeError: 'module' object is not callable
3. NameError: name 'a' is not defined
4. TypeError: must be str, not int
5. AttributeError: 'builtin_function_or_method' object has no attribute 'add'
6. AttributeError: 'builtin_function_or_method' object has no attribute 'mul'
7. TypeError: can't multiply sequence by non-int of type 'str'

CHAPTER 10

Object Oriented Programming Principles

Python supports both procedure oriented and object oriented features. This chapter discusses in detail about the various object oriented properties, viz., encapsulation, abstraction, inheritance and polymorphism.

10.1 Class Statement

Python supports object oriented programming. Object oriented programming (OOPs) has several advantages as compared to procedure oriented programming. They are

- Itfollows a bottom-up approach whereas procedure oriented programming follows top-down approach.
- It focuses on data and not on code.

The principles of object oriented programming are given below:

Encapsulation

Encapsulation means wrapping of data and the functions (operations on data) at a single place. An example is shown in Fig. 10.1.

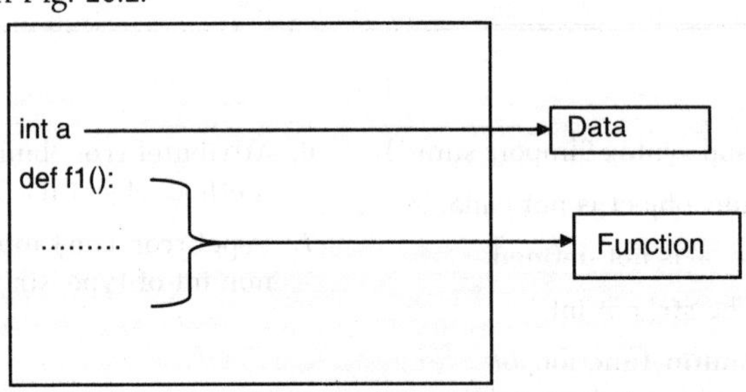

Figure **10.1** Representation of class properties

Data Abstraction

The data abstraction is the process by which only selected features of the object are highlighted while the internal details are suppressed.For example, consider mobile phones. The user can work with the desired feature of mobile phones without knowing the internal hardware connections, software code etc.Mobile phone manufacturers provide abstraction to their mobile device such that a lay user can handle the device without knowing the technical details. Thus, data abstraction reduces the complexity associated with data encapsulation.

Polymorphism

With the polymorphism concept, a single entity can act in multiple forms as shown in Fig. 10.2.

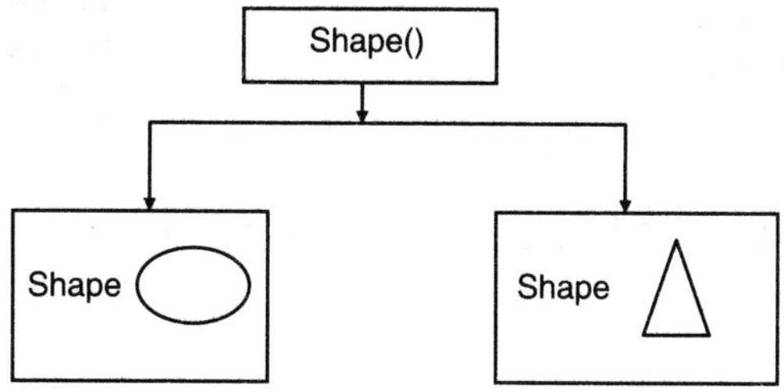

Figure 10.2. Example for polymorphism

Inheritance

Inheritance allows a class to derive the properties of another class. An example is shown in Fig. 10.3.

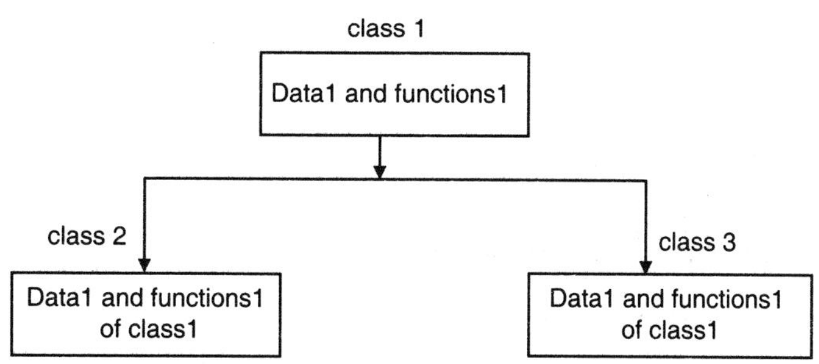

Figure 10.3. Example for inheritance

In Python, data encapsulation allows bundling of instance variables and methods in order to restrict access to certain class members. It packs the data and the functions into a single place and is implemented with the "class". The class contains both the data and the functions. The data in the class is represented with variables and are called as members of the class. The functions that can operate on the members arecalled as methods. In a class, we can write both members and methods.

When a class is defined with members and methods, the memory will not be allocated. So, with class definition, we cannot access the properties of the class. To overcome this, an object should be created for the class. When the object is created, then the memory is allocated. Then, with this object, the properties of the class can be accessible.

10.2 Class Body

In Python programming, data encapsulation is supported with "class". Class consists of both data and functions. The data in a class is called as members while functions in the class are called as methods. The definition of class is given below.

```
classclass_name:
    statement1_class
    statement2_class
    statement3_class
    statementn_class
    ...................
```

The statement in the class consists of either data or function. An example code for a class with members is given below.

```
class ex:
    x=100
    y="abadffa"
print("Member value of x= ",ex.x)
print("Member value of y= ",ex.y)
```

Output

```
D:\PythonPrograms>python a1.py
Member value of x= 100
Member value of y= abadffa
```

10.3 Objects

In Python programming, objects for class can be created in two different ways. They are

- Attribute referencing
- Instantiation.

Attribute referencing

In attribute referencing, Python class properties can be accessed by using the class name itself. The syntax of the attribute referencing is

```
class_name:propertyname
```

```
class ex:
    x=[]
ex.x=input("Enter the value of member x: ")
print("The value of ex.x is= ",ex.x)
```

Output

```
D:\PythonPrograms>python a1.py
Enter the value of member x: 355
The value of ex.x is= 355
```

Instantiation

During the instantiation process, an empty object is created and this object is assigned with the given object name. The syntax for the class instantiation is

```
object_name=class_name()
```

After creating the class instance, the properties of the class are accessed with the following syntax

```
object_name:propertyname
```

An example code for the class instantiation is given below.

```
class ex:
    x=[]
a=ex();
a.x=input("Enter the value of member x: ")
print("The value of a.x is= ",a.x)
```

Output

```
D:\PythonPrograms>python a1.py
Enter the value of member x: hello
The value of a.x is= hello
```

10.4 Class Methods

The class is used to pack the data for the functions. Functions will operate on the data given in the class. The functions defined with in the class are called as methods. In Python programming, the function is defined with the following syntax.

```
deffunction_name(arguments_list):
    statement_1
    statement_2
    ..............
    statement_n
```

The class method also follows the syntax of ordinary function. But, the class method should be defined within the class. The syntax for the class method is given below.

```
classclass_name:
    statements_classbody
    deffunction_name(arguments_list):
        statement_1
        statement_2
        ...............
        statement_n
    statements_classbody
```

The class method can also be accessed by using either attribute referencing or instantiation. An example code for the class method with attribute referencing is given below.

```
class ex:
    def f1():
        print("This is class method")
ex.f1()
```

Output

```
D:\PythonPrograms>python a1.py
This is class method
```

An example for class instantiation is given below.

```
class ex:
    def f1():
        print("This is class method")
a=ex()
a.f1()
```

Output

```
D:\PythonPrograms>python a1.py
Traceback (most recent call last):
    File "a1.py", line 6, in <module>
        a.f1()
TypeError: f1() takes 0 positional arguments but 1 was given
```

The above program is used to access the class methods by using class instantiation. Butthe program raises an error. To overcome this, the class method should always take atleast the current object as an argument.

```
class ex:
    deff1(ex):
        print("This is class method")
a=ex()
a.f1()
```

Output

```
D:\PythonPrograms>python a1.py
This is class method
```

10.5 Self Variable

In C++ and Java programming languages, "this" pointer is used to point to the current object. In Python programming, the "self" pointer is used to point to the current object. With the self pointer, all the properties of class, viz., members and methods can be accessed.

```
class ex:
    def read(self):
        self.a=input("Enter the value:")
    def disp(self):
        print("The value of a= ",self.a)
a=ex()
a.read()
a.disp()
```

Output

```
D:\PythonPrograms>python a1.py
Enter the value:good morning
The value of a= good morning
```

10.6 Class Properties and Instance Properties

A class contains two types of properties, viz., variable and method. The data in a class is maintained with the members. There are two types of variables.They are

1. Class variable
2. Instance variable

Class variable maintains only a single copy of the data. The value of a class variable is shared by all instances. The instance variable values change from one instance to another instance. An example code is given below.

```
class ex:
    var1=100
b=ex()
b.var1=200
print("Class variable of instance b: ",ex.var1)
print(«Instance b variable: «,b.var1)
c=ex()
c.var1=300
print("Class variable of instance c: ",ex.var1)
print(«Instance c variable: «,c.var1)
```

Output

```
D:\PythonPrograms>python a1.py
Class variable of instance b: 100
Instance b variable: 200
Class variable of instance c: 100
Instance c variable: 300
```

Similar to variables, methods are also of two types. They are

i. Class method
ii. Instance method

The class method should contain the class itself as an argument,whereas in instance method, the first argument should always be "self".

```
class ex:
    var1=100
    #instance method
    def disp(self):
        print("Value of var1= ",self.var1)
    #class method
    def disp1(ex):
        print("Value of var1= ",ex.var1)
a=ex()
a.disp()
a.disp1()
```

Output

```
D:\PythonPrograms>python a1.py
Value of var1= 100
Value of var1= 100
```

Built-in class properties

In Python, there are various built-in class properties, as listed below.

- ._dict_
- ._doc_
- ._name_
- ._module_
- ._bases_

._dict_ The__dict__ attribute represents the dictionary with the class namespace.

```
class ex:
    a=100
obj1=ex()
print("The value of __dict__ attribute= ",ex.__dict__)
```

Output

```
D:\PythonPrograms>python b2.py
The value of __dict__ attribute= {'__module__': '__main__', 'a': 100, '__dict__': <attribute '__dict__' of 'ex' objects>, '__weakref__': <attribute '__weakref__' of 'ex' objects>, '__doc__': None}
```

.__doc__ The.__doc__ attribute represents the class documentation string. If the string is undefined then "none" is represented.

```
class ex:
   a=100
obj1=ex()
print("The value of __doc__ attribute= ",ex.__doc__)
```

Output

```
D:\PythonPrograms>python b2.py
The value of __doc__ attribute= None
```

.__name__ The__name__ attribute represents the class name.

```
class ex:
   a=100
obj1=ex()
print("The value of __name__ attribute= ",ex.__name__)
```

Output

```
D:\PythonPrograms>python b2.py
The value of __name__ attribute= ex
```

.__module__ The__module__ attribute represents the name of the module in which the class definition is available.

```
class ex:
   a=100
obj1=ex()
print("The value of __module__ attribute= ",ex.__module__)
```

Output

```
D:\PythonPrograms>python b2.py
The value of __module__ attribute= __main__
```

.__bases_ The.__bases__ attribute is tuple that contains the base classes.

```
class ex:
   a=100
obj1=ex()
print(«The value of __bases__ attribute= «,ex.__bases__)
```

Output

```
D:\PythonPrograms>python b2.py
The value of __bases__ attribute= (<class 'object'>,)
```

Built-in functions for handling class attributes

Various built-in functions for handling class attributes are

- hasattr (obj, name)
- getattr (obj, name[, default])
- setattr (obj, name,value)
- delattr (obj, name)

hasattr() The hasattr() function checks whether or not the given attribute is available in the attributes of a given class. For this function, the first argument should be the class name and the second argument should be the name of the attribute.

```
class ex:
   a=100
obj1=ex()
print(hasattr(obj1,'a'))
```

Output

```
D:\PythonPrograms>python b2.py
True
```

getattr()The getattr() function returns the value of the given attribute in the given class. The first argument should be the name of the class and the second argument should be the name of the attribute.

```
class ex:
    a=100
obj1=ex()
print(getattr(obj1,'a'))
```

Output

```
D:\PythonPrograms>python b2.py
100
```

setattr() The setattr() function sets the value of the given attribute in the given class to the given value. The first argument should be the name of the class, the second argument should be the name of the attribute and the third argument should be the new value of the attribute.

```
class ex:
    a=100
obj1=ex()
print(getattr(obj1,'a'))
setattr(obj1,'a',200)
print(getattr(obj1,'a'))
```

Output

```
D:\PythonPrograms>python b2.py
100
200
```

delattr() The delattr() function deletes the given attribute in the given class. The first argument should be the name of the class and the second argument should be the name of the attribute.

```
class ex:
    a=100
    b=200
obj1=ex()
print(getattr(obj1,'a','b'))
delattr(obj1,'a')
print(getattr(obj1,'a'))
```

Output

```
D:\PythonPrograms>python b2.py
100
Traceback (most recent call last):
    File "b2.py", line 7, in <module>
        delattr(obj1,'a')
AttributeError: a
```

Public and private methods

In a class, the methods are of two types -public and private. The public method is available inside and outside of the class. The private method is available in only within the class. The private method name should begin with a double underscore "__".

```
class ex:
    def __init__(self,arg):
        self.a=arg
    def __read(self):
        self.a=input("Enter the new value of a: ")
    def disp(self):
        print("The value of a= ",self.a)
obj1=ex(300)
obj1.__read()
obj1.disp()
```

Output

```
D:\PythonPrograms>python b2.py
Traceback (most recent call last):
    File "b2.py", line 12, in <module>
        obj1.__read()
AttributeError: 'ex' object has no attribute '__read'
```

In the above program, read() method is a private method and disp() method is a public method. The private method is called outside the class. So, it leads to error.

```
class ex:
    def __init__(self,arg):
        self.a=arg
    def __read(self):
        self.a=input("Enter the new value of a: ")
    def disp(self):
        obj1.__read()
        print("The value of a= ",self.a)
obj1=ex(300)
obj1.disp()
```

Output

```
D:\PythonPrograms>python b2.py
Enter the new value of a: 500
The value of a= 500
```

Special functions

In a Python class, various special functions can be defined. Some of them are

- repr_( )
- _cmp_( )
- _len_( )

__repr__() The __repr__() is a method used to return the object in printable format.

```
class ex:
    def __init__(self,arg):
        self.a=arg
    def __repr__(self):
        return("the object value is %s" %(self.a))
obj1=ex(300)
print(obj1)
```

Output

```
D:\PythonPrograms>python b2.py
the object value is 300
```

__cmp__() The __cmp__() method is used to compare two input objects. It returns False when the two objects are not equal. If the two objects are equal then it returns True.

```
class ex:
    def __init__(self,arg):
        self.a=arg
    def __repr__(self):
        return("the object value is %s" %(self.a))
    def __cmp__(self,other):
        return(cmp(self.a,other.a))
obj1=ex(300)
obj2=ex(400)
print(obj1)
print(obj2)
if(obj1==obj2):
    print("The obj1 and obj2 are not equal")
```

Output

```
D:\PythonPrograms>python b2.py
the object value is 300
the object value is 400
False
```

__len__() The len() function returns the length of a input sequence or mapping object. The __len__() is a special method which can be defined within a class and can be callable by the object. On the top of len() function execution, the __len__() will be executed.

```
class ex:
    def __init__(self,arg):
        self.a=arg
obj1=ex(300)
print(len(obj1))
```

Output

```
D:\PythonPrograms>python b2.py
Traceback (most recent call last):
    File "b2.py", line 8, in <module>
        print(len(obj1))
TypeError: object of type 'ex' has no len()
```

```
class ex:
    def __init__(self,arg):
        self.a=arg
    def __len__(self):
        return(1)
obj1=ex(300)
print(len(obj1))
```

Output

```
D:\PythonPrograms>python b2.py
```

10.7 Static Method

The static method is a method used to access the static variables. The class variables are also called as static variables. The static method should not have any arguments. The static method should be defined by using the "@staticmethod" statement. The syntax of static method is

```
classclass_name:
    statements_classbody
        @staticmethod
    deffunction_name(arguments_list):
        statement_1
        statement_2
        ..............
        statement_n
    statements_classbody
```

An example code is given below.

```
class ex:
    a=100
    @staticmethod
    def read():
        ex.a=int(input("Enter the value:"))
    @staticmethod
    def disp():
        print("The value of a= ",ex.a)
b=ex()
b.read()
b.disp()
```

Output

```
D:\PythonPrograms>python a1.py
Enter the value:200
The value of a= 200
```

In the above example code, the variable "a" is a static variable. The method **read()** and **disp()** are the static methods. These static methods can access the static variable and do not have any arguments. In the body of the method, the static variable is accessed with the **classname.variablename.**

10.8 Data Hiding

In Python programming, the properties of a class can be hidden by using "__" (double underscore). An example code is given below.

```
class ex:
    a=200
    __b=100
print("Public Variable value: ",ex.a)
print("Hidden Variable value: ",ex.__b)
```

Output

```
D:\PythonPrograms>python a1.py
Public Variable value: 200
Traceback (most recent call last):
File "a1.py", line 7, in <module>
print("Hidden Variable value: ",ex.__b)
AttributeError: type object 'ex' has no attribute '__b'
```

In the above example code, **b** is a hidden variable. So, the variable **b** cannot be accessed outside the class. The value of hidden variable **b** can be accessible only within the class "ex".

```
class ex:
    a=200
    __b=100
    def f1():
        print("Hidden Variable value: ",ex.__b)
print("Public Variable value: ",ex.a)
ex.f1()
```

Output

```
D:\PythonPrograms>python a1.py
Public Variable value: 200
Hidden Variable value: 100
```

The methods can be hidden by using "__". These methods cannot be accessed outside the class.

```
class ex:
    a=200
    __b=100
    def f1():
        print("Hidden Variable-b value: ",ex.__b)
    def __f2():
        print("Hidden Method")
        print(«Variable-a value: «,ex.__b)
ex.f1()
ex.__f2()
```

Output

```
D:\PythonPrograms>python a1.py
Hidden Variable-b value: 100
Traceback (most recent call last):
File "a1.py", line 13, in <module>
ex.__f2()
AttributeError: type object 'ex' has no attribute '__f2'
```

The hidden methods are accessible only within a class.

```
class ex:
    a=200
    __b=100
    def f1():
        ex.__f2()
        print("Hidden Variable-b value: ",ex.__b)
    def __f2():
        print("Hidden Method")
        print("Variable-a value: ",ex.a)
ex.f1()
```

Output

```
D:\PythonPrograms>python a1.py
Hidden Method
Variable-a value: 200
Hidden Variable-b value: 100
```

10.9 Deleting an Object

In Python programming, the **del** keyword is used to delete an object. The syntax for deleting the object is

```
delobject_name
```

An example code is given below.

```
class ex:
    a=200
    deff1(ex):
        print(«Variable-a value: «,ex.a)
obj1=ex()
obj1.f1()
obj2=ex()
obj2.f1()
del(obj1)
obj1.f1()
```

Output

```
D:\PythonPrograms>python a1.py
Variable-a value: 200
Variable-a value: 200
Traceback (most recent call last):
    File "a1.py", line 15, in <module>
        obj1.f1()
NameError: name 'obj1' is not defined
```

In the above program, two objects, viz., obj1 and obj2 are created for the class "ex". The method n "ex" is called by these two objects. Then the object "obj1" is deleted. So, calling method "f1()" with the object "obj1" raised an error.

10.10 Constructor

In Python programming, the __int__() method will be executed during object creation. Hence, this method is used as a constructor for the class. The __int__() method or the constructor is used to initialize the class variables. The constructor method should always take the self pointer as the first argument. The remaining arguments will be passed during the object creation. An example for the constructor is given below.

```
class ex:
    def __init__(self,arg):
        self.a=arg
obj1=ex(300)
print("Value defined by the constructor= ",obj1.a)
```

Output

```
D:\PythonPrograms>python a1.py
Value defined by the constructor= 300
```

10.11 Method Overriding

In Python programming, method overriding allows the same method in both the sub-class and base class. In case of method overriding, the object for the sub-class will always points to the definition provided in the sub-class only. The definition of the base class is overridden by the sub-class definition. An example for method overriding is as shown:

```
class super:
    def disp(self):
        print("Super class method")
class sub:
    def disp(self):
        print("Sub class method")
x=sub()
x.disp()
```

Output

```
D:\PythonPrograms>python a1.py
Sub class method
```

10.12 Inheritance

Inheritance is used to derive the properties of one class to another class. In general, the properties from the base class can be derived into subclasses. So, the subclass contains the properties of base class as well as its own properties.

There are three types of inheritances in Python. They are

- Single inheritance
- Multiple inheritance
- Multilevel inheritance

Single inheritance

In single inheritance, the subclass can derive the properties of only one base class. The syntax for single inheritance is given below.

```
class base_class:
    #body of base class
class subclass_name(base_class):
    #body of the subclass
```

The single inheritance is shown in Fig. 10.4.

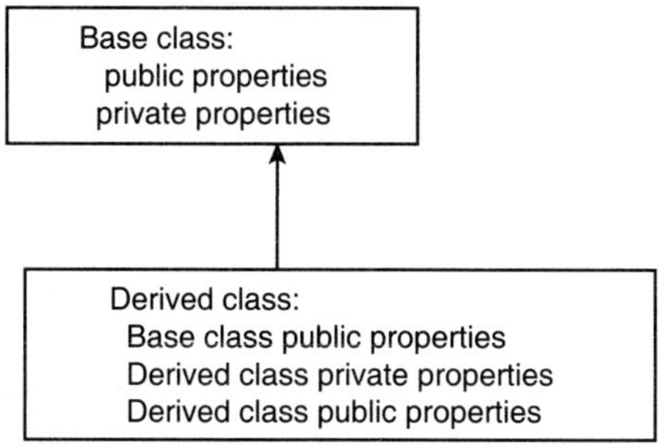

Figure 10.4 Representation of single inheritance

An example for single inheritance is given below.

```
class a:
    x=200
class b(a):
    y=300
def f1(self):
    print("Properties of sub class: ",self.x,self.y)
obj1=b()
obj1.f1()
```

Output

```
D:\PythonPrograms>python a1.py
Properties of sub class: 200 300
```

The hidden properties of base class cannot be derived into subclass. If an attempt is made to use them, it will raise an error.

Multiple inheritance

In multiple inheritance, the subclass derives the properties of more than one base class. Multiple base classes are separated with ",". The syntax of multiple inheritance is given below.

```
class base_class1:
    #body of base class1
class base_class2:
    #body of base class2
classsubclass_name(base_class1,base_class2):
    #body of the sub class
```

Multiple inheritance is shown in Fig. 10.5.

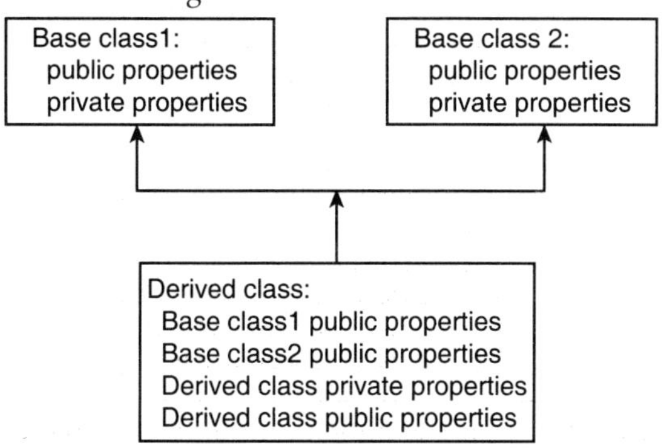

Figure 10.5 Representation of multiple inheritance

An example for multiple inheritance is given below.

```
class a:
    x=200
class b:
    y=100
class c(a,b):
    z=300
    def f1(self):
        print("Properties of sub class: ",self.x,self.y,self.z)
obj1=c()
obj1.f1()
```

Output

```
D:\PythonPrograms>python a1.py
Properties of sub class: 200 100 300
```

Multilevel inheritance

In multilevel inheritance, the properties of base class1 are derived into subclass1. The properties of subclass 1 are derived in to subclass2. The syntax of multilevel inheritance is given below.

```
class base_class1:
    #body of base class1
class sub_class1(base_class1):
    #body of subclass1
class subclass_name2(sub_class1):
        #body of the sub class2
```

Multilevel inheritance is shown in Fig.10.6.

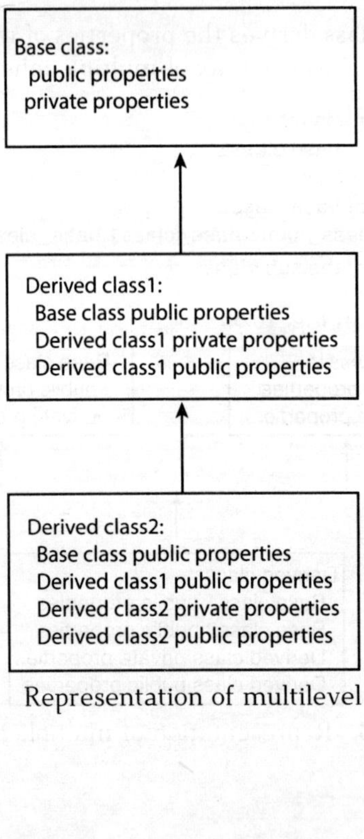

Figure **10.6** Representation of multilevel inheritance

An example code is given below.

```
class a:
    x=200
    def disp(self):
        print("Properties of base class1: ",self.x)
class b(a):
    y=300
    def f1(self):
        self.disp()
        print("Properties of sub class1: ",self.y)
class c(b):
    z=300
    def f2(self):
        self.f1()
        print("Properties of sub class3: ",self.z)
obj1=c()
obj1.f2()
```

Output

```
D:\PythonPrograms>python a1.py
Properties of base class1: 200
Properties of sub class1: 300
Properties of sub class3: 300
```

Multipath inheritance

Multipath inheritance is a combination of multilevel and multiple inheritances. Thus, in this type of inheritance, the public properties of base class are derived into various subclasses. All the public properties of subclasses are further derived into the final subclass. The multipath inheritance is shown in Fig. 10.7. The syntax of the multiple inheritance is given below.

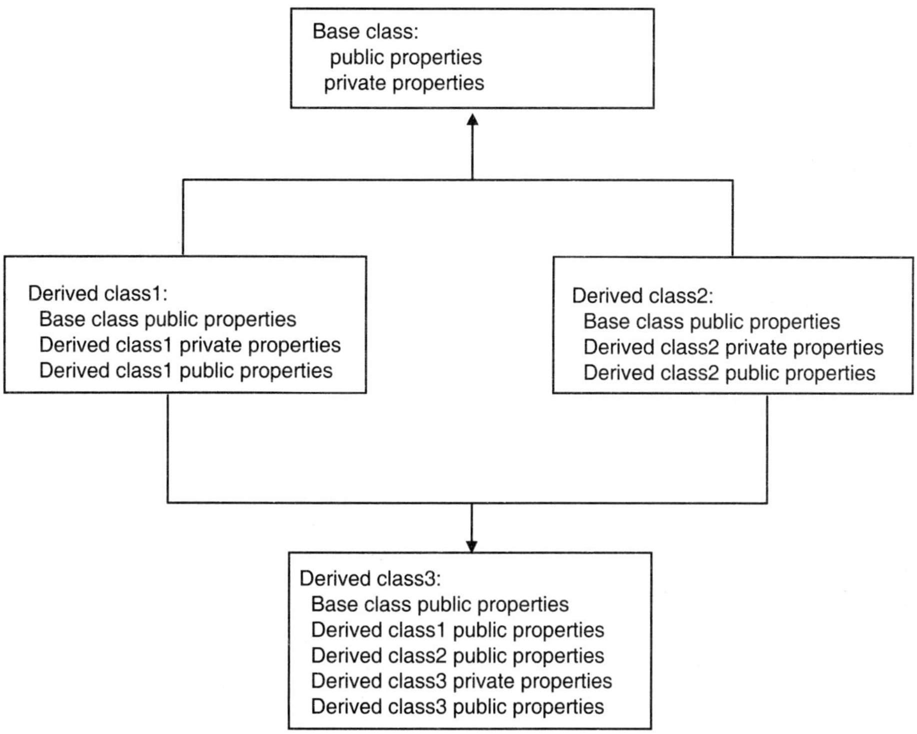

Figure **10.7**. Representation of Multipath inheritance

```
class base_class1
    #body of base class1
class sub_class1(base_class1):
    #body of subclass1
class sub_class2(base_class1):
        #body of the sub class2
class sub_class3(sub_class1,sub_class2):
        #body of the sub class3
```

```
class a:
   x=100
class b(a):
   y=200
class c(a):
   z=300
class d(b,c):
   p=500
def f1(self):
   print("Properties of sub class: ",self.x,self.y,self.z,self.p)
obj1=d()
obj1.f1()
```

Output

```
D:\PythonPrograms>python b2.py
Properties of sub class: 100 200 300 500
```

In case of multipath inheritance, the diamond problem can occur. The diamond problem is also called as "deadly diamond of death". It occurs due to repeatedly deriving the public properties of base class to the final sub-derived classes. In this case, if the method is overridden, then the new definition in the subclass will be executed. If the new definition is not available in the final sub-derived class, then the definition is available in the first class which is given in the order during inheritance definition.

```
class a:
   x=100
   def f(self):
       print("f function in class a")
class b(a):
   y=200
   def f(self):
       print("f function in class b")
class c(a):
   z=300
   def f(self):
       print("f function in class c")
class d(b,c):
   p=500
   def f(self):
       print("f function in class d")
obj1=d()
obj1.f()
print("base classes=",obj1.__class__.__bases__)
```

Output

```
D:\PythonPrograms>python b2.py
f function in class d
base classes= (<class '__main__.b'>, <class
'__main__.c'>)
```

In the above program, f() method is derived from class "a" to classes "b" and "c" and further to class "d". In class "d", this method is overridden and when the method is called then the new definition is executed.

```
class a:
    x=100
    def f(self):
        print("f function in class a")
class b(a):
    y=200
    def f(self):
        print("f function in class b")
class c(a):
    z=300
    def f(self):
        print("f function in class c")
class d(b,c):
    p=500
obj1=d()
obj1.f()
print("base classes= ",obj1.__class__.__bases__)
```

Output

```
D:\PythonPrograms>python b2.py
f function in class b
base classes= (<class '__main__.b'>, <class
'__main__.c'>)
```

In the definition of class "d", the base classes are specified in the order of "b" and then "c". So, when the method is called, the method in class "b" is executed. Python overcomes this problem by providing a facility to change the order of classes in the inheritance definition. The new order should be given to **__bases__** class attribute.

```
class a:
    x=100
    def f(self):
        print("f function in class a")
class b(a):
    y=200
    def f(self):
        print("f function in class b")
class c(a):
    z=300
    def f(self):
        print("f function in class c")
class d(b,c):
    p=500
    def r(self,parent1,parent2):
self.__class__.__bases__=(parent2,parent1)
obj1=d()
obj1.r(b,c)
obj1.f()
print("base classes= ",obj1.__class__.__bases__)
```

Output

```
D:\PythonPrograms>python b2.py
f function in class c
base classes= (<class '__main__.c'>, <class
'__main__.b'>)
```

10.13 Composition or Containership or Complex Object

Composition allows defining a class with objects of other classes. For example, in class 'a' definition, if objects of class 'b' are included then it is called as "composition". In this case, class 'a' is called as container class and class 'b' is called as content class. The object of the container class is called as complex object.

```
class a:
    def __init__(self,m):
        self.x=m
    def getx(self):
        return(self.x)
```

```
class a:
    def __init__(self,m):
        self.x=m
    def getx(self):
        return(self.x)
```

Output

```
D:\PythonPrograms>python b2.py
15
```

In the above program, the class 'a' is called content class and class 'b' is called container class. If the object of the container class is deleted then the object of the content class will also be deleted.

10.14 Abstract Classes and Interfaces

Abstract class is a class which does not allow the creation of objects. The abstract class should contain abstract method. The definition of the abstract method is not provided in the abstract class. Itis provided in the implanting subclass. In Python, the "abc" module provides support for the abstract class. To declare a method as an abstract method **@abstractmethod** statement is used. In Python, the interface can be defined with abstract class only.

```
fromabc import abstractmethod
class a:
    @abstractmethod
    def getx(self): pass
class b(a):
    def getx(self):
        print("abstract method is implemented in sub class")
obj2=b()
obj2.getx()
```

Output

```
D:\PythonPrograms>python b2.py
abstract method is implemented in sub class
```

In the above example, class "a" is considered as abstract class or interface. Class "b" is implementing the interface. The **getx()** method is the abstract method in the abstract class and it does not have any definition. Thus, the definition of the abstract method is provided in the implanting class "b".

10.15 Metaclass

The meta class is the class of all the classes. In general,**type()** function returns the type as "class" whereas with the metaclass feature, the **type()** function returns the metaclass name as its response. It contains **new()** and **__init__()** methods.

```
class abc:
    def __init__(self):
        pass
class pqr(type):
    pass
class xyz(metaclass=pqr):
    def __init__(self):
        pass
print(type(abc))
print(type(xyz))
```

Output

```
D:\PythonPrograms>python b2.py
<class 'type'>
<class '__main__.pqr'>
```

10.16 Operator Overloading

Common operator overloading methods in Python includes indexing and slicing, iterable objects, attribute access, string representation, right-side and in-places uses, call expressions, comparisons, Boolean test and object destruction.In Python programming, all operators are executed by using magic function. The magic method is a special method used to perform operator overloading. It is also called as **dunder method**. For each operator, the Python interpreter will execute the corresponding function. The magic function for the "+" operator syntax is given below.

```
object.__add__(self, other)
```

For example "a+b" statement is converted into
a.__add__(self,b)
a and b are considered as number objects.

Other methods are **__sub__**, **__mul__** and **__div__**. To overload the operators in Python, we can provide new definition for the corresponding magic method. An example code for adding two class objects is given below.

```
class ex:
    def __init__(self,a=0):
        self.var1=a
    def __add__(self,obj2):
        return self.var1+obj2.var1
    def disp(self):
        print("The value of var1= ",self.var1)
x=ex(100)
y=ex(200)
x.disp()
y.disp()
z=x+y
print("The value of overloaded + operator= ",z)
```

Output

```
D:\PythonPrograms>python a1.py
The value of var1= 100
The value of var1= 200
The value of overloaded + operator= 300
```

With the help of operator overloading, the user can provide multiple definitions for the same operator. Thus, operator overloading is one of the ways to implement polymorphism in Python. This type of polymorphism is called as "adhoc polymorphism".

Example **1**

```
class ex:
    def __init__(self):
        self.var1=[10,20]
def __add__(self,obj2):
    l=list()
    for i in range(0,len(self.var1)):
        l.append(self.var1[i]+obj2.var1[i])
    return(l)
    def disp(self):
        print("The value of var1= ",self.var1)
x=ex()
y=ex()
x.disp()
y.disp()
z=x+y
print("The value of overloaded + operator= ",z)
```

Output

```
D:\PythonPrograms>python b2.py
The value of var1= [10, 20]
The value of var1= [10, 20]
The value of overloaded + operator= [20, 40]
```

Example 2

```
class ex:
    def __init__(self,a):
        self.var1=a
    def __add__(self,obj2):
        return(self.var1+" "+obj2.var1)
    def disp(self):
        print("The value of var1= ",self.var1)
x=ex(«good»)
y=ex(«morning»)
x.disp()
y.disp()
z=x+y
print("The value of overloaded + operator= ",z)
```

Output

```
D:\PythonPrograms>python b2.py
The value of var1= good
The value of var1= morning
The value of overloaded + operator= good morning
```

10.16.1 Reverse adding

During operator overloading, the overloaded operator can work in the order specified in its definition. For example, if "+" operator is overloaded with `__add__()` method, then the overloaded operator can work according to its definition only. If A and B are two objects, then `__add__()` is used to perform the A+B operation by its method definition. In this case, the overloaded operator with `__add__()` is not responsible for performing the reverse operation B+A.

```
class ex:
    def __init__(self,a):
        self.var1=a
    def __add__(self,a):
        return(self.var1+a)
    def disp(self):
        print("The value of var1= ",self.var1)
x=ex(10)
x.disp()
z=x+2
print("The value of overloaded + operator= ",z)
m=2+x
print("The value of overloaded + operator= ",z)
```

Output

```
D:\PythonPrograms>python b2.py
The value of var1= 10
The value of X+2 = 12
Traceback (most recent call last):
    File "b2.py", line 19, in <module>
        m=2+x
TypeError: unsupported operand type(s) for +: 'int'
and
'ex'
```

In the above program, the value '2' is added to the member of object 'x" (x+2). So the `__add__()` definition contains code for object+2, whereas when an attempt is made to perform 2+x, it raises an error.

Python programming supports the reverse operation of the overloaded operator with various functions. To perform the reverse addition operation `__radd__()` method should be used.

```
class ex:
    def __init__(self,a):
        self.var1=a
    def __add__(self,a):
        return(self.var1+a)
    def __radd__(self,a):
        return(self.var1+a)
    def disp(self):
        print("The value of var1= ",self.var1)
x=ex(10)
```

```
y=ex(20)
x.disp()
y.disp()
z=x+2
print("The value of X+2 = ",z)
m=2+x
print("The value of 2+X= ",z)
```

Output

```
D:\PythonPrograms>python b2.py
The value of var1= 10
The value of var1= 20
The value of X+2 = 12
The value of 2+X= 12
```

10.16.2 getitem() and setitem()

Python programming supports two built-in functions, **getitem()** and **setitem()**. The **getitem(listobj,index)** is used to return the element in the input list at the index position. The **setitem(listobj,index,value)** is used to assign the index position of the list to the value. Python programming allows overloading these two built-in functions. With this overloading, these two functions can be applied to class objects also.

```
class ex:
    def __init__(self,a):
        self.var1=a
    def __getitem__(self,a):
        print("the item at ",a+1," position is= ",self.var1[a])
    def __setitem__(self,a,b):
        self.var1[a]=b
    def disp(self):
        print("The value of var1= ",self.var1)
x=ex([10,20])
x.disp()
x[0]
x[1]=100
x.disp()
```

Output

```
D:\PythonPrograms>python b2.py
The value of var1= [10, 20]
the item at 1 position is= 10
The value of var1= [10, 100]
```

10.16.3 Membership operators

Python programming contains two membership operators. These are operators used to check whether or not the given element is a member of the input set of elements. The two membership operators are "in" and "not in". These two operators can also be overloaded for the objects. For overloading the membership operators, **__contains__()** method should be defined in the class.

```
class ex:
    def __init__(self,a):
        self.var1=a
    def __contains__(self,b):
        if(b in self.var1):
            return(True)
        else:
            return(False)
    def disp(self):
        print("The value of var1= ",self.var1)
x=ex([10,20,30])
x.disp()
print(30 in x)
print(10 not in x)
```

Output

```
D:\PythonPrograms>python b2.py
The value of var1= [10, 20, 30]
True
False
```

10.16.4 Miscellaneous functions

Various miscellaneous functions can also be overloaded in Python programming.

1. The **abs()** function is used to return the absolute value. This function can be overloaded with the **__abs__()** method.

```
class ex:
    def __init__(self,a):
        self.var1=a
    def __abs__(self):
        for i in range(0,len(self.var1)):
            self.var1[i]=abs(self.var1[i])
    def disp(self):
        print("The value of var1= ",self.var1)
x=ex([-10, -20])
x.disp()
abs(x)
x.disp()
```

Output

```
D:\PythonPrograms>python b2.py
The value of var1= [-10, -20]
The value of var1= [10, 20]
```

2. The **float()** function is used to convert the integer argument to float type. The **__float__()** is used to overload the **float()** function.

```
class ex:
    def __init__(self,a):
        self.var1=a
    def __float__(self):
        return(float(self.var1))
    def disp(self):
        print("The value of var1= ",self.var1)
x=ex(3)
x.disp()
print(float(x))
```

Output

```
D:\PythonPrograms>python b2.py
The value of var1= 3
3.0
```

3. The **pow(a,b)** function is used to compute a^b. The **__pow__()** is used to overload the **pow()** function.

```
class ex:
    def __init__(self,a):
        self.var1=a
    def __pow__(self,a):
        for i in range(0,len(self.var1)):
            self.var1[i]=pow(self.var1[i],a)
    def disp(self):
        print("The value of var1= ",self.var1)
x=ex([3, 4])
x.disp()
pow(x,2)
x.disp()
```

Output

```
D:\PythonPrograms>python b2.py
The value of var1= [3, 4]
The value of var1= [9, 16]
```

4. Python programming has function call operator. This operator can be overloaded with the **__call__()**. For each function call of the object, this overloaded method can be executed.

```
class ex:
    def __init__(self,a):
        self.var1=a
    def __pow__(self,a):
        for i in range(0,len(self.var1)):
            self.var1[i]=pow(self.var1[i],a)
    def disp(self):
        print("The value of var1= ",self.var1)
    def __call__(self,a,b=0):
        print("the __call__() is called")
x=ex(3)
x.disp()
x(1)
x(1,2)
```

Output

```
D:\PythonPrograms>python b2.py
The value of var1= 3
the __call__() is called
the __call__() is called
```

10.17 Garbage Collection

In Python, when the object is initialized memory is allocated automatically. The de-allocation of memory is also automatic in Python. For this, it uses two types of techniques. They are

- Reference counting

In reference counting, a counter is maintained for each object. If any one of the other object refers to the current object, then the current object counter is incremented. When reference to the current object is removed, then its counter is decremented. If the counter value is zero, then automatically the corresponding object is de-allocated. Though the usage of this process is efficient, it suffers from the problem of reference cycle, where there is a dependency among the objects and when there is strong referencing, they cannot be de-allocated.

- Garbage collection

To overcome the problem of reference cycle, garbage collection is used. In Python, the threshold value for garbage collection process is predefined. If the difference value between the allocated and de-allocated objects is greater than the threshold, then garbage collection is executed automatically. In Python "gc" module is used for performing the garbage collection process.

10.18 Sample Programs

Program 1: Write a Python program to print "hello" world automatically when the object is created.

> Programming Tip:
>
> During the objection creation, constructor will be called.

```
class hello:
    def __init__(self):
        print("Hello World")
p1 = hello()
p2 = hello()
p3 = hello()
```

Output

```
D:\PythonPrograms>python a1.py
Hello World
Hello World
Hello World
```

Program 2: Write a Python program to print the docstring value of a class.

In a class, the docstrings are maintained with the """ and """. They can be accessed with the __doc__ member.

```
class ex:
    """this is docstringmemebr value"""
    x=100
    y="abadffa"
print("Member value of __doc__= ",ex.__doc__)
print("Member value of x= ",ex.x)
print("Member value of y= ",ex.y)
```

Output

```
D:\PythonPrograms>python a1.py
Member value of __doc__= this is docstringmemebr value
Member value of x= 100
Member value of y= abadffa
```

Program 3: Write a Python program to store the class method into another object.

In Python programming, an object used to store the class method reference is called as "method object".

> Programming Tip:
> Class definition contains members and methods.

```
class ex:
    def f1():
        print("This is class method")
a=ex.f1
a()
```

Output

```
D:\PythonPrograms>python a1.py
This is class method
```

Program 4: Write a Python program to develop single inheritance to derive the method.

> Programming Tip:
> The single inheritance will derive the properties of base class into derived class.

```
class a:
    x=200
    def disp(self):
        print("Properties of base class: ",self.x)
class b(a):
    y=300
    def f1(self):
        self.disp()
        print("Properties of subclass: ",self.y)
obj1=b()
obj1.f1()
```

Output

```
D:\PythonPrograms>python a1.py
Properties of base class: 200
Properties of subclass: 300
```

Program 5: Write a Python program to develop a method that can take any number of arguments.

```
class abc:
    def f1(self,*a):
        print("Received arguments: ",a)
x=abc()
x.f1()
x.f1(10)
x.f1(10,20)
```

Output

```
D:\PythonPrograms>python a1.py
Received arguments: ()
Received arguments: (10,)
Received arguments: (10, 20)
```

Program 6: Write a Python program for __eq__()

```
class ex:
    def __init__(self,arg):
        self.a=arg
    def __repr__(self):
        return("the object value is %s" %(self.a))
    def __eq__(self,other):
        return(self.a==other.a)
obj1=ex(300)
obj2=ex(400)
print(obj1)
print(obj2)
print(obj1==obj2)
```

Output

```
D:\PythonPrograms>python b2.py
the object value is 300
the object value is 400
False
```

Program 7: Write a Python program for __ne__()

```
class ex:
    def __init__(self,arg):
        self.a=arg
    def __repr__(self):
        return("the object value is %s" %(self.a))
    def __nq__(self,other):
        return(self.a!=other.a)
obj1=ex(300)
obj2=ex(400)
print(obj1)
print(obj2)
print(obj1!=obj2)
```

Output

```
D:\PythonPrograms>python b2.py
the object value is 300
the object value is 400
True
```

Program 8: Write a Python program for __lt__()

```
class ex:
    def __init__(self,arg):
        self.a=arg
    def __repr__(self):
        return("the object value is %s" %(self.a))
    def __lt__(self,other):
        return(self.a<other.a)
obj1=ex(300)
obj2=ex(400)
print(obj1)
print(obj2)
print(obj1<obj2)
```

Output

```
D:\PythonPrograms>python b2.py
the object value is 300
the object value is 400
True
```

Program 9: Write a Python program for __gt__()

```
class ex:
    def __init__(self,arg):
        self.a=arg
    def __repr__(self):
        return("the object value is %s" %(self.a))
    def __gt__(self,other):
        return(self.a>other.a)
obj1=ex(300)
obj2=ex(400)
print(obj1)
print(obj2)
print(obj1>obj2)
```

Output

```
D:\PythonPrograms>python b2.py
the object value is 300
the object value is 400
False
```

Program 10: Write a Python program for __le__()

```
class ex:
    def __init__(self,arg):
        self.a=arg
    def __repr__(self):
        return("the object value is %s" %(self.a))
    def __le__(self,other):
        return(self.a<=other.a)
obj1=ex(300)
obj2=ex(300)
print(obj1)
print(obj2)
print(obj1<=obj2)
```

Output

```
D:\PythonPrograms>python b2.py
the object value is 300
the object value is 300
True
```

Program 11: Write a Python program for __ge__()

```
class ex:
    def __init__(self,arg):
        self.a=arg
    def __repr__(self):
        return("the object value is %s" %(self.a))
    def __ge__(self,other):
        return(self.a>=other.a)
obj1=ex(300)
obj2=ex(200)
print(obj1)
print(obj2)
print(obj1>=obj2)
```

Output

```
D:\PythonPrograms>python b2.py
the object value is 300
the object value is 200
True
```

Program 12: Write a Python program to read the values of object properties and display them with the built in function.

```
class ex:
    def read(self):
        self.a=int(input("Enter the value of a:"))
        self.b=int(input("Enter the value of b:"))
obj1=ex()
obj1.read()
print(getattr(obj1,'a'))
print(getattr(obj1,'b'))
```

Output

```
D:\PythonPrograms>python b2.py
Enter the value of a:10
Enter the value of b:20
10
20
```

Program 13: Write a Python to addtwo complex numbers objects.

```
class ex:
    def __init__(self):
        self.c=0
        self.v=0
    def read(self):
        self.c=int(input("Enter the real part value:"))
        self.v=int(input("Enter the imaginary part value:"))
    def disp(self):
        print("The complex number: ",self.c,"+i",self.v)
    def __add__(self,m):
        x=ex()
        x.c=self.c+m.c
        x.v=self.v+m.v
```

```
return(x)
p=ex()
p.read()
q=ex()
q.read()
p.disp()
q.disp()
r=ex()
r=p+q
r.disp()
```

Output

```
D:\PythonPrograms>python b2.py
Enter the real part value:10
Enter the imaginary part value:5
Enter the real part value:3
Enter the imaginary part value:4
The complex number: 10 +i 5
The complex number: 3 +i 4
The complex number: 13 +i 9
```

Program 14: Write a Python to perform the subtraction operation on object.

```
class ex:
    def __init__(self,a):
        self.m=a
    def disp(self):
        print(self.m)
    def __sub__(self,n):
        return(self.m-n)
p=ex(100)
p.disp()
print(p-10)
```

Output

```
D:\PythonPrograms>python b2.py
100
90
```

Program 15: Write a Python to __mul__() for performing multiplication operation on object.

```
class ex:
    def __init__(self,a):
        self.m=a
    def disp(self):
        print(self.m)
    def __mul__(self,n):
        return(self.m*n)
p=ex(100)
p.disp()
print(p*50)
```

Output

```
D:\PythonPrograms>python b2.py
100
5000
```

Program 16: Write a Python to perform overload of the division operator.

```
class ex:
    def __init__(self,a):
        self.m=a
    def disp(self):
        print(self.m)
    def __floordiv__(self,n):
        return(self.m/n)
    def __truediv__(self,n):
        return(self.m/n)
p=ex(100)
p.disp()
print("floor div: ",p//50)
print("true div: ",p/25)
```

Output

```
D:\PythonPrograms>python b2.py
100
floor div: 2.0
true div: 4.0
```

Program 17: Write a Python to __and__().

```
class ex:
    def __init__(self,a):
        self.m=a
    def __and__(self,n):
        return(self.m and n)
p=ex(100)
print(p and 57)
print(p and 0)
```

Output

```
D:\PythonPrograms>python b2.py
57
0
```

Program 18: Write a Python program to perform += operator on an object.

```
class ex:
    def __init__(self,a):
        self.m=a
    def __iadd__(self,n):
        self.m+=n
        return self
    def disp(self):
        print(self.m)
p=ex(100)
p.disp()
p+=25
p.disp()
```

Output

```
D:\PythonPrograms>python b2.py
100
125
```

Program 19: Write a Python program to ** __ispow__()

```
class ex:
    def __init__(self,a):
        self.m=a
    def __ipow__(self,n):
        self.m**=n
        return self
    def disp(self):
        print(self.m)
p=ex(3)
p.disp()
p**=2
p.disp()
```

Output

```
D:\PythonPrograms>python b2.py
3
9
```

Program 20: Write a Python to override the disp() method in base and subclass.

```
class ex:
    def __init__(self,a):
        self.m=a
    def disp(self):
        print(self.m)
classab(ex):
    def __init__(self,x,y):
        self.m=x
        self.n=y
    def disp(self):
        print(self.m, " ",self.n)
obj=ab(10,50)
obj.disp()
```

Output

```
10 50
```

Program 21: Write a Python to overload disp() method with two definitions.

```
class ex:
    def __init__(self,a):
        self.m=a
    def disp(self,n=None):
        if n is None:
            print(self.m)
        else:
            print(self.m, " ",n)
obj=ex(10)
obj.disp()
obj.disp(50)
```

Output

```
D:\PythonPrograms>python b2.py
10
10 50
```

Program 22: Write a Python to perform reverse subtraction.

```
class ex:
    def __init__(self,a):
        self.m=a
    def disp(self):
        print(self.m)
    def __sub__(self,n):
        return(self.m-n)
    def __rsub__(self,n):
        return(self.m-n)
p=ex(100)
p.disp()
print(p-5)
print(5-10)
```

Output

```
D:\PythonPrograms>python b2.py
100
95
-5
```

Program 23: Write a Python to perform reverse multiplication.

```
class ex:
    def __init__(self,a):
        self.m=a
    def disp(self):
        print(self.m)
    def __mul__(self,n):
        return(self.m*n)
    def __rmul__(self,n):
        return(self.m*n)
p=ex(100)
p.disp()
print(p*5)
print(5*p)
```

Output

```
D:\PythonPrograms>python b2.py
100
500
500
```

Program 24: Write a Python to compute the area of a shape by using interface.

```
fromabc import abstractmethod
class ab:
    @abstractmethod
    def area(self): pass
class square(ab):
    def __init__(self,a=0):
```

```
        self.x=a
    def area(self):
        print("Area of square= ",self.x*self.x)
class rect(ab):
    def __init__(self,a=0,b=0):
        self.x=a
        self.y=b
    def area(self):
        print("Area of rectangle= ",self.x*self.y)
s=square(5)
s.area()
t=rect(3,10)
t.area()
```

Output

```
D:\PythonPrograms>python b2.py
Area of square= 25
Area of rectangle= 30
```

Glossary

- Encapsulation means wrapping of data and the functions
- Data abstraction represents only the highlighted features of the object by suppressing the internal details.
- With the polymorphism concept, a single entity can act in multiple forms.
- Inheritance allows a class to derive the properties of another class

Summary

- Class is used to wrap both data and code at a single place. With this, Python supports encapsulation property.
- Memory will be created for objects in a class.
- The class consists of members and methods.
- The properties of one class can be derived into another class by using inheritance concept.
- Polymorphism can enable a single entity to act in multiple forms.

Multiple Choice Questions

1. Self pointer in Python is similar to
   (a) **super** in Java
   (b) **virtual** in Java
   (c) **this** pointer in Java
   (d) None of the above
2. Which function will be automatically executed when the object is created?
   (a) **__run__()**
   (b) **__init__()**
   (c) **__void__()**
   (d) **__auto__()**
3. What are the default arguments for **__init__**() method?
   (a) self (b) self, void
   (c) void (d) void, void
4. Which will create an empty object?
   (a) Class (b) Method
   (c) Member (d) Instantiation
5. Class variables are
   (a) void (b) non-void
   (c) static (d) non-static
6. Which keyword is used to delete an object?
   (a) **del**
   (b) **remove**
   (c) **clear**
   (d) None of the above.
7. The static variable can be accessed with
   (a) method name
   (b) variable name
   (c) object name
   (d) class name
8. In Python, destructor is implemented with
   (a) **del**
   (b) **remove**

(c) clear
(d) None of the above.

9. In method overriding, which is correct?
(a) The definition of base class will override the sub class.
(b) Both the definitions are available in base class.
(c) The definition of subclass will override the base class.
(d) None of the above.

10. Which of the following supports data hiding?
(a) @@ (b) @
(c) _ (d) __

11. Python supports
(a) procedure oriented programming
(b) object oriented programming
(c) Both (a) and (b)
(d) None of the above

12. Object oriented approach follows?
(a) Top-down approach
(b) Bottom-up approach
(c) Both (a) and (b)
(d) None of the above

13. Procedure-oriented approach follows
(a) Top-down approach
(b) Bottom-up approach
(c) Both (a) and (b).
(d) None of the above.

14. Procedure-oriented approach focuses on
(a) data
(b) code
(c) both data and code
(d) None of the above.

15. Object oriented approach focuses on
(a) data
(b) code
(c) both data and code
(d) None of the above.

16. Wrapping of data and code into a single entity is called as
(a) Abstraction
(b) Inheritance
(c) Polymorphism
(d) Encapsulation

17. Highlighting only the features by suppressing the internal details is called as
(a) Abstraction
(b) Inheritance
(c) Polymorphism
(d) Encapsulation

18. Which of the following features allow an entity to act in multiple forms?
(a) Abstraction
(b) Inheritance
(c) Polymorphism
(d) Encapsulation

19. Which of the following features can derive the properties of one class to another class?
(a) Abstraction
(b) Inheritance
(c) Polymorphism
(d) Encapsulation

20. In Python, data encapsulation is achieved with
(a) Class
(b) Object
(c) Attributes
(d) Methods

21. The class contains
(a) data
(b) functions
(c) both data and functions
(d) None of the above.

22. Memory is allocated for
(a) class
(b) object
(c) both class and object.
(d) None of the above.

23. The keyword for defining a class is
(a) def
(b) class
(c) assign
(d) None of the above.

24. With attribute referencing, the class properties can be accessed with
(a) property value
(b) property name
(c) class name with property
(d) class name itself

25. The functions defined within a class are called as
(a) members
(b) methods
(c) submembers
(d) submethods

26. In case of class instantiation, the minimum number of arguments of a function is
(a) 1 (b) 2 (c) 3 (d) 4

27. self variable can access
(a) members
(b) methods

(c) both members and methods.
(d) None of the above.

28. How many copies of class variable are maintained in memory?
(a) 0 (b) 1
(c) 2 (d) Many

29. Which variable will be shared by all the instances?
(a) class (b) instance
(c) member (d) method

30. How many copies of instance variable are maintained in memory?
(a) 0 (b) 1
(c) 2 (d) Many

31. The class method contains which of the following argument?
(a) static (b) dynamic
(c) class itself (d) self

32. The instance method contains which of the following argument?
(a) static (b) dynamic
(c) class itself (d) self

33. The class variables are
(a) static (b) dynamic
(c) volatile (d) non-volatile

34. The static method should be defined with which statement?
(a) !staticmethod
(b) &staticmethod
(c) @staticmethod
(d) *staticmethod

35. In Python, data hiding is supported with?
(a) _ (b) __ (c) " (d) ""

36. The hidden methods are accessible
(a) within the class
(b) outside the class
(c) within the function
(d) outside the function

37. The first argument of the constructor is
(a) none (b) self
(c) int (d) float

38. In Python, the operators are executed by using?
(a) self function
(b) more function
(c) less function
(d) magic function

39. Which of the following are magic functions?
(a) __add__ (b) __sub__
(c) __mul__ (d) All the above.

40. Which of the following module is responsible for performing garbage collection process?
(a) gc
(b) gm
(c) gcc
(d) None of the above.

Fill in the Blanks

1. When compared to procedure oriented approach, ______________ is efficient.

2. Python supports ______________, ______________ features.

3. Data is focused on in ______________ approach.

4. Code is focused on in ______________ approach.

5. Class supports ______________ feature of OOPs.

6. A class contains ______________, ______________

7. In Python, by using ______________, data and code can be grouped into a single place.

8. A single entity can act in multiple forms by using ______________.

9. Memory will not be created for ______________.

10. For allocating memory, ______________ should be created.

11. The data in a class is called as ______________.

12. Objects can be created by using ______________ and ______________.

13. An empty object is created by using ______________.

14. With self pointer, the properties of ______________ can be accessible.

15. There are ______________ types of members.

16. There are ______________ types of methods.

17. The static method should have ______________ arguments.

18. ______________ statement is used for defining static method.

19. del keyword is used for ______________.

20. ______________ method is called as constructor in Python.

21. ________________ methods can be accessible only within the class.
22. ________________ methods can be accessible within the class and outside the class.
23. The private member contains __________ symbol.
24. The __________________ built-in function is used to get the class attribute value.
25. The __________________ built-in function is used to set the class attribute value.
26. The _______________ built-in attribute returns all the base classes.
27. The multi-path inheritance suffers with ______________________ problem.
28. The abstract class contains ____________________.
29. The ____________ module supports abstract class.
30. The ___________ statement is used to define the abstract method.
31. The ______________ is another name of abstract class.
32. The definition of the methods in interface should be implemented in ____________.
33. The __________ class contains object of another class.
34. __________________ is a parent class of other classes.
35. __________ allows providingadhoc polymorphism.
36. In Python overloading __________, _____________ is allowed.
37. ___________ allows providing multiple definitions within a class.
38. ___________ allows providing multiple definitions with inheritance.

State True/False

1. Method overriding allows the same method in both subclass and base class.
2. The definition of the base class is not overridden by the subclass definition.
3. The subclass object points to subclass definition only.
4. Operators cannot be overloaded in Python.
5. Operators can be overloaded with magic methods.
6. `__xyz__()` is a magic method.
7. Reference counting is one of the garbage collection processes in Python.
8. Garbage collection process of Python will overcome the problems in reference counting.
9. The "gc" module supports reference counting process.
10. The deallocation process is automatic in Python.
11. Indexing is an operator overloading method.
12. Slicing is not an operator overloading method.
13. Multilevel inheritance derives the properties of one class to another class and further can be inherited.
14. Multiple inheritance derives the properties of one base class to subclass.
15. In case of multiple inheritance, multiple base classes are separated with ":".
16. In single inheritance, only one level of inheritance is allowed.
17. `subclass(baseclass)` will perform the inheritance.
18. The constructor is used to delete the objects.
19. The members of the class can be initialized with constructor.
20. Other than first argument, the remaining arguments should be passed to constructor during the object creation.
21. `__init__()` is a constructor.
22. `__init__()` requires two arguments
23. Self argument should be passed to `__init__()`.
24. In Python, destructor can be defined.
25. With `del()`, destructor can be defined.
26. Default arguments are not allowed in method definition.
27. `__dict__` attribute represents the dictionary with the class namespace.
28. [] is not used for referencing.

29. The current module is represented with __module__ attribute.
30. The class method should contain the class itself as an argument.
31. The class variable maintains multiple single copy of the data.
32. The **delattr()** function deletes the given attribute in the given class.
33. Private attributes are declared with **.
34. **__repr__()** is a method used to return the object in printable format.
35. Double underscore provides data hiding.
36. The hidden methods can be accessible outside the class.
37. Method overriding allows the same method in both subclass and base class.
38. In single inheritance, the subclass can derive the properties of only one base class.
39. Diamond problem occurs in single inheritance
40. Python class allows creation of complex object
41. In Python, the "bca" module provides support for the abstract class
42. **__add__()** overloads the addition operator
43. **__radd__()** provides reverse addition feature
44. **__contains__()** is used to overload the membership operator

Find the Output

1.
```
class x:
    a=100
print(x.a)
```
2.
```
class x:
    def b():
        a=100
print(x.b())
```
3.
```
class x:
    def b():
        print(100)
print(x.b())
```
4.
```
class x:
    a=40
z=x()
z.a=50
print(z.a)
```
5.
```
class x:
    def y():
        print(50)
z=x()
print(z.y)
```
6.
```
class x:
    def y(x):
        print("50")
z=x()
z.y()
```
7.
```
class x:
    a=50
    def y(self):
        print(self.a)
z=x()
z.y()
```
8.
```
class x:
    a=50
p=x()
q=x()
p.a=40
q.a=60
print(x.a,p.a,q.a)
```
9.
```
class x:
    a=[]
    def __init__():
        a=50
print(x.a)
```
10.
```
class x:
    def __init__(self):
        self.a=50
y=x()
print(y.a)
```
11.
```
class x:
    _a=100
b=x()
```

```
print(b._a)
```

12.
```
class x:
    a=100
class y(x):
    a=10
b=y()
print(b.a)
```

13.
```
class x:
    def __init__(self):
        self.a=list()
b=x()
print(b)
```

14.
```
class x:
    def __init__(self):
        self.a=list()
b=x()
print(len(b.a))
```

15.
```
class x:
    def __init__(self):
        self.a=10
        self.__b=20
b=x()
print(b.a)
```

16.
```
class x:
def __init__(self):
        self.a=10
        self.__b=20
        print(self.__b)
b=x()
```

17.
```
class x:
def __init__(self):
        self.a=10
b=x()
print(x.__dict__)
```

18.
```
class x:
    def __init__(self):
        self.a=10
b=x()
print(x.__doc__)
```

19.
```
class x:
    def __init__(self):
        self.a=10
b=x()
print(x.__name__)
```

20.
```
class x:
    def __init__(self):
        self.a=10
b=x()
print(x.__module__)
```

21.
```
class x:
    def __init__(self):
        self.a=10
class y(x):
        pass
print(y.__bases__)
```

22.
```
class x:
    """This is class x"""
print(x.__doc__)
```

23.
```
class x:
    pass
if(hasattr(x,'z')):
        print("class x has z attribute")
else:
        print("class x has no z attribute")
```

24.
```
class x:
    z=100
n=getattr(x,'z')
if(n):
        print("value=",n)
else:
        print("class x has no z attribute")
```

25.
```
class x:
    z=100
setattr(x,'z',500)
if(x.z):
        print("value=",x.z)
else:
        print("class x has no z attribute")
```

26. class x:

```
    a=[100]
        def __len__(self):
return(len(self.a)+len(self.a))
m=x()
print(len(m))
```

27. class x:

```
    a=[100,200]
    def __gt__(self,b):
        return(self.a[0]>b.a[1])
m=x()
n=x()
print(m>n)
```

28. class x:

```
    a=[100,200]
    def __lt__(self,b):
        return(self.a[0]<b.a[1])
m=x()
n=x()
print(m<n)
```

29. class x:

```
    a=[100,200]
    def __eq__(self,b):
        return(self.a[0]==b.a[1])
m=x()
n=x()
print(m==n)
```

30. class x:

```
    def __init__(self,a=None):
        if(a==None):
            self.m=10
        else:
            self.m=10
            self.n=20
l=x()
print(hasattr(l,'n'))
```

31. class x:

```
    def __init__(self,a=None):
        if(a==None):
            self.m=10
        else:
            self.m=10
            self.n=20
l=x(100)
print(hasattr(l,'n'))
```

32. class x:

```
    def __init__(self,a=None):
        if(a!=None):
            self.m=a.m
            self.n=a.n
        else:
            self.m=10
            self.n=20
    def d(self):
        print(self.m, self.n)
l=x()
p=x(l)
l.d()
p.d()
```

33. class x:

```
    a=100
class y():
    b=200
    c=x()
    def f1(self):
        print(self.b, self.c.a)
l=y()
l.f1()
```

34. class ex:

```
    b=100
    @staticmethod
    def disp():
        print(ex.b)
b=ex()
b.disp()
```

Find the Error

1.
```
class x:
    a=100
print(a)
```

2.
```
class x:
    def b():
        print(a=100)
print(x.b())
```

3.
```
class x:
        a=40
z=x(400)
z.a=50
print(z.a)
```

4.
```
class x:
    def y():
        print(50)
z=x()
print(z.y())
```

5.
```
class x:
    def y(x):
        print(self)
z=x()
z.y()
```

6.
```
class x:
    a=50
    def y(x):
        print(self.a)
z=x()
z.y()
```

7.
```
class x:
        a=40
        __b=50
print(x.a)
print(x.b)
```

8.
```
class x:
def __init__(self):
        a=50
print(x.a)
```

9.
```
class x:
    def __init__(self):
        self.a=50
y=x(300)
print(y.a)
```

10.
```
class x:
    a=50
class b(x):
    def xy(self):
        print(self.a)
b.xy()
```

11.
```
class x:
    __init__():
        pass
o=x()
```

12.
```
class x:
    __init__(self):
        pass
o=x()
```

13.
```
class x:
    def __init__(self):
        self.a=10
    def __add_(self,b):
        return(self.a+b)
o=x()
print(o+2)
```

14.
```
class a:
    @abstractmethod
    def b(self):
        pass
```

15.
```
class x:
    __a=100
b=x()
print(b.__a)
```

16.
```
class x:
    __a=100
b=x()
print(len(b))
```

17.
```
class x:
    a=100
class y(x):

b=y()
print(b.a)
```

18.
```
class x:
    a=100
class y():
    c=80
b=y()
print(b.a)
```

Long Answer Questions

1. What are various OOP principles? Explain about them.
2. How data encapsulation is achieved in Python?
3. With an example, discuss in detail about inheritance.
4. List the drawbacks of conventional programming. Explain how object oriented programming overcomes them.
5. With an example, clearly explain encapsulation in Python.
6. Discuss in detail about constructor with an example.
7. What is inheritance? Present the advantages and disadvantages of inheritance.
8. Explain the role of self pointer in Python with a programming example.
9. What is method overloading? What are the principles of method overloading in Python?
10. What is method overriding? How method overriding is different than method overloading?
11. Explain single inheritance with schematic representation?
12. Explain multilevel inheritance with a schematic representation.
13. Explain multiple inheritance with a schematic representation.
14. Explain the multipath inheritance with a schematic representation.
15. What is abstract class? Discuss in detail about the importance of abstract class.
16. What are the drawbacks of monolithic, procedural and structural programming languages?
17. Differentiate between method and function.
18. How does Python support the definition of parameterized constructor? Discuss with an example.
19. Explain containership with an example.
20. Write a detailed note on garbage collection in Python?

Short Answer Questions

1. Does Python support data hiding? Justify your answer.
2. How can an object be deleted?
3. Differentiate between class and instance variables.
4. What is a class? Give examples.
5. What is a constructor?
6. Define inheritance.
7. Define data hiding.
8. What is a destructor?
9. Differentiate between class and object.
10. List some of the operators that can be overloaded in Python.
11. What is the usage of double score?
12. Define adhoc polymorphism.
13. How does Python support destructor?
14. What happens if all the members of the class are private?
15. What is containership?
16. Give the importance of meta class.
17. List any four magic methods.
18. Discuss about reverse multiplication.
19. How many methods should be defined for overloading a division operator?
20. List the methods for overloading compound assignment operators.

Exercise Programs

1. Write a Python program to handle complex number addition and subtraction by using classand integer number objects?
2. Write a Python program to overload {-,* and /} operators.
3. Write a Python program to implement encapsulation.
4. Write Python program to implement data hiding.
5. Write a Python program to overload + operator to add matrices.
6. Write a Python program to overload * operator to multiply matrices.
7. Write a Python program to find the area of a circle, rectangle and triangle using method overloading.
8. Write a Python program that defines a class and declare an array of objects to that class.
9. Write a Python program to add two complex numbers by using class.
10. Write a Python program for calculating the total marks and grade of 60 students in a class.
11. Write a Python program to initialize objects for a fixed deposit system.
12. Write a Python program to illustrate the nesting of a method.
13. Write a Python program to overload the data conversion functions.
14. Write a Python program to define the copy constructor.
15. Write a Python program to demonstrate the usage of static method.
16. Write a Python programto print the class properties.
17. Write a Python program to print the instance properties.
18. Write a Python programto print the reverse of object properties.
19. Write a Python program to swap two numbers by using method.
20. Write a Python programto read 5 subject marks of 5 students and print the total marks of each student.
21. Write a Python program to find the area and perimeter of square and circle using interface.
22. Write a Python program to use basic overloading methods.
23. Write a Python program to use self variable in methods.
24. Write a Python program to demonstrate the use of subclass.
25. Write a Python programto demonstrate the use of inner class.
26. Write a Python program to implement inheritance and demonstrate the use of method overriding.
27. Write a Python program to create a sales tax calculator class and perform various operations.
28. Write a Python program to create a room object and initialize its properties length, breadth and height with default values during the creation of object.
29. Write a Python programto perform constructor overloading.
30. Write a Python program to create **vehicle** class and derive its properties into **bike** class.
31. Write a Python programto create an animal interface and implement it with **tiger** class.
32. Write a Python program to perform various operations on a bank account.
33. Write a Python program to perform base class initialization.
34. Write a Python programpass and return from method.
35. Write a Python programto read and add two distances.
36. Write a Python program to create a class for employee to get and print the details of employee.
37. Write a Python programto create class to read different times.
38. Write a Python program to create a class to add times.
39. Write a Python program to create a class to read date and print the week day.
40. Write a Python program to overload the right-shift operator.
41. Write a Python program to overload the left-shift operator.

42. Write a Python program to overload the AND operator.
43. Write a Python program to overload the OR operator.
44. Write a Python program to overload the INVERT operator.
45. Write a Python program to overload the XOR operator
46. Write a Python program to overload the compound subtraction operator.
47. Write a Python program to overload the compound multiplication operator.
48. Write a Python program to overload the compound division operator.
49. Write a Python program to overload the compound mod operator.
50. Write a Python program to overload the compound right-shift operator.
51. Write a Python program to overload the compound left-shift operator
52. Write a Python program to overload the compound AND operator.
53. Write a Python program to overload the compound OR operator.
54. Write a Python program to overload the compound XOR operator.
55. Write a Python program to overload the compound invert operator.
56. Write a Python program to overload the __main__.
57. Write a Python program to create a college container with faculty content object.
58. Write a Python program to change the meta class name as attribute name.
59. Write a Python program to create two objects for a class and display total length by adding the length of all attributes in all objects.

Answers

Multiple Choice Questions

1. (c)	7. (d)	13. (a)	19. (b)	25. (b)	31. (c)	37. (b)
2. (b)	8. (a)	14. (b)	20. (a)	26. (a)	32. (d)	38. (d)
3. (a)	9. (c)	15. (a)	21. (c)	27. (c)	33. (a)	39. (d)
4. (d)	10. (d)	16. (d)	22. (a)	28. (b)	34. (c)	40. (a)
5. (c)	11. (c)	17. (a)	23. (b)	29. (a)	35. (b)	
6. (a)	12. (b)	18. (c)	24. (d)	30. (d)	36. (a)	

Fill in the Blanks

1. object oriented approach
2. Procedure oriented, object oriented
3. object oriented
4. procedure oriented
5. encapsulation
6. members and functions
7. class
8. polymorphism
9. class definition
10. object
11. Members
12. attribute referencing, Instantiation.
13. instantiation
14. class
15. two
16. two
17. zero
18. deleting the object.
20. __init__()
21. Private
22. Public
23. __
24. hasattr()
25. setattr()
26. __bases__
27. diamond
28. abstract method
29. abc
30. @abstractmethod
31. interface
32. subclass
33. container
34. Metaclass
35. Operator overloading
36. operator, method
37. Method overloading
38. Method overriding

State True/False

1. True
2. False
3. True
4. False
5. True
6. False
7. True
8. True
9. False
10. True
11. True
12. False
13. True
14. False
15. False
16. True
17. True
18. False
19. True
20. True
21. True
22. False
23. True
24. True
25. true
26. False
27. True
28. False
29. True
30. True
31. False
32. True
33. False
34. True
35. True
36. False
37. True
38. True
39. False
40. True
41. False
42. True
43. True
44. True

Find the Output

1. 100
2. None
3. 100
   None
4. 50
5. <bound method x.y of <__main__.x object at 0x02F3AA10>>
6. 50
7. 50
8. 50 40 60
9. []
10. 50
11. 100
12. 10
13. <__main__.x object at 0x02D32530>
14. 0
15. 10
16. 20
17. {'__module__': '__main__', '__init__': <function x.__init__ at 0x0145E660>, '__dict__': <attribute '__dict__' of 'x' objects>, '__weakref__': <attribute '__weakref__' of 'x' objects>, '__doc__': None}
18. None
19. x
20. __main__
21. (<class '__main__.x'>,)
22. This is class x
23. class x has no z attribute
24. value= 100
25. value= 500
26. 2
27. False
28. True
29. False
30. False
31. True
32. 10 20
    10 20
33. 200 100
34. 100

Find the Error

1. NameError: name 'a' is not defined
2. TypeError: 'a' is an invalid keyword argument for this function
3. TypeError: object() takes no parameters
4. TypeError: y() takes 0 positional arguments but 1 is given
5. NameError: name 'self' is not defined
6. NameError: name 'self' is not defined
7. AttributeError: type object 'x' has no attribute 'b'
8. AttributeError: type object 'x' has no attribute 'a'
9. TypeError: __init__() takes 1 positional argument but 2 is given
10. TypeError: xy() missing 1 required positional argument: 'self'
11. invalid syntax
12. invalid syntax
13. unsupported operand type(s) for +: 'x' and 'int'
14. name 'abstractmethod' is not defined
15. 'x' object has no attribute '__a'
16. TypeError: object of type 'x' has no len()
17. IndentationError: expected an indented block
18. AttributeError: 'y' object has no attribute 'a'

CHAPTER 11 Packages

Python programming allows the data and code for outside the program by using module and package concepts. The present chapter discusses in detail about handling the packages in Python. For this, a package management system called "PIP" should be used.

11.1 Introduction to PIP

In Python, a module is a single python file that contains various definitions and executable statements. The package contains a group of module files. It also contains __init__.py file. A module contains multiple definitions and executable statements and can be written in a single file.

```
def x1():
    print("x1 function")
def x2():
    print("x2 function")
```

With the help of import statement, all the definitions and executable statements available in a module can be used by other programs. But, with module, only one file can be imported.

The dir(module) will give the list of methods and attributes of the given module.

```
>>> dir(sum)
['__call__', '__class__', '__delattr__', '__dir__',
'__doc__', '__eq__', '__format__', '__ge__', '__
getattribute__', '__gt__', '__hash__', '__init__', '__
init_subclass__', '__le__', '__lt__', '__module__',
'__name__', '__ne__', '__new__', '__qualname__', '__
reduce__', '__reduce_ex__', '__repr__', '__self__', '__
setattr__', '__sizeof__', '__str__', '__subclasshook__',
'__text_signature__']
```

To overcome this problem, packages are used. By using multiple modules, classes can be grouped into a single place. All the components of a package are thus placed in a single directory. The package directory should be differentiated from the ordinary directory. For this, the package directory contains __int__.py file. Every package directory contains this file.

11.2 Installing Packages via PIP

PIP stands for package installer for python.

- PIP is installed by using the following syntax
  python -m pip install -U pip setuptools

```
D:\PythonPrograms>python -m pip install -U pip setuptools
Requirement already up-to-date: pip in d:\python\python36-32\lib\site-packages
Collecting setuptools
    Downloading setuptools-35.0.2-py2.py3-none-any.whl (390kB)
        100%    | 399kB 16kB/s
Collecting appdirs>=1.4.0 (from setuptools)
    Downloading appdirs-1.4.3-py2.py3-none-any.whl
Collecting six>=1.6.0 (from setuptools)
    Downloading six-1.10.0-py2.py3-none-any.whl
Collecting packaging>=16.8 (from setuptools)
    Downloading packaging-16.8-py2.py3-none-any.whl
Collecting pyparsing (from packaging>=16.8->setuptools)
    Downloading pyparsing-2.2.0-py2.py3-none-any.whl (56kB)
        100%    |61kB 17kB/s
Installing collected packages: appdirs, six, pyparsing, packaging, setuptools
    Found existing installation: setuptools 28.8.0
        Uninstalling setuptools-28.8.0:
            Successfully uninstalled setuptools-28.8.0
Successfully installed appdirs-1.4.3 packaging-16.8 pyparsing-2.2.0 setuptools-35.0.2 six-1.10.0
```

- Download the “get-pip.py” file
- Run the “get-pip.py” file

```
D:\PythonPrograms>python get-pip.py
Requirement already up-to-date: pip in d:\python\python36-32\lib\site-packages
Collecting wheel
    Downloading wheel-0.29.0-py2.py3-none-any.whl (66kB)
        100%    |71kB 15kB/s
Installing collected packages: wheel
Successfully installed wheel-0.29.0
```

- Set the PATH variable to the pip PATH

```
D:\PythonPrograms>pip help
'pip' is not recognized as an internal or external command, operable program or batch file.
D:\PythonPrograms>echo %PATH%
C:\WINDOWS\system32;C:\WINDOWS;C:\WINDOWS\System32\Wbem;C:\WINDOWS\System32\
WindowsPowerShell\v1.0\;     D:\Python\Python36-32;C:\Users\T     SRIKANTH\AppData\Local\
Microsoft\WindowsApps;
D:\PythonPrograms>set PATH=%PATH%;D:\Python\Python36-32\Scripts
```

```
D:\PythonPrograms>pip help
Usage
pip <command> [options]
Commands
install                     Install packages.
download                    Download packages.
uninstall                   Uninstall packages.
freeze                      Output installed packages in requirements format.
list                        List installed packages.
show                        Show information about installed packages.
check                       Verify installed packages have compatible dependencies.
search                      Search PyPI for packages.
wheel                       Build wheels from your requirements.
hash                        Compute hashes of package archives.
completion                  A helper command used for command completion.
help                        Show help for commands.
```

```
General Options
-h, --help                    Show help.
--isolated                    Run pip in an isolated mode, ignoring environment variables and user
                              configuration.
-v, --verbose                 Give more output. Option is additive, and can be used up to 3 times.
-V, --version                 Show version and exit.
-q, --quiet                   Give less output. Option is additive, and can be used up to 3 times
                              (corresponding to WARNING, ERROR, and CRITICAL logging levels).
--log <path>                  Path to a verbose appending log.
--proxy <proxy>               Specify a proxy in the form [user:passwd@]proxy.server:port.
--retries <retries>           Maximum number of retries each connection should attempt (default 5
                              times).
--timeout <sec>               Set the socket timeout (default 15 seconds).
--exists-action <action>      Default action when a path already exists:
                              (s)witch, (i)gnore, (w)ipe, (b)ackup, (a)bort.
--trusted-host <hostname>     Mark this host as trusted, even though it does
                              not have valid or any HTTPS.
--cert <path>                 Path to alternate CA bundle.
--client-cert <path>          Path to SSL client certificate, a single file containing the private key
                              and the certificate in PEM format.
--cache-dir <dir>             Store the cache data in <dir>.
--no-cache-dir                Disable the cache.
--disable-pip-version-check
Do not periodically check PyPI to determine whether a new version of pip is available for
download. Implied with --no-index.
```

- Install the virtual environment

```
D:\PythonPrograms>pip install virtualenv
Collecting virtualenv
   Downloading virtualenv-15.1.0-py2.py3-none-any.whl (1.8MB)
      100%    1.8MB 17kB/s
Installing collected packages: virtualenv
Successfully installed virtualenv-15.1.0
```

```
D:\PythonPrograms>easy_install virtualenvwrapper-win
Searching for virtualenvwrapper-win
Reading https://pypi.python.org/simple/virtualenvwrapper-win/
Downloading https://pypi.python.org/packages/af/f1/
d2fbc0c65353e3aaa02dd414102158f097abe77c34df48e864ee7afef822/
virtualenvwrapper-win-1.2.1.zip#md5=26e16b4c64d2060198789d3f066247e4
Best match: virtualenvwrapper-win 1.2.1
Processing virtualenvwrapper-win-1.2.1.zip
Writing C:\Users\TSRIKA~1\AppData\Local\Temp\easy_install-czqh2hes\virtualenvwrapper-
win-1.2.1\setup.cfg
Running virtualenvwrapper-win-1.2.1\setup.py -q bdist_egg --dist-dir C:\Users\
TSRIKA~1\AppData\Local\Temp\easy_install-czqh2hes\virtualenvwrapper-win-1.2.1\
egg-dist-tmp-fd2_i702
warning: install_lib: 'build\lib' does not exist -- no Python modules to install
creating d:\python\python36-32\lib\site-packages\virtualenvwrapper_win-1.2.1-py3.6.egg
Extracting virtualenvwrapper_win-1.2.1-py3.6.egg to d:\python\python36-32\lib\site-packages
Adding virtualenvwrapper-win 1.2.1 to easy-install.pth file
Installing add2virtualenv.bat script to d:\python\python36-32\Scripts
Installing cd-.bat script to d:\python\python36-32\Scripts
Installing cdproject.bat script to d:\python\python36-32\Scripts
```

```
Installing cdsitepackages.bat script to d:\python\python36-32\Scripts
Installing cdvirtualenv.bat script to d:\python\python36-32\Scripts
Installing folder_delete.bat script to d:\python\python36-32\Scripts
Installing lssitepackages.bat script to d:\python\python36-32\Scripts
Installing lsvirtualenv.bat script to d:\python\python36-32\Scripts
Installing mkvirtualenv.bat script to d:\python\python36-32\Scripts
Installing rmvirtualenv.bat script to d:\python\python36-32\Scripts
Installing setprojectdir.bat script to d:\python\python36-32\Scripts
Installing toggleglobalsitepackages.bat script to d:\python\python36-32\Scripts
Installing whereis.bat script to d:\python\python36-32\Scripts
Installing workon.bat script to d:\python\python36-32\Scripts
Installed d:\python\python36-32\lib\site-packages\virtualenvwrapper_win-1.2.1-py3.6.egg
Processing dependencies for virtualenvwrapper-win
Finished processing dependencies for virtualenvwrapper-win
```

- Make a virtual environment called "exp"

```
(HELLOW~1) D:\PythonPrograms>mkvirtualenv exp
Using base prefix 'd:\\python\\python36-32'
New python executable in C:\Users\TSRIKA~1\Envs\exp\Scripts\python.exe
Installing setuptools, pip, wheel...done.
(exp) D:\PythonPrograms>
```

A directory "exp" is created in the "Envs" folder. In this folder, various files such as python.exe, setuptools and pip etc. will be available. All the installations for this are specific to this particular project only.

- A new project called "dir1" is created and in this, a new directory with the same project name is created. This folder will be considered as the root folder.

```
(exp) D:\PythonPrograms>mkdir dir1
(exp) D:\PythonPrograms>cd dir1
(exp) D:\PythonPrograms\dir1>mkdir exp
(exp) D:\PythonPrograms\dir1>cd exp
(exp) D:\PythonPrograms\dir1\exp>
```

- Set the current directory as the project directory.

```
(exp) D:\PythonPrograms\dir1\exp>setprojectdir .
"D:\PythonPrograms\dir1\exp" is now the project directory for
virtualenv "C:\Users\TSRIKA~1\Envs\exp"
"D:\PythonPrograms\dir1\exp" added to
C:\Users\TSRIKA~1\Envs\exp\Lib\site-packages\virtualenv_path_extensions.pth
```

- The virtual setup is created. We can deactivate it by using **deactivate**.

```
(exp) D:\PythonPrograms\dir1\exp>deactivate
D:\PythonPrograms\dir1\exp>
```

After deactivating, the change will happen at the left side of the prompt.

- To activate it we can use **workon name_of_virtual_space**

```
D:\PythonPrograms\dir1\exp>workon exp
(exp) D:\PythonPrograms\dir1\exp>
```

- The **lsvirtualenv** is used to list the all the environments in the **workson** home directory.

```
D:\PythonPrograms\dir1\exp>workon exp
(exp) D:\PythonPrograms\dir1\exp>
```

- Install a package **timely** by using pip

```
    (exp) D:\PythonPrograms\dir1\exp>pip install timely
Collecting timely
    Using cached timely-0.1.tar.gz
Building wheels for collected packages: timely
    Running setup.py bdist_wheel for timely ... done
    Stored in directory: C:\Users\T SRIKANTH\AppData\Local\pip\Cache\wheels\42\
d0\54\c1de7574f60e7fea676f08409eb6123ff3c9065cb2516ae803
Successfully built timely
Installing collected packages: timely
Successfully installed timely-0.1
```

- Python package **timely** is a stopwatch interface.

11.3 Using Python Packages

- Create a file **exp.py** in the environment where the Python package is installed.

```
from flask import Flask
app= Flask(__name__)
@app.route("/")
def exp():
    return "Hai Exp"
if __name__ == "__main__":
    app.run()
```

Output

```
(exp) D:\PythonPrograms\dir1\exp>python exp.py
* Running on http://127.0.0.1:5000/ (Press CTRL+C to quit)
127.0.0.1 - - [21/May/2017 22:43:45] "GET / HTTP/1.1" 200 -
127.0.0.1 - - [21/May/2017 22:43:45] "GET /favicon.ico
HTTP/1.1" 404 -
127.0.0.1 - - [21/May/2017 22:43:45] "GET /favicon.ico
HTTP/1.1" 404 -
```

Open the browser and type the URL as "http://127.0.0.1:5000"

11.4 Absolute and Relative Imports

In Python programming, we use **import** statement for importing the modules in the package. The modules can be imported in two different ways, viz., absolute and relative.

- "from package import module" is an absolute import. In this process, the parent package folder and the corresponding module name should be specified in absolute import statement. So, in this, the path from the top level to the sub-module should be clearly mentioned.
- In relative import statement, "." represents the parent of the present module. The net level is indicated with another ".". So, in case of relative import the statement is modified as "from . import module".

11.5 Namespace Package

In Python, the namespace packages are used to install the sub-packages by splitting across various locations. If parent package is having __init__.py file (not a valid Python package) then an implicit namespace is created. For this **pkgutil** package should be used. In the __init__.py file, add the following code.

```
from pkgutil import extend_path
_path__=extend_path(__path__,__name__)
import pkg_resources
pkg_resources.declare_namespace(__name__)
```

11.6 Sample Programs

Program 1: Write a Python program to create a package with two classes.

- Create a new directory with the name of the package **p1**.
- Create the class **class1** in the directory **p1**.

> **Programming Tip:** To group multiple Python files with their definitions, package is required

```
class class1:
    def __init__(self):
        print("Class1 object is created")
```

- Create the class **class2** in the directory **p1**.

```
class class2:
    def __init__(self):
        print("Class2 object is created")
```

- Create the __init__.py
- With this, the package **p1** with two classes {**c1 and c2**} is created. In the same directory, create another python file that crates objects for these classes. For this, create **a1.py**.

```
from c1 import class1
from c2 import class2
obj1=class1()
obj2=class2()
```

Output

```
D:\PythonPrograms\p1>python a1.py
Class1 object is created
Class2 object is created
```

Program 2: Write a Python program to create the package in **program 1** to make it as pip installer.

- The structure of the package should be

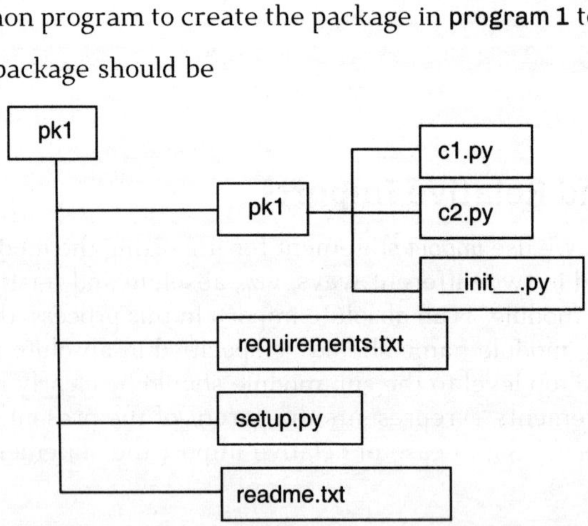

- Create the requirements.txt file
  - o Install the **pipreqs**

```
D:\PythonPrograms>pip install pipreqs
Collecting pipreqs
  Using cached pipreqs-0.4.7-py2.py3-none-any.whl
Requirement already satisfied: yarg in d:\python\
python36-32\lib\site-packages (from pipreqs)
Requirement already satisfied: docopt in d:\python\
python36-32\lib\site-packages (from pipreqs)
Requirement already satisfied: requests in d:\python\
python36-32\lib\site-packages (from yarg->pipreqs)
Installing collected packages: pipreqs
Successfully installed pipreqs-0.4.7
```

> **Programming Tip:**
> PIP is used for installing a package in Python.

  - o Generate the automated **requirements.txt** file

```
D:\PythonPrograms>pipreqs --force D:\PythonPrograms\pk1
INFO: Successfully saved requirements file in D:\PythonPrograms\pk1\
requirements.txt
```

  - o The content of the **requirements.txt** file is

```
setuptools==35.0.2
```

```
D:\PythonPrograms\pk1>pip install -r requirements.txt
Requirement already satisfied: setuptools==35.0.2 in d:\python\python36-32\lib\site-packages
(from -r requirements.txt (line 1))
Requirement already satisfied: six>=1.6.0 in d:\python\python36-32\lib\site-packages (from
setuptools==35.0.2->-r requirements.txt (line 1))
Requirement already satisfied: packaging>=16.8 in d:\python\python36-32\lib\site-packages
(from setuptools==35.0.2->-r requirements.txt (line 1))
Requirement already satisfied: appdirs>=1.4.0 in d:\python\python36-32\lib\site-packages
(from setuptools==35.0.2->-r requirements.txt (line 1))
Requirement already satisfied: pyparsing in d:\python\python36-32\lib\site-packages (from
packaging>=16.8->setuptools==35.0.2->-r requirements.txt (line 1))
```

- The **readme.txt** file should be created with all specifications /instructions for installing the package **pk1**.
- The **setup.py** file should be created in the folder **p1**

```
from setuptools import setup
setup(
    name='pk1',
    version='1.0',
    description='Example',
    author='public',
    author_email='public@yahoo.com',
    url="http://www.yahoo.com/",
    packages=['pk1'],
)
```

- Register the package i.e. the **setup.py file** with PYPI.

```
D:\PythonPrograms\pk1>python setup.py register
running register
running egg_info
writing pk1.egg-info\PKG-INFO
writing dependency_links to pk1.egg-info\dependency_links.txt
writing top-level names to pk1.egg-info\top_level.txt
reading manifest file 'pk1.egg-info\SOURCES.txt'
writing manifest file 'pk1.egg-info\SOURCES.txt'
running check
We need to know who you are, so please choose either:
    1. use your existing login,
    2. register as a new user,
    3. have the server generate a new password for you (and email it to you), or
    4. quit
Your selection [default 1]:
1
Username: PUBLIC
Password:
Registering pk1 to https://upload.pypi.org/legacy/
```

After this, the login information is saved in .pypirc file.

- Next, upload the registered package

```
D:\PythonPrograms\pk1>python setup.py sdist upload
running sdist
running egg_info
writing pk1.egg-info\PKG-INFO
writing dependency_links to pk1.egg-info\dependency_links.txt
writing top-level names to pk1.egg-info\top_level.txt
reading manifest file 'pk1.egg-info\SOURCES.txt'
writing manifest file 'pk1.egg-info\SOURCES.txt'
running check
creating pk1-1.0
creating pk1-1.0\pk1
creating pk1-1.0\pk1.egg-info
copying files to pk1-1.0...
copying setup.py -> pk1-1.0
copying pk1\__init__.py -> pk1-1.0\pk1
copying pk1\c1.py -> pk1-1.0\pk1
copying pk1\c2.py -> pk1-1.0\pk1
copying pk1.egg-info\PKG-INFO -> pk1-1.0\pk1.egg-info
copying pk1.egg-info\SOURCES.txt -> pk1-1.0\pk1.egg-info
copying pk1.egg-info\dependency_links.txt -> pk1-1.0\pk1.egg-info
copying pk1.egg-info\top_level.txt -> pk1-1.0\pk1.egg-info
Writing pk1-1.0\setup.cfg
Creating tar archive
removing 'pk1-1.0' (and everything under it)
running upload
Password:
Submitting dist\pk1-1.0.tar.gz to https://upload.pypi.org/legacy/
```

With this, the package `pk1` is uploaded into pip.

- Whenever we want, we can install the package and the classes in the package can be used. So, come out of `pk1` directory and install the `pk1` package.

```
D:\PythonPrograms\p1>cd..
D:\PythonPrograms>pip install pk1
Requirement already satisfied: pk1 in d:\pythonprograms\pk1
```

- Create a new python file **a2.py** and then import the package **pk1** and use the classes.

```
from pk1.c1 import class1
from pk1.c2 import class2
obj1=class1()
obj2=class2()
obj3=class1()
obj4=class2()
```

Output

```
D:\PythonPrograms>python a2.py
Class1 object is created
Class2 object is created
Class1 object is created
Class2 object is created
```

Glossary

- Package contains a group of files with various definitions and executable statements.
- __init__.py is the mandatory file for the definition of the package.

Package Installer for Python (PIP) allows the user to install packages in Python.

Summary

- A module is a single file used to group multiple definitions and executable code.
- Package is a collection of multiple files where each file can be a module.
- All multiple files should be placed in a single directory.
- The __init__ file should be maintained in the package directory.
- The elements of the package can be imported using either relative or absolute method.

Multiple Choice Questions

1. Which of the file is used for package?
   (a) __in__.py
   (b) __it__.py
   (c) __init__.py
   (d) None of the above
2. In Python, which is used to group multiple definitions and statements?
   (a) Module
   (b) Package
   (c) Both a and b
   (d) None of the abo
3. In Python, which is used to group class files?
   (a) Module
   (b) Package
   (c) Both a and b
   (d) None of the above.
4. During PIP installer package conversion process, which of these files are required?
   (a) setup.py
   (b) requirements.py
   (c) readme.py
   (d) All of the above.
5. For PIP, the PATH variable should be set to
   (a) Python
   (b) Python\Python36-32\Scripts
   (c) Python\Python36-32
   (d) None of the above

Fill in the Blanks

1. The module can import ____________________ number of files.
2. The package can import ____________________ number of files.
3. ____________________ is used to list the elements of a module.
4. All the components of a package are placed in a ____________________.
5. ____________________ is used to create a virtual environment.

State True/False

1. The **deactivate** command is used to activate the virtual setup.
2. The **workon** is used to activate the virtual setup.
3. There are two types of imports in Python.
4. "." is used to represent the current level in relative import.
5. **from package import module** is an absolute import.

Find the Output

1. Director p2:
C1.py
```
class class1:
def __init__(self):
print("Class1 object is created")
```
a1.py
```
from c1 import class1
obj1=class1()
```

Find the Error

1. Director p2:
C1.py
```
class class1:
def __init__(self):
print("Class1 object is created")
```
a1.py
```
import c1
obj1=class1()
```

Long Answer Questions

1. What is a package? With an example, write the step-by-step process for creating a package and using it within the same directory.
2. Explain the process of downloading packages by using PIP.
3. How does Python convert the user-defined package to a PIP installer?

Short Answer Questions

1. List the differences between module and package.
2. Which file is used to differentiate the package directory from others?
3. What are the required files to upload a user-defined package?

Exercise Programs

1. Write a Python program to create a package for Fibonacci, prime number and even/odd classes.
2. Write a Python program to upload the package designed for ex -**1** to make it as a PIP installer.

Answers

Multiple Choice Questions

1. (c) 2. (a) 3. (b) 4. (d) 5. (b)

Fill in the Blanks

1. one
2. multiple
3. dir(module_name)
4. single directory
5. mkvirtualenv

State True/False

1. False
2. True
3. True
4. False
5. True

Find the Output

1. Class1 object is created

Find the Error

1. NameError: name 'class1' is not defined

CHAPTER 12

Strings and Regular Expressions

This chapter elaborates on the handling of strings in Python. The string object uses ordinary string value. Other than ordinary strings, raw strings can be handled with regular expression. Regular expressions are used to handle text patterns efficiently.

12.1 Methods of String Objects

1. In Python programming, there is no character primitive data type. The character data is also considered as string data with size **1**. The string data can be defined with single quote or double quotes.

```
>>> a="hello"
>>> b='hello'
>>> a
'hello'
>>> b
'hello'
>>> type(a)
<class 'str'>
>>> type(b)
<class 'str'>
```

2. The string content can be accessed with the index and starts with **0**.

```
>>> a[0]
'h'
>>> a[0:2]
'he'
>>> a[3:6]
'lo'
>>> a[1:4]
'ell'
```

3. The elements of a string cannot be deleted. However, the complete string object can be deleted by using 'del' keyword.

```
>>> a="this is string"
>>> a
'this is string'
>>> a[0]
't'
>>> del(a[0])
Traceback (most recent call last):
    File "<stdin>", line 1, in <module>
```

```
TypeError: 'str' object doesn't support item deletion
>>> del a
>>> a
Traceback (most recent call last):
    File "<stdin>", line 1, in <module>
NameError: name 'a' is not defined
```

4. The slice operator ":" is used to extract the characters in the input string. For this, the starting position of the string and the length should be specified.

```
>>> st='abcd'
>>> st
'abcd'
>>> st[1:2]
'b'
>>> st[0:3]
'abc'
```

5. Two strings can be concatenated by using "+" operator. The "*" operator is used to repeat the string.

```
>>> a="good"
>>> b="morning"
>>> a
'good'
>>> b
'morning'
>>> c=a+b
>>> c
'goodmorning'
>>> d=a*2
>>> d
'goodgood'
```

6. Two strings can be concatenated by placing the strings together. They can also be combined by using parenthesis. In these cases, the strings should be defined in the current statement only.

```
>>> 'good''morning'
'goodmorning'
>>> ('good'
... 'morning')
'goodmorning'
```

7. In a string object, the index and the character is given as a pair by the **enumerate()** method.

```
a=input("Enter the input string:")
b=list(enumerate(a))
print(a)
print(b)
```

Output

```
D:\PythonPrograms>python a1.py
Enter the input string: this is a prg
this is a prg
[(0, 't'), (1, 'h'), (2, 'i'), (3, 's'), (4, ' '),
(5, 'i'), (6, 's'), (7, ' '), (8, 'a'), (9, ' '),
(10, 'p'), (11, 'r'), (12, 'g')]
```

8. The **len()** returns the length of the object.

```
>>> a="good morning"
>>> a
'good morning'
>>> len(a)
12
```

Various Python string methods are listed below.

- The string first character is capitalized with **capitalize()** method.

```
>>> a
'good morning'
>>> a.capitalize()
'Good morning'
```

- The **center()** method will place the input string at the center in the prescribed width.

```
>>> a
'good morning'
>>> a.center(15)
' good morning '
```

- The **count()** method is used to count the frequency occurrence of the input substring in the input string.

```
>>> a
'good morning'
>>> a.count('o')
3
```

- The **endswith()** function will check whether the input string ends with the input substring or not.

```
>>> a
'good morning'
>>> a.endswith('ng')
True
```

- The **isalpha()** method checks whether all the characters in the string are empty or not. If any one of the character is not an alphabet, then it returns FALSE; otherwise it returns TRUE.

```
>>> a
'good morning'
>>> a.isalpha()
False
>>> b=»hai»
>>> b.isalpha()
True
```

- The **isdecimal()**method returns TRUE if all the characters in the string are decimal; otherwise it returns FALSE.

```
>>> z="100"
>>> z.isdecimal()
True
```

- The isupper() method checks whether or not the all characters in the input string are in upper case. The islower() method checks whether or not all characters in the input string are in lower case or not.

```
>>> q="ABC"
>>> q.isupper()
True
>>> q.islower()
False
```

- The lower() method will return the string with all the lower case letters, whereas the upper() method will return the string with all the upper case letters.

```
>>> q="ABC"
>>> w=q.lower()
>>> w
'abc'
>>> x=w.upper()
>>> x
'ABC'
```

- The partition() method will partition the input string into various parts. The partition is performed according to the substring.

```
>>> a="this is a program"
>>> a
'this is a program'
>>> a.partition(" ")
('this', ' ', 'is a program')
>>> a.partition("s ")
('thi', 's ', 'is a program')
```

- The swapcase() method will return the string by swapping lower case to uppercase and upper case to lower case.

```
>>> z="ABcdEFgh"
>>> z
'ABcdEFgh'
>>> z.swapcase()
'abCDefGH'
```

12.1.1 Escape sequencing

The escape sequencing character is used to represent special characters in a string. Python supports escape sequencing. Various characters used for escape sequencing are listed below

- In the string "\" can be represented with "\\".

```
>>> a="ab\"
   File "<stdin>", line 1
      a="ab\"
            ^
SyntaxError: EOL while scanning string literal
>>> a="ab\\"
>>> a
'ab\\'
>>> len(a)
3
```

- In string, the single quote can be represented with “\’”.

```
>>> a='ab''
  File "<stdin>", line 1
    a='ab''
          ^
SyntaxError: EOL while scanning string literal
>>> a='ab\''
>>> a
"ab'"
```

- The escape sequence character \” is used to represent the double quote.

```
>>> x="ab""
  File "<stdin>", line 1
    x="ab""
          ^
SyntaxError: EOL while scanning string literal
>>> x="ab\""
>>> x
'ab"'
```

- “\a” is used to represent the ASCII Bell

```
>>> z="a\ab"
>>> z
'a\x07b'
```

- “\b” is used to represent the ASCII backspace.

```
>>> z="qw\ber"
>>> z
'qw\x08er'
```

- “\f” is used to represent the ASCII Formfeed.

```
>>> z="qw\fer"
>>> z
'qw\x0cer'
```

- “\n” is used to represent the ASCII Linefeed

```
>>> z="qw\ner"
>>> z
'qw\ner'
```

- “\r” is used to represent the ASCII carriage return

```
>>> z="qw\rer"
>>> z
'qw\rer'
```

- "\t" is used to represent the ASCII horizontal tab.

```
>>> z="qw\ter"
>>> z
'qw\ter'
```

- "\v" is used to represent the ASCII vertical tab.

```
>>> z="qw\ver"
>>> z
'qw\x0ber'
```

12.2 Iterating Strings

In Python, iteration can be applied on the strings using "for" loop.

```
st="hello!"
print("Iterating strings:")
for i in st:
    print(i)
```

Output

```
D:\PythonPrograms>python s1.py
Iterating strings:
h
e
l
l
o
!
```

12.3 String Module

The string module has several functions to handle Python strings. The module contains various constants. They are given below.

- The "ascii_letters" represents both the uppercase and lowercase letters.
- The "ascii_uppercase" represents the uppercase letters.
- The "ascii_lowercase" represents the lowercase letters.
- The "digits" represents the decimal digits.
- The "hexdigits" represents the hexadecimal digits.
- The "octdigits" represents the octagonal digits.
- The "punctuation" represents the possible letters used for punctuation.
- The "printable" represents the printable letters.
- The "whitespace" represents the characters used for whitespace.

```
import string
print("The value of digits constant: ",string.digits)
print("The value of letters constant: ",string.ascii_letters)
print("The value of lowercase constant: ",string.ascii_lowercase)
print("The value of uppercase constant: ",string.ascii_uppercase)
print("The value of hexdigits constant: ",string.hexdigits)
print("The value of octdigits constant: ",string.octdigits)
print("The value of punctuation constant: ",string.punctuation)
print("The value of whitespace constant: ",string.whitespace)
print("The value of printable constant: ",string.printable)
```

```
Output
D:\PythonPrograms>python a1.py
The value of digits constant: 0123456789
The value of letters constant: abcdefghijklmnopqrstuvwxyzABCDEFGHIJKLMNOPQRSTUVWXYZ
The value of lowercase constant: abcdefghijklmnopqrstuvwxyz
The value of uppercase constant: ABCDEFGHIJKLMNOPQRSTUVWXYZ
The value of hexdigits constant: 0123456789abcdefABCDEF
The value of octdigits constant: 01234567
The value of punctuation constant: !"#$%&'()*+,-./:;<=>?@[\]^_`{|}~
The value of whitespace constant:
The value of printable constant:
0123456789abcdefghijklmnopqrstuvwxyzABCDEFGHIJKLMNOPQRSTUVWXYZ!"#$%&'()*+,-./:;<=>?@
[\]^_`{|}~
```

In Python 3, all these functions are available as string methods. Various functions in this module are listed below.

- The **startswith()** method is used to check whether the given substring is started within the input string or not. For this, the start and end index can also be specified within the method.

```
s=input("Enter the input string:")
s1=input("enter the substring to be matched:")
a=s.startswith(s1)
if(a==1):
    print(s1," is started in ", s)
else:
    print(s1," is not started in ", s)
```

```
Output
D:\PythonPrograms>python b2.py
Enter the input string: good morning
enter the substring to be matched: good
good is started in good morning
D:\PythonPrograms>python b2.py
Enter the input string: good morning
enter the substring to be matched: mor
mor is not started in good morning
```

- The **find()**method is used to search for the given substring in the input string. If the substring is found then the index of the position will be returned.

```
s=input("Enter the input string:")
s1=input("enter the substring to be matched:")
a=s.find(s1)
if(a>0):
    print(s1," is found in ", s, "at ",a," position ")
else:
    print(s1," is not found in ", s)
```

```
Output
D:\PythonPrograms>python b2.py
Enter the input string: good morning
enter the substring to be matched: mor
mor is found in good morning at 5 position
```

- The **index()** method is used to return the index of the substring in the given string. If the substring is not found, then an exception will be raised.

```
s=input("Enter the input string:")
s1=input("enter the substring to be matched:")
a=s.index(s1)
if(a>0):
    print(s1," is found in ", s, "at ",a," position ")
else:
    print(s1," is not found in ", s)
```

Output

```
D:\PythonPrograms>python b2.py
Enter the input string: good
morning
enter the substring to be matched:
mor
mor is found in good morning at 5
position
```

- The rfind() method returns the highest index position of the substring in the input string. If the substring is not available in the input string, then -1 will be returned.

```
s=input("Enter the input string:")
s1=input("enter the substring to be matched:")
a=s.rfind(s1)
if(a>0):
    print(s1," is found in ", s, "at ",a," position ")
else:
    print(s1," is not found in ", s)
```

Output

```
D:\PythonPrograms>python b2.py
Enter the input string:this is very
very good and is happy
enter the substring to be
matched:is
is is found in this is very very good
and is happy at 27 position
```

- The rindex() method is similar to rfind() method. If the substring is not available in a given string, then rfind() method will return "-1" where as the rindex() method will throws an exception.

```
s=input("Enter the input string:")
s1=input("enter the substring to be matched:")
a=s.rindex(s1)
if(a>0):
    print(s1," is found in ", s, "at ",a," position ")
else:
    print(s1," is not found in ", s)
```

Output

```
D:\PythonPrograms>python b2.py
Enter the input string:this is very
very good and is happy
    enter the substring to be
matched:is
is is found in this is very very good
and is happy at 27
    position
```

- The isalnum()method checks whether or not all characters in the input string are alphanumeric If all the characters are alphanumeric, then it returns TRUE; otherwise, it returns FALSE.

```
s=input("Enter the input string:")
a=s.isalnum()
if(a):
    print("All the characters in the string are alphanumeric")
else:
    print("All the characters in the string are not
alphanumeric")
```

Output

```
D:\PythonPrograms>python b2.py
Enter the input string: good
morning
All the characters in the string are
not alphanumeric
D:\PythonPrograms>python b2.py
Enter the input string: good
All the characters in the string are
alphanumeric
```

- The isdigit() method returns TRUE if all the characters in the input string are digits. If all the characters are not digits, then it returns FALSE.

```
s=input("Enter the input string:")
a=s.isdigit()
if(a):
    print("All the characters in the string are digits")
else:
    print("All the characters in the string are not digits")
```

Output

```
D:\PythonPrograms>python b2.py
Enter the input string:456
All the characters in the string are digits
```

- The isspace() method returns TRUE when the input string is a space character. If not, then it returns FALSE.

```
s=input("Enter the input string:")
flag=0;
for i in range(0,len(s)):
    if(s[i].isspace()):
        flag=1;
        print("Space is available in input string")
if(flag==0):
    print("Space is not available in input string")
```

Output

```
D:\PythonPrograms>python b2.py
Enter the input string: good morning
Space is available in input string
```

- The ljust() method returns the left justified input string within the specified width. It can also use fillchar() method to fill the empty positions during justification.

```
s=input("Enter the input string:")
t=int(input("Enter the width to be justified:"))
u=input("Enter the character to be filled:")
a=s.ljust(t,u)
print("The left justified string= ",a)
```

Output

```
D:\PythonPrograms>python b2.py
Enter the input string: good
Enter the width to be justified:7
Enter the character to be filled:#
The left justified string= good###
```

- The rjust() method returns the right justified input string within the specified width. It can also use fillchar() method to fill the empty positions during justification.

```
s=input("Enter the input string:")
t=int(input("Enter the width to be justified:"))
u=input("Enter the character to be filled:")
a=s.rjust(t,u)
print("The right justified string= ",a)
```

Output

```
D:\PythonPrograms>python b2.py
Enter the input string:good
Enter the width to be justified:7
Enter the character to be filled:#
The right justified string= ###good
```

- The zfill() method extends the width of the input string to the specified size by placing "0" in the empty positions.

```
s=input("Enter the input string:")
t=int(input("Enter the width to be filled:"))
a=s.zfill(t)
print("The zero filled string= ",a)
```

Output

```
D:\PythonPrograms>python b2.py
Enter the input string: good
Enter the width to be filled:7
The zero filled string= 000good
```

- The lower() method takes a string and returns the equivalent string with all lowercase characters.

```
s=input("Enter the input string:")
print("The lower case string= ",s.lower())
```

Output

```
D:\PythonPrograms>python b2.py
Enter the input string: GOOD
The lower case string= good
```

- The upper() method takes a string and returns the equivalent string with all uppercase characters.

```
s=input("Enter the input string:")
print("The upperr case string= ",s.upper())
```

Output

```
D:\PythonPrograms>python b2.py
Enter the input string: good
The upper case string= GOOD
```

- The lstrip() method returns the input string by removing the specified character in the left position. The default character considered for removal is whitespace.

```
s=input("Enter the input string:")
t=input("Enter the left character to be stripped:")
z=s.lstrip(t)
print("the result of lstrip= ",z)
```

Output

```
D:\PythonPrograms>python b2.py
Enter the input string: tttttttthis is good
Enter the left character to be stripped: t
the result of lstrip= his is good
```

- The rstrip()method returns the input string by removing the specified character in the right position. The default character considered for removal is whitespace.

```
s=input("Enter the input string:")
t=input("Enter the right character to be stripped:")
z=s.rstrip(t)
print("the result of rstrip= ",z)
```

Output

```
D:\PythonPrograms>python b2.py
Enter the input string: this is gooddddddddddddd
Enter the right character to be stripped: d
the result of rstrip= this is goo
```

- The strip()"() method returns the input string by removing the specified character in either left or right positions. The default character considered for removal is whitespace.

```
s=input("Enter the input string:")
t=input("Enter the character to be stripped:")
z=s.strip(t)
print("the result of strip= ",z)
```

Output

```
D:\PythonPrograms>python b2.py
Enter the input string: this is good
Enter the character to be stripped:
t
the result of strip= his is good
D:\PythonPrograms>python b2.py
Enter the input string: this is good
Enter the character to be stripped:
d
the result of strip= this is goo
```

- The max() method returns the maximum element in the iterable arguments.

```
s=[10,20,30,40,50]
z=max(s)
print("the max result= ",z)
```

Output

```
D:\PythonPrograms>python b2.py
the max result= 50
```

- The min() method returns the minimum element in the iterable arguments.

```
s=[10,20,30,40,50]
z=min(s)
print("the min result= ",z)
```

Output

```
D:\PythonPrograms>python b2.py
the min result= 10
```

- The **replace()**method replaces the existing substring within the input string with the new substring.

```
s=input("Enter the input string:")
t=input("Enter the existing substring:")
z=input("Enter the new substring:")
print("the result of strip= ",s.replace(t,z))
```

Output

```
D:\PythonPrograms>python b2.py
Enter the input string: this is good
Enter the existing substring :is
Enter the new substring: can be
the result of strip= thcan be can be
good
```

- The title() method converts the first character of each word in the input string to the upper case character.

```
s=input("Enter the input string:")
print("the result= ",s.title())
```

Output

```
D:\PythonPrograms>python b2.py
Enter the input string:this is good
the result= This Is Good
```

- The split() method splits the input string into various substrings. The splitting can be performed based on the number of required lines or based on the delimiter for splitting the string.

```
s=input("Enter the input string:")
t=input("Enter the delimiter:")
print("the result= ",s.split(t))
```

Output

```
D:\PythonPrograms>python b2.py
Enter the input string:this is good
Enter the delimiter:is
the result= ['th', ' ', ' good']
```

- The join()method joins the two input strings. During the join operation, the first string will be joined after each character in the second string.

```
s=input("Enter the first string:")
t=input("Enter the second string:")
print("the result= ",s.join(t))
```

Output

```
D:\PythonPrograms>python b2.py
Enter the first string: ab
Enter the second string: python
the result= pabyabtabhaboabn
```

- The isidentifier() returns TRUE when the input string is a identifier. If the input string is not a identifier then FALSE will be returned.

```
s=input("Enter the first string:")
t=s.isidentifier()
if(t):
    print("input string is a identifier")
else:
    print("input string is not a identifier")
```

Output

```
D:\PythonPrograms>python b2.py
Enter the first string: if
input string is a identifier
```

- The ord() function returns the ascii code of the input character.

```
s=input("Enter the string: ")
for i in s:
    print("The ascii code of ",i, " is ",ord(i))
```

Output

```
D:\PythonPrograms>python b2.py
Enter the string: abc
The ascii code of a is 97
The ascii code of b is 98
The ascii code of c is 99
```

- The chr() function returns the equivalent character of the input ascii code.

```
s=int(input("Enter the ascii code: "))
print("The character for the given ascii code of ",s, " is ",chr(s))
```

Output

```
D:\PythonPrograms>python b2.py
Enter the ascii code: 97
The character for the given ascii code of 97 is a
```

12.4 String Formatting

Similar to C Programming, Python programming also offers usage of various format specifiers. Various format specifiers are listed below.

- The %d is used for formatting the integer data.

```
a=int(input("Enter integer value:"))
print("Integer value: %d" %a)
```

Output

```
D:\PythonPrograms>python a1.py
Enter integer value:10
Integer value: 10
```

- The %f is used for formatting the floating point data.

```
a=float(input("Enter floating point value:"))
print("Floating Point value: %f" %a)
```

Output

```
D:\PythonPrograms>python a1.py
Enter floating point value:25.344
Floating Point value: 25.344000
```

- The %.<size>f is used to format the floating with the fixed size of fractional number.

```
a=float(input("Enter floating point value:"))
print("Floating Point value: %f" %a)
print("Floating Point value: %.2f" %a)
```

Output

```
D:\PythonPrograms>python a1.py
Enter floating point value:100.56
Floating Point value: 100.560000
Floating Point value: 100.56
```

- The %s is used to format the string objects.

```
a=input("Enter String value:")
print("String value: %s" %a)
```

Output

```
D:\PythonPrograms>python a1.py
Enter String value:hello
String value: hello
```

- The %s is also used to handle other data objects.

```
b=[100,200,300]
print("b value: %s" %b)
```

Output

```
D:\PythonPrograms>python a1.py
b value: [100, 200, 300]
```

Specifying the position of the string

Python uses format()method to format the input string according to the user requirement. The format()method uses placeholders ({}) for specifying the position of the string. There are four types of arguments as listed below.

- Default arguments: It takes the arguments according to their order. No need to specify the index of the argument.
- Positional arguments: It takes the arguments according to their position. The initial argument index starts with 0.
- Keyword arguments: It takes the arguments based on the keywords.
- Mixed arguments: It takes the both the positional and keyword arguments.

```
a=int(input("Enter the Year: "))
b=input("Enter the Month Name: ")
c=int(input("Enter the Date:"))
print("Default argument data:\n year {}, month {} date {}.".format(a,b,c))
print("Positional argument data:\n year {0}, month {1} date {2}.".format(a,b,c))
print("Keyword argument data:\n year {x}, month {y} date {z}.".format(x=a,z=c,y=b))
print("Mixed argument data:\n year {0}, month {1} date {z}.".format(a,b,z=c))
```

Output

```
D:\PythonPrograms>python a1.py
Enter the Year: 2015
Enter the Month Name: sep
Enter the Date:25
Default argument data:
year 2015, month sep date 25.
Positional argument data:
year 2015, month sep date 25.
Keyword argument data:
year 2015, month sep date 25.
Mixed argument data:
year 2015, month sep date 25.
```

In case of mixed arguments, the positional arguments should be placed before the keyword arguments.

12.5 Regular Expression

Python programming supports a feature called as "regular expressions". With this, text patterns can be efficiently handled. They are the basic building blocks for machine text processing. Python is using **REGREX** to support regular expression. For this, input data is given as a string. Within the input string, the required pattern is analyzed. In Python programming, "re" module is used to handle various functions for regular expressions.

12.5.1 Re-module

The "re" module is mainly used to provide various functions for regular expressions. Each of these functions takes two arguments. They are 1) the input string and 2) the pattern.

The input string used by the regular expression is not an ordinary string. An ordinary string contains escape sequence characters. To overcome this, the regular expressions are maintained by "raw strings". The raw string starts with "r" character followed by the opening single quote.

```
>>> a="hel\tlo"
>>> a
'hel\tlo'
>>> print(a)
hel lo
>>> a=r'hel\tlo'
>>> print(a)
hel\tlo
```

In Python programming, the patterns need not be characters. Various patterns are listed below.

- The exact match of ordinary characters is represented by pattern a,X,9,<
- Any single character other than "\n" is represented by pattern . (a period)
- Any single word character pattern is \w.
- Any non word character pattern is \W.
- Boundary pattern between word and non word is \b.
- Single white space character pattern is \s.
- Non single white space character pattern is \S.
- Pattern for tab is \t
- Pattern for new line is \n
- Pattern for return is \r.
- Decimal digit pattern is \d.
- Pattern for special character is \special character
- ^ is used for matching the beginning of the line.
- $ is used for matching the end of the line.
- [. . .] is used for matching any single character in the bracket.
- [^. . .] is used for matching any single character not in the bracket.

Various operators can be applicable to the pattern. They are

- The "+" operator is used to represent one or more repetitions of the pattern to its left.
- The "*" operator is used represent zero or more repetitions of the pattern to its left.
- The "?" is used to match the zero or one repetitions of the pattern to its left.

Various functions available in the "re" module are listed below.

- re.match ()

  The syntax is

```
match_obj=re.match(pattern,string,flags)
```

- o The pattern is a regular expression with raw string
- o The string represents the data to be matched with the pattern
- o The flags represent the modifiers. For example, **re.I** is used for case in sensitive matching.
- o The **match_obj** maintains the groups matched.

```
import re
a = "this is regular expression program and is a match program"
m = re.match( r'(.*)\s(.*)\s(.*)', a)
if m:
    print("m.group() : ", m.group())
    print("m.group(1) : ", m.group(1))
    print("m.group(2) : ", m.group(2))
    print("m.group(3) : ", m.group(3))
else:
    print("No match found")
```

Output

```
D:\PythonPrograms>python a1.py
m.group() : this is regular expression program and is a match program
m.group(1) : this is regular expression program and is a
m.group(2) : match
m.group(3) : program
```

- re.search()

The **match()** will perform checking operation only at the beginning of the string where as the **search()** will perform checking operation within the string. The syntax of the search() function is

```
search_obj=re.search(pattern,string,flags)
```

```
import re
a = "this is regular expression program and is a match program"
m = re.search( r'(i.*)\s(.*)\s(.*)', a)
if m:
    print("m.group() : ", m.group())
    print("m.group(1) : ", m.group(1))
    print("m.group(2) : ", m.group(2))
    print("m.group(3) : ", m.group(3))
else:
    print("No match found")
```

Output

```
D:\PythonPrograms>python a1.py
m.group() : is is regular expression program and is a match program
m.group(1) : is is regular expression program and is a
m.group(2) : match
m.group(3) : program
```

The above program with **match()** function will not find anything and the result is "No match found".

- re.sub()

The **sub()** is used to substitute the new sub string in the input string matched with the pattern. The syntax is

```
sub_obj=re.sub(pattern,newstring,string,max=0)
```

```
import re
a = "this is regular expression program and is a match program"
m = re.sub( r'(i.*)\s(.*)\s(.*)', "",a)
print("After matching and substitution result: ",m)
```

Output

```
D:\PythonPrograms>python a1.py
After matching and substitution result: th
```

- re.split()

The **split()** function will partition the input text into various parts based on delimiters.

```
import re
a = "this is regular expression program and is a match
program"
m = re.split( r'(.*)\s(e.*)', a)
print("After matching and substitution result: ")
for i in m:
    print(i)
```

Output

```
D:\PythonPrograms>python a1.py
After matching and substitution
result:
this is regular
expression program and is a match
program
```

- re.findall()

It is similar to **split()** function except that partition is not performed based on delimiter. Other than this, the partitioning is performed based on the matching.

```
import re
a = "this is regular expression program and is a match
program"
m = re.findall( r'(.*)\s(e.*)', a)
print("After matching and substitution result: ")
for i in m:
    print(i)
```

Output

```
D:\PythonPrograms>python a1.py
After matching and substitution
result:
('this is regular', 'expression
program and is a match program')
```

12.6 Dictionary-based Formatting Expressions

Dictionary elements can also be placed as part of a string. For this, "%" operator is used to represent the elements of the dictionary.

```
di={"a":1,"b":2.6,"c":"hai"}
st1="%(a)d"%di
st2="%(b)f"%di
st3="%(c)s"%di
print(st1)
print(st2)
print(st3)
```

Output

```
D:\PythonPrograms>python bb.py
1
2.600000
hai
```

12.7 Sample Programs

Program 1: Write a Python program to check whether or not the given substring exists in the input string.

```
a=input("Enter the input string: ")
b=input("Enter the substring to be searched: ")
if(b in a):
    print(b," is in ",a)
else:
    print(b," is not in ",a)
```

Output

```
D:\PythonPrograms>python a1.py
Enter the input string: good evening
Enter the substring to be searched:
eve
eve is in good evening
```

Program 2: Write a Python program to check whether or not the given two input strings same.

```
a=input("Enter the first input string: ")
b=input("Enter the second input string: ")
if not(b is a):
    print(b," is same as ",a)
else:
    print(b," is not same as ",a)
```

Output

```
D:\PythonPrograms>python a1.py
Enter the first input string: abc
Enter the second input string: abc
abc is same as abc
```

Program 3: Write a Python program to convert the decimal number to other formats by using format() method.

```
a=int(input("Enter the Decimal Value: "))
b=float(input("Enter the Floating Point Value: "))
print("Input decimal Value= {:d}".format(a))
print("Binary Value={0:b}".format(a))
print("Octal Value={0:o}".format(a))
print("Hexa Decimal Value={0:x}".format(a))
print("Input decimal float value= {:f}".format(b))
```

Output

```
D:\PythonPrograms>python a1.py
Enter the Decimal Value: 100
Enter the Floating Point Value: 5.8
Input decimal Value= 100
Binary Value=1100100
Octal Value=144
Hexa Decimal Value=64
Input decimal float value= 5.800000
```

Program 4: Write a Python program to read the string and print the reverse of the string.

```
s=input("Enter the input string: ")
r=''
for i in range(len(s)-1,-1,-1):
    r=r+s[i]
print("Reverse string= ",r)
```

Output

```
D:\PythonPrograms>python b2.py
Enter the input string: abc
Reverse string= cba
```

Program 5: Write a Python program to check whether the input string is a palindrome or not.

```
s=input("Enter the input string: ")
r=''
for i in range(len(s)-1,-1,-1):
    r=r+s[i]
if(s==r):
    print("Input string is a palindrome")
else:
    print("Input string is not a palindrome")
```

Output

```
D:\PythonPrograms>python b2.py
Enter the input string: aba
Input string is a palindrome
```

Program 6: Write a Python program to find the frequency of characters occurring in a string?

```
s=input("Enter the input string: ")
res=[]
du=set()
u=[]
for l in s:
    if l not in du:
        u.append(l)
        du.add(l)
for i in range(0,len(u)):
    t=u[i]
    v=0
    for j in range(0,len(s)):
        if(t==s[j]):
            v=v+1;
    res.append(v)
print("Input string= ",s)
print("Frequency Occurrence= ",res)
```

Output

```
D:\PythonPrograms>python b2.py
Enter the input string: abab
Input string= abab
Frquency Occurrence= [2, 2]
```

Program 7: Write a Python program to find the number of vowels in an input string.

> **Programming Tip:**
> In Python, the membership operators are "in" and "not in".

```
s=input("Enter the input string: ")
c=0
for i in s:
    if i in ['a','e','i','o','u']:
        c=c+1
print("The count of vowels: ",c)
```

Output

```
D:\PythonPrograms>python b2.py
Enter the input string: good
The count of vowels: 2
```

Program 8: Write a Python program to find the number of consonants in the input string.

```
s=input("Enter the input string: ")
c=0
for i in s:
    if i not in ['a','e','i','o','u']:
        c=c+1
print("The count of consonants: ",c)
```

Output

```
D:\PythonPrograms>python b2.py
Enter the input string: morning
The count of consonants: 5
```

Program 9: Write a Python program to find the number of digits in the input string.

```
s=input("Enter the input string: ")
c=0
for i in s:
    if i.isdigit():
        c=c+1
print("The count of digit characters: ",c)
```

Output

```
D:\PythonPrograms>python b2.py
Enter the input string: a1b2c345
The count of digit characters: 5
```

Program 10: Write a Python program to find the number of whitespaces in the input string.

```
s=input("Enter the input string: ")
c=0
for i in s:
    if i.isspace():
        c=c+1
print("The count of white space characters: ",c)
```

Output

```
D:\PythonPrograms>python b2.py
Enter the input string: good
morning
The count of white space
characters: 1
```

Program 11: Write a Python program to reverse a sentence.

```
s=input("Enter the input string: ")
r=''
for i in range(len(s)-1,-1,-1):
    r=r+s[i]
print("Reverse sentence= ",r)
```

Output

```
D:\PythonPrograms>python b2.py
Enter the input string: hello hai\n
good
Reverse sentence= doog n\iah
olleh
```

Program 12: Write a Python program to remove the duplicate characters in aqn input string.

```
s=input("Enter the input string: ")
du=set()
u=""
for l in s:
    if l not in du:
        u=u+l
        du.add(l)
print("The string without duplicates= ",u)
```

Output

```
D:\PythonPrograms>python b2.py
Enter the input string: hello good morning
The string without duplicates= helo gdmrni
```

Program 13: Write a Python program to sort the elements of a string.

```
s=input("Enter the input string: ")
x=''.join(sorted(s))
print("The alphabetical order sorted string= ",x)
```

Output

```
D:\PythonPrograms>python b2.py
Enter the input string: hello
The alphabetical order sorted string= ehllo
```

Program 14: Write a Python program to remove non alphabet characters in the input string.

```
import re
s=input("Enter the input string: ")
t = re.sub('[^A-Za-z]', '', s)
print("The string with alphabets= ",t)
```

Output

```
D:\PythonPrograms>python b2.py
Enter the input string: abc123def
The string with alphabets= abcdef
```

Program 15: Write a Python program to sort the letters and print the distinct letters.

```
s=input("Enter the input string:")
s2=''.join(sorted(set(s.lower())))
print(s2)
```

Output

```
D:\PythonPrograms>python b2.py
Enter the input string:hello good morning
deghilmnor
```

Program 16: Write a Python program to print all permutations of a given string.

```
from itertools import permutations
x=int(input("Enter the number:"))
li = list(permutations(range(1, x+1)))
print("The list of permutations are:")
print(li)
```

Output

```
D:\PythonPrograms>python b2.py
Enter the number:3
The list of permutations are:
[(1, 2, 3), (1, 3, 2), (2, 1, 3), (2, 3, 1), (3, 1, 2), (3, 2, 1)]
```

Program 17: Write a Python program to print the first non-repeating character in the input string.

```
x=input("Enter the string:")
for i in x:
    if(x.count(i)==1):
        print("The first non repeated chracter in the string: ",i)
        break
```

Output

```
D:\PythonPrograms>python b2.py
Enter the string:aaabccc
The first non repeated chracter in the string: b
```

Program 18: Write a Python program to print the run length encoding.

```
x=input("Enter the string:")
s=''
for i in x:
    if(i not in s):
        s=s+i
        s=s+str(x.count(i))
print("original string: ",x)
print("The run length code: ",s)
```

Output

```
D:\PythonPrograms>python b2.py
Enter the string:aaaabbbcccccc
original string: aaaabbbcccccc
The run length code: a4b3c6
```

Program 19: Write a Python program to check whether the input strings are anagrams of each other or not.

```
x=input("Enter the first string:")
y=input("Enter the second string:")
if(sorted(x.upper())==sorted(y.upper())):
    print("The two strings are anagrams")
else:
    print("The two strings are not anagrams")
```

Output

```
D:\PythonPrograms>python b2.py
Enter the first string:abc
Enter the second string:bca
The two strings are anagrams
```

Program 20: Write a Python program to print all the words in an input string.

```
x=input("Enter the string:")
y=x.split()
print("The words in the input string: ",y)
```

Output

```
D:\PythonPrograms>python b2.py
Enter the string: hello good morning
The words in the input string: ['hello', 'good',
'morning']
```

Program 21: Write a Python program to remove the words beginning with vowels.

```
x=input("Enter the string:")
y=x.split()
z=""
for i in y:
    if(i[0] not in ['a','e','i','o','u']):
        z=z+i+" "
print(z)
```

Output

```
D:\PythonPrograms>python b2.py
Enter the string: an apple is good fruit
good fruit
```

Program 22: Write a Python program to remove the words beginning with consonants.

```
x=input("Enter the string:")
y=x.split()
z=""
for i in y:
    if(i[0] in ['a','e','i','o','u']):
        z=z+i+" "
print(z)
```

Output

```
D:\PythonPrograms>python b2.py
Enter the string:an apple is good fruit
an apple is
```

Program 23: Write a Python program to remove the words ending with vowels.

```
x=input("Enter the string:")
y=x.split()
z=""
for i in y:
    if(i[len(i)-1] not in ['a','e','i','o','u']):
        z=z+i+" "
print(z)
```

Output

```
D:\PythonPrograms>python b2.py
Enter the string:an apple is good fruit
an is good fruit
```

Program 24: Write a Python program to remove the words ending with consonants.

```
x=input("Enter the string:")
y=x.split()
z=""
for i in y:
    if(i[len(i)-1] in ['a','e','i','o','u']):
        z=z+i+" "
print(z)
```

Output

```
D:\PythonPrograms>python b2.py
Enter the string:an apple is good fruit
apple
```

Program 25: Write a Python program to find the index of second string in the first string.

```
x=input("Enter the string:")
y=input("Enter the string to be searched:")
z=x.index(y)
if(z>-1):
    print("The string2 is found in string1 at ",z, "index")
```

Output

```
D:\PythonPrograms>python b2.py
Enter the string:abcd
Enter the string to be searched:bc
The string2 is found in string1 at 1 index
```

Glossary

- The string object uses ordinary string value.
- Raw strings can be handled with regular expression.
- Regular expressions are used to handle text patterns efficiently.

Summary

- The string is used to represent character data.
- Each character of the string is accessed with the corresponding index value.
- The string can be iterated. Various operations can be performed on the string object.
- The string module provides various functions for handling strings in Python.
- Other than ordinary strings, raw strings can be efficiently handled by the regular expression.
- The Re module is used for performing various operations with the regular expressions.

Multiple Choice Questions

1. The access specifier for the int is
   (a) %c (b) %d
   (c) %f (d) None
2. The access specifier for the float is
   (a) %f (b) %d
   (c) %l (d) %s
3. The access specifier for the string is
   (a) %a (b) %t
   (c) %s (d) %i
4. Which module provides functions for regular expression?
   (a) reg (b) rex
   (c) rge (d) re
5. Which of the string function supports string formatting?
   (a) format()
   (b) formats()
   (c) formatting()
   (d) None of the above.
6. How many types of arguments are allowed in format() function?
   (a) 1 (b) 2
   (c) 3 (d) 4
7. Which function will check only the initial character of the string?
   (a) search()
   (b) match()
   (c) look()
   (d) None of the above.
8. Which function will check any character in the string?
   (a) search()
   (b) match()
   (c) look()
   (d) None of the above.
9. Which function requires delimiter for partitioning the string?
   (a) match() (b) search()
   (c) findall() (d) split()
10. Which function does not require delimiter for portioning the string?
    (a) match() (b) search()
    (c) findall() (d) split()
11. In Python, character data is considered as
    (a) int (b) float
    (c) string (d) class
12. The string can be defined with
    (a) single quote
    (b) double quote
    (c) Either (a) or (b).
    (d) None of the above.
13. The length of the string for character data is?
    (a) 0 (b) 1
    (c) 2 (d) 3
14. The initial value of the index for a string is
    (a) 0 (b) 1
    (c) 2 (d) 3
15. By placing the multiple strings together, they can be?
    (a) repeated (b) deleted
    (c) created (d) concatenated
16. To concatenate strings by using parenthesis, the strings should be defined in
    (a) previous statement
    (b) current statement
    (c) next statement
    (d) All the above.
17. The pair of character and index of a string is given by
    (a) enumerate()
    (b) get()
    (c) getpair()
    (d) getindexpai()
18. Which of the following is used to divide the string into various substrings?
    (a) substr() (b) sub()
    (c) str() (d) partition()
19. In case of escape sequencing, '\' is represented with
    (a) \\ (b) /
    (c) // (d) \
20. "\a" is used to represent
    (a) backspace (b) formfeed
    (c) bell (d) lineffed
21. The iteration can be applied on strings by using
    (a) condition
    (b) for loop
    (c) if statement
    (d) if..else statement
22. Which of the following is required for taking arguments in Default arguments?
    (a) Value (b) Keywords
    (c) Index (d) Order

23. Which of the following is required for taking arguments in Positional arguments?
(a) Value (b) Keywords
(c) Index (d) Order

24. Which of the following is required for taking arguments in Keyword arguments?
(a) Value (b) Keywords
(c) Index (d) Order

25. Mixed arguments represent
(a) positional arguments
(b) keyword arguments
(c) Both positional and keyword arguments.
(d) None of the above.

26. In Python, text patterns are handled efficiently with
(a) module
(b) package
(c) string
(d) regular expression

27. Which of the following module supports regular expression?
(a) Re-module
(b) ReE-module
(c) ReEx-module
(d) None of the above.

28. The regular expressions are maintained with
(a) ordinary strings
(b) enumerated strings
(c) raw strings
(d) enumerated raw strings

29. Raw strings start with which character?
(a) r (b) a (c) s (d) d

30. Raw string contains
(a) single quote
(b) double quote
(c) Both (a) and (b).
(d) None of the above.

Fill in the Blanks

1. The string is defined with ___________.
2. The string can have ___________ characters.
3. The elements of the string cannot be ___________.
4. The slice operator is used to ___________ the characters in the string.
5. For slice operator, ___________ and ___________ should be specified.
6. Two strings can be concatenated by using ___________, ___________ and ___________.
7. ___________ is used to check whether all the characters in the string are empty or not.
8. ___________ is used to check whether all the characters in the string are decimal or not.
9. ___________ will exchange the case of the character in the string.
10. The escape character \" is used to represent ___________.
11. ___________ is used to represent the ASCII linefeed.
12. In string module, ___________ represent the decimal digits.
13. In string module, ___________ represents the printable letters.
14. In string module, ___________ represents the hexadecimal digits.
15. In string module, ___________ represents the octagonal digits.
16. In string module, ___________ is used to change all the characters to upper case.
17. In string module, ___________ is used to change all the characters to lower case.
18. In string module, ___________ is used to divide the input string into various parts.
19. In string module, ___________ is used to join the input strings.
20. In string module, ___________ is used to search a substring in the given string.
21. In string module, ___________ is used to update the substring with new substring.
22. ___________ formatter is used to handle other data objects.
23. The **format()** method uses ___________ placeholders.
24. There are ___________ types of arguments for **format()** method.
25. The Python uses ___________ for supporting regular expressions.
26. With regular expressions, ___________ can be handled efficiently.

State True/False

1. There is a character primitive data type in Python.
2. Quotes are used to represent the value of the string.
3. Index is required to access the individual character of the string.
4. The elements of the string can be deleted.
5. The complete string can be deleted.
6. **del** keyword is used to delete the individual element of the string.
7. **del** keyword is used to delete the complete string.
8. The slice operator requires two arguments.
9. The **endswith()** function will check whether the string ends with a substring or not.
10. The escape character \r is used to represent line feed.
11. **for** loop is used for iterating strings.
12. String module is not available in Python.
13. Python allows the usage of format specifiers.
14. The %.<size>f is used to format floating with fixed size of fractional number.
15. Regular expressions use ordinary strings.
16. Any single word character pattern is \w
17. Decimal digit pattern is \n.
18. ^ is used for matching the beginning of line.
19. Non-single white space character pattern is \S
20. Any non-word character pattern is \X.

Find the Output

1.
```
a=('hai'
'xyz'
'hello')
print(a)
```
2.
```
a='abcdef'
c=a.center(6)
print(c)
```
3.
```
a='abcdef'
c=a.partition('z')
print(c)
```
4.
```
a='hai'
l=len(a)
i=0
while(i<l):
    print(a[i])
    i=i+1
```
5.
```
import string
a="goodmorning"
print(a.upper())
```
6.
```
s="HAI"
print(s.lower())
```
7.
```
s="HAI"
print(s.isalnum())
```
8.
```
s="HAI"
print(s.isdigit())
```
9.
```
s="HAI"
print(s.startswith('a'))
```
10.
```
s="HAI"
print(s.find('a'))
```
11.
```
s="hai"
print(s.index('a'))
```
12.
```
s="hai"
z='i' in s
print(z)
```
13.
```
s="hai"
z='x' not in s
print(z)
```
14.
```
s="hai"
print(s.isdigit())
```
15.
```
s="1050"
print(s.isdigit())
```
16.
```
s="1050"
s1="ab"
x=s is s1
print(x)
```
17.
```
s="1050"
print(s.rfind("0"))
```
18.
```
s="1050"
print(s.rindex("0"))
```
19.
```
s="1050"
print(s.isalnum())
```

20. s="a@0"
print(s.isalnum())

21. s="a@0"
print(s.isdigit())

22. s="a b"
print(s.isspace())

23. s=" "
print(s.isspace())

24. s="abc"
print(s.ljust(5))

25. s="abc"
print(s.ljust(5,'*'))

26. s="abc"
print(s.rjust(5,'*'))

27. s="abc"
print(s.rjust(5))

28. s="abc"
print(s.zfill(5))

29. s="abcdefa"
print(s.lstrip('a'))

30. s="abcdefa"
print(s.rstrip('a'))

31. s="abcdefa"
print(s.strip('a'))

32. s=[22,42,1,62]
print(max(s))

33. s=[22,42,1,62]
print(min(s))

34. s="this is first line"
print(s.replace("is", "was"))

35. s="this is first line"
print(s.replace("is", "was",1))

36. s="this is first line"
print(s.replace("is", "was",-1))

37. s="this is first line"
print(s.split())

38. s="this is first line"
print(sorted(s.split()))

39. s="this is"
t="first line"
z=s.join(t)
print(z)

40. s="this is"
t="first line"
z=s+t
print(z)

41. s="python"
print(s.isidentifier())

42. s="main"
print(s.isidentifier())

Find the Error

1. import string
a="goodmorning"
a.replace("xyz")
print(a)

2. a=10
print("%d"a)

3. a="hellogoodmorning"
for i in len(a)
print(a[i])

4. a="hellogoodmorning"
for i in a:
    del(a[i])

5. a="hai\"
print(a)

Long Answer Questions

1. What is a regular expression? How does Python provide this feature?
2. What are the differences between string and raw string? With a program, discuss it.
3. In Python, how string object is used to refer non-string objects?
4. Explain the functions in Re-module.
5. List and explain the string methods.
6. Explain string formatting in Python.

Short Answer Questions

1. List any four constants and their values defined in a string module.
2. What are escape sequence characters?
3. Discuss about Re-module in Python.
4. Explain string slicing?
5. Are Strings mutable? Justify your answer.

Exercise Programs

1. Write a Python program to check count number of characters in a string.
2. Write a Python program to read the given set of words and print the min and max sized words.
3. Write a Python program to remove any non digit character in the input string.
4. Write a Python program to format the input string to left, right and center of the padding.
5. Write a Python program to print "gOOGLE cASE" in the input string.
6. Write a Python program to print the maximum length palindromes in the input string.
7. Write a Python program to print the lexicographic rank of a string with duplicate characters.
8. Write a Python program to print the lexicographic rank of a string without duplicate characters.
9. Write a Python program to count the even decimal value substrings in a binary string.
10. Write a Python program to read the binary string and print the equivalent decimal value.
11. Write a Python program to read the binary string and print the equivalent octal value.
12. Write a Python program to read the binary string and print the equivalent hexadecimal value
13. Write a Python program to read a binary string and print the logical left-shift result.
14. Write a Python program to read a binary string and print the logical right-shift result.
15. Write a Python program to read a binary string and print the circular left-shift result.
16. Write a Python program to read a binary string and print the circular right-shift result.
17. Write a Python program to read a binary string and print the arithmetic left-shift result.
18. Write a Python program to read a binary string and print the arithmetic right-shift result.
19. Write a Python program to read the digit string and compute the exponential value of the string.
20. Write a Python program to read the digit string and compute the power of the string.
21. Write a Python program to read the digit string and compute the logarithmic value of the string.
22. Write a Python program to read the digit strings and compute all the arithmetic operations between them.
23. Write a Python program to read the complex digit strings and compute all the arithmetic operations between them.
24. Write a Python program to swap the first and second half of the input string.
25. Write a Python program to read the number of bits and display all possible binary strings with n bits.
26. Write a Python program to compute the Euclidean distance between two digit strings.
27. Write a Python program to compute the City-block distance between two digit strings.
28. Write a Python program to compute the Manhattan distance between two digit strings.
29. Write a Python program to compute the Euclidean distance between each element of the string.
30. Write a Python program to compute the City-block distance between each element of the string.
31. Write a Python program to compute the Manhattan distance between each element of the string.
32. Write a Python program to expand the given string with specified length.

33. Write a Python program to check whether the input string is Heterogram or not.
34. Write a Python program to convert the input string into ASCII form.
35. Write a Python program to convert the input ASCII form to string.
36. Write a Python program to convert the input sentence into ASCII form.
37. Write a Python program to convert the input ASCII form to a sentence.
38. Write a Python program to swap the first and second half of a sentence.
39. Write a Python program to swap the first and last letter of a sentence.
40. Write a Python program to fill the input string with the specified character.
41. Write a Python program to fill the input sentence with the specified character.
42. Write a Python program to print the length of all possible subsequence strings.
43. Write a Python program to check whether or not the input mobile number string is valid.
44. Write a Python program to check whether the input string a pangram or not.
45. Write a Python program to replace each element of the string with the associated vowel character.
46. Write a Python program to print the initial and last name of the input names in a set of strings.
47. Write a Python program to perform the Wild-Card pattern matching with the input string.
48. Write a Python program to check whether the input string of expression is balanced or not.
49. Write a Python program to move all the vowels in the input string to the front of the string.
50. Write a Python program to move all the vowels in the input string to the end of the string.
51. Write a Python program to move all the consonants in the input string to the front of the string?
52. Write a Python program to move all the consonants in the input string to the end of the string.
53. Write a Python program to move all the white spaces in the input string to the front of the string.
54. Write a Python program to move all the white spaces in the input string to the end of the string.
55. Write a Python program to print the rotated string with the slice operator.
56. Write a Python program to find the mirror characters in the input string.
57. Write a Python program to print various arithmetic operator patterns.
58. Write a Python program to swap the vowel and consonant element positions in the input string.
59. Write a Python program to search for a substring in the input string.
60. Write a Python program to concatenate multiple strings.
61. Write a Python program to join multiple strings.

Answers

Multiple Choice Questions

1. (b)	7. (b)	13. (b)	19. (a)	25. (c)
2. (a)	8. (a)	14. (a)	20. (c)	26. (d)
3. (c)	9. (d)	15. (d)	21. (b)	27. (a)
4. (d)	10. (c)	16. (b)	22. (d)	28. (c)
5. (a)	11. (c)	17. (a)	23. (c)	29. (a)
6. (d)	12. (c)	18. (d)	24. (b)	30. (a)

Fill in the Blanks

1. single or double quote.
2. escape sequence
3. deleted
4. extract
5. starting position, length
6. +, parenthesis, placing strings together
7. isalpha()
8. isdecimal()
9. swapcase()
10. double quote
11. \n
12. digits
13. printable
14. hexdigits
15. octdigits
16. upper()
17. lower()
18. split()
19. join()
20. find()
21. replace()
22. %s
23. {}
24. four
25. REGREX
26. text patterns

State True/False

1. False
2. True
3. True
4. False
5. True
6. False
7. True
8. True
9. True
10. False
11. True
12. False
13. True
14. True
15. False
16. True
17. False
18. True
19. True
20. False

Find the Output

1. haixyzhello
2. abcdef
3. ('abcdef', '', '')
4. h
   a
   i
5. GOODMORNING
6. hai
7. True
8. False
9. False
10. -1
11. 1
12. True
13. True
14. False
15. True
16. False
17. 3
18. 3
19. True
20. False
21. False
22. False
23. True
24. abc
25. abc**
26. **abc
27. abc
28. 00abc
29. bcdefa
30. abcdef
31. bcdef
32. 62
33. 1
34. thwas was first line
35. thwas is first line
36. thwas was first line
37. ['this', 'is', 'first', 'line']
38. ['first', 'is', 'line', 'this']
39. fthis isithis isrthis issthis istthis is this islthis isithis isnthis ise
40. this isfirst line
41. True
42. True

Find the Error

1. TypeError: replace() takes at least 2 arguments (1 given)
2. SyntaxError: invalid syntax (print("%d"a))
3. SyntaxError: invalid syntax
4. TypeError: 'str' object does not support item deletion
5. SyntaxError: EOL while scanning string literal

CHAPTER

13 Files and Directory Access

Python programming can handle various operations on a file by using streams. There are two different streams, viz., I/O and file streams. The present chapter discusses about various operations performed on a file.

13.1 Files and Streams

A file contains data stored in memory. All programming languages provide file handling features. Python also supports various file handling operations. Python uses streams for handling files. Stream represents continuous flow of data. There are two types of streams. They are

- Input/Output (I/O) stream
- File stream

The I/O stream is used to handle various operations related to input devices and output devices. The input stream is used to handle the input devices. input is used to represent the input stream. print is used to represent the output stream.

```
a=input("Enter the input for input: ")
print("Entered String: ",a)
```

Output

```
D:\PythonPrograms>python a1.py
Enter the input for raw_input: 1+2
Entered String: 1+2
```

A file can be created, deleted or modified using only the file stream. Import of module is not necessary to use the file stream. The file object has various attributes as given below.

- The "closed" attribute represents whether the input file object is closed or not.
- The "mode" attribute represents the mode of the file
- The "name" attribute represents the name of the file.

13.2 Opening a File

In Python, open() function is used to open a file. This function will take two arguments. The first argument represents the name of the file. The second argument represents the mode of the file to be opened. The mode of the file can be any one of the following

- Read
- Write
- Append

13.2.1 The read mode

The **read** mode allows performing read operations on the input file. The various types of read mode are

- r mode is used to open the file for reading purpose only. This is the default mode for opening any file. In this case, the file pointer is always placed at the starting point of the file.
- r+ mode is used to open the file for performing both read and write operations. In this case, the file pointer is always placed at the starting point of the file.
- rb mode is used to open the file for reading it in binary format. In this case, the file pointer is always placed at the starting point of the file.
- rb+ mode is used to open the file for performing both read and write operations in only binary format. In this case, the file pointer is always placed at the starting point of the file.

Content of abc.text

```
This is first line in abc.
```

```
f=open("abc.txt","r")
for line in f:
    print(line)
```

Output

```
D:\PythonPrograms>python a1.py
This is first line in abc.
```

13.2.2 The write mode

The **write** mode is used to perform the write operation in the file. Various types of write mode are

- w+ mode is used to create a new file to perform both reading and writing operations. If the file already exists, then the file is overwritten. In this case, the file pointer is always placed at the starting point of the file.
- w mode is used to create a new file to perform only writing operation. If the file already exists then the file is overwritten. In this case, the file pointer is always placed at the starting point of the file.
- wb mode is used create a new file to perform only writing operation in binary format. If the file already exists, then the file is overwritten. In this case, the file pointer is always placed at the starting point of the file.
- wb+ mode is used to create a new file to perform both reading and writing operations in binary format. If the file already exists then the file is overwritten. In this case, the file pointer is always placed at the starting point of the file.

Content of abc.text

```
This is first line in abc.
```

```
f=open("abc.txt","w+")
f.write("This is second line abc.txt")
```

Output

```
Content of abc.text
This is second line abc.txt
```

In this example, the file **abc.txt** is already available. So, the **w+** mode overwrites the existing file with the given content. If the file is not available, then it creates a new file.

13.2.3 The append mode

The **append** mode is used to append the data at the end of the file. If the file is already available, then the data is appended at the end of the file; otherwise a new file will be created and the content will be appended to the new file.

- a mode is used to open the file for appending purpose only. In this case, the file pointer is always placed at the end point of the file.
- a+ mode is used to open the file for performing both read and append operations. In this case, the file pointer is always placed at the end point of the file.
- ab mode is used to open the file for appending it in binary format. In this case, the file pointer is always placed at the end point of the file.
- ab+ mode is used to open the file for performing both read and append operations in only binary format. In this case, the file pointer is always placed at the end point of the file.

Content of abc.text

This is second line abc.txt

```
f=open("abc.txt","a")
f.write("\nThis is third line abc.txt")
```

Output

```
Content of abc.text
This is second line abc.txt
This is third line abc.txt
```

13.3 Reading/Writing Operations on a File

The open()function is used to open the file. The mode in which the file is opened decides which operation is to be performed in the file. In a file, we can perform two operations. They are

- Read
- Write

13.3.1 The read operation

1. The read operation is performed with the **read()** method. The **read()** method should be used with the file stream object.

```
f=open("abc.txt")
s=f.read()
print(s)
```

Output

```
D:\PythonPrograms>python a1.py
This is second line abc.txt
This is third line abc.txt
```

The **read()** method reads the data from the beginning of the file. It reads the data and returns it as string object. For **read()** method, we can also specify the size limit of the data to be read.

```
f=open("abc.txt")
s=f.read(6)
print(s)
```

Output

```
D:\PythonPrograms>python a1.py
This i
```

In the above example code, only 6 string objects (characters) are returned from "abc.txt" by the read() method.

2. The readline() method is used to return the line-by-line data from the input file.

```
f=open("abc.txt")
s=f.readline()
print(s)
```

Output

```
D:\PythonPrograms>python a1.py
This is second line abc.txt
```

2. The **readlines()** method is used to return all lines of data from the input file.

```
f=open("abc.txt")
s=f.readlines()
print(s)
```

Output

```
D:\PythonPrograms>python bb.py
['This is second line abc.txt\n', 'This is third line abc.txt\n']
```

13.3.2 The write operation

1. Similar to **read()** method, the **write()** method is used to write the data into the file. If the file is opened in the write mode, then the **write()** method starts the writing operation from the beginning of the file; otherwise the **write()** method starts writing from the end of the file.

Content of abc.text

```
This is second line abc.txt
This is third line abc.txt
```

```
f=open("abc.txt","w")
s="This is a Python programming book"
f.write(s)
```

Output

```
Content of abc.text
This is a Python programming book
```

2. The **writelines()** method is used to write multiple lines of data at a time into the file. If the file is opened in the write mode, then the **writelines()** method starts the writing operation from the beginning of the file; otherwise the **writelines()** method starts writing from the end of the file.

Content of abc.text

```
This is second line abc.txt
This is third line abc.txt
```

```
f=open("abc.txt","w")
s=["This is a Python programming book", "\nThis is file
   chapter"]
f.writelines(s)
```

Output

```
Content of abc.text
This is a Python programming book
This is file chapter
```

13.4 Other File Operations

Other than read and write operations, various other operations are also allowed. They are given below.

- The **close()** method is used to close the file object that is already created.

```
f1=open("abc.txt")
s2=f1.read()
print("The data from file:")
print(s2)
f1.close()
```

Output

```
D:\PythonPrograms>python a1.py
The data from file:
This is a Python programming book
This is file chapter
```

- The **rename()** method is used to rename the existing file name with a new file name. This method is available in **os** module. So, to use this function, the **os** module should be imported.

```
import os
f1=open("abc.txt")
print("Name of the file: ",f1.name)
f1.close()
os.rename("abc.txt","h1.txt")
print("Opening with new name")
f1=open("h1.txt")
print("Name of the file: ",f1.name)
f1.close()
print("Opening with old name:")
f1=open("abc.txt")
print("Name of the file: ",f1.name)
f1.close()
```

Output

```
D:\PythonPrograms>python a1.py
Name of the file: abc.txt
Opening with new name
Name of the file: h1.txt
Opening with old name:
Traceback (most recent call last):
  File "a1.py", line 15, in <module>
    f1=open("abc.txt")
FileNotFoundError: [Errno 2] No such file or directory: 'abc.txt'
```

- The **os** module also contains **remove()** function. This function deletes the input file. To use this function, **os** module should be imported.

```
import os
print("Opening with new name")
f1=open("h1.txt")
print("Name of the file: ",f1.name)
f1.close()
os.remove("h1.txt")
print("Opening the deleted file:")
f1=open("h1.txt")
print("Name of the file: ",f1.name)
f1.close()
```

Output

```
D:\PythonPrograms>python a1.py
Opening with new name
Name of the file: h1.txt
Opening the deleted file:
Traceback (most recent call last):
  File "a1.py", line 12, in <module>
    f1=open("h1.txt")
FileNotFoundError: [Errno 2] No such file or
directory: 'h1.txt'
```

- The **tell()** method is used to represent the current position of the file object.

Content of hello.text

```
This is first line
This is second line
This is third line
```

```
f3=open("hello.txt","a")
x=f3.tell()
f3.write(" abc")
print("the current position of f3: ",x)
f3.close()
```

Output

```
D:\PythonPrograms>python a1.py
the current position of f3: 61
```

Content of hello.text

```
This is first line
This is second line
This is third line abc
```

- The **seek()** method is used to relocate current position of a file object to the specified position. It contains two arguments, as listed below.
  - o The first argument specifies the number of bytes to be moved.
  - o The second argument specifies the position from which **seek()** method should work.

Generally, it can move from beginning, current or ending position of the file. The corresponding values are {0,1,2}. These are defined as constants in **os** module. The names of the constants are SEEK_SET, SEEK_CUR and SEEK_END.

Content of hello.text

```
This is first line
This is second line
This is third line
```

```
import os
f3=open("hello.txt","a")
x=f3.tell()
print("the current position of f3: ",x)
f3.write(" abc")
x=f3.tell()
print("the current position of f3: ",x)
f3.seek(5,os.SEEK_SET)
x=f3.tell()
print("the current position of f3: ",x)
f3.close()
```

Output

```
D:\PythonPrograms>python a1.py
the current position of f3: 61
the current position of f3: 65
the current position of f3: 5
```

Content of hello.text

```
This is first line
This is second line
This is third line abc
```

- The truncate() function is used to delete the content of a file. The deletion is performed from the specified position.

Content of hello.text

```
This is first line
This is second line
This is third line
```

```
f3=open("hello.txt","r+")
f3.truncate(10)
y=f3.read()
print("The data from file:")
print(y)
f3.close()
```

Output

```
D:\PythonPrograms>python a1.py
The data from file:
This is fi
```

Content of hello.text

```
This is fi
```

13.5 Iterating through Files

In Python programming, the os module provides several methods for iterating through all files in the directory. These methods are listed below.

- The os.listdir() method returns all components within the specified directory. It can also display all the files within the specified directory. The example code below displays the names of the files available in the subdirectory aa.

```
import os
for f in os.listdir('./aa'):
    if os.path.isfile(f):
        print ("Name of the file: ",f)
```

Output

```
D:\PythonPrograms>python a1.py
Name of the file: a2.py
Name of the file: bitwise.py
Name of the file: del.py
```

- The os.walk() method is used to walk all the components within the specified directory. The example code below displays the names of all components within the current directory.

```
import os
for root, dirs, filenames in os.walk('.'):
    for f in filenames:
        print ("Name of the component: ",f)
```

Output

```
D:\PythonPrograms>python a1.py
Name of the component: get-pip.py
Name of the component: hello.txt
Name of the component: new.txt
Name of the component: __pycache__
```

13.6 Splitting Words

In Python, the words in the file can be split by using regular expressions. After iterating the result of the regular expression, the frequency occurrence of each word can be estimated.

```
import re
import string
f = {}
d = open('one.txt', 'r')
t = d.read().lower()
m = re.findall(r'\b[a-z]{3,15}\b', t)
for w in m:
    c = f.get(w,0)
    f[w] = c + 1
f_list = f.keys()
for w in f_list:
    print(w, f[w])
```

one.txt

```
hello this is first line
hai this is second line
```

Output

```
D:\PythonPrograms>python s1.py
hello 1
this 2
first 1
line 2
hai 1
second 1
```

13.7 Serialization and De-serialization

Serialization is a process used to reduce data loss. In this process, the data is not maintained with their names, but with the objects. The de-serialization process is the reverse process of serialization. It ungroups data from the corresponding object. In Python programming, the serialization and de-serialization process is performed with the help of **pickle** module. This module contains various methods for serialization and de-serialization of Python objects. In the serialization process, the objects are converted into a byte stream and in the de-serialization process, the byte stream is converted into objects. Various functions in **pickle** module are given below.

- The **dump()** function is used to perform the serialization process.

```
import pickle
fruits = ["apple", "orange", "banana", "grape","papya"]
fh = open("ser1.txt", "wb")
pickle.dump(fruits, fh)
print("Serilization process is completed")
fh.close()
```

Output

```
D:\PythonPrograms>python a1.py
Serilization process is completed
```

- The de-serialization process is performed with the **load()** function.

```
import pickle
file1 = open("ser1.txt", "rb")
f = pickle.load(file1)
print("The de-serialized data: ")
print(f)
```

Output

```
D:\PythonPrograms>python a2.py
The de-serialized data:
['apple', 'orange', 'banana', 'grape', 'papya']
```

13.8 Hash Files

Hash functions are used to provide security to the files. The hash function will take the variable length file as an input and generate a fixed-length hash code. The generated hash code is called as Message Digest. The Python programming provides support for two types of hash functions viz., MD5 and SHA-1. For this, Python provides **hashlib** module for handling hashing functions. To generate the digest for any type of file, it is mandatory that the file should be read in binary mode. The below code discusses about **md5** and **sha-1** functions.

```
import hashlib
    h = hashlib.md5()
with open('one.txt', 'rb') as f1:
    b= f1.read()
    h.update(b)
print("message Digest for one.txt file:")
print(h.hexdigest())
```

Output

```
D:\PythonPrograms>python s1.py
message Digest for one.txt file:
8fc2cf39909a8164eac88ab924781de8
```

```
import hashlib
    h = hashlib.sha1()
with open('one.txt', 'rb') as f1:
    b= f1.read()
    h.update(b)
print("message Digest for one.txt file:")
print(h.hexdigest())
```

Output

```
D:\PythonPrograms>python s1.py
message Digest for one.txt file:
2117821b56253165e37b145547e37309ebf304fe
```

13.9 Directory Access

The directory contains multiple files. In Python programming, the os module provides various functions to handle the operations of the directory. These functions are listed below.

- The mkdir() function is used to create a new directory in the current directory.

```
import os
os.mkdir("newdir")
print("New directory is created")
```

Output

```
D:\PythonPrograms>python a1.py
New directory is created
```

- The chdir() function is used to change the directory from current to the specified directory.

```
import os
os.chdir("newdir")
print("changed to newdir directory")
```

Output

```
D:\PythonPrograms>python a1.py
changed to newdir directory
```

- The getcwd() function is used to get the name of the current working directory.

```
import os
os.chdir("newdir")
print("changed to newdir directory")
print("current directory: ",os.getcwd())
```

Output

```
D:\PythonPrograms>python a1.py
changed to newdir directory
current directory: D:\PythonPrograms\newdir
```

- The rmdir() function is used to remove the specified directory.

```
import os
os.rmdir("newdir")
print("newdir directory is deleted")
```

Output

```
D:\PythonPrograms>python a1.py
newdir directory is deleted
```

- The content of the directory can be accessed with the help of glob() defined in glob package.

```
import glob
ac = glob.glob("d:\\Python\\**\\**")
print("Content of Python directory:")
print(ac)
```

Output

```
D:\PythonPrograms>python bb.py
Content of Python directory:
['d:\\Python\\Python36-32\\DLLs',
'd:\\Python\\Python36-32\\Doc',
'd:\\Python\\Python36-32\\include',
'd:\\Python\\Python36-32\\Lib',
'd:\\Python\\Python36-32\\libs',
'd:\\Python\\Python36-32\\LICENSE.txt',
'd:\\Python\\Python36-32\\NEWS.txt',
'd:\\Python\\Python36-32\\python.exe',
'd:\\Python\\Python36-32\\python3.dll',
'd:\\Python\\Python36-32\\python36.dll',
'd:\\Python\\Python36-32\\pythonw.exe',
'd:\\Python\\Python36-32\\README.txt',
'd:\\Python\\Python36-32\\Scripts',
'd:\\Python\\Python36-32\\tcl',
'd:\\Python\\Python36-32\\Tools',
'd:\\Python\\Python36-32\\vcruntime140.dll']
```

13.10 Sample Programs

Program 1: Write a Python program to print the attributes of a file.

```
f=open("abc.txt","w+")
print("The attributes of file stream are:")
print("Name of the file: ",f.name)
print("Mode of the file: ",f.mode)
print("Response of closed attribute: ",f.closed)
```

Output

```
D:\PythonPrograms>python a1.py
The attributes of file stream are:
Name of the file: abc.txt
Mode of the file: w+
Response of closed attribute: False
```

Program 2: Write a Python program to read all lines in the input file.

```
f=open("abc.txt")
s=f.readlines()
print(s)
```

Output

```
D:\PythonPrograms>python a1.py
['This is second line abc.txt\n', 'This
is third line
abc.txt']
```

Program 3: Write a Python program to write and read the data in the input file.

```
n=int(input("Enter number of lines in the data: "))
s=[]
print("Enter the data line by line")
for i in range(n):
    s1=input("Enter data: ")
    s.append(s1)
    s.append("\n")
print(s)
f=open("abc.txt","w")
f.writelines(s)
f.close()
f1=open("abc.txt","r")
s2=f1.read()
print("The data from file:")
print(s2)
```

Output

```
D:\PythonPrograms>python a1.py
Enter number of lines in the data: 2
Enter the data line by line
Enter data: hai readers
Enter data: good morning
['hai readers', '\n', 'good morning', '\n']
The data from file:
hai readers
good morning
```

Program 4: Write a Python program to read and write with a single file object.

```
import os
f3=open("new.txt","w+")
x=f3.tell()
print("the current position: ",x)
f3.write(" this is first line in new.txt")
x=f3.tell()
print("the current position: ",x)
f3.seek(0,os.SEEK_SET)
x=f3.tell()
print("the current position: ",x)
y=f3.read()
print("The data from file:")
print(y)
x=f3.tell()
print("the current position: ",x)
f3.close()
```

When the file is opened in the write mode, the file pointer is at the starting position of the file. After performing the write operation, the file moves to the end of the file. So, if a file is opened in the w+ mode, then we can perform both read and write operations. The file object is positioned initially at the beginning of the file. After performing the write operation, the current position indicates the end of the file. Then to perform the read operation, no data is found from the end of the file position. Hence, the current position should be moved to the specified location. For this, seek() method is used.

Output

```
D:\PythonPrograms>python a1.py
the current position: 0
the current position: 30
the current position: 0
The data from file: this is first line in new.txt
the current position: 30
```

Program 5: Write a Python program to serialize and de-serialize multiple objects.

Serialization process: (a1.py)

```
import pickle
fruits1 = ["apple", "orange", "banana", "grape","papya"]
colors=["red","green","blue"]
fh = open("ser1.txt", "wb")
x=(fruits1,colors)
pickle.dump(x, fh)
print("Serilization process is completed")
fh.close()
```

De-serialization process: (a2.py)

```
import pickle
file1 = open("ser1.txt", "rb")
(x,y) = pickle.load(file1)
print("The de-serialized data: ")
print(x)
print(y)
```

Output

```
D:\PythonPrograms>python a1.py
Serilization process is completed
D:\PythonPrograms>python a2.py
The de-serialized data:
['apple', 'orange', 'banana', 'grape', 'papya']
['red', 'green', 'blue']
```

Program 6: Write a Python program to display each word of a file in reverse order.

```
with open('a.txt', 'r') as myfile:
    data=myfile.read().replace('\n', '')
print("Content of a file: ", data)
a1=data.split()
print("reverse words:")
for i in a1:
    r=''
    for j in range(len(i)-1,-1,-1):
        r=r+i[j]
    print(r,end=" ")
```

Output

```
D:\PythonPrograms>python b2.py
Content of a file: this is a sample
program
reverse words:
siht si a elpmas margorp
```

Program 7: Write a Python program to change the content of a file to uppercase letters.

```
with open('a.txt', 'r') as myfile:
    data=myfile.read().replace('\n', '')
print("Content of a file: ", data)
a1=data.split()
print("uppercase words:")
for i in a1:
    i=i.upper()
    print(i,end=" ")
```

Output

```
D:\PythonPrograms>python b2.py
Content of a file: this is a sample
program
uppercase words:
THIS IS A SAMPLE PROGRAM
```

Program 8: Write a Python program to justify the content of a file and fill it with "*"?

```
with open('a.txt', 'r') as myfile:
    data=myfile.read().replace('\n', '')
print("Content of a file: ", data)
a1=data.split()
print("justified words:")
for i in a1:
    i=i.ljust(len(i)+3,"*")
    print(i,end=" ")
```

Output

```
D:\PythonPrograms>python b2.py
Content of a file: this is a sample
program
justified words:
this*** is*** a*** sample*** program***
```

Program 9: Write a Python program to merge two files.

> Programming Tip:
> When a file is opened, then the file pointer is in the first location of the file.

```
f1=open("a.txt","r")
f2=open("a1.txt","r")
f3=open("aq.txt","w+")
s1=f1.read()
s2=f2.read()
f3.write(s1)
f3.write(s2)
f3.seek(0,0)
s3=f3.read()
print("content of first file:\n",s1)
print("content of second file:\n",s2)
print("content of merged file:\n",s3)
```

Output

```
D:\PythonPrograms>python b2.py
content of first file:
this is the content of first file
content of second file:
this is the content of second file
content of merged file:
this is the content of first filethis is
the content of
second file
```

Program 10: Write a Python program to display the size of a file.

```
f1=open("a.txt","r")
s1=f1.read()
a=f1.tell()
print("content of first file:\n",s1)
print("Size of file is: ",a," bytes")
```

Output

```
D:\PythonPrograms>python b2.py
content of first file:
this is the content of first file
Size of file is: 33 bytes
```

Program 11: Write a Python program to copy the content of one file to another file.

```
f1=open("a.txt","r")
f2=open("a1.txt","w+")
s1=f1.read()
f2.write(s1)
f2.seek(0,0)
s2=f2.read()
print("content of original file:\n",s1)
print("content of Copied file:\n",s2)
```

Output

```
D:\PythonPrograms>python b2.py
content of original file:
this is the content of first file
content of Copied file:
this is the content of first file
```

Glossary

- A stream represents the flow of data. The I/O stream represents the flow of data towards I/O devices and file stream represents the flow of data towards files.
- The os module provides various methods for iterating through all files in the directory.
- Serialization is a process used to reduce data loss.

Summary

- The input stream is used to handle the various operations of input devices.
- The output stream is used to handle the various operations of output devices.
- The file stream is used to handle various operations on files.
- The file object is used to handle the given file.
- The os module provides various operations for the files.
- Serialization and de-serialization processes can be performed in Python programming.

Multiple Choice Questions

1. How many types of streams are available in Python?
(a) 1 (b) 2
(c) 3 (d) 4

2. Which of the following stream is used for input devices?
(a) input (b) read
(c) print (d) output

3. Which of the following stream is used for output devices?
(a) input (b) read
(c) print (d) output

4. How many types of modes available for open() ?
(a) 1 (b) 2
(c) 3 (d) 4

5. What are various modes of open()?
(a) read (b) write
(c) append (d) All of the above

6. Which of the following creates a file in binary format?
(a) rb
(b) wb
(c) Both a and b.
(d) None of the above.

7. Which module defines the constants for seek()?
(a) seek (b) tell
(c) read (d) os

8. Which of the following module supports serialization?
(a) os
(b) pickle
(c) Both a and b.
(d) None of the above.

9. The name of the current working directory is given by
(a) getcwd() (b) getcpwd()
(c) getcd() (d) getpd()

10. The os.walk() method return
(a) root (b) files
(c) directories (d) All of the above.

11. Which of the following is used for handling files in Python?
(a) object (b) pointer
(c) streams (d) classes

12. The stream is used to represent
(a) continuous flow of data
(b) continuous flow of control
(c) random flow of data
(d) random flow of control

13. The input stream is used to handle
(a) input control (b) input data
(c) output control (d) output data

14. The output stream is used to handle
(a) input control (b) input data
(c) output control (d) output data

15. The "print" represents
(a) input stream
(b) output stream
(c) control stream
(d) None of the above

16. read represents?
(a) input stream
(b) output stream
(c) control stream
(d) None of the above

17. A file can be created with
(a) input stream (b) output stream
(c) file stream (d) control stream

18. To use the file stream, which of the following is required?
(a) Importing a module
(b) Importing a package
(c) Inheriting a file class
(d) None of the above

19. Which of the following are file attributes?
(a) Closed (b) Mode
(c) Name (d) All the above

20. To open a file, which of the following is required?
    (a) create()
    (b) open()
    (c) file()
    (d) None of the above.

21. How many arguments are required for open()?
    (a) 0 (b) 1
    (c) 2 (d) 3

22. A file can be opened in how many modes?
    (a) 0 (b) 1
    (c) 2 (d) 3

23. Which of the following mode represent ab+ ?
    (a) read (b) write
    (c) append (d) All the above.

24. The current position of the object is represented with
    (a) tell() (b) current()
    (c) position() (d) curr_position()

25. Which of the following module supports iterating through files?
    (a) stdin (b) stdout
    (c) flask (d) os

Fill in the Blanks

1. A file contains data stored in _______________.
2. Python uses _______________ for handling files.
3. The stream represents the continuous flow of _______________.
4. There are_______________ number of streams.
5. closed is a _______________.
6. mode is a_______________.
7. name is a _______________.
8. The first argument of open() is the _______________.
9. The second argument of open() is the _______________.
10. There are _______________ numbers of read modes.
11. The wb mode represents _______________.
12. The read operation is performed with _______________.
13. The writelines() method starts writing operation from the _______________ of the file.
14. _______________ is used to close the file object.
15. _______________ is used to rename the existing file name.
16. _______________ is used to relocate the file object.
17. _______________ is used to delete the content of the file.
18. _______________ is a process used to reduce the data loss.
19. The de-serialization process is performed with the help of _______________ module.
20. _______________ is used to perform the serialization process.
21. _______________ is used to perform the de-serialization process.
22. To provide security to the files, _______________ are used.
23. The generated hash code is _______________.
24. The hash code can be generated for only _______________ mode files.
25. The dictionary can have _______________.
26. _______________ is used to create a new directory.
27. _______________ is used to change the directory from current directory.
28. _______________ is used to get the name of the current working directory.
29. _______________ is used to remove the specified directory.
30. The content of the directory can be accessed with the help of _______________.

State True/False

1. A file is stored in memory.
2. I/O stream is used to handle files.
3. File stream is used to handle files.
4. File can be created with file stream.

5. File cannot be deleted with file stream.
6. File stream usage does not require importing module step.
7. The file attribute can specify whether the object is closed or not.
8. The file attribute cannot specify the mode of the file.
9. The name of the file can be represented with file attribute.
10. The append mode will create a new file.
11. The write mode will create a new file.
12. The read mode will create a new file.
13. The **read()** method should not be used with the file stream object.
14. A file stream object is required to perform various operations of a file.
15. The **read()** method returns data as a string object.
16. The size limit can be specified for **read()** method.
17. The **readlines()** method is used to return a single line of data from a file.
18. The **read()** method is used to return multiple lines from a file.
19. In write mode, the **write()** method will write the data from the beginning of the file.
20. In append mode, the **write()** method will write the data from the beginning of the file.
21. Data can be written from the end of the file.
22. With **os** module, a file name can be renamed.

Find the Output

1. a.txt

   Hello good morning

```
f=open("a.txt","r")
for a in f:
    print(a)
```

2.

```
f=open("a1.txt","a+")
print("file is created")
for a in f:
    print(a)
```

3.

```
f=open("a.txt","r")
s=f.read()
print(type(s))
```

Find the Error

1.

```
f=open("a.txt","w")
for a in f:
    print(a)
```

2.

```
f=open("a1.txt","r")
for a in f:
    print(a)
```

3.

```
f=open("a.txt","r")
for a in f:
    print(a)
f1.close()
```

Long Asnwer Questions

1. What is importance of file stream as compared to the I/O stream?
2. In Python, what are various ways to create a new file?
3. By using **open()** function, how many types of files can be created? Write a program to explain the procedure.
4. Discuss in detail about the various operations of files.
5. How does Python support serialization?
6. Discuss in detail about hash files.
7. With an example, explain how the directory can be accessed in Python?

Short Answer Questions

1. Define the stream? Discuss the relation between stream and files.
2. Which module supports serialization? List two functions of the module.

3. What is the importance of os module?
4. How many types of streams are available in Python?
5. Discuss about I/O streams.
6. Explain the process of splitting words.
7. What is functionality of **writelines()**?

Exercise Programs

1. Write a Python program to count the number of lines, words and characters in the input file.
2. Write a Python program to merge two input files content into a single file.
3. Write a Python program to display the content of all files within the specified directory.
4. Write a Python program to display the dimensions of the input image.
5. Write a Python program to perform the mail merge process.
6. Write a Python program to compute the message digest.
7. Write a Python program to read the student name and marks and store them in a file.
8. Write a Python program to read the student name and marks from the file and estimate the average mark.
9. Write a Python program to add a new sentence to the existing file.
10. Write a Python program to read, line by line, from a file and display it.
11. Write a Python program to print the content of a file in the reverse order.
12. Write a Python program to swap the first and second half of the input file content.
13. Write a Python program to display the frequency of vowels and consonants in a file.
14. Write a Python program to identify palindromes in the input file.
15. Write a Python program to identify anagrams in the input file.
16. Write a Python program to compare the content of two files.

Answers

Multiple Choice Questions

1. b	6. c	11. c	16. a	21. c
2. a	7. d	12. a	17. c	22. d
3. c	8. b	13. b	18. d	23. c
4. c	9. a	14. d	19. d	24. a
5. c	10. d	15. b	20. b	25. d

Fill in the Blanks

1. memory
2. streams
3. data
4. two
5. file object attribute.
6. file object attribute
7. file object attribute
8. name of the file
9. mode in which the file to be opened
10. four
11. **write** mode
12. **read()**
13. beginning
14. **close()**
15. **rename()**
16. **seek()**
17. **truncate()**
18. Serialization
19. **pickle**
20. **dump()**
21. **load()**
22. hash functions
23. Message Digest
24. binary
25. multiple files
26. **mkdir()**
27. **chdir()**
28. **getcwd()**
29. **rmdir()**
30. **glob()**

State True/False

1. True	6. True	11. True	16. True	21. True
2. False	7. True	12. False	17. False	22. True
3. True	8. False	13. False	18. False	
4. True	9. True	14. true	19. True	
5. False	10. True	15. True	20. False	

Find the Output

1. Hello good morning
2. File is created
3. <class 'str'>

Find the Error

1. io.UnsupportedOperation: not readable
2. FileNotFoundError: [Errno 2] No such file or directory: 'a1.txt'
3. NameError: name 'f1' is not defined

CHAPTER

14 Errors and Exceptions

In Python, errors and exceptions are handled efficiently. The **try**, **except** and **else** blocks are used to handle the exceptions. The **finally** block is used to execute the set of statements without checking the condition of the exception. The present chapter discusses in detail about errors and exceptions.

14.1 Motivation

During the execution of a program, there may be a possibility of perceiving errors. There are three types of errors. They are

- Syntax error
- Logic error
- Exception

Syntax errors are errors generated during the parsing. So, they are also called as parsing errors. In the program, if there is any syntax error, then the program will not be executed.

```
x=input("Enter data: ")
print("Entered data:"
```

Output

```
D:\PythonPrograms>python a1.py
File "a1.py", line 4
                    ^
SyntaxError: unexpected EOF while parsing
```

The above example code has a syntax error. The print statement does not end with ")". So, during the program parsing, this error is generated and the program is not executed.

The second type of error is called as logic error. Logic errors do not interrupt the execution of the program but they are responsible for getting unwanted result. Fixing logic errors has been found to be difficult.

```
a=int(input("Enter the first number:"))
b=int(input("Enter the second number:"))
c=a-b;
print("The first number:",a)
print("The second number:",b)
print("Result of addition:",c)
```

Output

```
D:\PythonPrograms>python s1.py
Enter the first number:10
Enter the second number:3
The first number: 10
The second number: 3
Result of addition: 7
```

The above program is intended to perform the addition of given two numbers. But due to logical error, the subtraction result is obtained.

The third type of error is called as "exception". Exceptions are the errors generated during the run time. During the execution of the program, if the exception is generated, then the execution is terminated immediately.

```
x=int(input("Enter number1: "))
y=int(input("Enter number2: "))
print("Number1 value: ",x)
print("Number2 value: ",y)
print("result of number1/number2: ",x/y)
print("result of number1*number2: ",x*y)
```

Output

```
D:\PythonPrograms>python a1.py
Enter number1: 15
Enter number2: 0
Number1 value: 15
Number2 value: 0
Traceback (most recent call last):
  File "a1.py", line 7, in <module>
    print("result of number1/number2: ",x/y)
ZeroDivisionError: division by zero
```

In the above example code, there is no syntax error. So, the program execution is started. During the execution process, the operation "15/0" has to be executed. This is an error such that the result is infinity. This value cannot be represented. To overcome this problem, a runtime error called as Exception "ZeroDivisionError" is generated.

14.2 Examples of Exception

Some examples of exceptions in Python are listed below.

- When the floating point calculation fails, then `FloatingPointError` will be generated.
- When an error is generated during the arithmetic operations then `ArithmeticError` will be generated.
- When an import statement is failed, then `ImportError` will be generated.
- In the dictionary, if the input key is not identified then `KeyError` will be generated.
- In the sequence, if the input index is not found then `IndexError` will be generated.
- `OSError` will be generated for any issues in operating system.

14.3 Handling Exceptions

In Python programming, exceptions can be handled efficiently. The exception can be handled by using **try** block. The **try** block may contain multiple **except** statements. The syntax of the **try** block is

```
........
try:
......
except exception-n:
......
else:
......
............
```

In the program, the code that is expected to raise an exception will be placed in the try block. If an exception is raised, then the corresponding **except** block will be executed. If the exception is not raised in the **try** block, then the **else** block will be executed.

14.4 Try Keyword

The syntax of the exception handling mechanism in Python contains three blocks. They are **try**, **except** and **else** blocks.

```
x=int(input("Enter the number1:"))
y=int(input("Enter the number2:"))
print("The value of number1:",x)
print("The value of number2:",y)
try:
    z=x/y
except ZeroDivisionError:
        print("Number2 value is zero")
else:
        print("The result=",z)
```

Output

```
D:\PythonPrograms>python a1.py
Enter the number1:15
Enter the number2:0
The value of number1: 15
The value of number2: 0
Number2 value is zero
```

While executing the above program, the two values entered are 15 and 0. So, the **ZeroDivisionError** exception can be raised. To handle this exception, **except** block is executed. If the exception is not raised, then the **else** block will be executed.

Output

```
D:\PythonPrograms>python a1.py
Enter the number1:15
Enter the number2:3
The value of number1: 15
The value of number2: 3
The result= 5.0
```

In any Python program, for a single **try** block, we can write multiple **except** statements. Each **except** block handles the corresponding exception.

```
try:
    x=int(input("Enter the number1:"))
    y=int(input("Enter the number2:"))
    print("The value of number1:",x)
    print("The value of number2:",y)
    z=x/y
except ZeroDivisionError:
        print("Number2 value is zero")
except KeyboardInterrupt:
        print("\nuser is interrupted by pressing ctrl+c")
else:
        print("The result=",z)
```

Output

```
D:\PythonPrograms>python a1.py
Enter the number1:15
Enter the number2:
user is interrupted by pressing ctrl+c
```

Now, let us assume that while entering the value of the second data, the user interrupted by pressing ctrl+c. This will raise an exception called as **KeyboardInterrupt**. This exception is handled by using **second except** block. This program can also handle the **ZeroDivisionError** exception.

In Python, multiple exceptions can be declared within a single **except** block. In this case, multiple exceptions should be specified within() sepearted by ",".

```
try:
    x=int(input("Enter the number1:"))
    y=int(input("Enter the number2:"))
    print("The value of number1:",x)
    print("The value of number2:",y)
    z=x/y
except (ZeroDivisionError,KeyboardInterrupt):
        print("\nException is raised")
else:
        print("The result=",z)
```

Output

```
D:\PythonPrograms>python a1.py
Enter the number1:15
Enter the number2:0
The value of number1: 15
The value of number2: 0
Exception is raised
D:\PythonPrograms>python a1.py
Enter the number1:87
Enter the number2:
Exception is raised
```

In Python, **except** block can be defined such that it can handle any type of exception.

```
try:
    x=int(input("Enter the number1:"))
    y=int(input("Enter the number2:"))
    print("The value of number1:",x)
    print("The value of number2:",y)
    z=x/y
except:
        print("\nException is raised")
else:
        print("The result=",z)
```

Output

```
D:\PythonPrograms>python a1.py
Enter the number1:54
Enter the number2:0
The value of number1: 54
The value of number2: 0
Exception is raised
D:\PythonPrograms>python a1.py
Enter the number1:
Exception is raised
```

14.5 Finally Keyword

The **finally** block can also be included within the **try** block. If an exception is raised within the **try** block, then **except** block will be executed; otherwise, the **else** block will be executed. So, either **except** or **else** blocks will be executed for the corresponding **try** block. The **finally** block will be executed whether any condition of exception is raised or not. In both of these cases, the **finally** block code will be executed.

```
try:
    x=int(input("Enter the number1:"))
    y=int(input("Enter the number2:"))
    print("The value of number1:",x)
    print("The value of number2:",y)
    z=x/y
except (ZeroDivisionError,KeyboardInterrupt):
        print("\nException is raised")
else:
        print("The result=",z)
finally:
        print("This is finally block")
```

Output

```
D:\PythonPrograms>python a1.py
Enter the number1:25
Enter the number2:5
The value of number1: 25
The value of number2: 5
The result= 5.0
This is finally block
D:\PythonPrograms>python a1.py
Enter the number1:25
Enter the number2:
Exception is raised
This is finally block
D:\PythonPrograms>python a1.py
Enter the number1:25
Enter the number2:0
The value of number1: 25
The value of number2: 0
Exception is raised
This is finally block
```

From the above example code output, it may be seen that the **finally** block is executed irrespective of the condition of the exception.

14.6 Handling Exception in Invoked Functions

Python programming allows the handling of the exceptions raised in the invoked functions. Let us say function A() invokes function B() and function B() invokes function C(). If the exception is raised in the function C(), then the exception handling mechanism handles the raised exception in the tray block of function C() and continues the execution of catch handlers. Then the flow of control is continued for executing functions B() and A().

```
def x():
    print("Invoking y function")
    y()
    print("y is invoked successfully")
def y():
    print("Invoking z function")
    z()
    print("z is invoked successfully")
def z():
    try:
        x=int(input("Enter the number1:"))
        y=int(input("Enter the number2:"))
        print("The value of number1:",x)
        print("The value of number2:",y)
        z=x/y
    except (ZeroDivisionError,KeyboardInterrupt):
            print("\nException is raised")
    else:
            print("The result=",z)
    finally:
            print("This is finally block")
print("Invoking x function")
x()
```

Output

```
D:\PythonPrograms>python b2.py
Invoking x function
Invoking y function
Invoking z function
Enter the number1:10
Enter the number2:0
The value of number1: 10
The value of number2: 0
Exception is raised
This is finally block
z is invoked successfully
y is invoked successfully
```

14.7 With and Except Statements

The **with** statement in Python will reduce the complexity of the exception handling mechanism. It wraps all the related tasks of clean ups and required operations. The best usage of **with** statement is the opening of a file. In this case, there is no need to specify the statements for close operation. The **with** statement automatically closes the opened file object.

The exceptions raised within the **with** block can also be handled. For this case, the **with** block should be placed inside a **try** block and the corresponding except blocks should be defined.

```
a=0
b=2
try:
    with (b/a) as f:
        print("no exception in with block")
except:
    print("exception in with block")
```

Output

```
D:\PythonPrograms>python a1.py
exception in with block
```

14.8 Raising Exceptions

The previous sections discussed about handling exceptions that are raised by default. However, in Python programming, the exceptions can also be raised manually. This type of exception is also handled efficiently in Python. The syntax for raising an exception manually is given below.

```
raise type_of_exception[,value_exception[,object_traceback]]
```

Manual exceptions are also handled by using **except** block. Most of these raised exceptions can be objects of a string or class.

```
try:
    a=int(input("Enter the value of a: "))
    b=int(input("Enter the value of b: "))
    print("The value of a= ",a)
    print("The value of b= ",b)
    if(a-b)<0:
        raise Exception("value of a-b is <0")
except Exception as e:
    print("Received exception: ",e)
```

Output

```
D:\PythonPrograms>python a1.py
Enter the value of a: 15
Enter the value of b: 20
The value of a= 15
The value of b= 20
Received exception: value of a-b is <0
```

14.9 Re-raising Exception

In Python programming, the last exception can be re-raised. The re-raising of an exception is performed with the **raise** statement. For this, multiple **try-except** blocks are used.

```
try:
    a=int(input("Enter the value of a: "))
    b=int(input("Enter the value of b: "))
    print("The value of a= ",a)
    print("The value of b= ",b)
    if(a-b)<0:
        raise Exception("Exception raised")
except Exception as e:
    try:
        print("Received exception: ",e)
        if(a<10):
            raise e
    except Exception as e1:
        print("Received raised exception:",e)
```

Output

```
D:\PythonPrograms>python s1.py
Enter the value of a: 4
Enter the value of b: 7
The value of a= 4
The value of b= 7
Received exception: Exception raised
Received raised exception: Exception raised
```

14.10 Instantiating Exception

In Python programming, whenever an exception is raised, an instance of the exception base class will be created. The arguments that are passed during the exception raise will be stored in **instance.args** and the string is represented with **__str__()**.

```
try:
    a=int(input("Enter the value of a: "))
    b=int(input("Enter the value of b: "))
    print("The value of a= ",a)
    print("The value of b= ",b)
    if(a-b)<0:
        raise Exception("value of a-b is <0")
except Exception as e:
    print("Exception caught")
    print("type of instance:",type(e))
    print("Arguments stored:",e.args)
    print("__str__() value=",e)
    x=e.args
    print("argument:",x)
```

Output

```
D:\PythonPrograms>python s1.py
Enter the value of a: 4
Enter the value of b: 8
The value of a= 4
The value of b= 8
Exception caught
type of instance: <class 'Exception'>
Arguments stored: ('value of a-b is <0',)
__str__ value= value of a-b is <0
argument: ('value of a-b is <0',)
```

14.11 Custom Exceptions

In Python programming, there are two types of exceptions. They are

- Built-in exceptions
- Custom exceptions

For built-in-exceptions, the definition is available with Python. So, the user need not provide the definition of built-in exceptions. The built-in exceptions can be raised either manually or automatically. Some of the built-in exceptions are listed below.

- BufferedError – Raised during the execution of buffer related operations.
- LookupError– Raised when the key or index of a sequence or mapping is invalid.
- AssertionError– Raised during the failure of assert statement execution
- AttributeError– Raised for referencing invalid attribute reference.
- FloatingPointError– Raised during the failure of floating point operation.
- IOError– Raised during the failure of I/O operation.
- ImportError– Raised during the failure of import statement.

In Python programming, the definitions of user-defined exceptions should initially be defined within the program for effective handling. Each of the user-defined exception requires its class definition. In general, the class of user-defined exception should be very less in size.

```
class ne(Exception):
    pass
try:
    a=int(input("Enter the value of a: "))
    b=int(input("Enter the value of b: "))
    print("The value of a= ",a)
    print("The value of b= ",b)
    if(a-b)<0:
        raise ne
except ne:
    print("custom exception is raised")
```

Output

```
D:\PythonPrograms>python a1.py
Enter the value of a: 5
Enter the value of b: 14
The value of a= 5
The value of b= 14
custom exception is raised
```

14.12 Assert Statement

To trap the user-defined constants, **assert** statement is used in Python programming. By using the **assert** statement, line-by-line debugging will be performed. The **assert** statement is also called as conditional raise statement. If the condition is not satisfied, then the **assert** statement will raise an exception. The syntax for assert statement is

```
assert expression[,argument]
```

The **assert** statement is handled by the **try...except** block. If the asserted exception is not handled, then the program will be immediately terminated.

```
a=int(input("Enter the value of a: "))
b=int(input("Enter the value of b: "))
print("The value of a= ",a)
print("The value of b= ",b)
assert a<b, "custom exception is raised"
```

Output

```
D:\PythonPrograms>python a1.py
Enter the value of a: 9
Enter the value of b: 5
The value of a= 9
The value of b= 5
Traceback (most recent call last):
    File "a1.py", line 8, in <module>
        assert a<b, "custom exception is raised"
AssertionError: custom exception is raised
```

14.13 Pre-defined Clean-up Actions

Pre-defined clean-up actions are used to clean the memory by removing the objects that are not used for a long time.

one.txt

```
hello
```

s1.py

```
for i in open("one.txt","r"):
    print(i)
```

Output

```
D:\PythonPrograms>python s1.py
hello
```

In the above program, the **one.txt** is open even after the execution of the program. So, to avoid this, the pre-defined clean-up action is performed with the **with** statement. After this statement is executed, the file will automatically be closed.

```
with open("one.txt","r") as x:
    for i in x:
        print(i)
```

Output

```
D:\PythonPrograms>python s1.py
hello
```

14.14 Sample Programs

Program 1: Write a Python program to handle the **ImportError** exception.

> **Programming Tip:**
> Exceptions are raised during the run time.

```
try:
    import os1
except ImportError as e:
    print("Raised Error: ",e)
```

Output

```
D:\PythonPrograms>python a1.py
Raised Error: No module named 'os1'
```

Program 2: Write a Python program to handle the **IOError** and **IndexError**.

```
try:
    import sys
    print(sys.argv[1])
except IOError as e:
    print("Raised Error: ",e)
except IndexError as f:
    print("Raised Error: ",f)
```

Output

```
D:\PythonPrograms>python a1.py
Raised Error: list index out of range
```

Program 3: Write a Python program to manually raise an exception when the number is positive.

```
try:
    x=int(input("Enter the number: "))
    if(x>0):
        raise Exception
except Exception:
    print("Raised Error:")
else:
    print("The input nuber: ",x)
```

Output

```
D:\PythonPrograms>python a1.py
Enter the number: 5
Raised Error:
D:\PythonPrograms>python a1.py
Enter the number: -5
The input nuber: -5
```

Glossary

- Syntax errors are errors generated at the time of parsing.
- Logic errors do not interrupt the execution of the program but they are responsible for getting unwanted results.
- Exceptions are errors generated during the run time. During the execution of the program, if the exception is generated, then the execution is terminated immediately.
- The **try, except** and **else** blocks are used to handle the exceptions.
- The **finally** block is used to execute a set of statements without checking the condition of the exception.

Summary

- There are three types of errors viz., syntax error, logical error and exception. The syntax errors are also called as parsing errors.
- Fixing logical errors is difficult. If an exception is raised, then the program execution is automatically terminated.
- The **try** block is used to handle the statements that raise exceptions.
- The raised exceptions can be handled with **except** block.
- If the exception is not raised, then the **else** block is executed.
- Irrespective of the condition of the exception, the **finally** block will be executed.

Multiple Choice Questions

1. How many types of exceptions are available in Python?
(a) 1 (b) 2
(c) 3 (d) 4

2. Exceptions are
(a) run time error
(b) syntax error
(c) Both a and b.
(d) None of the above.

3. The code expected to raise an error should be placed in which block?
(a) **else** (b) **finally**
(c) **except** (d) **try**

4. The exception raised in **try** block is handled by which block?
(a) **else** (b) **finally**
(c) **except** (d) **try**

5. Which block will be executed at any condition?
(a) **else** (b) **finally**
(c) **except** (d) **try**

6. Which block will be executed in case exception is not raised?
(a) **else** (b) **finally**
(c) **except** (d) **try**

7. Which keyword is used to raise the exceptions manually?
(a) **else** (b) **finally**
(c) **except** (d) **raise**

8. Which of the following is a generic exception?
(a) **Exception**
(b) **ImportError**
(c) **EOFError**
(d) None of the above.

9. Assertion is used for
(a) line debugging
(b) complete code debugging
(c) Both a and b.
(d) None of the above.

10. Custom exceptions can be defined as
(a) module
(b) class
(c) package
(d) None of the above.

11. How many types of errors are there?
(a) 0 (b) 1 (c) 2 (d) 3

12. Which type of error is generated during the parsing?
(a) Syntax error (b) Logic error
(c) Exception (d) All the above

13. Which type of error will not interrupt the execution of a program?
(a) Syntax error (b) Logic error
(c) Exception (d) All the above.

14. Fixing which type of error is found to be difficult?
(a) Syntax error (b) Logic error
(c) Exception (d) All the above

15. Which type of error will be generated during the runtime?
(a) Syntax error (b) Logic error
(c) Exception (d) All the above.

16. **ZeroDivisionError** is
(a) a syntax error (b) a logic error
(c) an exception (d) All the above.

17. How many **except** statements are allowed in **try** block?
(a) 1 (b) 2 (c) 3 (d) Many

18. If an exception is raised then which block is executed?
(a) **try** block
(b) **except** block
(c) **else** block
(d) All the above.

19. If an exception is not raised within the **try** block, then which block is executed?
(a) **try** block (b) **except** block
(c) **else** block (d) All the above.

20. Which of the following block will be executed at any condition?
    (a) **finally** block (b) **except** block
    (c) **else** block (d) All the above.
21. Which of the following statement will be used for clean-up operation?
    (a) **try** (b) **with**
    (c) **except** (d) **finally**
22. Which of the following keyword is used for manual raising of exception?
    (a) **raise** (b) **raising**
    (c) **raised** (d) All the above.
23. The manually raised exceptions are handled by
    (a) **raise**
    (b) **with**
    (c) **except**
    (d) None of the above.
24. In Python, which exceptions can be re-raised?
    (a) first (b) second
    (c) third (d) last
25. In Python, how many types of exceptions are there?
    (a) **0** (b) **1** (c) **2** (d) **3**
26. The built-in exceptions can be raised in how many ways?
    (a) Manually
    (b) Automatically
    (c) Both (a) and (b).
    (d) None of the above.

Fill in the Blanks

1. During the program execution, there may be a chance of getting ________________.
2. Syntax errors are also called as ________________.
3. ________________ does not interrupt the execution of the program.
4. During arithmetic operations, ________________ will be generated.
5. During floating point calculation fails, ________________ will be generated.
6. When an import statement fails, then ________________ will be generated.
7. ________________ will be generated for any issues in the operating system.
8. In the dictionary, if the input key is not identified then ________________ will be generated.
9. In a sequence, if the input index is not found then ________________ will be generated.
10. Exceptions can be handled by using ________________ block.
11. The **try** block may contain multiple ________________ statements.
12. If an exception is raised, then the corresponding ________________ will be executed.
13. The syntax of the exception handling mechanism contains ________________ blocks.
14. The three blocks of exception handling mechanism are ________________.
15. For a single **try** block, ________________ number of **except** statements is allowed.
16. ________________ will be generated if the user interrupts the program execution.
17. A single **except** block can handle ________________ number of exceptions.
18. ________________ block can handle any type of exception.
19. Within **try** block, ________________ will be executed if the exception is raised.
20. Within **try** block, ________________ will be executed if the exception is not raised.
21. Within **try** block, ________________ will be executed at any condition of the exception.

State True/False

1. An error will be generated during coding of the program.
2. An error will be generated during execution of the program.
3. There are four types of errors.
4. Syntax errors can occur within the program.
5. Logic errors can occur within the program.
6. Exceptions can occur within the program.
7. Logic errors can occur at the time of parsing.

8. Parsing errors are exceptions.
9. Parsing errors are logic errors.
10. Parsing errors are syntax errors.
11. A program can be executed if there are syntax errors.
12. A program cannot be executed if there are logic errors.
13. A program cannot be executed if there are exceptions.
14. Syntax errors are difficult to fix.
15. Logic errors are difficult to fix.
16. The execution of a program can be terminated immediately if the exception is raised.
17. **ZeroDivisionError** is a syntax error
18. **ZeroDivisionError** is a logical error
19. **ZeroDivisionError** is an exception
20. **try** block consists of three blocks.

Find the Output

1.
```
x=100
y=200
print("The value of number1:",x)
print("The value of number2:",y)
try:
   z=x/y
except ZeroDivisionError:
   print("Number2 value is zero")
else:
   print("The result=",z)
```

2.
```
x=100
y=0
try:
   z=x/y
except ZeroDivisionError:
   print("Number2 value is zero")
else:
   print("The result=",z)
```

3.
```
x=100
y=10
try:
      z=x/y
      except ZeroDivisionError:
   print("Number2 value is zero")
finally:
   print("finally block")
```

Find the Error

1.
```
x=100
y=0
print("The value of number1:",x)
print("The value of number2:",y)
try:
   z=x/y
```

2.
```
x=100
y=0
print("The value of number1:",x)
print("The value of number2:",y)
z=x/y
```

3.
```
import osad
print("Hello")
```

4.
```
x=100
y=0
try:
      z=x/y
      else:
   print("The result=",z)
```

Long Answer Questions

1. What is the importance of **try** block in Python?
2. How are exceptions raised in **try** block handled in Python?
3. Write a program to display an end message irrespective of exception.
4. Discuss the procedure for raising user-defined exception.

Short Answer Questions

1. Differentiate between error and exception.
2. Explain **try** block.
3. How can an exception be raised manually?
4. Define assertion.

Exercise Programs

1. Write a Python program to use the with statement for opening a file and handling various exceptions.
2. Write a Python program to create a user-defined exception if the input number is even?

Answers

Multiple Choice Questions

1. b	5. b	9. a	13. b	17. d	21. b	25. c
2. a	6. a	10. b	14. b	18. b	22. a	26. c
3. d	7. d	11. d	15. c	19. c	23. c	
4. c	8. a	12. a	16. c	20. a	24. d	

Fill in the Blanks

1. errors
2. parsing errors
3. Logic error
4. ArithmeticError
5. FloatingPointError
6. ImportError
7. OSError
8. KeyError
9. IndexError
10. try
11. except
12. except block
13. three
14. try, except and else blocks
15. multiple
16. KeyboardInterrupt
17. multiple
18. except
19. except block
20. else block
21. finally block

State True/False

1. False	5. True	9. False	13. True	17. False
2. True	6. True	10. True	14. False	18. False
3. False	7. False	11. False	15. True	19. True
4. True	8. False	12. False	16. True	20. True

Find the Output

1. The value of number1: 100
   The value of number2: 200
   The result= 0.5
2. Number2 value is zero
3. finally block

Find the Error

1. SyntaxError: unexpected EOF while parsing
2. ZeroDivisionError: division by zero
3. ModuleNotFoundError: No module named 'osad'
4. SyntaxError: invalid syntax

CHAPTER

15 Multithreading

Each program consists of multiple statements. Execution of each statement can further create multiple processes. Execution of each process, in turn, leads to the creation of multiple threads. Python programming can efficiently handle the execution of multiple threads. A thread is a light-weight process. Multiple threads can share the memory space of the associated process. The present chapter discusses in detail about how multithreading is handled in Python.

15.1 Introduction to Thread

A thread is a single flow of the process. It is used for exploiting the latency and concurrency in parallel, distributed processing. They are mainly intended for designing event-driven software. The thread can be of three types:

- User thread
- Kernel thread
- Hybrid thread

A multithreaded program contains multiple threads that are executed parallely. All these multiple threads will share a common memory space. So, the data is shared among all the multiple threads.

15.2 Differences Between Process and Thread

For executing a program, there are two types of units, viz., process and thread. When a program is executing, multiple processes or threads can be created from itself. A program contains various sets of instructions. For the execution of each instruction, a process is required. In some cases, each process contains multiple threads. The differences between process and thread are listed below.

- The process can be considered as a heavy-weight task while the thread is a light-weight task. Here, weight represents the memory usage.
- In case of multiprocessing, each process maintains its own copy of the data in a separate memory space. In case of multithreading, all multiple threads maintain only one copy in memory space, which is shared by all the processes.
- Multiple processes can easily communicate with one another. However, multiple threads use a complex procedure to communicate with one another.
- Each process requires maintaining its own copy of process table to maintain the duplicated data from the parent process. Each of the thread shares common memory; so they do not require additional tables.
- Changes made by one process will not be reflected to other processes, whereas changes made by one thread will be reflected on all other threads.

- The parent process will have control over the child processes, whereas threads of the same process will have control over one another.
- Processes are independent, whereas threads are dependent.

15.3 Threading Module

The **threading** module is used to provide various functions for handling threads in Python. This module considers each thread as an object. Various functions and constants defined in **threading** module are listed below.

- The **active_count()** function returns the number of live threads for the currently executing program.
- The **current_thread()** function returns the name of the current thread being executed.
- The **get_ident()** function returns the thread identifier.
- The list of all live multiple threads list is given by the **enumerate()**function.
- The name of the main thread is given by the **main_thread()**function.
- The maximum time allocated for each of the thread is given by the IMEOUT_MAX constant.

```
import threading
print("No. of Alive threads: ",threading.active_count())
print("Current Thread Object: ",threading.current_thread())
print("Thread Identifier: ", threading.get_ident())
print("List of Alive Threads: ",threading.enumerate())
print("Main Thread Object: ",threading.main_thread())
print("Thread Max. Time: ", threading.TIMEOUT_MAX)
```

Output

```
D:\PythonPrograms>python a1.py
No. of Alive threads: 1
Current Thread Object: <_MainThread(MainThread, started
5964)>
Thread Identifier: 5964
List of Alive Threads: [<_MainThread(MainThread, started
5964)>]
Main Thread Object: <_MainThread(MainThread, started
5964)>
Thread Max. Time: 4294967.0
```

15.4 Thread Synchronization

- Local object information can be obtained with the usage of **local()** function.

```
import threading
x=threading.local()
print("Local Thread Object: ",x)
```

Output

```
D:\PythonPrograms>python a1.py
Local Thread Object: <_thread._local object at 0x03887AB0>
```

- In earlier versions of Python, two modules, **thread** and **threading**, are available. But in Python3, _thread and **threading** modules are available. All the functions of a thread are available in threading module.

```
>>> import thread
Traceback (most recent call last):
   File "<stdin>", line 1, in <module>
ModuleNotFoundError: No module named 'thread'
>>> import _thread
>>>
```

- In Python programming, a new thread can be created in two different ways. They are
  - o By using **_thread** module
  - o By using **threading** module

  In case of **_thread** module, a new thread can be created by defining the action of the thread in a function. The syntax is given below

```
_thread.start_new_thread(function_name_obj,(arg1,arg2...))
```

```
import _thread
def abc(arg1):
    print("Thread Name: ",arg1)
_thread.start_new_thread(abc,("Thread1",))
_thread.start_new_thread(abc,("Thread2",))
_thread.start_new_thread(abc,("Thread3",))
_thread.start_new_thread(abc,("Thread4",))
_thread.start_new_thread(abc,("Thread5",))
_thread.start_new_thread(abc,("Thread6",))
while True:
    pass
```

Output

```
D:\PythonPrograms>python a1.py
Thread Name: Thread1
Thread Name: Thread6
Thread Name: Thread5
Thread Name: Thread2
Thread Name: Thread3
Thread Name: Thread4
```

- Creating threads by using **_thread** module is a low-level threading.
- In case of creating a child thread by using **threading** module, the **Thread** class is used by the following procedure
  - o Defining the new subclass from the **Thread** class in **threading** module.
  - o Method overriding of **__init__()** to provide new arguments to the child thread.
  - o Method overriding of **run()** to provide the action of the thread.

```
import threading
class newthread(threading.Thread):
    def __init__(self,tname):
        threading.Thread.__init__(self)
        self.name=tname
t1=newthread("t1")
print("t1 thread is created")
t2=newthread("t2")
print("t2 thread is created")
```

Output

```
D:\PythonPrograms>python a1.py
t1 thread is created
t2 thread is created
```

- The **threading** module contains a class called as **Thread**. The **Thread** class contains various methods as listed below.
  - o The thread activity is started with the **start()** method.

```
import threading
class newthread(threading.Thread):
    def __init__(self,tname):
        threading.Thread.__init__(self)
        self.name=tname
        print("Name in __int__: ",self.name)
t1=newthread("t1")
t2=newthread("t2")
t1.start()
t2.start()
```

Output

```
D:\PythonPrograms>python a1.py
Name in __int__: t1
Name in __int__: t2
```

o The run() method will perform the actual execution of the thread. Whenever a new thread is created, new definition for the run() method can be provided by using method overriding.

```
import threading
class newthread(threading.Thread):
    def __init__(self,tname):
        threading.Thread.__init__(self)
        self.name=tname
    def run(self):
        print(self.name," thread is running")
t1=newthread("t1")
t2=newthread("t2")
t1.start()
t2.start()
```

Output

```
D:\PythonPrograms>python a1.py
t1 thread is running
t2 thread is running
```

o The getname() method is used to return the name of the thread.

```
import threading
class newthread(threading.Thread):
    def __init__(self,tname):
        threading.Thread.__init__(self)
        self.name=tname
    def run(self):
        print(self.name," thread is running")
t1=newthread("t1")
t2=newthread("t2")
t1.start()
t2.start()
print("Result of getname(): ",t1.getName())
print("Result of getname(): ",t2.getName())
```

Output

```
D:\PythonPrograms>python a1.py
t1 thread is running
t2 thread is running
Result of getname(): t1
Result of getname(): t2
```

o The setname() method is used to set a new name for the thread.

```
import threading
class newthread(threading.Thread):
    def __init__(self,tname):
        threading.Thread.__init__(self)
        self.name=tname
    def run(self):
        print(self.name," thread is running")
t1=newthread("t1")
t2=newthread("t2")
t1.start()
t2.start()
print("Result before setname(): ",t1.getName())
print("Result before setname(): ",t2.getName())
t1.setName("thread1")
t2.setName("thread2")
print("Result after setname(): ",t1.getName())
print("Result after setname(): ",t2.getName())
```

Output

```
D:\PythonPrograms>python a1.py
t1 thread is running
t2 thread is running
Result before setname(): t1
Result before setname(): t2
Result after setname(): thread1
Result after setname(): thread2
```

o is_alive() method checks whether the thread is alive or terminated. It returns True when the thread is alive; otherwise it returns False.

```
import threading
class newthread(threading.Thread):
    def __init__(self,tname):
        threading.Thread.__init__(self)
        self.name=tname
    def run(self):
        print(self.name," thread is running")
t1=newthread("t1")
t2=newthread("t2")
print("Active threads count: ", threading.active_count())
print("result of is_alive(t1): ",t1.is_alive())
print("result of is_alive(t2): ",t2.is_alive())
t1.start()
t2.start()
print("Active threads count: ", threading.active_count())
print("result of is_alive(t1): ",t1.is_alive())
print("result of is_alive(t2): ",t2.is_alive())
```

Output

```
D:\PythonPrograms>python a1.py
Active threads count: 1
result of is_alive(t1): False
result of is_alive(t2): False
t1 thread is running
t2 thread is running
Active threads count: 2
result of is_alive(t1): False
result of is_alive(t2): False
```

- Waiting of termination of thread is handled by using join() method.
- isDaemon() method is used to check whether the input thread is a Daemon thread or not.
- setDaemon() method is used to set the thread as Daemon.

- In Python programming, synchronization is achieved with locks. If one thread locks then other threads should wait until the lock is opened. Thus, locks are an efficient way of supporting thread synchronization. A thread lock can be in any one of the two states as given below.
  - Locked
  - Unlocked

When the lock is created for a thread, then the default state is "unlocked". A new lock can be created by using lock() function in threading module.

On a thread lock, the following two functions can be applicable.

- acquire():If any of the lock is in unlocked state, then any thread can get the lock by using acquire() method.
- release():If any of the lock is in "locked state" then the corresponding thread can release the lock by using release() method.

```
import threading
class newthread(threading.Thread):
    def __init__(self,tname,l):
        threading.Thread.__init__(self)
        self.name=tname
        self.lock=l
    def run(self):
        print(self.name," thread is running")
    def x(self):
        self.lock.acquire()
        print(self.name, "is locked")
    def y(self):
        self.lock.release()
        print(self.name, "is released")
l=threading.Lock()
t1=newthread("t1",l)
t2=newthread(«t2»,l)
t1.start()
t2.start()
t1.x()
t1.y()
t2.x()
t2.y()
```

Output

```
D:\PythonPrograms>python a1.py
t1 thread is running
t2 thread is running
t1 is locked
t1 is released
t2 is locked
t2 is released
```

The **Lock()** method allows the thread to acquire only one lock. The lock can be acquired by another thread only after it has been released by the current thread.

```
import threading
class newthread(threading.Thread):
    def __init__(self,tname,l):
        threading.Thread.__init__(self)
        self.name=tname
        self.lock=l
    def run(self):
        print(self.name," thread is running")
    def x(self):
        self.lock.acquire()
        print(self.name, "is locked")
    def y(self):
        self.lock.release()
        print(self.name, "is released")
l=threading.Lock()
t1=newthread("t1",l)
t2=newthread(«t2»,l)
t1.start()
t2.start()
t1.x()
t2.x()
```

Output

```
D:\PythonPrograms>python a1.py
t1 thread is running
t2 thread is running
t1 is locked
```

To overcome this problem, locks are created using the **RLock()**method. These locks are called as reentrant locks.

```
import threading
class newthread(threading.Thread):
    def __init__(self,tname,l):
        threading.Thread.__init__(self)
        self.name=tname
        self.lock=l
    def run(self):
        print(self.name," thread is running")
    def x(self):
        self.lock.acquire()
        print(self.name, "is locked")
    def y(self):
        self.lock.release()
        print(self.name, "is released")
l=threading.RLock()
t1=newthread("t1",l)
t2=newthread(«t2»,l)
t1.start()
t2.start()
t1.x()
t2.x()
```

Output

```
D:\PythonPrograms>python a1.py
t1 thread is running
t2 thread is running
t1 is locked
t2 is locked
```

15.5 Sample Program

***Program 1*:** Write a Python program to exit the thread by using _thread module.

```
import _thread
def abc(arg1):
    print("Started Thread Name: ",arg1)
```

```
    print("The thread1 is now exit")
    _thread.exit()
_thread.start_new_thread(abc,("Thread1",))
while True:
    pass
```

Output

```
D:\PythonPrograms>python a1.py
Started Thread Name: Thread1
The thread1 is now exit
```

Glossary

- A thread is a light-weight process. Multiple threads can share the memory space of the associated processes.
- A process is called as heavy-weight task while a thread is called as light-weight task. Here, weight represents the memory usage.

Summary

- In Python, threads can be created by using _thread or threading modules.
- The _thread uses low-level threading and threading module uses high-level threading.
- Various operations can be applied on the thread. The threading module consists of Thread class and it contains various methods.
- Thread synchronization is achieved with locks. A lock can be created. The created object can acquire an additional lock or release a lock.

Multiple Choice Questions

1. Daemon threads are stopped at
   (a) shutdown
   (b) restart
   (c) Both a and b.
   (d) None of the above.
2. Thread can be created in how many ways?
   (a) 1 (b) 2 (c) 3 (d) 4
3. Which module is responsible for low-level threading?
   (a) thread
   (b) threading
   (c) _thread
   (d) None of the above.
4. Which module is responsible for high-level threading?
   (a) thread
   (b) threading
   (c) _thread
   (d) None of the above.
5. Which of the following gives the number of live current threads?
   (a) threading.get_ident()
   (b) threading.current_thread()
   (c) threading.active_count()
   (d) None of the above.
6. Thread class is available in
   (a) _thread
   (b) threading
   (c) Both a and b.
   (d) None of the above.
7. Which method should be overwritten for creating a thread using Thread class?
   (a) __init__
   (b) run()
   (c) Both a and b.
   (d) None of the above.
8. What are the various method(s) for using lock?
   (a) acquire()
   (b) release()
   (c) Both a and b.
   (d) None of the above.
9. Thread synchronization is achieved
   (a) with lock of the thread
   (b) by running the thread
   (c) by sleeping the thread
   (d) None of the above.
10. When will the main thread exit?
    (a) After completion of entire thread
    (b) After completion of entire process
    (c) After completion of entire instruction
    (d) After completion of entire program
11. Various applications of thread are?
    (a) exploiting the latency
    (b) exploiting concurrency
    (c) distributed processing
    (d) All the above.

12. What are the various types of threads?
    (a) User thread (b) Kernel thread
    (c) Hybrid thread (d) All the above
13. A multithreaded program contains
    (a) single execution of single thread
    (b) single execution of multiple threads
    (c) multiple execution of multiple threads
    (d) multiple execution of single thread
14. All multiple threads use
    (a) shared memory space
    (b) separate memory space
    (c) Both (a) and (b).
    (d) None of the above.
15. The process is called as?
    (a) light-weight task
    (b) heavy-weight task
    (c) medium-weight task
    (d) None of the above.
16. The thread is called as?
    (a) light-weight task
    (b) heavy-weight task
    (c) medium-weight task
    (d) None of the above.
17. Each Python module considers the thread as?
    (a) class
    (b) object
    (c) Both (a) and (b).
    (d) None of the above.
18. The time allocated for each thread is represented by?
    (a) MAX (b) OUT_MAX
    (c) IME_MAX (d) IMEOUT_MAX
19. Thread lock states are
    (a) locked
    (b) unlocked
    (c) Both (a) and (b).
    (d) None of the above.
20. Reentrant locks are created with?
    (a) Lock() (b) Rock()
    (c) RLock() (d) All the above.

Fill in the Blanks

1. A thread is a _______________ flow of process.
2. A thread is designed for _______________.
3. There are_______________ number of threads in Python.
4. _______________, _______________ and _______________ are types of threads.
5. _______________ is shared among all multiple threads.
6. When a program is executing, _______________ can be created.
7. Each program statement can further create _______________.
8. Each process can further create _______________.
9. A process is a _______________.
10. A thread is a _______________.
11. The weight represents _______________.
12. Communication among multiple threads is _______________.
13. Communication among multiple processes is _______________.
14. Each process requires maintaining its own copy of _______________.
15. Changes of one process _______________ in another process.
16. Changes of one thread _______________ in another thread.
17. For handling threads, _______________ module is used.
18. _______________ is used for counting alive threads.
19. The name of the currently executing thread is represented by _______________.
20. The thread identifier is represented with _______________.

State True/False

1. The local() function is used to get the local object information.
2. All functions of thread are available in threading module.
3. In Python, a thread can be created by using only one method.
4. By using _thread module, a thread can be created.

5. By using threading module, a thread can be created.
6. Creating a thread by using **_thread** module is high-level threading.
7. The **Thread** class is available in **_thread** module.
8. The **Thread** class is available in **threading** module.
9. The thread activity is started with **start()** method.
10. The execution of the thread is performed with **start()** method.
11. The execution of the thread is performed with **run()** method.
12. Waiting of termination of thread is handled by using **alive()** method.
13. **join()** method will wait for the termination of the thread.
14. In Python, synchronization is achieved with threads.
15. There are two states used for thread synchronization.
16. The default state of a lock is “locked”
17. Thread module handles locks.
18. **lock()** in threading module can create a lock.
19. **acquire()** method is used to get the lock.
20. **release()** method is used to get the lock.

Find the Output

1.
```
import threading
print("Current Thread Object: ",threading.current_thread())
```
2.
```
import threading
print(threading.local())
```
3.
```
import threading
class newthread(threading.Thread):
  def __init__(self,tname):
threading.Thread.__init__(self)
  self.name=tname
t1=newthread("t1")
t1.start()
print("List of Alive Threads: ",threading.enumerate())
```

Find the Error

1.
```
import Threading
print("Current Thread Object: ",threading.current_thread())
```
2.
```
import threading
print(local())
```
3.
```
import threading
class newthread(Thread):
  def __init__(self,tname):
threading.Thread.__init__(self)
self.name=tname
t1=newthread("t1")
t1.start()
print("List of Alive Threads: ",threading.enumerate())
```

Long Answer Questions

1. List the differences between thread and process.
2. What is the procedure to create a thread by using threading module?
3. In Python, how is thread synchronization supported?

Short Answer Questions

1. Differentiate **Lock** and **RLock**.
2. List the various attributes of **_thread** module?
3. In Python, how many ways are there to create a thread?
4. Write the syntax for creating a thread by using **_thread** module.

Exercise Programs

1. Write a Python program to handle multiple threads for 10 milliseconds.
2. Write a Python program to handle the producer–consumer problem.

Answers

Multiple Choice Questions

1. (a)
2. (b)
3. (c)
4. (b)
5. (c)
6. (b)
7. (c)
8. (c)
9. (a)
10. (d)
11. (d)
12. (d)
13. (c)
14. (a)
15. (b)
16. (a)
17. (b)
18. (d)
19. (c)
20. (c)

Fill in the Blanks

1. single
2. even driven software
3. three
4. User, Kernel and Hybrid
5. Data
6. multiple processes or threads
7. multiple processes
8. multiple threads.
9. heavy-weight task
10. light-weight task
11. memory usage
12. complex
13. easy
14. process table
15. will not be reflected
16. will be reflected
17. threading
18. active_count()
19. current_thread()
20. get_ident()

State True/False

1. True
2. True
3. False
4. True
5. True
6. False
7. False
8. True
9. True
10. False
11. True
12. False
13. True
14. False
15. True
16. False
17. False
18. True
19. True
20. False

Find the Output

1. Current Thread Object: <_MainThread(MainThread, started 5592)>
2. <_thread._local object at 0x0392E630>
3. List of Alive Threads: [<_MainThread(MainThread, started 7736)>]

Find the Error

1. ModuleNotFoundError: No module named 'Threading'
2. NameError: name 'local' is not defined
3. NameError: name 'Thread' is not defined

CHAPTER

16 Tkinter

Python supports Graphical User Interface (GUI) by using wxPython, JPython and Tkinter. Among these, the present chapter discuses about Tkinter based GUI. The tkinter module contains various classes for supporting widgets.

16.1 Introduction

The earlier chapters of this book discussed command line interface parameters in Python. However, Python programming supports both the command line interface and graphical user interface (GUI). The Python supports GUI in three ways viz., wxPython, JPython and Tkinter.

- The wxPython is a platform independent toolkit for supporting GUI in Python. The implementation of GUI with this toolkit is easy, but since wxPython gets frequently updated, frequent patch updations are required for new feature requests.
- The JPython supports GUI for integrating with the Java platform. It is majorly used for embedded scripting, interactive interpreter and rapid application development.
- The Tkinter is also called as Tk interface. It is a standard toolkit in Python for GUI. It binds the Tk widgets to Python objects. To use this, a working Tcl/Tk system is required. The advantage of Tkinter is that it is more portable than other GUI toolkits.

In Python 3, the tkinter module is responsible for handling the various operations of GUI. It provides an easy way to create GUI applications in Python. In case of using this toolkit, from tkinter import * statement should be included. With this, all the attributes of tkinter module are available in the current program. After importing, create a GUI application main window. For this, use Tk() method. Then add the required widgets to the main window. Finally, call the mainloop() method for executing the events.

```
from tkinter import *
a = Tk()
a.title('First Tkinter program')
a.mainloop()
```

Output

D:\PythonPrograms>python a1.py

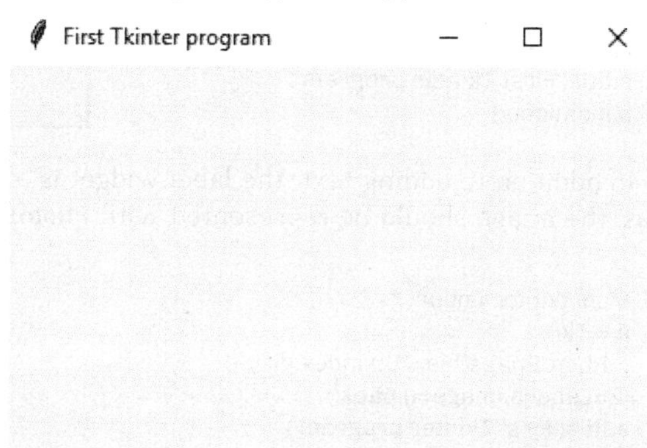

16.2 Widget

Tkinter widgets represent various objects for handling GUI. For each GUI component, an object is maintained for the corresponding widget class. Various widgets are listed below

- button
- canvas
- checckbutton
- combobox
- entry
- frame
- label
- labelframe
- listbox
- menu
- menubutton
- message
- notebook
- optionMenu
- panedwindow
- progressbar
- radiobuttion
- scale
- scrollbar
- separator
- sizegrip
- spinbox
- text
- treeview

The common properties of widgets include colors, fonts, dimensions, anchors, bitmaps and cursors. The tkinker places all the components in the main window by using any one of the following methods:

- pack() method places components in blocks of parent widget.
- grid() method places components in table structure of parent widget.
- place() method places components within the specified position of parent widget.

16.3 Label Widget

The label widget is used to add the labels and images in the GUI window. For this widget component, Label class is used.

```
from tkinter import *
a = Tk()
l = Label(a, text="This is a Label")
l.pack()
a.title('First Tkinter program')
a.mainloop()
```

Output

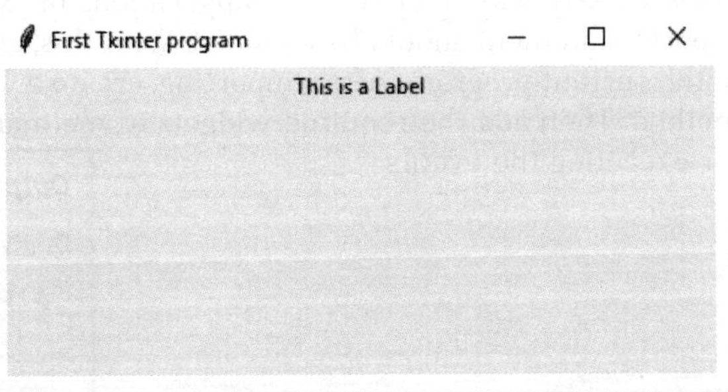

In addition to adding text, the label widget is also used to add images in the GUI window. For this, the image should be represented with PhotoImage() method.

```
from tkinter import *
a = Tk()
i=PhotoImage(file="D:\index.gif")
l2=Label(a,image=i).pack()
a.title('First Tkinter program')
a.mainloop()
```

Output

16.4 Button Widget

The button widget is used to add a button in the GUI window.

```
from tkinter import *
def abc():
    print("OK button is clicked")
a = Tk()
b1=Button(a, text="OK", width=30, command=abc).pack()
a.mainloop()
```

Output

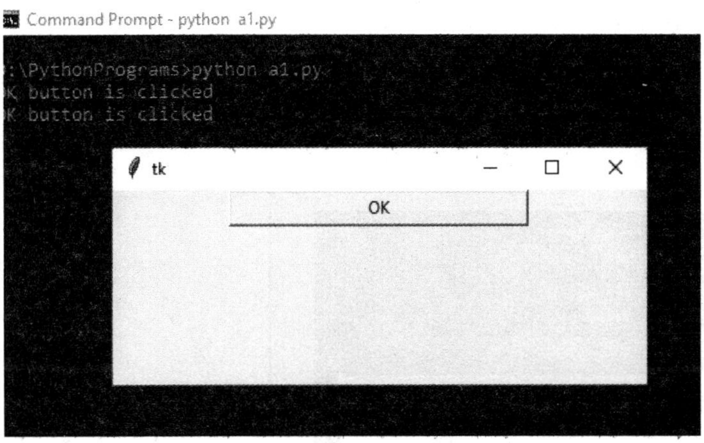

In case of buttons, the arguments can be passed to the command function by using lambda expressions.

```
from tkinter import *
def abc(number):
    print(number, "button is clicked")
a = Tk()
b1=Button(a, text="OK", width=30, command=lambda:abc(1)).pack()
b2=Button(a, text="RESET", width=30, command=lambda:abc(2)).pack()
a.mainloop()
```

Output

In the above example code, the command for the button widget is a function. Other than function, method can also be used for representing the command for the widget. These types of methods are called as "Bound Methods". They should be defined within a class. In case of using bound methods, __init__ method should be overridden.

```
from tkinter import *
class xyz:
    def abc(number):
        print(number, "button is clicked")
a = Tk()
b1=Button(a, text="OK", width=30, command=lambda:xyz.abc(1)).pack()
b2=Button(a, text="RESET", width=30, command=lambda:xyz.abc(2)).pack()
a.mainloop()
```

Output

16.5 Checkbutton Widget

The Checkbutton widget is used to add the checkbutton in the GUI window. It allows multiple selections of options.

```
from tkinter import *
a = Tk()
var1=IntVar()
var2=IntVar()
var3=IntVar()
var4=IntVar()
c1=Checkbutton(a, text="Value1", variable=var1).pack()
c2=Checkbutton(a, text="Value2", variable=var2).pack()
c3=Checkbutton(a, text="Value3", variable=var3).pack()
c4=Checkbutton(a, text="Value4", variable=var4).pack()
print(“Value of var1: “,var1)
print(“Value of var2: “,var2)
print(“Value of var3: “,var3)
print(“Value of var4: “,var4)
a.mainloop()
```

Output

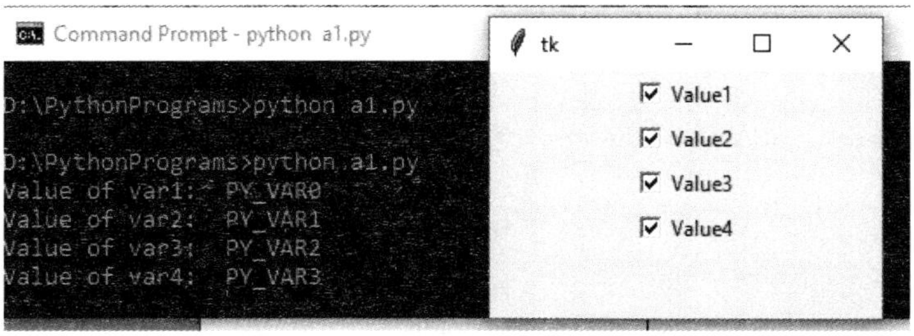

16.6 Entry Widget

The entry widget is used to add the textbox in the GUI window. The entry widget will take single line text input from the user.

```
from tkinter import *
a = Tk()
l1=Label(a, text="Enter your name").pack()
e1=Entry(a).pack()
b1=Button(a,text="SUBMIT").pack()
a.mainloop()
```

Output

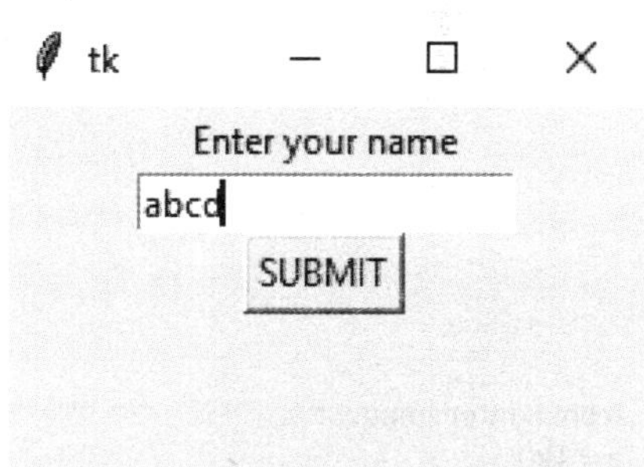

16.7 Listbox Widget

The Listbox widget is used to add the drop down list box component in the GUI window. It allows user to select multiple options. The elements can be added with insert() method and deleted with delete() method.

```
from tkinter import *
a = Tk()
l1=Listbox(a,height=5)
l1.pack()
l1.insert(END, “item1”)
l1.insert(END, “item2”)
l1.insert(END, “item3”)
l1.insert(END, “item4”)
l1.insert(END, “item5”)
a.mainloop()
```

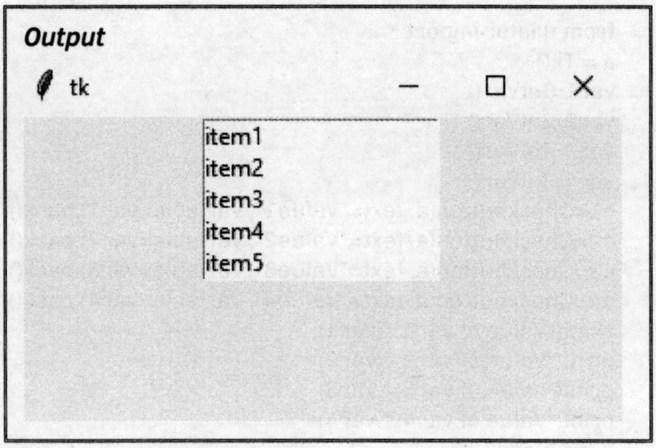

16.8 Radiobutton Widget

The Radiobutton widget is used to add combo of options (multiple options) in the GUI window. It allows only option selection among multiple options.

```
from tkinter import *
a = Tk()
var = IntVar()
Radiobutton(a, text="radio1", variable=var, value=1).pack(anchor=W)
Radiobutton(a, text="radio2", variable=var, value=2).pack(anchor=W)
Radiobutton(a, text="radio3", variable=var, value=3).pack(anchor=W)
a.mainloop()
```

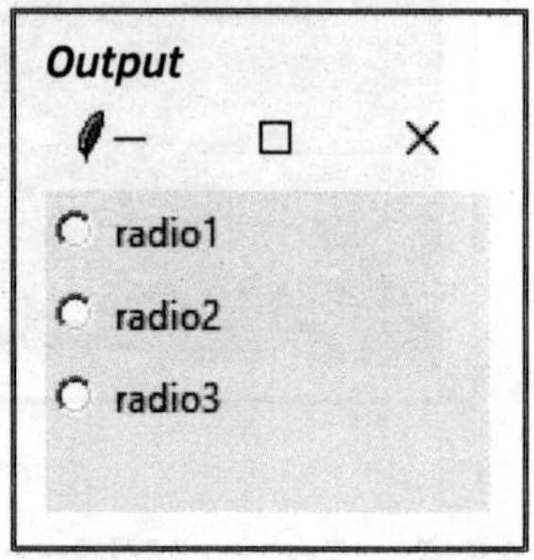

16.9 Scrollbar Widget

The Scrollbar widget is used to add the scrollbar component in the GUI window.

```
from tkinter import *
a = Tk()
scrollbar = Scrollbar(a)
scrollbar.pack(side=RIGHT, fill=Y)
a.mainloop()
```

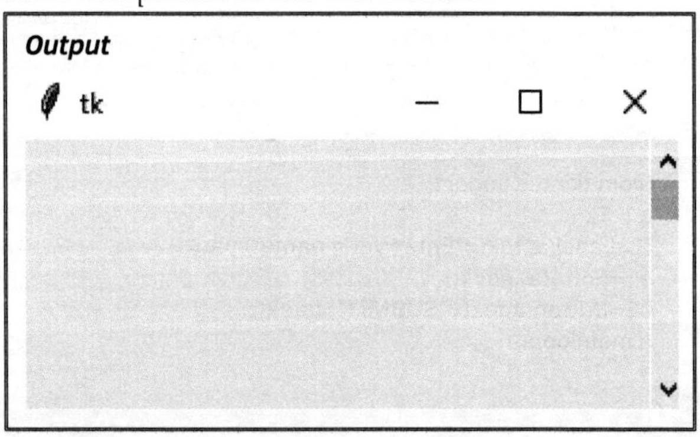

16.10 Text Widget

The Text widget is used to add multiple lines of text in the GUI window.

```
from tkinter import *
a = Tk()
t1 = Text(a, height=3, width=50)
t1.pack()
t1.insert(END, "This is first line\n This is second line\n This is third line")
a.mainloop()
```

Output

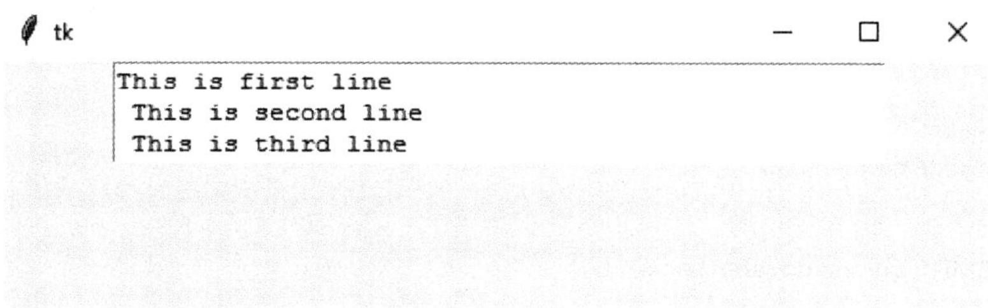

16.11 Container Widgets

Container widgets are used to place the widget objects in a proper order. In general, they are also called as layout managers. For this, it can use grid widget or frame widget. The grid layout widget is found to be more efficient than pack(). The grid consists of various rows and columns. If any widget is placed with the grid widget, then the position of the cell in the grid should be specified with the corresponding row and column numbers.

```
from tkinter import *
a = Tk()
l1=Label(a, text="Enter user name").grid(row=0,column=0)
e1=Entry(a)
e1.grid(row=0,column=1)
l2=Label(a, text="Enter password").grid(row=1,column=0)
e2=Entry(a)
e2.grid(row=1,column=1)
b1=Button(a,text="SUBMIT").grid(row=2,column=0)
a.mainloop()
```

Output

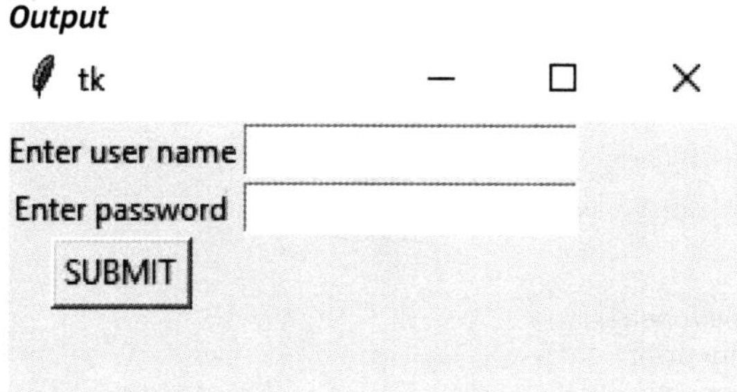

16.12 Frame Widget

The Frame widget is used to arrange other widgets in the container. In general, the other widgets are under the control of geometry manager.

```
from tkinter import *
a = Tk()
def abc():
    #print(e1.get())
    te=e1.get()
    f=Frame(a)
    f.pack()
    l=Label(f, text=te).pack()
l1=Label(a, text="Enter your name").pack()
e1=Entry(a)
e1.pack()
b1=Button(a,text="SUBMIT", command=abc).pack()
a.mainloop()
```

Output

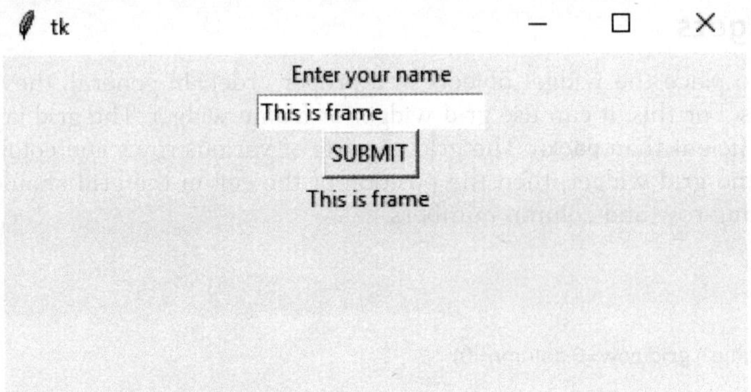

16.13 Menu Widget

The menu widget is used to create a new menu or various menu items. Each menu item can also have sub-menu items.

```
from tkinter import *
a = Tk()
def open1():
    print("File Menu is selcted")
def print():
    print("File Menu is selcted")
me=Menu(a)
mainmenu = Menu(me)
filemenu=Menu(me)
filemenu.add_command(label=»Open», command=open1)
filemenu.add_command(label=»print», command=print)
mainmenu.add_cascade(label=»File», menu=filemenu)
mainmenu.add_command(label="Exit", command=a.quit)
a.config(menu=mainmenu)
a.mainloop()
```

Output

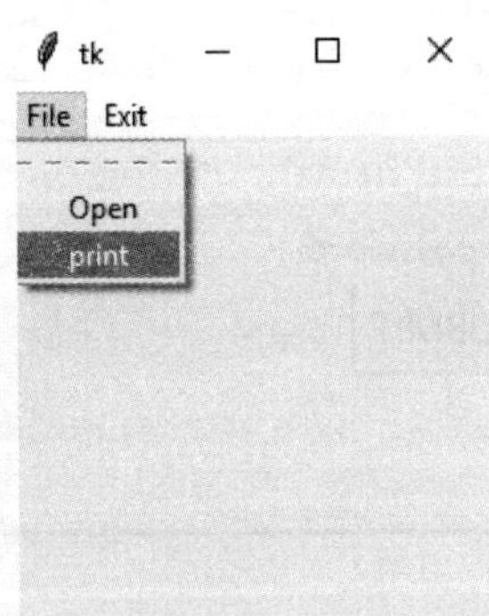

16.14 Labelframe Widget

The LabelFrame widget is a variant of Frame widget. The LabelFrame widget draws a border around its child widgets. It also contains the title display property. The LabelFrame widget is used for grouping multiple related widgets.

```
from tkinter import *
m = Tk()
g = LabelFrame(m, text="Entry widget group", padx=10, pady=10)
g.pack(padx=20, pady=20)
w1 = Entry(g)
w1.pack()
w2 = Entry(g)
w2.pack()
mainloop()
```

Output

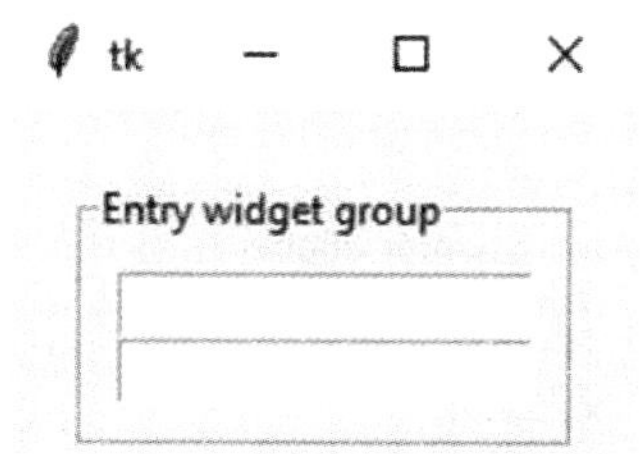

16.15 Message Widget

The message widget is used to display multiple lines of text. It is a variant of Label widget where the Label widget is used to display single widget.

```
from tkinter import *
m = Tk()
w = Message(m, text="this is a message widget-multi line message")
w.pack()
mainloop()
```

Output

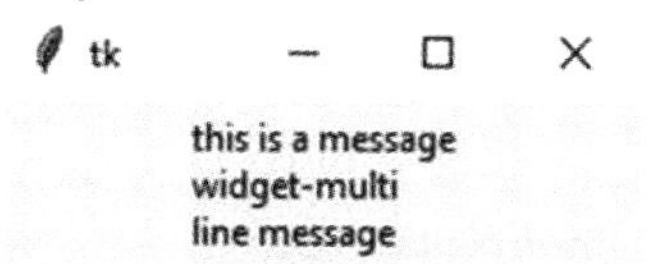

16.16 Combobox Widget

The Combobox widget is used to add the drop-down selection element in the window.

```
from tkinter import *
from tkinter import ttk
m = Tk()
ttk.Label(m, text="Choose the color:").grid(column=1, row=0)
n = ttk.Combobox(m, width=12) #3
n[‘values’] = (“red”,”green”,”blue”,”orange”,”yellow”)
n.grid(column=1, row=1)
n.current(0)
mainloop()
```

Output

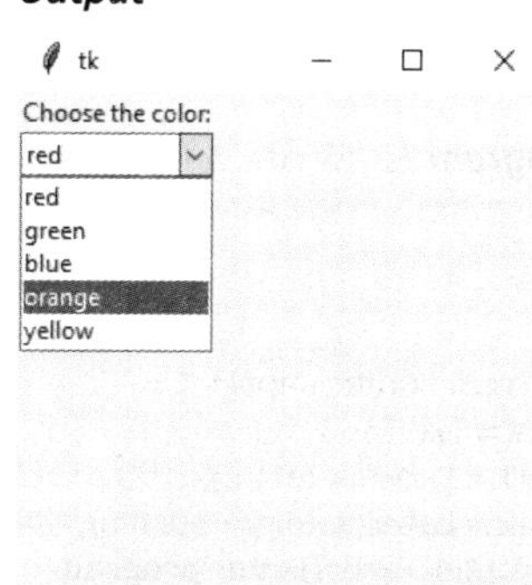

16.17 Scale Widget

The Scale widget allows the user to give a numerically bounded input and use the scale bar. It is similar to Entry widget but it will select the data by using the scale bar.

```
from tkinter import *
m = Tk()
x1 = Scale(m, from_=0, to=5)
x1.pack()
x2 = Scale(m, from_=0, to=6, orient=HORIZONTAL)
x2.pack()
x3 = Scale(m, from_=0, to=7, orient=VERTICAL)
x3.pack()
mainloop()
```

Output

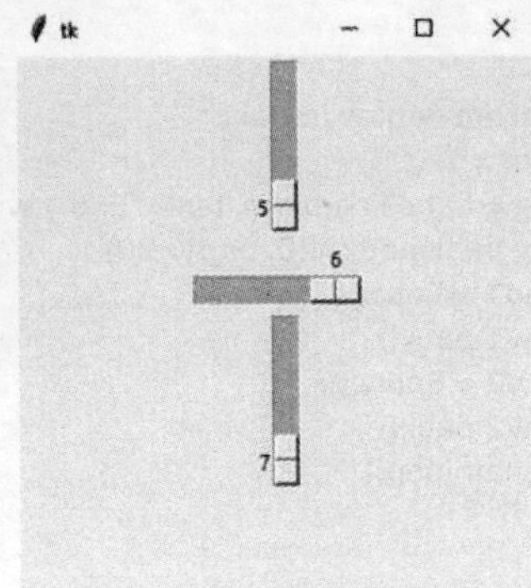

16.18 Canvas Widget

The Canvas widget is used to draw the plots and graphics in Tkinter. It is used for designing the various custom widgets.

```
from tkinter import *
m = Tk()
x = Canvas(m, width=200, height=100)
x.pack()
x.create_line(0, 0, 200, 100)
x.create_rectangle(50, 25, 150, 75, fill="red")
x.create_oval(100, 20, 150, 75, fill="green")
x.create_oval(50, 20, 100, 75, fill="blue")
mainloop()
```

Output

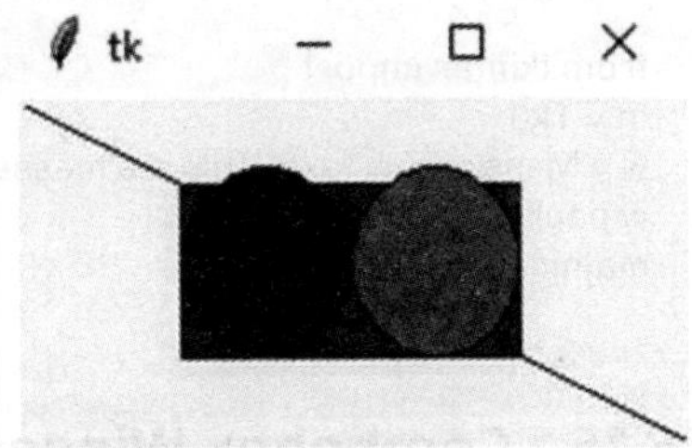

16.19 Sample Programs

Program 1: Write a Python program to add labels at the left and right side of the window.

```
from tkinter import *
a = Tk()
l1 = Label(a, text="good").pack(side="left")
l2 = Label(a, text="morning").pack(side="right")
a.title('First Tkinter program')
a.mainloop()
```

Output

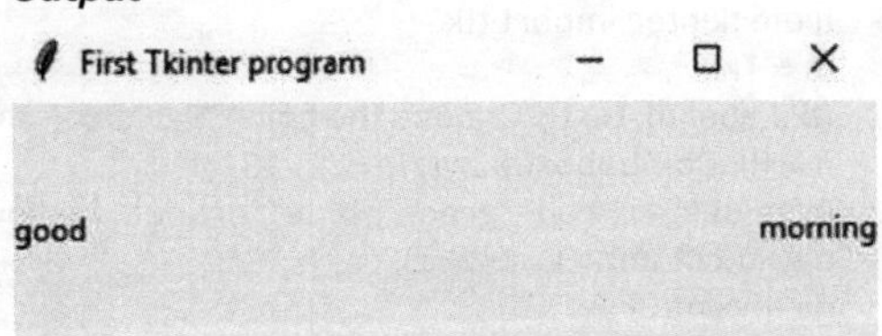

> **Programming Tip:**
> Widget is used to handle GUI in Python.

Program 2: Write a Python program to add different colors labels.

```
from tkinter import *
a = Tk()
l1 = Label(a, text="good",fg="red").pack(side="left")
l2 = Label(a, text="morning",fg="blue").pack(side="right")
a.title('First Tkinter program')
a.mainloop()
```

Output

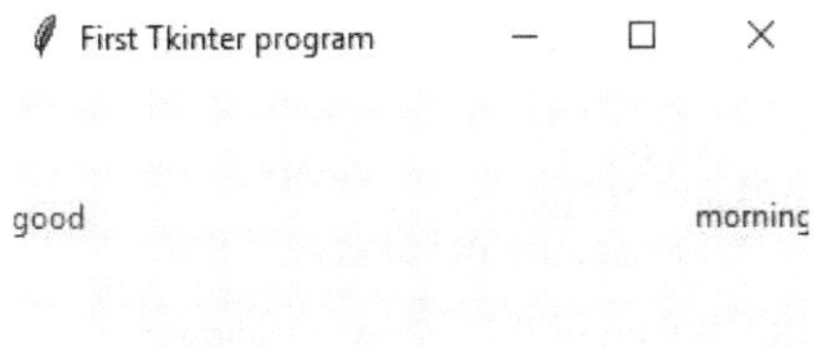

Program 3: Write a Python program to display the value of the selected checkbutton.

```
from tkinter import *
a = Tk()
var1=IntVar()
var2=IntVar()
var3=IntVar()
def abc(v):
    print("checkbox",v, "is selected:")
c1=Checkbutton(a, text="Value1", variable=var1, command=lambda:abc(var1)).pack()
c2=Checkbutton(a, text="Value2", variable=var2, command=lambda:abc(var2)).pack()
c3=Checkbutton(a, text="Value3", variable=var3, command=lambda:abc(var3)).pack()
a.mainloop()
```

Output

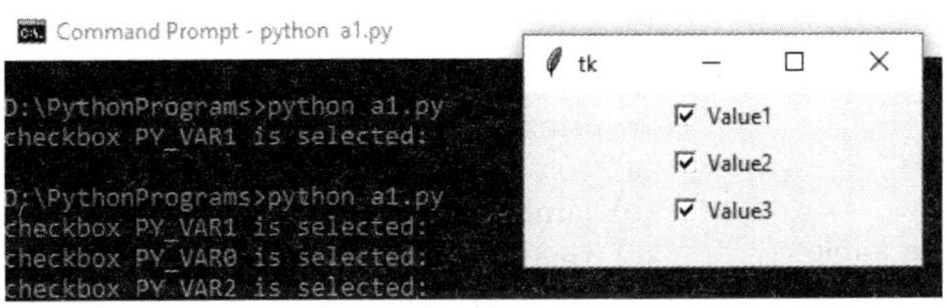

Glossary

- Tkinter is a package used by Python to support Graphical User Interface (GUI).
- Widget represents objects for handling GUI.

Summary

The Tkinter supports design of various GUI based applications. For each widget, create an object and then place it in the corresponding GUI window using **pack()**, **grid()** or **place()** methods. With this, various widgets such as label, button, entry, listbox, etc., can be created and placed in the GUI application window.

Multiple Choice Questions

1. To use the tkinter in Python3, which of the following statement is used?
(a) import *
(b) import sys
(c) from tkinter import*
(d) from * import tkinter

2. A single line text is handled with which widget?
(a) label
(b) entry
(c) labelbutton
(d) None of the above.

3. Which of the following widget is used to place the images?
(a) label
(b) entry
(c) labelbutton
(d) None of the above.

4. tkinter supports ?
(a) command line interfacing
(b) GUI
(c) threading
(d) None of the above.

5. The scrollbar widget can place scrollbar at?
(a) left
(b) right
(c) Either a or b.
(d) None of the above.

6. Which of the following places other widgets in current window?
(a) pack()
(b) grid()
(c) place()
(d) None of the above.

7. Which of the following places data in table structure?
(a) pack() (b) grid()
(c) place() (d) None of the above

8. What are the ways to support GUI in Python?
(a) wxPython (b) JPython
(c) Tkinter (d) All the above

9. Frequently updated GUI support is
(a) wxPython (b) JPython
(c) Tkinter (d) All the above.

10. Which of the following is a Java based GUI?
(a) wxPython (b) JPython
(c) Tkinter (d) All the above.

11. Which of the following is a Tk interface?
(a) wxPython (b) JPython
(c) Tkinter (d) All the above.

12. A GUI application is created with?
(a) new() (b) create()
(c) Tk() (d) All the above.

13. Which of the following method is used for executing the events?
(a) loop() (b) mainloop()
(c) run() (d) mainrun()

14. An example of widgets is
(a) button (b) canvas
(c) entry (d) All the above.

15. For adding images in GUI, which of the following is used to represent the image?
(a) Image()
(b) Photo()
(c) PhotoImage()
(d) All the above.

16. For Button widget, the arguments are passes by using
(a) command line arguments
(b) lambda expression
(c) regular expression
(d) None of the above.

Fill in the Blanks

1. The entry widget is used to add __________________ in the GUI window.

2. The entry widget will take __________________ line(s) of text from the user.

3. The __________________ is used to add the drop down component.

4. For Listbox widget, __________________ is used to insert an element.

5. For Listbox widget, __________________ is used to delete an element.

6. The __________________ is used to add multiple options in GUI window.

7. The Radiobutton allows __________________ selection among multiple options.

8. Multiple lines of text can be added by using __________________ widget.

9. ____________________ is used to place the widgets in a proper order.

10. Container widgets are also called as ____________________.

11. The other widgets are under the control of ____________________.

12. ____________________ is used to arrange other widgets in the container.

13. ____________________ is used to create a new menu.

State True/False

1. The wxPython patches are not updated frequently.
2. The wxPython is used for supporting GUI in Python.
3. The JPython is used for supporting GUI in Python.
4. The Tkinter is used for supporting GUI in Python.
5. Tkinter and Tk interface are different.
6. The Tkinter is not portable.
7. The **Tk()** method will create a new GUI application.
8. For each widget, a new object is not created.
9. Color is a property of a widget.
10. Dimensions are not object properties.
11. **packs()** places components in current widget.
12. **grid()** places components in table structure of parent widget.
13. **place()** places components within the unspecified position of parent widget.

Find the Output

1.
```
from tkinter import *
a = Tk()
a.title('First Tkinter program')
a.mainloop()
```

2.
```
from tkinter import *
a = Tk()
b1=Button(a, text="OK").grid()
b2=Button(a, text="CANCEL").grid()
a.mainloop()
```

3.
```
from tkinter import *
a = Tk()
b1=Button(a, text="OK").pack()
b2=Button(a, text="CANCEL").pack()
a.mainloop()
```

4.
```
from tkinter import *
a = Tk()
b1=Button(text="OK").pack()
print("hello")
```

Find the Error

1.
```
from tkinter import *
l = Label(a, text="This is a Label")
l.pack()
a.title('First Tkinter program')
a.mainloop()
```

2.
```
from tkinter import *
a = Tk()
b1=Button(a,text="OK" size=30).pack()
print("hello")
```

Long Answer Questions

1. What are the various widgets in Python?
2. Write a Python program to display an alert message when the user data is negative?
3. Discuss about any four widget objects in Tkinter.

Short Answer Questions

1. List the various GUI providers in Python.
2. Write about layout manager widgets.

Exercise Programs

1. Write a Python program to design a calculator.
2. Write a Python program to draw various shapes.
3. Write a Python program to design a registration form.

Answers

Multiple Choice Questions

1. (b)
2. (a)
3. (a)
4. (b)
5. (c)
6. (a)
7. (b)
8. (d)
9. (a)
10. (b)
11. (c)
12. (c)
13. (b)
14. (c)
15. (c)
16. (b)

Fill in the Blanks

1. textbox
2. single
3. Listbox
4. insert()
5. delete()
6. Radiobutton.
7. single
8. Text
9. Container widget
10. layout managers
11. geometry manager
12. Frame widget
13. Menu widget

State True/False

1. False
2. True
3. True
4. True
5. False
6. False
7. True
8. False
9. True
10. False
11. False
12. True
13. False

Find the Output

1. 

2. 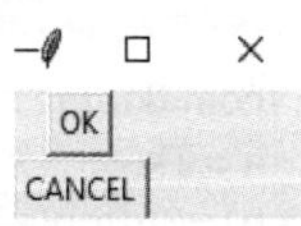

3. 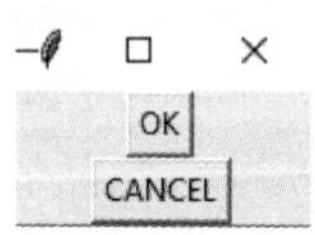

4. hello

Find the Error

1. NameError: name ‘a’ is not defined
2. SyntaxError: invalid syntax (b1=Button(a,text=”OK” size=30).pack())

CHAPTER

17 Events

The present chapter discusses about advanced concepts of GUI programming. This chapter elaborates on handling events in Python. An event is an object connected to a thread. With Python, the mouse event and key events can be handled efficiently.

17.1 Event Object

An event object can handle various program inputs. Python uses event objects to handle inputs. Among them popular inputs are

- Thread
- Widget

An event object for the thread will maintain an internal flag. All the threads in a program can be connected to the event. Any thread can use the event object. The event object for the thread is available in threading class.

```
import threading
import time
class newthread(threading.Thread):
    def __init__(self,tname,event):
        threading.Thread.__init__(self)
        self.name=tname
        self.threadEvent=event
    def run(self):
        print(self.name," thread is running")
e=threading.Event()
t1=newthread("t1",e)
t2=newthread("t2",e)
t1.start()
t2.start()
e.clear()
print("The thread event object is cleared")
time.sleep(5)
e.set()
print("the thread event object is set")
```

Output

```
D:\PythonPrograms>python a1.py
t1 thread is running
t2 thread is running
The thread event object is cleared
the thread event object is set
```

Various methods for the thread event object are listed below.

- set() is used to set the internal flag of the thread
- clear() is used to clear the internal flag of the thread
- wait(time_period) is used to block the internal flag of the thread for a specified amount of time.
- isSet() is used to check whether the internal flag value is set or not.

The event object can be applied to the tkinter widgets also. For this, the attribute of the event object should be a widget. The widget attribute indicates the widget for which the event object is created. The x,y attributes indicates the position of mouse. The x_root,y_root attributes indicates the relative position of mouse from top left corner position. The **char** attribute indicates the key value given from the keyboard. The **keysym** attribute indicates the key symbol given from the keyboard. The **keycode** attribute indicates the key code given from the keyboard. The **num** attribute indicates the number of the button pressed by the mouse. The **width** indicates the width of the input widget. The **height** indicates the height of the input widget. The **type** indicates the type of the widget.

17.2 Binding Callbacks to Events

In Python, binding is a process to connect the widget event object to the corresponding callback. In general, this is also called as "Event Handler". For this, the tkinter module contains a method called **bind()**. The **bind()** method is applicable in four different cases

- Applicable to widget instance
  In this, the **bind()** is applied on the instance. The syntax of the **bind()** method is

```
widget_object.bind(event_name,handler)
```

```
from tkinter import *
a = Tk()
def abc(event):
    x=event.widget
    f=Frame(a)
    f.pack()
    l1=Label(f, text=x).pack()
t1 = Text(a, width=30, height=10)
t1.bind('<KeyPress>', abc)
t1.pack()
t1.focus_set()
a.mainloop()
```

Output

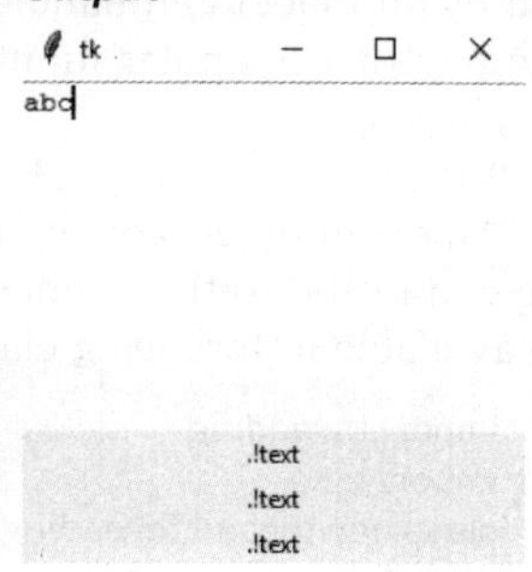

- Applicable to top level window
  In this, the **bind()** method is applied on the top level window in the GUI application. The syntax of the **bind()** is

```
top_level_object.bind(event_name,handler)
```

```
from tkinter import *
a = Tk()
def abc(event):
    print("mouse entered")
frame = Frame(a, width=200, height=200)
frame.bind('<Enter>', abc)
frame.pack()
a.mainloop()
```

Output

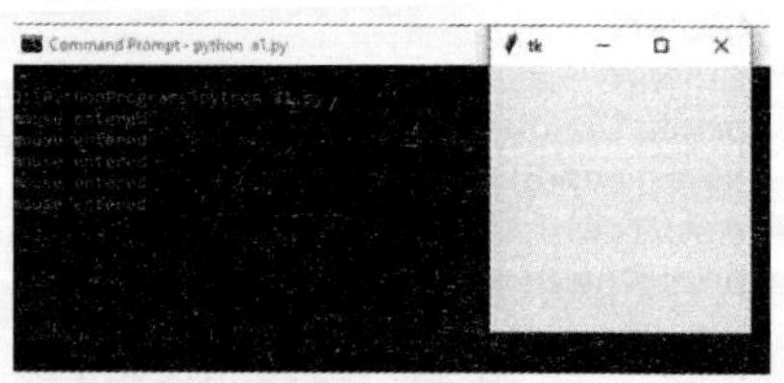

- Applicable to widget class
  In this case, the **bind_class()** method is used. This will perform binding operation for all widgets of the same class. the **bind_class()** method is applied on the top-level window in the GUI application. The syntax of the **bind_class()** is

```
top_level_object.bind_class("widget_class", event_name,handler)
```

```
from tkinter import *
a = Tk()
def abc(event):
    x=event.widget
    f=Frame(a)
    f.pack()
    l1=Label(f, text=x).pack()
b1 = Button(a, text="Button1")
b1.bind_class('Button','<Button-1>', abc)
b1.pack()
b2 = Button(a, text="Button2")
b2.bind_class('Button','<Button-1>', abc)
b2.pack()
a.mainloop()
```

Output

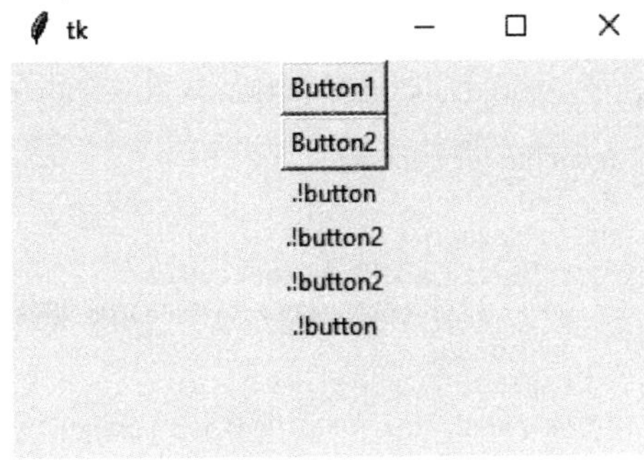

- Applicable to complete GUI application

In this case, bind_all() is used. This will perform binding process for all the widgets in the GUI application. The syntax for the bind_all() is given below.

```
top_level_object.bind_all(event_name,handler)
```

```
from tkinter import *
a = Tk()
def abc(event):
    x=event.widget
    f=Frame(a)
    f.pack()
    l1=Label(f, text=x).pack()
b1 = Button(a, text="Button1")
b1.pack()
b2 = Button(a, text="Button2")
b2.pack()
a.bind_all('<Button-1>', abc)
a.mainloop()
```

Output

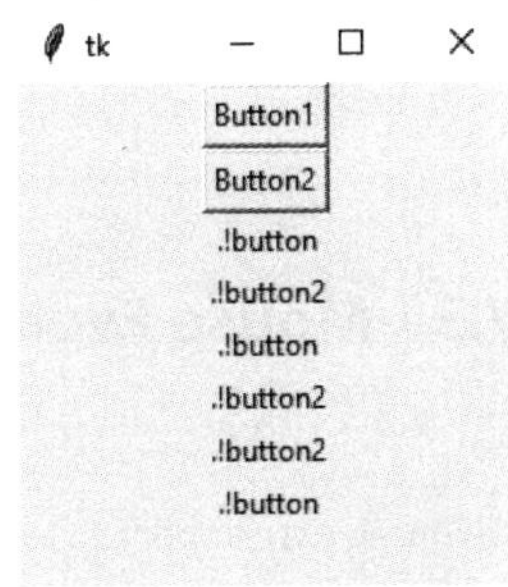

17.3 Events Names

The various event names in Python are listed below.

- Button-1
- B1-Motion
- ButtonRelease-1
- Double-Button-1
- Enter
- Leave
- FocusIn
- FocusOut
- Return
- Key
- <Shift-Up>
- <Configure>

17.4 Keyboard Events

The keyboard events will 'listen' to the state of input from the keyboard and whenever an event occurs, the associated action will be performed.

```
from tkinter import *
a = Tk()
def abc(event):
    x="Key Symbol: "+event.keysym
    y="Key Symbol Number: "+str(event.keysym_num)
    f=Frame(a)
    f.pack()
    l4=Label(f, text="Key Pressed").pack()
    l1=Label(f, text=x).pack()
    l2=Label(f, text=y).pack()
def abc1(event):
    f=Frame(a)
    f.pack()
    l4=Label(f, text="Key Released").pack()
text = Text(a, width=20, height=5)
text.bind('<KeyPress>', abc)
text.bind('<KeyRelease>', abc1)
text.pack(expand=1, fill="both")
text.focus_set()
a.mainloop()
```

Output

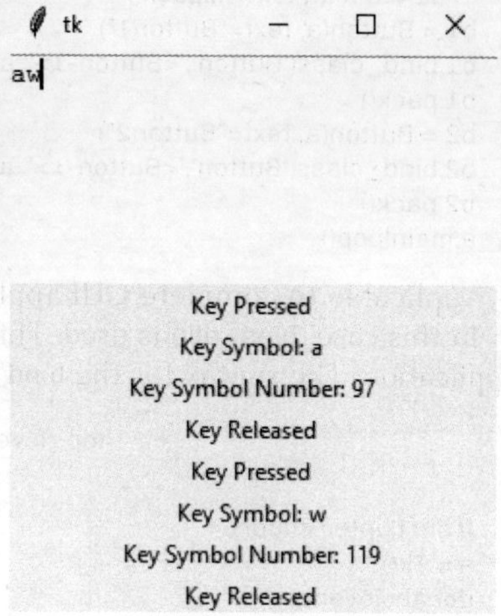

17.5 Mouse Events

Mouse events are used to handle changes in the mouse and to perform the corresponding action.

```
from tkinter import *
a = Tk()
def abc(event):
    x=str(event.x)
    y=str(event.y)
    x1=str(event.x_root)
    y1=str(event.y_root)
    f=Frame(a)
    f.pack()
    l4=Label(f, text="Mouse clicked at ("+x+","+y+")").pack()
    l5=Label(f, text="Mouse relative position("+x1+","+y1+")").pack()
def abc1(event):
    f=Frame(a)
    f.pack()
    l4=Label(f, text="Mouse Entered").pack()
def abc2(event):
    f=Frame(a)
    f.pack()
    l4=Label(f, text="Mouse Leaved").pack()
def abc3(event):
    f=Frame(a)
    f.pack()
    l4=Label(f, text="Mouse Dragged").pack()
```

```
def abc4(event):
    f=Frame(a)
    f.pack()
    l4=Label(f, text="Mouse Released").pack()
a.bind('<Enter>',abc1)
a.bind('<Button-1>',abc)
a.bind('<Leave>',abc2)
a.bind('<B1-Motion>',abc3)
a.bind('<ButtonRelease-1>',abc4)
a.mainloop()
```

Output

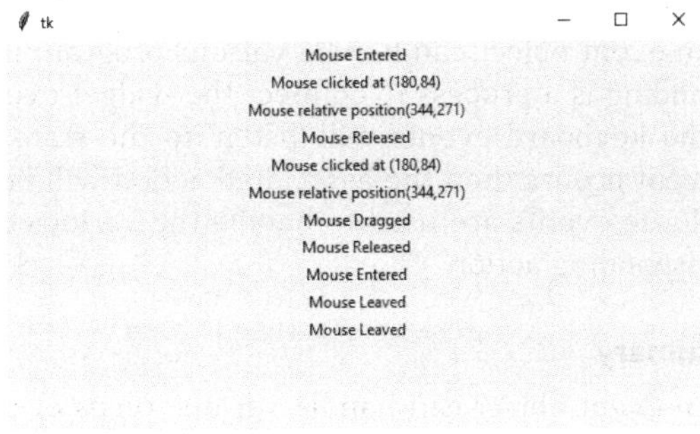

17.6 Sample Programs

Program 1: Write a Python program to wait the thread event object for a specified time.

```
import threading
import time
class newthread(threading.Thread):
    def __init__(self,tname,event):
        threading.Thread.__init__(self)
        self.name=tname
        self.threadEvent=event
    def run(self):
        print(self.name," thread is running")
e=threading.Event()
t1=newthread("t1",e)
t2=newthread("t2",e)
t1.start()
t2.start()
x=int(input("Enter the time period for wait: "))
print("The thread event object is waiting")
e.wait(x)
print("The thread event object is cleared")
```

> **Programming Tip:** Event object handles various inputs.

Output

```
D:\PythonPrograms>python a1.py
t1 thread is running
t2 thread is running
Enter the time period for wait: 5
The thread event object is waiting
The thread event object is cleared
```

Program 2: Write a Python program to print whether the mouse click is at right or left.

```
from tkinter import *
a = Tk()
    def abc(event):
        f=Frame(a)
        f.pack()
        l1=Label(f, text="Left is clicked").pack()
    def abc1(event):
        f=Frame(a)
        f.pack()
        l1=Label(f, text="Middle is clicked").pack()
    def abc2(event):
        f=Frame(a)
        f.pack()
        l1=Label(f, text="Right is clicked").pack()
a.bind('<Button-1>',abc)
a.bind('<Button-2>',abc1)
a.bind('<Button-3>',abc2)
a.mainloop()
```

Output

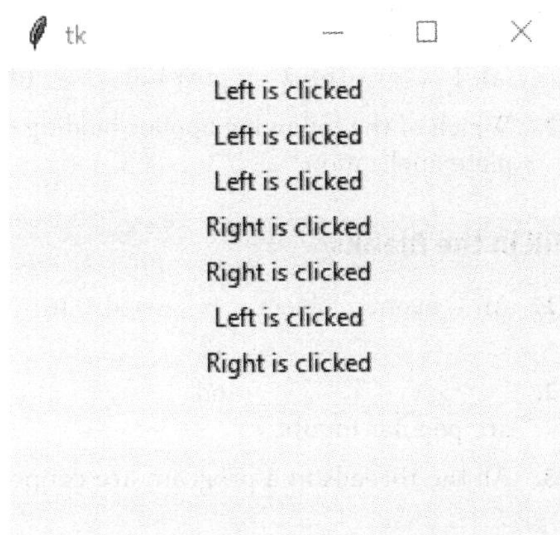

Glossary

- An event object can handle various program inputs.
- Binding is a process to connect the widget event object to the corresponding callback.
- The keyboard events will 'listen' to the state of input from the keyboard and whenever an event occurs then the associated action will be performed.
- Mouse events are used to handle the various changes in the mouse and can perform the corresponding action.

Summary

- An event object can handle various types of objects. Binding is a process to connect the callback to the event object.
- The event object can bind four different cases in Python.

Multiple Choice Questions

1. Event object can handle
   (a) thread
   (b) widget
   (c) Both a and b.
   (d) None of the above.
2. Thread event object contains how many internal flags?
   (a) 1 (b) 2 (c) 3 (d) 4
3. What are various methods of thread supported by an event object?
   (a) set (b) wait
   (c) clear (d) All of the above.
4. Which module supports thread event object?
   (a) thread (b) Thread
   (c) threading (d) All of the above.
5. Which method will return the status of the thread event object?
   (a) is_Set() (b) is_Status()
   (c) is_Get() (d) is_Getstatus
6. In Python, how many ways are there to perform binding?
   (a) 1 (b) 2 (c) 3 (d) 4
7. Which of the following applies binding to complete application?
   (a) bind()
   (b) bind_all()
   (c) bind_class()
   (d) bind_complete()
8. Which of the following event represents left mouse click?
   (a) Button-1 (b) Button-2
   (c) Button-3 (d) Button-4
9. Which of the following event represents right mouse click?
   (a) Button-1 (b) Button-2
   (c) Button-3 (d) Button-4
10. Which of the following event represent middle mouse click?
    (a) Button-1 (b) Button-2
    (c) Button-3 (d) Button-4
11. The bind() method is applicable in how many different cases?
    (a) 1 (b) 2 (c) 3 (d) 4
12. bind_class() is used for binding?
    (a) All widgets of same class
    (b) All widgets of different classes
    (c) Different widgets of different classes
    (d) None of the above.

Fill in the Blanks

1. An event object is used to handle __________________.
2. __________________ and __________________ are popular inputs.
3. All the threads in a program are connected to __________________.
4. Any __________________ can use the event object.
5. __________________ is used to set the internal flag of the object.
6. __________________ is used to clear the internal flag of the object.

7. Event handler is used to perform __________________ process.
8. Binding will connect __________________ to the corresponding callback.
9. __________________ is sued to bind the call back to the widget instance.
10. __________________ is used to bind all widgets of the same class.

State True/False

1. An event object can handle only one type of input.
2. Multiple types of inputs can be handled by an event object.
3. An event object for the thread will maintain multiple flags.
4. Single flag is maintained by the event object.
5. All the threads in a program can be connected to the event.
6. Only selected threads can use the event object.
7. The **threading** module is responsible for handling threads and events.
8. **isSet()** is used to check whether the event object is deleted or not.
9. **wait()** will block the internal flag of the thread.
10. Event handler uses **bind()** method.

Find the Output

1.
```
import threading
e=threading.Event()
print(e.isSet())
```
2.
```
import threading
e=threading.Event()
e.set()
print(e.isSet())
```
3.
```
import threading
e=threading.Event()
e.set()
print(e.isSet())
e.clear()
print(e.isSet())
```
4.
```
from tkinter import *
a = Tk()
def abc(event):
    x=event.widget
    f=Frame(a)
    f.pack()
    l1=Label(f, text="key pressed").pack()
t1 = Text(a, width=30, height=10)
t1.bind('<KeyPress>', abc)
t1.pack()
t1.focus_set()
a.mainloop()
```

Find the Error

1.
```
from tkinter import *
def abc(event):
    x=event.widget
    f=Frame(a)
    f.pack()
    l1=Label(f, text=x).pack()
t1 = Text(a, width=30, height=10)
t1.bind('<KeyPress>', abc)
t1.pack()
t1.focus_set()
a.mainloop()
```
2.
```
from tkinter import *
a = Tk()
t1 = Text(a, width=30, height=10)
t1.bind('<KeyPress>', abc)
t1.pack()
t1.focus_set()
a.mainloop()
```

Long Answer Questions

1. In Python, how is thread synchronization achieved with an event object?
2. Discuss in detail about tkinter objects.
3. How does Python handle key events?

Short Answer Questions

1. What is an event?
2. What is an event object?
3. How are listeners supported in Python?
4. List the various attributes of an event.

Exercise Programs

1. Write a Python program to design a calculator by using key and mouse events.
2. Write a Python program to handle event objects of text and entry widgets by using bind_class() method.

Answers

Multiple Choice Questions

1. (c)
2. (a)
3. (d)
4. (c)
5. (a)
6. (d)
7. (b)
8. (a)
9. (c)
10. (b)
11. (d)
12. (a)

Fill in the Blanks

1. various inputs
2. Thread, widget
3. events
4. thread
5. set()
6. clear()
7. binding
8. event object
9. bind()
10. bind_class()

State True/False

1. False
2. True
3. False
4. True
5. True
6. False
7. True
8. False
9. True
10. true

Find the Output

1. False
2. True
3. True, False
4. 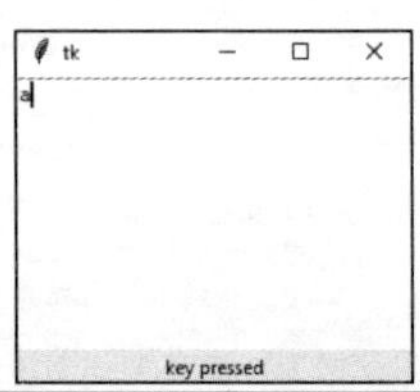

Find the Error

1. NameError: name 'a' is not defined
2. NameError: name 'abc' is not defined

CHAPTER

18 Standard Library

18.1 Operating System Interface

Python programming runs under an operating system. It contains a feature to communicate with the operating system. These features are available in os module. So, in any Python program, import os statement is required to communicate with the operating system. The various functions defined in the os module are listed below.

- The system() function is sued to execute any operating system command. For this function, the command to be executed should be passed as an argument. The command should be specified as a string.

```
import os
os.system("dir m*.*")
```

Output

```
D:\PythonPrograms>python a1.py
Volume in drive D has no label.
Volume Serial Number is 4006-8C06
Directory of D:\PythonPrograms
05/17/201   12:18   275 main.py
05/11/201   12:24   611 math functions.py
05/11/201   02:41   152 member op.py
3 File(s) 1,038 bytes
0 Dir(s) 271,706,546,176 bytes free
```

- getcwd() function returns the current working directory.

```
import os
print("Name of OS:", os.name)
print("Current working directory: ", os.getcwd())
```

Output

```
D:\PythonPrograms>python a1.py
Name of OS: nt
Current working directory: D:\PythonPrograms
```

- mkdir(dir_name) function creates a new directory with the name dir_name in the current directory.

```
import os
print("Creating D1 directory: ",os.mkdir("dir1"))
```

Output

```
D:\PythonPrograms>dir
 Volume in drive D has no label.
 Volume Serial Number is 4006-8C06

 Directory of D:\PythonPrograms

06/07/2017  21:56    <DIR>          .
06/07/2017  21:56    <DIR>          ..
06/07/2017  21:54                83 a1.py
06/05/2017  17:44    <DIR>          aa
06/07/2017  21:56    <DIR>          Old prgs
05/17/2017  14:56    <DIR>          __pycache__
               1 File(s)             83 bytes
               5 Dir(s)  271,706,537,984 bytes free

D:\PythonPrograms>python a1.py
Creating D1 directory:  None

D:\PythonPrograms>dir
 Volume in drive D has no label.
 Volume Serial Number is 4006-8C06

 Directory of D:\PythonPrograms

06/07/2017  21:56    <DIR>          .
06/07/2017  21:56    <DIR>          ..
06/07/2017  21:56                64 a1.py
06/05/2017  17:44    <DIR>          aa
06/07/2017  21:56    <DIR>          dir1
06/07/2017  21:56    <DIR>          Old prgs
05/17/2017  14:56    <DIR>          __pycache__
               1 File(s)             64 bytes
               6 Dir(s)  271,706,537,984 bytes free
```

- getpid() function returns the process id of the current process.
- chdir("path_dir") function changes the current directory to path_dir.

18.2 Text Processing

Python contains standard libraries for providing services for text processing. The various modules used for text processing are listed below.

- string module is used to handle string objects.
- re module is used to handle regular expressions and pattern matching.
- difflib module is used to compute the deltas.

- o The **SequenceMatcher** class is used to match sequence pairs of text.
- o The **Differ** class is used to compare lines of text. The Differ delta contains three possible symbols, viz., '- ', '+ ', '? '.
- o The **HtmlDiff** class is used to compare text side by side and line by line and display the result in a HTML table.
- o The **context_diff** class is used to compare the given string lists and the result is placed in the format of context diff.
- o The **get_close_matches()** returns a perfect matched result.
- o The **ndiff()** compares the given string lists and returns the differ delta.

- **textwrap** module is used to wrap and fill the text.
  - o The **wrap()** wraps each and every line of the string to make the line width uniform.
  - o The **fill()** wraps each and every line of the string to make the line width uniform and returns the wrapped text.
  - o The **shorten()** will shorten or reduce the input text by removing the exceeded text.
  - o The **dedent()** removes all leading whitespaces in each and every line.
  - o The **intent()** adds prefix data to the specified lines of text.
- **unicodedata** module is used for Unicode Database (UCD), which contains all character properties.
  - o The **lookup()** returns the character of the input string.
  - o The **name()** returns the name of the character.
  - o The **decimal()** returns the input character decimal value.
  - o The **digit()** returns the digit value of the input integer character.
  - o The **numeric()** returns the numeric value of the input float character.

18.3 Mathematics

Python contains standard libraries for handling numeric and mathematical data. Various modules used for this are listed below.

- The **numbers** module is used to handle number data.
- The **math** module is used to handle the various mathematical functions.
- The **cmath** module is used to handle the various mathematical functions for complex number data.
  - o The **phase()** function returns the phase of the input complex number.
  - o The **polar()** function returns the polar form of the input complex number.
  - o The **exp()** function returns the exponential value of the input complex number.
  - o The **log()** function returns the logarithmic value of the input complex number.
  - o The **log10()** function returns the base-10 logarithm value of the input complex number.
  - o The **acos()** returns the arc cosine value of the input complex number.
  - o The **atanh()** returns the inverse hyperbolic tangent value of the input complex number.

```
import cmath
a=complex(10,5)
print("Input number: ",a)
print("Phase: ",cmath.phase(a))
print("polar: ",cmath.polar(a))
print("log: ",cmath.log(a))
```

Output

```
D:\PythonPrograms>python a1.py
Input number: (10+5j)
Phase: 0.4636476090008061
polar: (11.180339887498949, 0.4636476090008061)
log: (2.4141568686511508+0.4636476090008061j)
```

- The **decimal** module is used to handle various arithmetic operations of decimal fixed point and floating point data.
    - o The **getcontext()** returns the current context.
    - o The **Decimal()** function is used to create a decimal object.
    - o The **as_integer_ratio()** function will represent the floating point data as a pair of integers.
    - o The **as_tuple()** function is used to represent the input number into a tuple with sign, digit and exponent component.
    - o The **compare()** function is used to compare two input decimal objects.
    - o The **copy_abs()** function is used to compute the absolute value of the input number.
    - o The **copy_negate()** function is used to compute the negative value of the input number.

```
import decimal
print(decimal.getcontext())
a=decimal.Decimal('5.1')
print("Decimal object= ",a)
print("Result of as_integer_ratio()= ",a.as_integer_ratio())
print("Result of as_tuple()= ",a.as_tuple())
print("Result of copy_abs()= ",a.copy_abs())
```

Output

```
D:\PythonPrograms>python a1.py
Context(prec=28, rounding=ROUND_
HALF_EVEN, Emin=-999999,
Emax=999999, capitals=1, clamp=0,
flags=[], traps=[InvalidOperation,
DivisionByZero, Overflow])
Decimal object= 5.1
Result of as_integer_ratio()= (51, 10)
Result of as_tuple()=
DecimalTuple(sign=0, digits=(5, 1),
exponent=-1)
Result of copy_abs()= 5.1
```

- The **fractions** module is used to handle the operations on rational number data.
    - o The **Fraction()** function is used to create an object for the Fraction from the input arguments.
    - o The **limit_denominator()** function represents the input fraction denominator to the input max limit.
    - o The **__floor__()** function returns the greatest integer value of the input fractional number.
    - o The **__ceil__()** function returns the least integer value of the input fractional number.
    - o The **__round__()** function returns the rounded value of the input fractional number.

```
import fractions
a=fractions.Fraction(35634,7568)
print("Fraction object= ",a)
print("Result of limit_denominator: ",a.limit_denominator(2))
print("Result of __floor__(): ",a.__floor__())
print("Result of __ceil__(): ",a.__ceil__())
print("Result of __round__(): ",a.__round__())
```

Output

```
D:\PythonPrograms>python a1.py
Fraction object= 17817/3784
Result of limit_denominator: 9/2
Result of __floor__(): 4
Result of __ceil__(): 5
Result of __round__(): 5
```

- The **random** module is used to handle the operations on pseudo random number data.
    - o The **getrandbits()** function is used to generate a random number with the specified number of bits.
    - o The **random()** function is used to generate random floating value data.
    - o The **randrange()** function generates a random integer number within the specified range.
    - o The **shuffle()** function will shuffle all the items in the list.

```
import random
print("Result of random(): ",random.random())
print("Result of randrange(): ",random.randrange(30))
print("Result of getrandbits(): ",random.getrandbits(6))
b=[1, 2, 43, 9]
print("Original list: ",b)
random.shuffle(b)
print("Result of shuffle: ",b)
```

Output

```
D:\PythonPrograms>python a1.py
Result of random():
0.2619957151196758
Result of randrange(): 18
Result of getrandbits(): 63
Original list: [1, 2, 43, 9]
Result of shuffle: [2, 9, 1, 43]
```

- The **statistics** module is used to handle various statistical operations.
  - o The **mean()** function is used to compute the mean of the input data.
  - o The **median()** function is used to compute the median of the input data.
  - o The **mode()** function is used to compute the mode of the input data.
  - o The **stdev()** function is used to compute the standard deviation of the input data.
  - o The **variance()** function is used to compute the variance of the input data.

```
import statistics
x=[45,21,93,73]
print("Input data: ",x)
print("Result of mean(): ",statistics.mean(x))
print("Result of median(): ",statistics.median(x))
print("Result of stdev(): ",statistics.stdev(x))
print("Result of variance(): ",statistics.variance(x))
```

Output

```
D:\PythonPrograms>python a1.py
Input data: [45, 21, 93, 73]
Result of mean(): 58
Result of median(): 59.0
Result of stdev(): 31.559467676119
Result of variance(): 996
```

18.4 Internet Access

In Python, there are two ways to access the internet. They are

- Open the required URL in the command line interface
  - o For this, **urllib** package should be used. In this package, there are four modules available, namely, **request**, **error**, **parse** and **robotparser**.
  - o Among these four modules, **request** module is used for opening the input URL.

```
import urllib.request
f = urllib.request.urlopen(«http://www.google.org»).read()
print(f)
```

Output

```
D:\PythonPrograms>python a1.py
b'<!DOCTYPE html>\n<html lang="en_US">\n <head>\n <meta charset="utf-8">\n <meta
content="IE=Edge" http-equiv="X-UA-Compatible">\n <!-- Google Tag Manager -->\n
<script>(function(w,d,s,l,i){w[l]=w[l]||[];w[l].push({\'gtm.start\':\n new Date().getTime(),event:\'gtm.
js\'});var f=d.getElementsByTagName(s)[0],\n j=d.createElement(s),dl=l!=\'dataLayer\'?\'&l=\'+l:\'\';j.
async=true;j.src=\n
...................................................
```

- Open the required URL in the web browser
  - o For this case, **webbrowser** module will be used.

```
import webbrowser
webbrowser.open(«http:://www.google.com»)
```

Output

D:\PythonPrograms>python a2.py

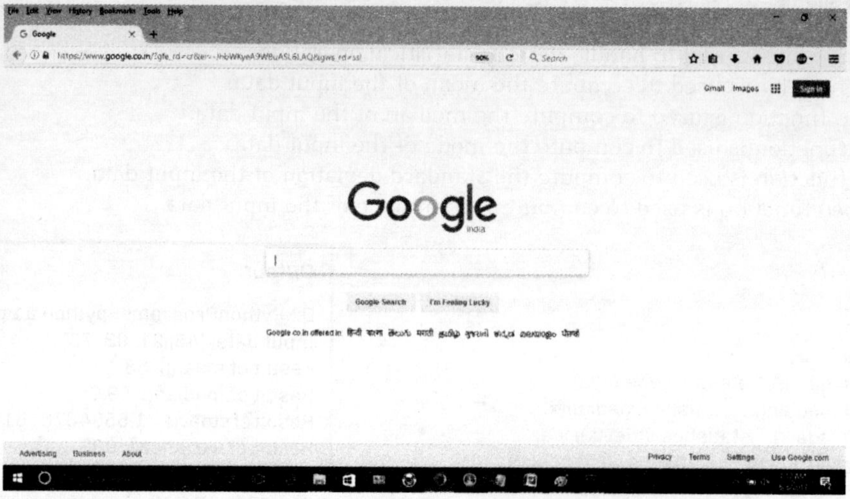

18.5 Dates and Times

Python contains **datetime** module for handling the various operations of date and time. Naïve and aware objects of date and time are allowed in Python. The aware object has pre knowledge about the input whereas the naïve object has no pre knowledge. Various methods in this module are

- The **MINYEAR** represents the minimum year allowed.
- The **MAXYEAR** represents the maximum year allowed.
- The **timedelta** object represents the duration difference of date or time.
- The **date()** creates a date with the input year, month and day.
- The **today()** returns the current date.

```
import datetime
d=datetime.date(2011,10,6)
print(datetime.MINYEAR)
print(datetime.MAXYEAR)
print("The date= ",d)
print("today= ",d.today())
```

Output

```
D:\PythonPrograms>python a1.py
1
9999
The date= 2011-10-06
today= 2018-02-22
```

18.6 Data Compression

In Python, data is compressed by using any one of the following algorithms.

- zlib
- gzip
- bz2
- lzma
- zipfile
- tarfile

In this section we discuss about **zipfile** based data compression in Python. For this, the **zipfile** module should be imported. It can compress the files within 4MB size. The various functions are

- The **is_zipfile()** checks whether the input file exists or not.
- The **Zipfile()** is used to create a new zip file.
- The **namelist()** returns all the files available in the input zip file
- The **infolist()** will return the information about the zip file.

The below program creates a zipfile with two text files.

```
import zipfile
a = zipfile.ZipFile('ex1.zip', 'w')
a.write("one.txt")
a.write("two.txt")
print(a.namelist())
```

Output

```
D:\PythonPrograms>python a1.py
['one.txt', 'two.txt']
```

Note: Make sure that "one.txt" and "two.txt" files are available in the current directory.

- The **read()** is used to read the content of file in zip file.

```
import zipfile
a = zipfile.ZipFile('ex1.zip')
c=a.read("one.txt")
print(repr(c))
c=a.read("two.txt")
print(repr(c))
```

Output

```
D:\PythonPrograms>python a1.py
b'this is one.txt file'
b'this is two.txt file'
```

- The **getinfo()** will return the information of a file in zip file.

```
import zipfile
a = zipfile.ZipFile('ex1.zip')
i=a.getinfo("one.txt")
print("Name of the file: ",i.filename)
i=a.getinfo("two.txt")
print("Name of the file: ",i.filename)
```

Output

```
D:\PythonPrograms>python a1.py
Name of the file: one.txt
Name of the file: two.txt
```

18.7 Turtle Graphics

The "turtle" is a module used to support graphics in Python. For this, **turtle** module should be imported in the Python program. Various functions in this module are

- **Screen()** – Creates a screen for the turtle
- **forward()** – Moves the turtle in forward direction

```
import turtle
x=turtle.Screen()
turtle.forward(200)
x.mainloop()
```

Output

D:\PythonPrograms>python a1.py

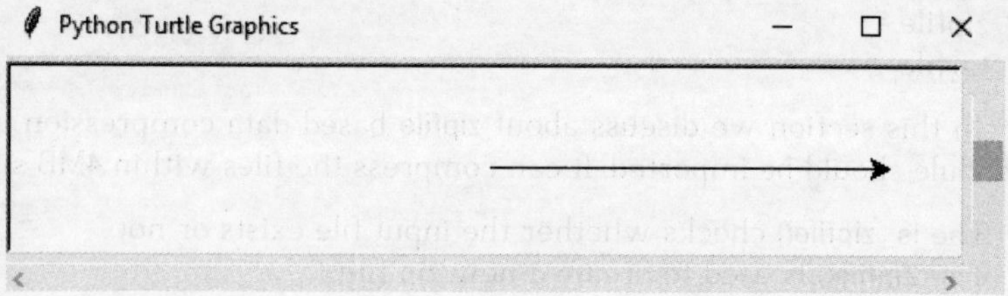

- backward() – Moves the turtle in backward direction

```
import turtle
x=turtle.Screen()
turtle.backward(200)
x.mainloop()
```

Output

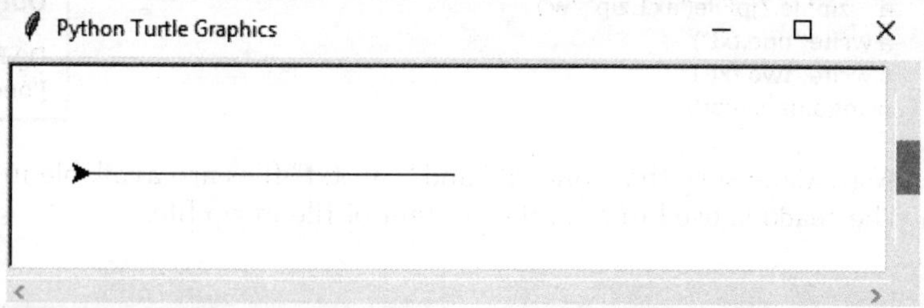

- right() – Moves the turtle in right direction

```
import turtle
x=turtle.Screen()
turtle.right(100)
turtle.forward(100)
x.mainloop()
```

Output

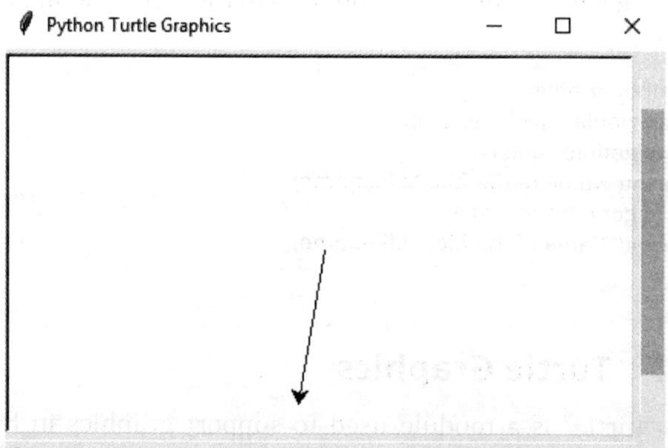

- left() – Moves the turtle in left direction

```
import turtle
x=turtle.Screen()
turtle.left(100)
turtle.forward(100)
x.mainloop()
```

Output

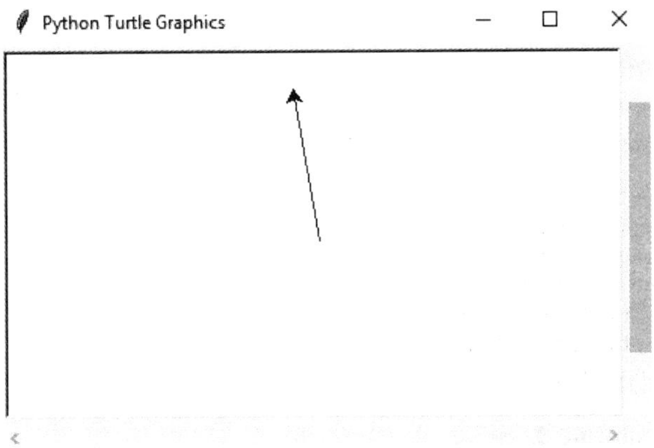

- circle() – draws the circle shape
- dot() – draws a dot shape

```
import turtle
x=turtle.Screen()
turtle.circle(100)
turtle.dot(100)
turtle.stamp()
x.mainloop()
```

Output

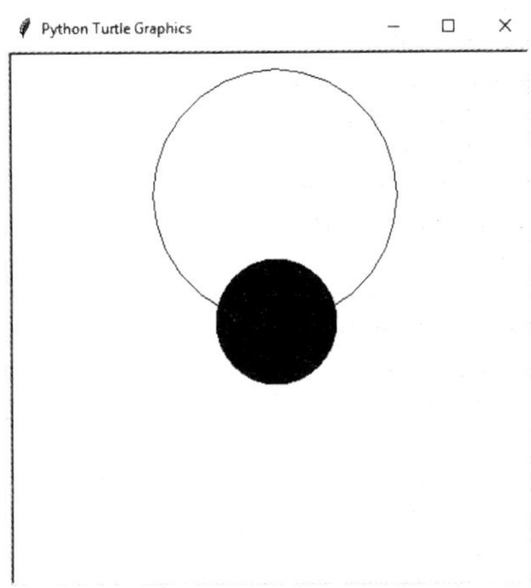

Example **1**

```
import turtle
x=turtle.Screen()
turtle.forward(100)
turtle.right(90)
turtle.forward(100)
turtle.right(90)
turtle.forward(100)
turtle.right(90)
turtle.forward(100)
turtle.right(90)
x.mainloop()
```

Output

Example 2

```
import turtle
x=turtle.Screen()
for i in range(5):
    turtle.forward(150)
    turtle.right(144)
x.mainloop()
```

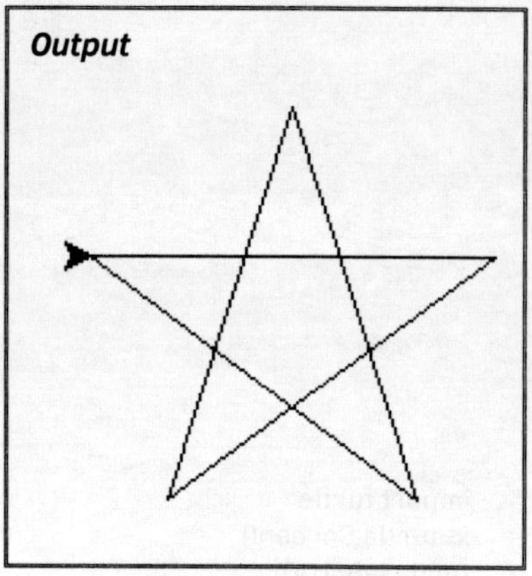

Example 3

```
import turtle
x=turtle.Screen()
turtle.pencolor("red")
turtle.forward(100)
turtle.right(90)
turtle.pencolor("green")
turtle.forward(100)
turtle.right(90)
turtle.pencolor("blue")
turtle.forward(100)
turtle.right(90)
turtle.pencolor("orange")
turtle.forward(100)
turtle.right(90)
x.mainloop()
```

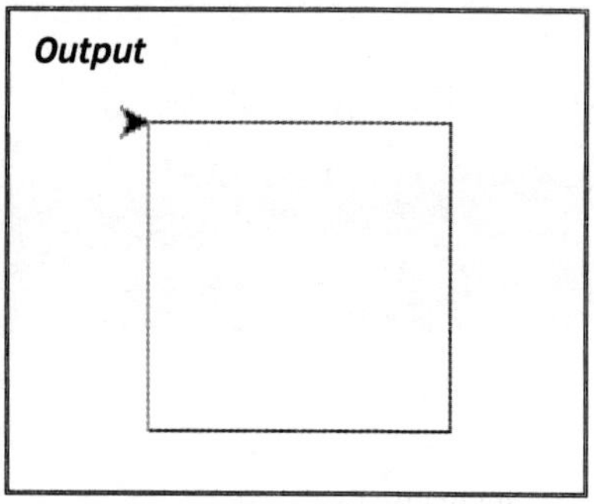

In the above output, the top and bottom lines are red and blue while the right and left lines are green and yellow respectively.

Example 4

```
import turtle
x=turtle.Screen()
turtle.pencolor("red")
for i in range(6):
turtle.forward(100)
turtle.right(60)
x.mainloop()
```

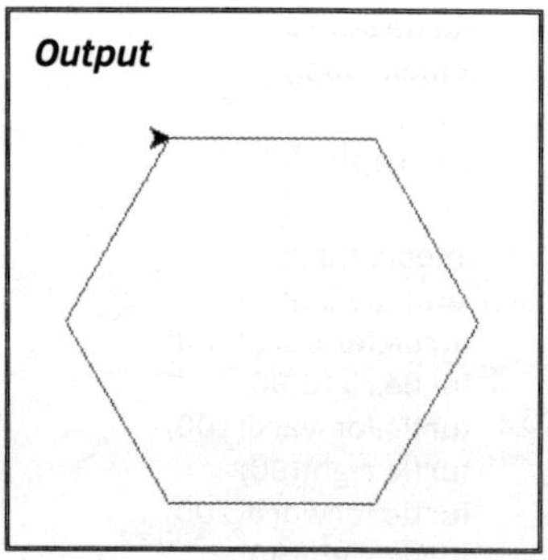

In the above output, the lines are red in color

Example **5**

```
import turtle
x=turtle.Screen()
x.bgcolor("yellow")
turtle.forward(200)
x.mainloop()
```

Output

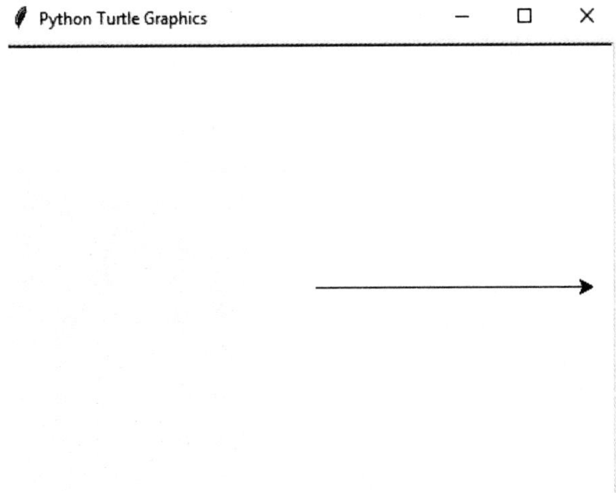

The background screen is yellow in the above output.

Example **6**

```
import turtle
x=turtle.Screen()
turtle.hideturtle()
x.bgpic("in.gif")
x.mainloop()
```

Output

Example **7**

```
import turtle
x=turtle.Screen()
turtle.shape("circle")
turtle.forward(50)
x.mainloop()
```

Output

18.9 Sample Programs

Program 1: Write a Python program to delete a file/directory by using operating system interface.

```
import os
os.remove("x.txt")
os.removedirs("dir1")
```

Output

```
D:\PythonPrograms>dir
 Volume in drive D has no label.
 Volume Serial Number is 4006-8C06

 Directory of D:\PythonPrograms

06/07/2017  21:59    <DIR>          .
06/07/2017  21:59    <DIR>          ..
06/07/2017  21:59                56 a1.py
06/05/2017  17:44    <DIR>          aa
06/07/2017  21:56    <DIR>          dir1
06/07/2017  21:56    <DIR>          Old prgs
06/07/2017  21:59                 0 x.txt
05/17/2017  14:56    <DIR>          __pycache__
               2 File(s)             56 bytes
               6 Dir(s)  271,706,509,312 bytes free

D:\PythonPrograms>python a1.py

D:\PythonPrograms>dir
 Volume in drive D has no label.
 Volume Serial Number is 4006-8C06

 Directory of D:\PythonPrograms

06/07/2017  21:59    <DIR>          .
06/07/2017  21:59    <DIR>          ..
06/07/2017  21:59                56 a1.py
06/05/2017  17:44    <DIR>          aa
06/07/2017  21:56    <DIR>          Old prgs
05/17/2017  14:56    <DIR>          __pycache__
               1 File(s)             56 bytes
               5 Dir(s)  271,706,509,312 bytes free
```

Program 2: Write a Python program to use difflib module.

```
import difflib
text1="abcdefgh"
text2="abcfabcf"
x=difflib.SequenceMatcher(None, text1, text2)
print(x)
```

Output

```
D:\PythonPrograms>python a1.py
<difflib.SequenceMatcher object at 0x02ED25F0>
```

Program 3: Write a Python program to wrap the text to a specified width.

```
import textwrap
s=input("Enter the text: ")
v=int(input("Enter the width: "))
x=textwrap.wrap(s,v)
print("Result of wrap: ",x)
y=textwrap.fill(s,v)
print("Result of fill: ",y)
```

Output

```
D:\PythonPrograms>python a1.py
Enter the text: kafkjjaf kfjdjfldjfldufdf dksfhksdfhdskfsdkf
Enter the width: 3
Result of wrap: ['kaf', 'kjj', 'af ', 'kfj', 'djf', 'ldj', 'fld', 'ufd', 'f d',
'ksf', 'hks', 'dfh', 'dsk', 'fsd', 'kf']
Result of fill: kaf
kjj
af
kfj
djf
ldj
fld
ufd
f d
ksf
hks
dfh
dsk
fsd
kf
```

Program 4: Write a Python program to read the character and print its UCD properties.

```
import unicodedata
s=input("Enter the charcter: ")
print("Name: ",unicodedata.name(s))
print("Category: ",unicodedata.category(s))
t=input(«Enter int character: «)
print(«decimal value: «,unicodedata.decimal(t))
print(«digit value: «,unicodedata.digit(t))
f1=input("Enter float character: ")
print("numeric value: ",unicodedata.numeric(f1))
```

Output

```
D:\PythonPrograms>python a1.py
Enter the charcter: d
Name: LATIN SMALL LETTER D
Category: Ll
Enter int character: 5
decimal value: 5
digit value: 5
Enter float character: 1
numeric value: 1.0
```

Program 5: Write a Python program to maintain data and time information.

```
import datetime
d=datetime.datetime(2011,10,6,hour=5,minute=45)
print("The date and time= ",d)
print("today= ",d.today())
```

Output

```
D:\PythonPrograms>python a1.py
The date and time= 2011-10-06 05:45:00
today= 2018-02-22 01:32:26.549778
```

Glossary

- Turtle module provides the facility for graphics in Python.

Summary

- Python programming supports various standard libraries to handle different operations.
- The **os** module is used for handling various operating system operations.
- The **difflib** and **textwrap** modules are used for handling text processing operations.
- Mathematical operations are handled with modules such as **numbers, math, cmath, decimal,** etc.
- The **zipfile** module is used to handle data compression operations.
- The graphics in Python is supported by **turtle** module.

Multiple Choice Questions

1. Which of the following modules support graphics?
(a) **tkinter**
(b) **turtle**
(c) Both a and b.
(d) None of the above.

2. Which module supports operating system interface?
(a) **osi**
(b) **osm**
(c) **os**
(d) None of the above.

3. Which of the following is an advantage of **os** module?
(a) It can execute os commands
(b) It can delete os commands
(c) Both a and b.
(d) None of the above.

4. In Python, which module provides text processing?
(a) **difflib** (b) **string**
(c) **re** (d) All the above

5. **unicode** module provides which feature?
(a) Mathematics
(b) Text wrapping
(c) Operating system interface
(d) Fractionals

6. **cmath** module functions work on which data?
(a) Complicated data (b) Mixed data
(c) Complex data (d) All of the above.

7. Which of the following modules open the URL in a browser?
(a) **urllib**
(b) **webbrowser**
(c) **browser**
(d) None of the above.

8. Which module will open the URL in command line interface?
(a) **urllib**
(b) **webbrowser**
(c) **browser**
(d) None of the above.

9. **gipfile** module provides which feature?
(a) Data reduction
(b) Data enrichment
(c) Data enhancement
(d) Data compression

10. **turtle** is added to which component?
(a) screen (b) widget
(c) frame (d) panel

Fill in the Blanks

1. Python programming will run under ________________________.

2. Python can communicate to an operating system by using ________________________.

3. ________________________ is used to execute any operating system command.

4. ________________________ returns the current working directory.

5. ________________________ creates a new directory.

6. ________________________ module is used to compute the deltas.

7. ________________________ module is used to handle various operations on rational data.

8. ________________________ module is used to handle pseudo random number data operations.

9. ________________________ is used to handle statistical operations.

10. ________________________ package is used for Internet Access in Python.

State True/False

1. The **webbrowser** module is used for internet access in Python.
2. The **datetime** module is used for handling date operations only.
3. The **datetime** module is used for handling both date and time operations.
4. **zlib** is the only compression algorithm supported in Python.
5. The **turtle** module is used to support graphics in Python.
6. **screen()** is used to create the screen of the turtle.
7. **forward()** is used to delete the screen of the turtle.
8. **backward()** is used to get the current position of the turtle.
9. **right()** is used to move the turtle in right direction.
10. **circle()** and **dot()** methods can be applicable on turtle.

Find the Output

1.
```
import turtle
x=turtle.Screen()
turtle.forward(100)
turtle.left(120)
turtle.forward(100)
turtle.left(120)
turtle.forward(100)
x.mainloop()
```
2.
```
import os
os.mkdir("a1")
print("a1 directory is created")
```
3.
```
import os
os.rmdir("a1")
print("a1 directory is deleted")
```

Find the Error

1.
```
import turtle
x=turtle.screen()
turtle.forward(100)
x.mainloop()
```
2.
```
import os
os.system(dir)
```
3.
```
import os
os.system("mkdir("aa")")
```

Long Answer Questions

1. Explain in detail about standard libraries in Python.
2. How Python can be used to draw graphics?
3. What are the different ways to access in Internet in Python?
4. List and explain about the various mathematical modules in Python?
5. In what way data compression is achieved in Python?

Short Answer Questions

1. What is turtle?
2. List the various ways to handle date and time data.
3. How can a Python program execute operating system commands?

Exercise Programs

1. Write a Python program to compare two input files by using difflib module.
2. Write a Python program to perform the following operations:
   - Limit the width of the text to a specified size
   - Remove all the leading whitespaces
   - Add a prefix to the selected lines of text

Answers

Multiple Choice Questions

1. (b) 2. (c) 3. (a) 4. (d) 5. (b) 6. (c) 7. (b) 8. (a) 9. (d) 10. (a)

Fill in the Blanks

1. an operating system
2. os module
3. system()
4. getcwd()
5. mkdir()
6. difflib
7. Fractions
8. Fractions
9. Statistics
10. urllib

State True/False

1. True
2. False
3. True
4. False
5. True
6. True
7. False
8. False
9. True
10. True

Find the Output

1.

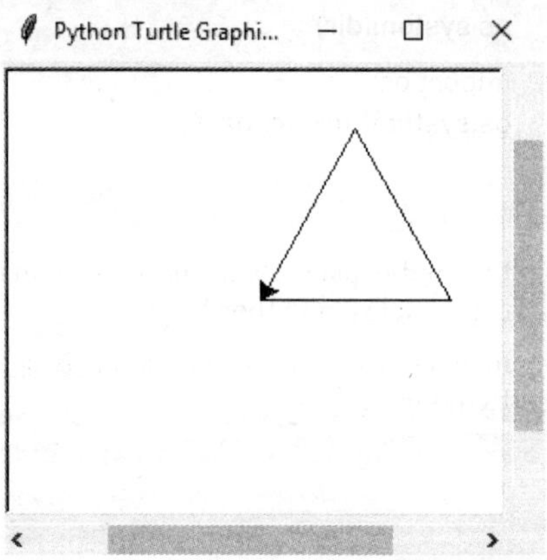

2. a1 directory is created
3. a1 directory is deleted

Find the Error

1. AttributeError: module 'turtle' has no attribute 'screen'
2. SyntaxError: invalid syntax (os.system("mkdir("aa")"))

CHAPTER 19 Testing

The process of software development includes several stages. After developing the code for the required product, the product will not be delivered directly to the client. If immediate delivery happens and the developed product failed, then it would lead to problems at the client's end. Hence, the testing phase is used. In the testing phase, the developed code will be tested in various conditions. The advantage of testing is that it enables the developer to deliver an error-free product. The product will be delivered to the client only if the result of the developed product is satisfied for all test conditions. The present chapter discusses in detail about testing in Python.

19.1 Basic Concepts of Testing

The testing process evaluates the developed product on whether it satisfies all the given requirements. Testing can be performed in two different ways. They are

- Manual testing
- Computer based testing – It is also called as unit testing.

During the testing process, it is hard to terminate the program. For termination, various details should be considered such as deadline of testing, identification of completion of testing process, management decision, etc.

In software development life cycle, verification and validation processes are mainly used to estimate the quality of the product. The verification process is used to verify if the developed product meets all the requirements. In general this process is performed by the software developers. The validation process is used to validate the developed product by checking whether the product is defective. In general, the validation process is performed by software testers.

During the testing process, the bugs, errors or defects in the developed product will be identified. So, it is recommended to perform the testing process in the initial stages of the systems development life cycle (SDLC). This will also help to reduce the time and cost associated with testing the product. During the testing process, if the identified bugs, errors or defects are solved then it is called as debugging.

19.2 Unit Testing in Python

The `unittest` module should be imported to test a Python program. A test case represents individual unit of the test. A collection of text cases is called as test suite. The test runner will perform the testing process. The test fixture represents the requirements for performing a test. There are several functions in `unittest` module:

- The `unittest.TestCase()` function is used to create a new test case.

- The function with **test_** as prefix represents the tests to be executed by the test runner.
- The **assertEqual()** will check each test for the expected result.
- The **assertTrue()** and **assertFalse()** verifies the condition for the test method.
- The **setup()** and **teardown()** methods define the statements to be executed before and after the test method.
- The **unittest.main()** provides command line interface.

```
import unittest
class t1(unittest.TestCase):
    def test_starting_out(self):
        self.assertEqual(1, 1)
if __name__ == "__main__":
    unittest.main()
```

Output

```
D:\PythonPrograms>python a1.py
.
------------------------------------------
Ran 1 test in 0.000s
OK
```

- From command line also, the unit test module can be executed.

```
D:\PythonPrograms>python -m unittest
----------------------------------------
Ran 0 tests in 0.000s
OK
```

- For each test, the outcome can be in three different values, namely, OK, FAIL and ERROR. If the test method is succeeded without any bugs/errors then "PASS" will be returned. If the test method is failed then raises **AssertionError** exception. If the test method raises an exception, then "ERROR" will be returned.

```
import unittest
class t1(unittest.TestCase):
    def test_ok(self):
        self.assertEqual(1,1)
    def test_fail(self):
        self.assertFalse(1<2)
    def test_error(self):
        raise RuntimeError("Test ERROR")

if __name__ == "__main__":
    unittest.main()
```

Output

```
D:\PythonPrograms>python a1.py
EF.
================================
ERROR: test_error (__main__.t1)
------------------------------------------
Traceback (most recent call last):
File "a1.py", line 11, in test_error
raise RuntimeError("Test ERROR")
RuntimeError: Test ERROR
================================
FAIL: test_fail (__main__.t1)
------------------------------------------
Traceback (most recent call last):
File "a1.py", line 8, in test_fail
self.assertFalse(1<2)
AssertionError: True is not false
------------------------------------------
Ran 3 tests in 0.000s
FAILED (failures=1, errors=1)
```

In the above program, three test methods are defined, viz., {test_ok(), test_fail(), test_error()}. The test_ok() test method checks the condition. The condition is tested and the result is okay. The test_fail() test method checks the condition for false output. However, the test condition yields true result. So, the result will be AssertionError. The test_error() raises an exception called as RuntimeError.

Various methods applicable on the test case are listed below.

- The assertEqual() checks whether or not the two input values.
- The assertNotEqual() checks whether or not the two input values are not equal.
- The assertTrue() checks if the result of the input condition is true or not.
- The assertFalse() checks if the result of the input condition is false or not.
- The assertRaises() checks whether the exception is raised or not.
- The assertAlmostEqual() checks whether or not the two input values are almost similar.
- The assertNotAlmostEqual() checks whether or not the two input values are not almost similar.
- The assertRegrex() checks whether or not the regrex search result is matched with the text or not.
- The assertIs() checks whether or not the first input is same as the second input.
- The assertIsNot() checks whether or not the first input is not the same as the second input.
- The assertIsNone() checks whether or not the input expression is none.
- The assertIsNotNone() checks whether or not the input expression is not none.
- The assertIn() checks whether or not the first input is in the second input.
- The assertNotIn() checks whether or not the first input is not in the second input.

19.3 Grouping Test Cases in Unit Testing

In Python unit testing, multiple test cases can be grouped by using "test suite". For this, TestSuite class in unit test module is used. The test case object is responsible for test whereas the test suite object is responsible for grouping multiple test case objects for test. Various methods in the test suite object are listed below.

- The addTest() method will add a test case or test suite to the current test suite.
- The addTests() method is used to add all the tests of the test case or test suite.
- The run() will run the tests and store the result in input result object.
- The countTestCases() counts the tests available in the test suite object.

19.4 Loading and Running Tests

In Python, multiple test cases are available in various classes and modules. All the test cases from these classes and modules can be loaded into a test suite by using TestLoader class. Various methods in this class are listed below.

- The loadTestsFromTestCase() method will load all the test cases from the input class to the current test suite object.
- The loadTestsFromModule() method will load all the test cases from the input module to the current test suite object.
- The loadTestsFromName() method will load all the test cases from the input name to the current test suite object.
- The getTestCaseNames() method will get the names of all test cases in the input class. The result will be in sorted order.

For running a test suite in Python, use the TextTestRunner() class. This class contains the run() method. The run() method will execute the input test suite.

```
import unittest
class t1(unittest.TestCase):
    def testm1(self):
        self.assertAlmostEqual(10,11)
    def testm2(self):
        self.assertNotAlmostEqual(10,11)
class t2(unittest.TestCase):
    def testm3(self):
        self.assertIsNone(none)
    def testm4(self):
        self.assertisNone("hello")
if __name__ == "__main__":
    l=unittest.TestLoader()
    s1=unittest.TestSuite()
    s2=unittest.TestSuite()
    r=unittest.TextTestRunner()
    s1.addTest(l.loadTestsFromTestCase(t1))
    r.run(s1)
    s2.addTest(l.loadTestsFromTestCase(t2))
    r.run(s2)
```

Output

```
D:\PythonPrograms>python a1.py
F.
==========================================
FAIL: testm1 (__main__.t1)
------------------------------------------
Traceback (most recent call last):
File "a1.py", line 5, in testm1
self.assertAlmostEqual(10,11)
AssertionError: 10 != 11 within 7 places
------------------------------------------
Ran 2 tests in 0.000s
FAILED (failures=1)
EE
==========================================
ERROR: testm3 (__main__.t2)
------------------------------------------
Traceback (most recent call last):
File "a1.py", line 12, in testm3
self.assertIsNone(none)
NameError: name 'none' is not defined
==========================================
ERROR: testm4 (__main__.t2)
------------------------------------------
Traceback (most recent call last):
File "a1.py", line 15, in testm4
self.assertisNone("hello")
AttributeError: 't2' object has no attribute 'assertisNone'
------------------------------------------
Ran 2 tests in 0.000s
FAILED (errors=2)
```

19.5 Sample Programs

Program 1: Write a Python program to check the test case whether the input expression is none or not.

```
import unittest
class t1(unittest.TestCase):
    def testm1(self):
        self.assertIsNone(None)
    def testm2(self):
        self.assertIsNone("hello")
if __name__ == "__main__":
    unittest.main()
```

Programming Tip:

Unit testing is a testing procedure conducted by Python.

```
Output

D:\PythonPrograms>python a1.py
.F
==============================
FAIL: testm2 (__main__.t1)
----------------------------------------------
Traceback (most recent call last):
File "a1.py", line 8, in testm2
self.assertIsNone("hello")
AssertionError: 'hello' is not None
----------------------------------------------
Ran 2 tests in 0.000s
FAILED (failures=1)
```

Program 2: Write a Python program to test whether the first input is in the second input or not.

```
import unittest
class t1(unittest.TestCase):
    def testm1(self):
        self.assertNotIn("hello","hello good morning")
    def testm2(self):
        self.assertIn("hello","hello good morning")

if __name__ == "__main__":
    unittest.main()
```

```
Output

D:\PythonPrograms>python a1.py
F.
========================================
FAIL: testm1 (__main__.t1)
--------------------------------------------------------
Traceback (most recent call last):
File "a1.py", line 5, in testm1
self.assertNotIn("hello","hello good morning")
AssertionError: 'hello' unexpectedly found in 'hello
good morning'
--------------------------------------------------------
Ran 2 tests in 0.000s
FAILED (failures=1)
```

Program 3: Write a Python program to test whether the two input values are almost same or not.

```
import unittest
class t1(unittest.TestCase):
    def testm1(self):
        self.assertAlmostEqual(10,11)
    def testm2(self):
        self.assertNotAlmostEqual(10,11)
if __name__ == "__main__":
    unittest.main()
```

```
Output

D:\PythonPrograms>python a1.py
F.
=============================================
FAIL: testm1 (__main__.t1)
--------------------------------------------------------
Traceback (most recent call last):
File "a1.py", line 5, in testm1
self.assertAlmostEqual(10,11)
AssertionError: 10 != 11 within 7 places
--------------------------------------------------------
Ran 2 tests in 0.000s
FAILED (failures=1)
```

Program 4: Write a Python program to create multiple test cases.

```
import unittest
class t1(unittest.TestCase):
    def testm1(self):
        self.assertAlmostEqual(10,11)
    def testm2(self):
        self.assertNotAlmostEqual(10,11)
class t2(unittest.TestCase):
    def testm3(self):
        self.assertIsNone(none)
    def testm4(self):
        self.assertisNone("hello")
if __name__ == "__main__":
    unittest.main()
```

Output

```
D:\PythonPrograms>python a1.py
F.EE
==========================================================
ERROR: testm3 (__main__.t2)
----------------------------------------------------------
Traceback (most recent call last):
File "a1.py", line 13, in testm3
self.assertIsNone(none)
NameError: name 'none' is not defined
==========================================================
ERROR: testm4 (__main__.t2)
----------------------------------------------------------
Traceback (most recent call last):
File "a1.py", line 16, in testm4
self.assertisNone("hello")
AttributeError: 't2' object has no attribute 'assertisNone'
==========================================================
FAIL: testm1 (__main__.t1)
----------------------------------------------------------
Traceback (most recent call last):
File "a1.py", line 5, in testm1
self.assertAlmostEqual(10,11)
AssertionError: 10 != 11 within 7 places
----------------------------------------------------------
Ran 4 tests in 0.000s
FAILED (failures=1, errors=2)
```

Program 5: Write a Python program to create multiple test cases and execute only one test case from the command line interface.

```
import unittest
class t1(unittest.TestCase):
    def testm1(self):
        self.assertAlmostEqual(10,11)
    def testm2(self):
        self.assertNotAlmostEqual(10,11)
class t2(unittest.TestCase):
    def testm3(self):
        self.assertIsNone(none)
    def testm4(self):
        self.assertisNone("hello")
if __name__ == "__main__":
    unittest.main()
```

Output

```
D:\PythonPrograms>python a1.py t1
F.
==========================================================
FAIL: testm1 (__main__.t1)
----------------------------------------------------------
Traceback (most recent call last):
File "a1.py", line 5, in testm1
self.assertAlmostEqual(10,11)
AssertionError: 10 != 11 within 7 places
----------------------------------------------------------
Ran 2 tests in 0.000s
FAILED (failures=1)
```

Glossary

- The testing process evaluates the developed product on whether it satisfies all the given requirements.
- Manual testing allows the user to perform the testing process manually.
- Unit testing allows Python to perform the testing process.

Summary

- Testing is an important step to validate the developed software product.
- The testing procedure can be either manual or computer based.
- The computer based testing procedure is called as unit testing.
- Python programming supports unit testing feature.
- Unit testing is supported by unittest module in Python.
- New test cases can be created for the unit testing process and thus can be evaluated.
- The result of the test case can be OK, FAILED or ERROR.

Multiple Choice Questions

1. Which of the following module provides testing in Python?
   (a) testing (b) alltesting
   (c) unittesting (d) classtesting
2. What are the various types of testing?
   (a) manual
   (b) computerized
   (c) Both a and b.
   (d) None of the above.
3. Verification process is performed by
   (a) developers
   (b) testers
   (c) Both a and b.
   (d) None of the above.
4. Validation process is performed by
   (a) developers
   (b) testers
   (c) Both a and b.
   (d) None of the above.
5. Unit testing is also called as
   (a) computerized testing
   (b) manual testing
   (c) Both a and b.
   (d) None of the above.
6. Test case is created by
   (a) TestCase
   (b) unittest.TestCase
   (c) Both a and b.
   (d) None of the above
7. Test case is a
   (a) collection of test modules
   (b) collection of test classes
   (c) collection of various tests
   (d) None of the above.
8. Test suite is a collection of test cases in
   (a) class (b) module
   (c) other test suites (d) All of the above.
9. Test suite is created by
   (a) TestSuite(b) unittest.TestSuite
   (c) Either a or b.
   (d) Both a and b.
10. Which method is responsible to execute the test suite?
    (a) unittest.TextTestRunner()
    (b) TextTestRunner()
    (c) Either a or b.
    (d) Both a and b.

Fill in the Blanks

1. The developed code is verified during _______________ phase.
2. There are _______________ types of testing methods.
3. _______________ and _______________ are the types of testing methods.
4. _______________ testing is a computer based testing.
5. During testing process, it is hard to perform _______________ operation.
6. During testing, _______________ in the developed product are identified.
7. The resolving process of bug/error/defect is called _______________.
8. _______________ is sued to create a new test case.
9. _______________ will check each test for the expected result.
10. _______________ provides command line interface.

State True/False

1. A unit test module can be executed from command line.
2. There is only one output for each test case.
3. "OK" is the output of the test case.
4. "FAIL" is the output of the test case.
5. "ERROR" is the output of the test case.
6. If a test method is fails, no exception is raised.
7. **AssertionError** exception can be raised when there is a test method failure.
8. Min unit testing and multiple test cases are grouped by using "test suite" module.
9. The **run()** will add a test case to the current test suite.
10. **TestLoader** class will load and run multiple test cases from various classes and modules.

Find the Output

1.
```
import unittest
class t1(unittest.TestCase):
    def test_starting_out(self):
        self.assertFalse(0)
if __name__ == "__main__":
    unittest.main()
```

2.
```
import unittest
class t1(unittest.TestCase):
    def test_starting_out(self):
        self.assertTrue(10)
if __name__ == "__main__":
    unittest.main()
```

3.
```
import unittest
class t1(unittest.TestCase):
    def test_starting_out(self):
        self.assertEqual("", "")
if __name__ == "__main__":
    unittest.main()
```

Find the Error

1.
```
import unittest
class t1(unittest.TestCase):
    def test_starting_out(self):
        self.assertEqual(1, 1)
if __name__ == "__main__":
    unittest.abc()
```

2.
```
import unittest
class t1(unittest.TestCase):
    def test_starting_out(self):
        self.assertEqual()
if __name__ == "__main__":
    unittest.main()
```

3.
```
import unittest
class t1(unittest.TestCase):
    def test_starting_out(self):
        self.assertFalse()
if __name__ == "__main__":
    unittest.main()
```

Long Answer Questions

1. Explain in detail about test cases.
2. What is unit testing? How does Python support unit testing?
3. Differentiate test and test case? Justify the answer with program.

Short Answer Questions

1. Differentiate test and test case.
2. What is the syntax to define a test in Python?
3. What is the loader and runner of Python?

Exercise Programs

1. Write a Python program for using setup() and tearDown() functions.
2. Write a Python program to create a test suite by loading test cases from module.

Answers

Multiple Choice Questions

1. c
2. c
3. a
4. b
5. a
6. b
7. c
8. d
9. b
10. a

Fill in the Blanks

1. testing
2. two
3. Manual testing, unit testing
4. Unit testing
5. termination
6. bugs/errors/defects
7. debugging
8. unittest.TestCase()
9. assertEqual()
10. unittest.main()

State True/False

1. True
2. False
3. True
4. True
5. True
6. False
7. True
8. True
9. False
10. True

Find the Output

1.
```
.
----------------------------------------------------
Ran 1 test in 0.000s
OK
```
2.
```
.
----------------------------------------------------
Ran 1 test in 0.000s
OK
```
3.
```
.
----------------------------------------------------
Ran 1 test in 0.000s
OK
```

Find the Error

1. AttributeError: module 'unittest' has no attribute 'abc' (unittest.abc())
2.
```
E
==============================
ERROR: test_starting_out (__main__.t1)
------------------------------
Traceback (most recent call last):
File "s1.py", line 5, in test_starting_out
self.assertEqual()
TypeError: assertEqual() missing 2 required positional arguments: 'first' and 'second'
------------------------------
Ran 1 test in 0.000s
FAILED (errors=1)
```
2.
```
E
==============================
ERROR: test_starting_out (__main__.t1)
------------------------------
Traceback (most recent call last):
File "s1.py", line 5, in test_starting_out
self.assertFalse()
TypeError: assertFalse() missing 1 required positional argument: 'expr'
------------------------------
Ran 1 test in 0.000s
FAILED (errors=1)
```

APPENDIX

A Networking

A.1 Introduction

Networking allows multiple systems to communicate. Using this concept, multiple devices can be connected and the data can be shared among them. A network can be created among multiple devices as shown in Fig. 19.1.

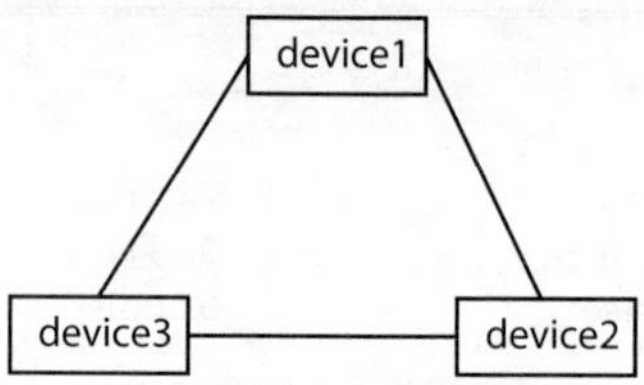

Fig. 19.1 Network with three devices

Within a network, each and every device can be recognized with its IP address. The IP addresses are unique and no more than one device can have same IP address. In the network as shown in Fig. 19.1, all the three devices have unique IP addresses. Within the network, any device can communicate with another device. Protocols are designed to enable communication among devices in a network. In general, TCP/IP or UDP protocols are used to establish communication among the devices. For each device, the port is acts as an interface to get connected to other devices. In general, the port is represented by numbers. In the device, a program or service is represented by a port number. Not more than one program or service should use the same port number.

A.2 Networking in Python

Python programming also supports the designing of a network to establish communication. Python supports networking at two different levels. They are

- Low-level networking

  In low-level networking, the "socket" is used to create the network underlying the operating system.

- High level networking

  In high-level networking, communication is preformed with application-specific protocols such as HTTP, FTP, SMTP etc.

A.3 Low-level Networking

In Python, low-level networking is performed with the socket. Thus, the communication between client and server happens through the socket. The socket used for the client is "client socket" and the socket used for the server is called as "server socket". A socket allows bidirectional communication.

In Python **socket** module provides several functions for low-level networking. So, in a low level networking python program, it is mandatory to use the statement **import socket**. Various functions of **socket** module are listed below.

- **socket()**is used to create a new socket. It can be created by using the following syntax.

```
socket_name=socket.socket(socket_family, socket_type)
```

- **socket_family** represents the type of the socket address family. The possible values for this are **AF_UNIX** and **AF_INET**. **AF_UNIX** is used for IPv4 protocol while **AF_INET** is used for IPv6 protocol. **AF_UNIX** is available only for UNIX-based operating system.
- **socket_type** represents the type of the socket. There are two types of sockets, viz., **SOCK_STREAM** and **SOCK_DGRAM**. **SOCK_STREAM** is used to represent the connection based streams for TCP. **SOCK_DGRAM** is used to represent the datagram streams for UDP.

```
import socket
s1=socket.socket(socket.AF_INET,socket.SOCK_STREAM )
print("Socket with AF_INET,SOCK_STREAM is created")
s2=socket.socket(socket.AF_INET,socket.SOCK_DGRAM )
print("Socket with AF_INET,SOCK_DGRAM is created")
```

Output

```
D:\PythonPrograms>python a1.py
Socket with AF_INET, SOCK_STREAM is created
Socket with AF_INET, SOCK_DGRAM is created
```

- **socket.gethostname()**will get the name of the host. It returns the local machine name.

```
import socket
print("host name: ",socket.gethostname())
print("host IPaddress: ",socket.gethostbyname(socket.
gethostname()))
```

Output

```
D:\PythonPrograms>python a1.py
host name: DESKTOP-6ECSOBG
host IPaddress: 192.168.1.100
```

A.4 Client-Server Network

Client-server communication allows connecting multiple devices in a network. Among multiple devices, one device will act as "server" and the remaining devices will act as "clients". The server is always the master controller or administrator of the entire network. Within the network, all the clients will be connected to the server. A client-server network is shown in Fig. 19.2.

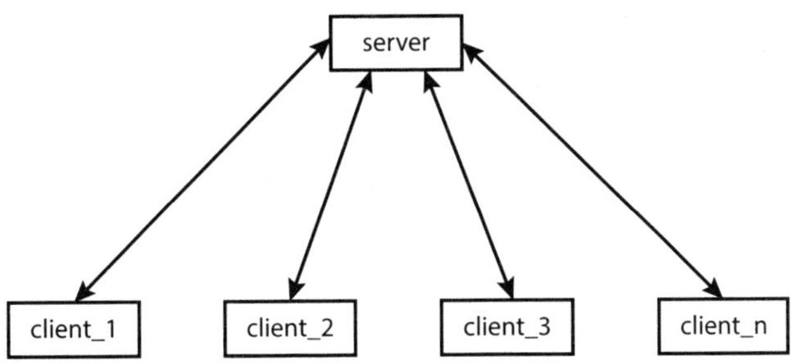

Fig. 19.2 Client-server network

In a client-server network, communication is allowed between any client and the server. All the clients can communicate with the server. The server can also communicate with all the clients in the network. The server or the client can be identified by its unique IP address. Both, client and server, have ports for connecting with the external environment.

For communication between the client and the server, a "socket" is required. The socket should be created at the client side and the server side. The socket created for the client is called as "client socket" whereas the socket created for the server is called as "server socket". After creating the socket at client or server side, the socket should be connected to the host and the port.

A.4.1. Server socket

The socket created at the server side is called as "server socket". The server socket can be created by using socket(). The server socket can be with TCP socket or UDP socket. The host represents either the IP address or the name of the device. For this purpose, bind() method is used. With this, the socket can 'listen' to the communication received from the specific IP address and the port. The socket can also send the messages from the specific IP address and the port. The syntax for the bind()method is

```
socket_object.bind((host_del,port_num))
```

- The socket_object represents the server socket object for which the bind() method should execute.
- The host_del represents the name or IP address or the name of the host device.
- The port_num is a number that represents the specific port.

```
import socket
s1=socket.socket(socket.AF_INET,socket.SOCK_STREAM )
print("TCP Socket is created")
s2=socket.socket(socket.AF_INET,socket.SOCK_DGRAM )
print("UDP Socket is created")
h=socket.gethostname()
p=255
s1.bind((h,p))
print("TCP socket is binded")
s2.bind((h,p))
print("UDP socket is binded")
```

Output

```
D:\PythonPrograms>python a2.py
TCP Socket is created
UDP Socket is created
TCP socket is binded
UDP socket is binded
```

In the above example code, the server socket is created and is connected to the local host device port 255. So, with this socket, the communication is allowed only to the local host device port 255.

After binding the server socket to the specific port of the host, the communication should be started between the client and the server socket. For this, initially the server socket should be connected with the client socket. The connection can be established only when the server socket receives a connection request from the client socket. So, the server socket should 'listen' for client socket requests. For this, listen()method is used. This method should be used only for server socket to receive the client socket requests. The syntax for the "listen()" method is

```
server_socket_object.listen(limit_req)
```

- The server_socket_object represents the server socket object for which the listen() method should execute.
- The limit_req represents the size of requests queue.

```
import socket
s1=socket.socket(socket.AF_INET,socket.SOCK_STREAM )
print("TCP Socket is created")
h=socket.gethostname()
```

```
p=255
s1.bind((h,p))
print("TCP socket is binded")
s1.listen(4)
print("TCP socket listen upto 4 connection requests")
```

Output

```
D:\PythonPrograms>python a2.py
TCP Socket is created
TCP socket is binded
TCP socket listen upto 4 connection requests
```

After the server socket is created, the server starts to listen for connection requests from the client. If it 'hears' any request, the server socket will accept the request and establish the connection with the requested client. For this accept()method is used. This method can be used only by the server socket. The syntax for the accept() method is

```
(client_socket,addr)=server_socket_object.accept()
```

- The server_socket_object represents the server socket object for which the listen() method should execute.
- The accept() method will establish the connection between the server socket and the client socket. It returns the client socket represented by client_socket and the address of the client socket, with addr.

A.4.2. Client socket

The client socket can be created by using the socket() method. After creating the client socket, it should be connected with the server socket. Communication is possible between the client and server sockets only when the connection is successful. In Python, the client-server socket can be connected to the server socket by using the following syntax.

```
client_socket_obj.connect((host_del,port_num))
```

- The client_socket_object represents the client socket object for which the connect() method should execute.
- The host_del represents the name or IP address or the name of the host device.
- The port_num is a number that represents the specific port.

When the client socket calls the connect()method, internally the client socket sends a request to the server socket. If the server socket listens to the client's connection requests, it will accept the request by using accept()and create a connection to the client socket. The example code below shows the usage of connect()method to connect between client and server sockets. In this example, both the sockets are created for the local host device. So, two command line interfaces are used for client and server sockets respectively.

a1.py

```
import socket
s1=socket.socket(socket.AF_INET,socket.SOCK_STREAM )
print("Server Socket is created")
h=socket.gethostname()
p=255
s1.bind((h,p))
print("Server socket is binded")
s1.listen(4)
print("Server socket listen upto 4 connection requests")
while True:
    (c,a)=s1.accept()
    print("Request is received from the client")
    print("Connected client address: ",a)
```

a2.py

```
import socket
s1=socket.socket(socket.AF_INET,socket.SOCK_STREAM )
print("Client Socket is created")
h=socket.gethostname()
p=255
print("Client socket is sending connection request")
s1.connect((h,p))
```

Output

Command Prompt - python a1.py

```
D:\PythonPrograms>python a1.py
Server Socket is created
Server socket is binded
Server socket listen upto 4 connection requests
```

Command Prompt

```
D:\PythonPrograms>python a2.py
Client Socket is created
Client socket is sending connection request

D:\PythonPrograms>
```

Command Prompt - python a1.py

```
D:\PythonPrograms>python a1.py
Server Socket is created
Server socket is binded
Server socket listen upto 4 connection requests
Request is received from the client
Connected client address: ('192.168.1.100', 58687)
```

A.5 Client–Server Communication

After establishing a connection between the client and server sockets, communication between them becomes allowed and messages are sent and received through the sockets. There are two types of sockets, viz., TCP and UDP. So, the communication between the sockets should be specific to the type of socket. In Python, various methods are available for handling communication between client and server sockets. They are listed below.

- The recv()method is used to receive the message with TCP socket.
- The send()method is used to send the message with TCP socket.
- The recvfrom()method is used to receive the message with UDP socket.

- The **sendto()**method is used to send the message with UDP socket.
- The **close()** method is used to close the socket for which the object it is called.

a2.py

```
import socket
s1=socket.socket(socket.AF_INET,socket.SOCK_STREAM )
print("Client Socket is created")
h=socket.gethostname()
p=255
print("Client socket is sending connection request")
s1.connect((h,p))
m=s1.recv(1000)
print(m.decode('ascii'))
```

a1.py

```
import socket
s1=socket.socket(socket.AF_INET,socket.SOCK_STREAM )
print("Server Socket is created")
h=socket.gethostname()
p=255
s1.bind((h,p))
print("Server socket is binded")
s1.listen(4)
print("Server socket listen upto 4 connection requests")
while True:
    (c,a)=s1.accept()
    print("Request is received from the client")
    print("Connected client address: ",a)
    t="Hello from server"
    c.send(t.encode('ascii'))
```

Output

Command Prompt - python a1.py

```
D:\PythonPrograms>python a1.py
Server Socket is created
Server socket is binded
Server socket listen upto 4 connection requests
Request is received from the client
Connected client address:  ('192.168.1.100', 58706)
```

Command Prompt

```
D:\PythonPrograms>python a2.py
Client Socket is created
Client socket is sending connection request
Hello from server

D:\PythonPrograms>
```

A.6 High-level Networking

Python programming has various standard library modules to interact with internet services. This process is called as high-level networking. In this, the local host device will act as a client and connect to Web servers. There are several modules in Python for handling internet services such as urllib, HTTP, NNTP, FTP, SMTP and POP3.

In Python, File Transfer Protocol (FTP) is supported by the ftblib module. In this module, the FTP() is used to get connected to the FTP host and port. login() is used to perform the login operation with the username and password. cwd() is used to change the directory. retrlines() is used to list the contents of the current working directory. quit()is used to close the FTP connection. storbinary()is used to send the file from client to the FTP server.

httplib is used for handling the client-side operations of an HTTP connection. The smtplib is used to send email messages from client-side program.

APPENDIX

B Sending E-mail

B.1 Introduction

Python programming provides high-level networking for handling internet services. It offers various libraries for supporting the different types of internet activities. Sending e-mail is a popular internet service that is supported by Python. In Python high-level networking, the local host device will act as client session object and connect to the requested mail server. When connection is established between client and the mail server, the client session object will be able to send mails. Python uses Simple Mail Transfer Protocol (SMTP) for sending the mails from one account to other account. The smtplib module is used for handling the mail sending process.

B.2 Creation of SMTP Object

Python has smtplib module for handling objects of SMTP. For creating an SMTP object, SMTP() function is used. The syntax is given below.

```
new_smtp_obj=smtp.SMTP(host_del,port_num)
```

- host_del represents the name of the SMTP mail server.
- port_num represents the port of the SMTP mail server for which the communication should be established.
- new_smtp_obj is the SMTP object created and returned by the SMTP() function.

```
import smtplib
try:
    s1 = smtplib.SMTP('smtp.mail.yahoo.com',587)
    print("SMTP object is created")
except SMTPException:
    print("Error: unable to use SMTP")
```

Output

```
D:\PythonPrograms>python a2.py
SMTP object is created
```

B.3 Mail Server Connection

After creating the SMTP object, a connection to the SMTP mail server is required. This connection is created by the connect()method. With this method, the connection between client side and the SMTP mail server side is established. The syntax for the connect()method is given below.

```
smtp_obj.conenct(host_del,port_num)
```

- smtp_obj represents the SMTP object for which the connection is established.
- host_del represents the name of the SMTP mail server.
- port_num represents the port of the SMTP mail server for which the communication should be established.

```
import smtplib
try:
    s1 = smtplib.SMTP('smtp.mail.yahoo.com',587)
    print("SMTP object is created")
    s1.connect('smtp.mail.yahoo.com',587)
    print("connected to mail.yahoo.com server via SMTP")
except SMTPException:
    print("Error: unable to use SMTP")
```

Output

```
D:\PythonPrograms>python a2.py
SMTP object is created
connected to mail.yahoo.com server
    via SMTP
```

B.4 Login to Mail Server

After creating the connection between the client side and the SMTP mail server side, the user will be able to login to the mail account by providing the username and password. For this, login( ) method should be used.

```
import smtplib
try:
    s1 = smtplib.SMTP('smtp.mail.yahoo.com',587)
    print("SMTP object is created")
    s1.connect('smtp.mail.yahoo.com',587)
    print("Connected to mail.yahoo.com server via SMTP")
    s1.ehlo()
    s1.starttls()
    s1.ehlo()
    s1.login("xxx@yahoo.com","xxx")
    print("Login is successful")
except SMTPException:
    print("Error: unable to use SMTP")
```

Output

```
D:\PythonPrograms>python a2.py
SMTP object is created
Connected to mail.yahoo.com server
    via SMTP
Login is successful
```

B.5 Sending E-mail

After logging into the SMTP mail server, e-mails can be sent from the user's account. The message can be sent by using sendmail()method. The syntax for the method is

```
ser_obj.sendmail(from_add,to_add,msg)
```

- ser_obj represents the server object for which the mail should be sent.
- from_add represents the From address.
- to_add represents the To address.
- mg represents the message delivered.

```
import smtplib
try:
    s1 = smtplib.SMTP('smtp.mail.yahoo.com',587)
    print("SMTP object is created")
    s1.connect('smtp.mail.yahoo.com',587)
    print("connected to mail.yahoo.com server via SMTP")
    s1.ehlo()
    s1.starttls()
    s1.ehlo()
    s1.login("xxx@yahoo.com","xxx"))
    print("login is successful")
    fad=" xxx@yahoo.com "
    taddr="yyy@yahoo.com"
    msg = "This mail is sent from python"
    s1.sendmail(fad, taddr, msg)
    s1.quit()
    print("mail sent successfully")
except SMTPException:
    print("Error: unable to use SMTP")
```

Output

```
D:\PythonPrograms>python a2.py
SMTP object is created
connected to mail.yahoo.com server
    via SMTP
login is successful
mail sent successfully
```

B.6 E-mail Package

The "email" package in Python can also send and parse e-mail messages. For this, two import statements should be used. The message can be a **MIMEMultipart** object. The message should be loaded with various headers, viz., "From", "To" and "Subject" and appended to the body of the mail. The complete message can be transferred using the SMTP server object.

```
import smtplib
from email.MIMEMultipart import MIMEMulipart
from email.MIMEText import MIMEText
try:
    s1 = smtplib.SMTP('smtp.mail.yahoo.com',587)
    print("SMTP object is created")
    s1.connect('smtp.mail.yahoo.com',587)
    print("Connected to mail.yahoo.com server via SMTP")
    s1.ehlo()
    s1.starttls()
    s1.ehlo()
    s1.login("xxx@yahoo.com","xxx"))
    print("Login is successful")
    fad=" xxx@yahoo.com "
    taddr=»yyy@yahoo.com»
    m=MIMEMultipart()
    m['From']=fad
    m['To']=taddr
    m['subject']=python mail
    b = "This mail is sent from python"
    m.attach(MIMEText(b,'plain'))
    t=m.as_string()
    s1.sendmail(fad, taddr, t)
    s1.quit()
    print("Mail sent successfully")
except SMTPException:
    print("Error: unable to use SMTP")
```

Output

```
D:\PythonPrograms>python a2.py
SMTP object is created
Connected to mail.yahoo.com server
    via SMTP
Login is successful
Mail sent successfully
```

APPENDIX

C Plotting Graphs

C.1 Introduction

To install the **plotly** package, use the following command. For this, the **pip** should be installed and the PATH environment variable should contain the address of the **scripts** folder.

```
python -m pip install plotly
```

```
C:\Users\T SRIKANTH>python -m pip install plotly
Collecting plotly
    Downloading plotly-2.1.0.tar.gz (1.1MB)
        100% | 1.1MB 504kB/s
Collecting decorator>=4.0.6 (from plotly)
    Downloading decorator-4.1.2-py2.py3-none-any.whl
Collecting nbformat>=4.2 (from plotly)
    Downloading nbformat-4.4.0-py2.py3-none-any.whl (155kB)
        100% | 163kB 936kB/s
Collecting pytz (from plotly)
    Downloading pytz-2017.2-py2.py3-none-any.whl (484kB)
        100% | 491kB 819kB/s
Requirement already satisfied: requests in d:\python\python36-32\lib\site-packages (from plotly)
Requirement already satisfied: six in d:\python\python36-32\lib\site-packages (from plotly)
Collecting traitlets>=4.1 (from nbformat>=4.2->plotly)
    Downloading traitlets-4.3.2-py2.py3-none-any.whl (74kB)
        100% | 81kB 1.0MB/s
Collecting jsonschema!=2.5.0,>=2.4 (from nbformat>=4.2->plotly)
    Downloading jsonschema-2.6.0-py2.py3-none-any.whl
Collecting ipython-genutils (from nbformat>=4.2->plotly)
    Downloading ipython_genutils-0.2.0-py2.py3-none-any.whl
Collecting jupyter-core (from nbformat>=4.2->plotly)
    Downloading jupyter_core-4.3.0-py2.py3-none-any.whl (76kB)
        100% | 81kB 1.0MB/s
Building wheels for collected packages: plotly
    Running setup.py bdist_wheel for plotly ... done
    Stored in directory: C:\Users\T SRIKANTH\AppData\Local\pip\Cache\wheels\33\4b\2f\
    b3651cc3166303da7676f5724865089d32f18b8685cc04cffd
Successfully built plotly
Installing collected packages: decorator, ipython-genutils, traitlets, jsonschema, jupyter-core, nbformat,
    pytz, plotly
Successfully installed decorator-4.1.2 ipython-genutils-0.2.0 jsonschema-2.6.0 jupyter-core-4.3.0
    nbformat-4.4.0 plotly-2.1.0 pytz-2017.2 traitlets-4.3.2
```

C.2 Working with plotly in Offline Mode

```
from plotly import __version__
from plotly.offline import download_plotlyjs, init_
    notebook_mode, plot, iplot
print(__version__)
```

Output

```
D:\PythonPrograms>python s1.py
2.1.0
```

In offline mode, graphs can be plotted and saved in the local system. There are two types of plotting in offline mode. They are

- With plotly.offline.plot()
- With plotly.offline.iplot()

C.3 Plotting with plotly.offline.plot()

plot() is used to plot the graph and save it in a local standalone HTML file. iplot() is used to plot the graph in a Jupyter notebook file. The HTML file will be opened in the local web browser and the Jupyter file will be opened in the notebook.

```
import plotly
from plotly.graph_objs import Scatter, Layout
plotly.offline.plot({
    "data": [Scatter(x=[10, 20, 30, 40], y=[40, 30, 20, 10])],
    "layout": Layout(title="with plot()")
})
```

Output

C.4 Plotting with plotly.offline.iplot()

For this mode of plotting graphs, initially the ipython is installed with all modes by using the following command.

```
pip install "ipython[all]"
```

Then install the Jupyter notebook App by using the following command.

```
jupyter notebook
```

With this command, the Jupyter notebook is openned as shown below.

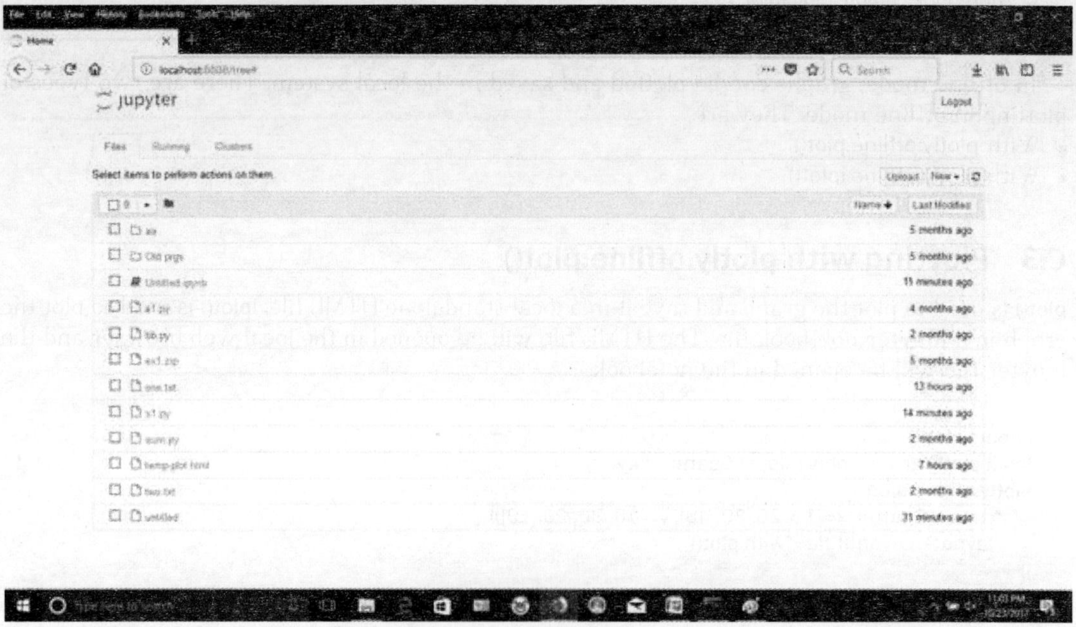

To create a new notebook, click on New → Python3

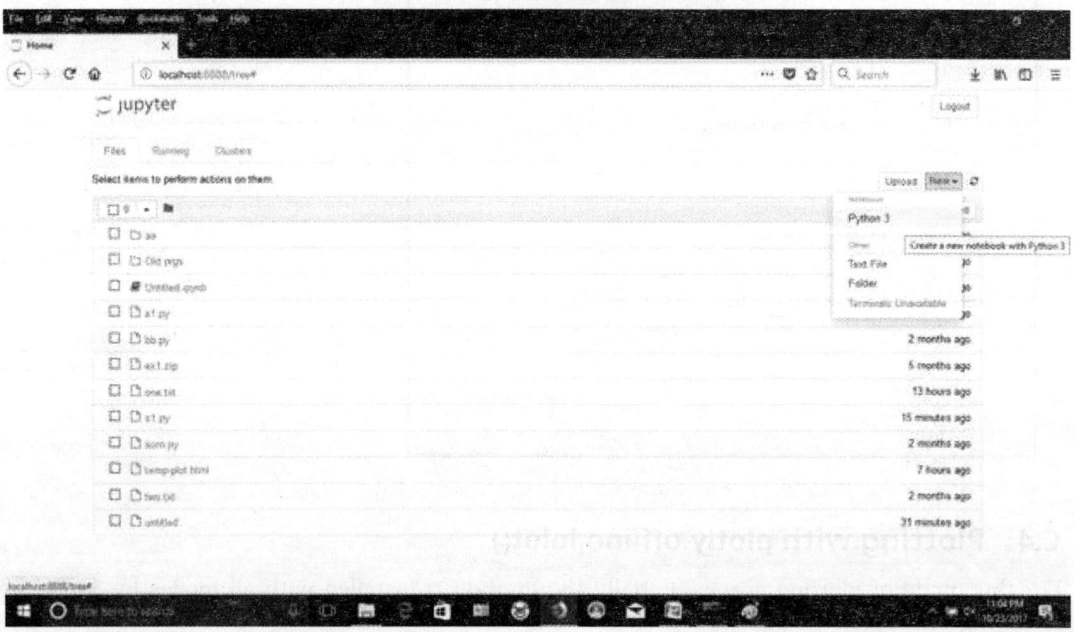

Type the code and click Run

```
import plotly
from plotly.offline import init_notebook_mode, iplot
from plotly.graph_objs import *
init_notebook_mode(connected=True)
trace0 = Scatter(
    x=[1, 2, 3, 4],
    y=[10, 15, 13, 17]
)
trace1 = Scatter(
    x=[1, 2, 3, 4],
    y=[16, 5, 11, 9]
)
data = Data([trace0, trace1])
plotly.offline.iplot(data,filename = 'basic-line')
```

Output

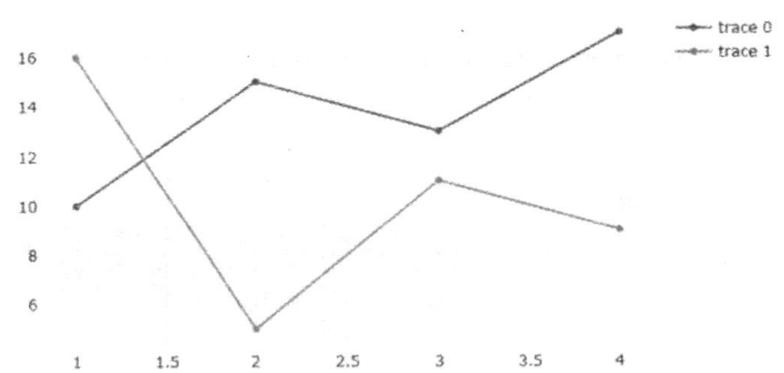

C.4.1 Bar graph

The bar graph can be plotted with Bar() function. It requires two arguments for x and y axes.

```
import plotly
from plotly.offline import init_notebook_mode,
    iplot, plot
import plotly.graph_objs as pg
init_notebook_mode(connected=True)
k=['first','second','third']
v=[10,20,30]
plotly.offline.iplot({
    "data": [pg.Bar(x=k, y=v)],
    "layout": pg.Layout(title="Bar Graph")
})
```

Output

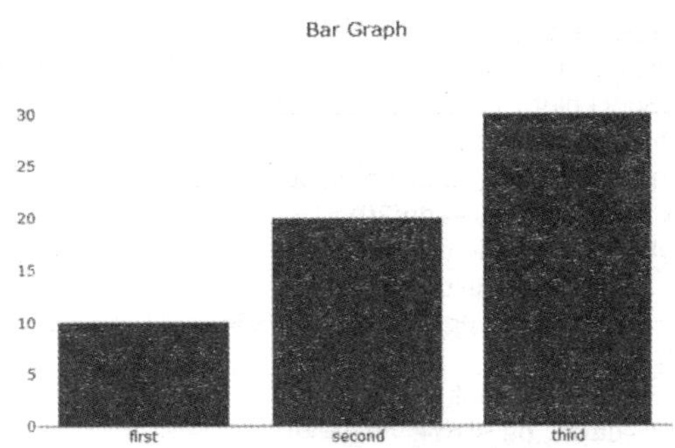

C.4.2 Box graph

The box graph can be plotted with **Box()** function. It requires two arguments for x and y axes.

```
import plotly
from plotly.offline import init_notebook_mode,
iplot, plot
import plotly.graph_objs as pg
init_notebook_mode(connected=True)
k=['first','second','third']
v=[10,20,30]
plotly.offline.iplot({
    "data": [pg.Box(x=k, y=v)],
    "layout": pg.Layout(title="Box Graph")
})
```

Output

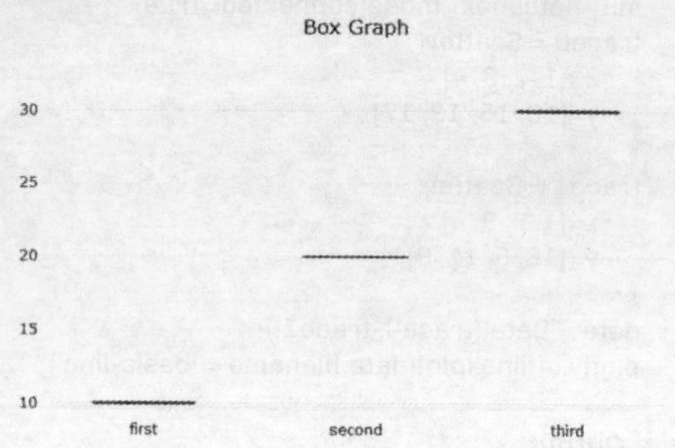

C.4.3 Heatmap graph

The heatmap graph can be plotted with **Heatmap()** function. It requires a matrix argument.

```
import plotly
from plotly.offline import init_notebook_mode,
    iplot, plot
import plotly.graph_objs as pg
init_notebook_mode(connected=True)
plotly.offline.iplot({
    "data": [pg.Heatmap(z=[[10, 20, 30],
                           [40, 50, 60],
                           [70, 80, 90]])],
        "layout": pg.Layout(title="Heatmap Graph")
})
```

Output

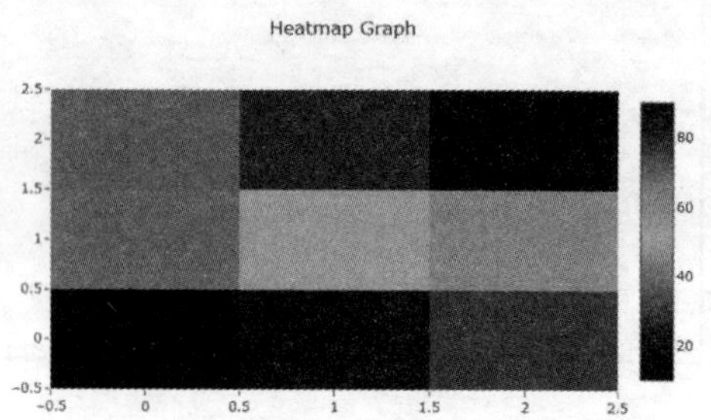

C.4.4 Histogram graph

The histogram graph can be plotted with **Histogram()** function. It requires array value as an argument.

```
import plotly
from plotly.offline import init_notebook_mode, iplot, plot
import plotly.graph_objs as pg
import numpy as np
init_notebook_mode(connected=True)
x = np.random.randn(20)
plotly.offline.iplot({
    "data": [pg.Histogram(x=x)],
        "layout": pg.Layout(title="Vertical Histogram Graph")
})
plotly.offline.iplot({
    "data": [pg.Histogram(y=x)],
        "layout": pg.Layout(title="Horizontal Histogram Graph")
})
```

Output

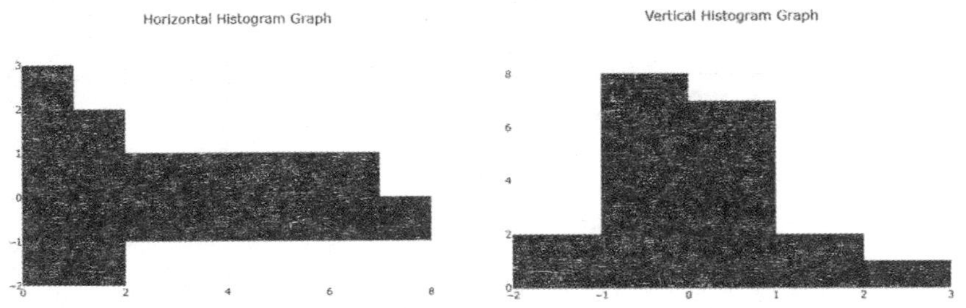

C.4.5 Pie graph

The pie graph can be plotted with Pie() function. It requires array label and value as arguments.

```
import plotly
from plotly.offline import init_notebook_mode, iplot, plot
import plotly.graph_objs as pg
import numpy as np
init_notebook_mode(connected=True)
x = [10,30,20,15,25]
y=['a','b','c','d','e']
plotly.offline.iplot({
    "data": [pg.Pie(labels=y, values=x)],
        "layout": pg.Layout(title="Pie Graph")
})
```

Output

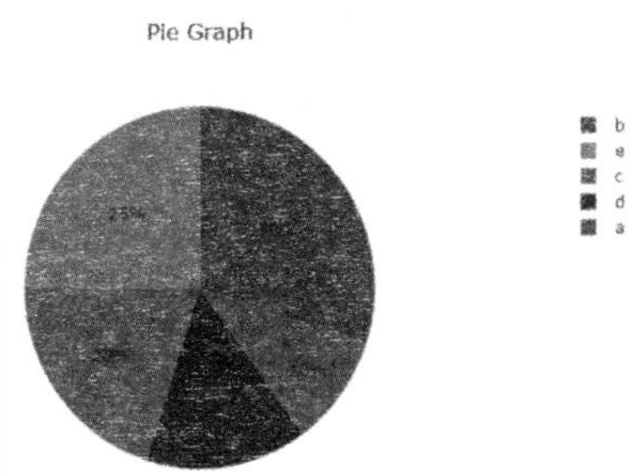

APPENDIX

D CGI/ Web Programming using Python

D.1 Introduction

Common Gateway Interface (CGI) is a standard protocol used to exchange information between the user script file and Web server. With this protocol, the Web pages can be dynamically generated at the Web server. These pages are generated by using CGI scripts. The CGI scripts are executed in the Web browser. The Web browser sends the requested CGI script name to the Web server, where it will be executed by the Web server and the response of the CGI script is transferred to the web browser.

D.2 Configuration of Apache Server

To execute Python-based CGI scripts, the following steps are required.

- The Python installation directory is

```
D:\Python\Python36-32
```

- Install the Web server in the system. In the present section we consider Tomcat Web server installed by using XAMPP. The path of the XAMPP installation directory is

```
C:\xampp
```

- In "xampp" folder, go to "apache" folder.
- In "apache" folder, go to "conf" directory.
- To configure the Apache web server and run the Python CGI scripts, add the following lines of code at the end of the **httpd.conf** file.

```
AddHandler cgi-script .py
ScriptInterpreterSource Registry-Strict
```

- Then open "xampp" control panel and restart the "Apache"

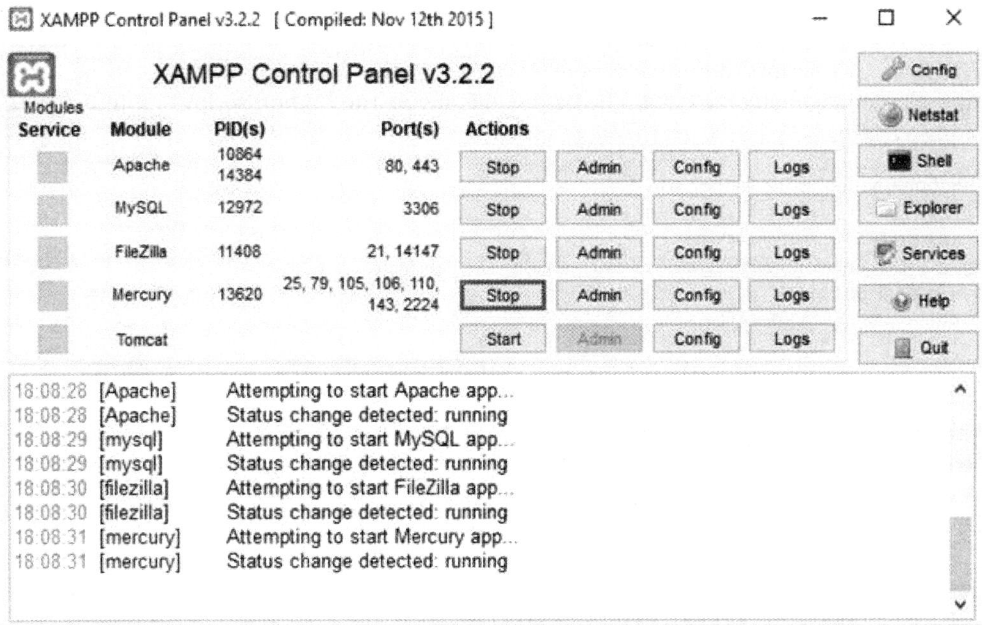

D.3 Running Python CGI Script with Apache Server

After configuring the Apache web server with the Python CGI script feature, perform the following steps.

- Create a folder (PP) in the "htdocs" folder.

```
C:\xampp\htdocs\PP
```

- In this folder, create a Python CGI script. The first line of the script should be the path of Python.

```
C:\xampp\htdocs\PP\s1.py
```

```
#!D:/Python/Python36-32/python.exe
print(«Content-Type: text/html\n»)
print ("Hello World!")
```

- Open the web browser, and type the following URL.

```
http://localhost/PP/s1.py
```

Output

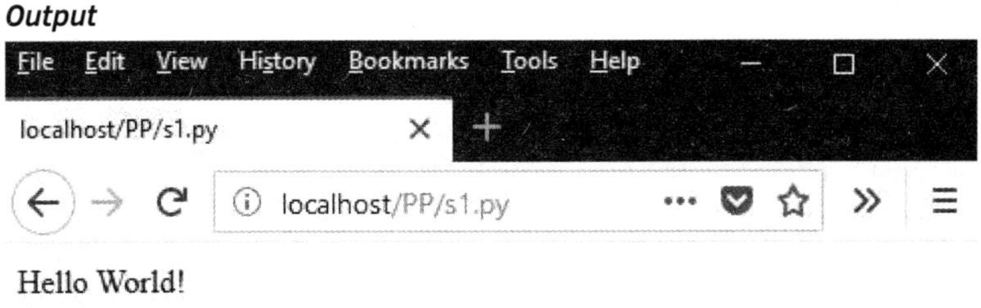

D.4 Python CGI Environment Variables

With Python CGI script, the environment variables of the operating system can be accessed. For this, **os** module should be used. The **os** module allows the Python script to interact with the operating system.

```
#!D:/Python/Python36-32/python.exe
import os
print(«Content-Type: text/html\n»)
print(«<h1>CGI Environment Variables </h1><br>»)
for p in os.environ.keys():
    print(p,»:»,os.environ[p],»</br>»)
```

Output

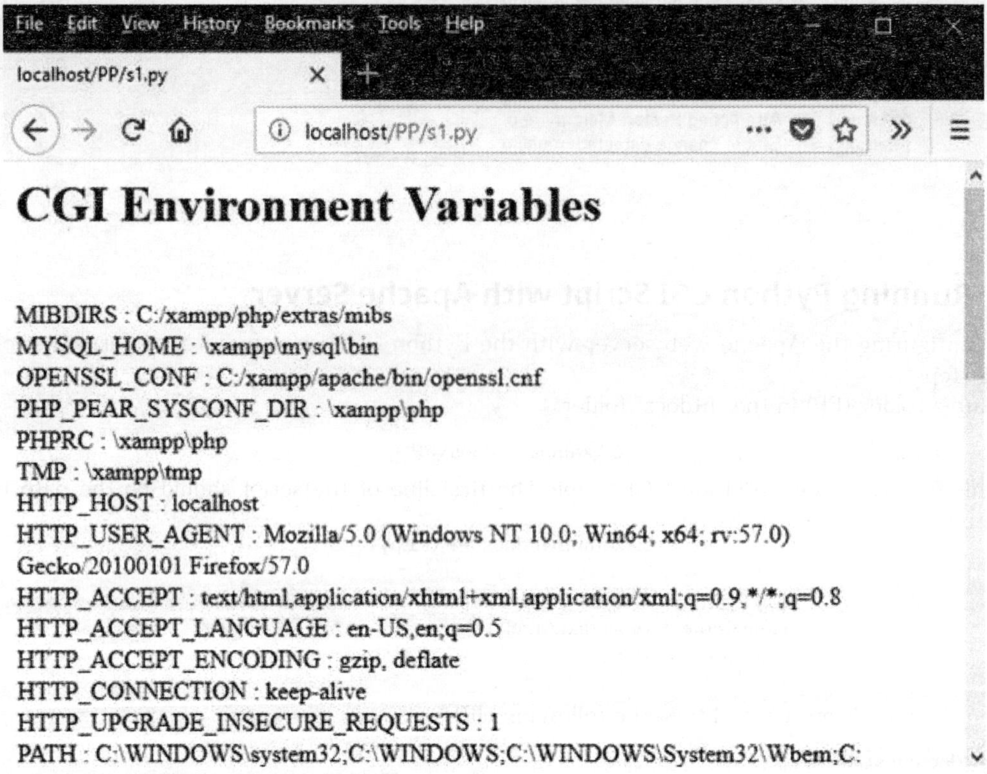

D.5 Form Handling with Python CGI Script

Data can be transferred between the Web browser and the Web server. Form data can be communicated by using either "post" or "get" methods (used to insert/update or retrieve remote data, respectively). The sample code below shows the form handling with Python CGI script.

- Create a form **a.html** which reads the name of the user. For this, the form contains a textbox and a button.

```
C:\xampp\htdocs\PP\a.html
```

```
<form action = "/PP/s1.py" method = "POST">
First Name: <input type = "text" name = "name"> </br>
<input type = "submit" value = "Click" />
</form>
```

- Then, write the Python CGI script, which receives the form data by using "POST" or "GET". The current example uses "POST" method. The CGI module in Python is used to handle form data with "POST" or "GET" requests. The **FieldStorage()**function in CGI module receives the data from the form.

```
C:\xampp\htdocs\PP\s1.py
```

```
#!D:/Python/Python36-32/python.exe
import cgi
f=cgi.FieldStorage()
name=f.getvalue('name')
print("Content-Type: text/html\n")
print("Hello",name)
```

Output

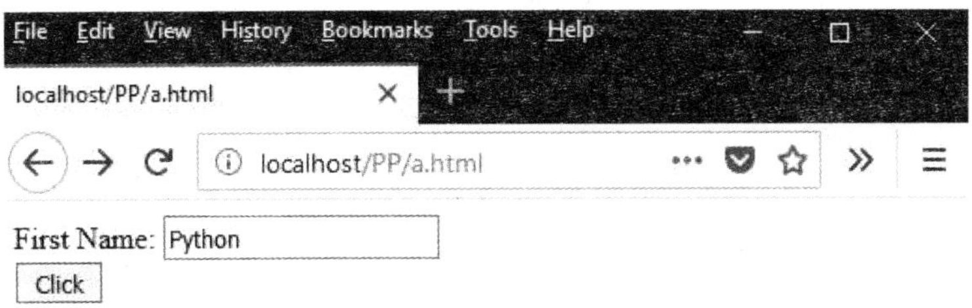

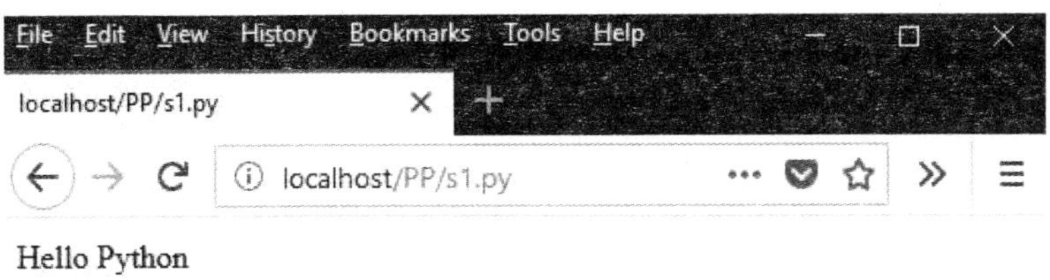

Index